Their Tattered Flags

TEXAS A&M UNIVERSITY

5

MILITARY HISTORY SERIES

The Epic of the Confederacy

Their
Tattered
Flags

FRANK E. VANDIVER

Texas A&M University Press

COLLEGE STATION

Originally published in 1970 by Harper's Magazine Press in association
with Harper & Row, Publishers, Inc. Simultaneously published in Canada
by Fitzhenry & Whiteside Limited.

Maps by Barbara Long

Library of Congress Cataloging-in-Publication Data

Vandiver, Frank Everson, 1925–
  Their tattered flags.

  (Texas A&M University military history series ;
no. 5)
  Reprint. Originally published: 1st ed. New York :
Harper's Magazine Press, 1970.
  Bibliography: p.
  Includes index.
  1. Confederate States of America—History.
I. Title.   II. Series: Texas A&M University military
history series ; 5.
E487.V33   1987   975'.03   87–6520
ISBN 0–89096–355–X

For
Wendell H. Stephenson
and D. L.

They are all gone now, with their tattered flags and faded uniforms. . . .

—BRUCE CATTON

Contents

Maps

Their Tattered Flags

History went against them almost from the start. And long after their dream ended at Appomattox their countrymen would argue whether or not Confederates ought to have existed at all. But they did exist, and they struggled mightily for four agonized years to ensure their future existence. They fought hard enough to exhaust their nascent nation, heroically enough to enlist against them the fiercest efforts of the United States, and honorably enough to linger on in legend for a hundred years.

But the question of whether or not they ought to have struggled and become legendary remains unanswered. Many Confederates would have argued that patriotism finds rectitude in any crusade for independence; surely, no real American could deny a quest for political liberty. Still, the argument has run since 1861 that politicians bartered away the South's future in the bankruptcy of secession.

Defeat—utter and abject—reinforces the accusation, of course, and serves to point up specifications. Reckless politicians are alleged to have led the South down the road to ruin without concern for the relative strengths of North and South, without qualms about casualties.

The fact is that most Southern leaders were men of good hope and progressive intent trapped by traditions and circumstances in the chilling realities of a new and massive war. That the South was not ready for engulfing war was not the fault of its leaders but an accident of time. Not all of the politicians in the South understood what the Confederacy or the war was about. Like so many trapped in transition they hewed hard to simple virtues while the verities went adrift.

Southerners who wanted secession, and there were many, hoped fervently for peaceful separation from the old Union. Even those Tories who longed for an unbroken United States hoped that secession, when it came, would run its course unhindered by conflict —and that perhaps some sort of compromise could then restore the nation. Some Southern enthusiasts hoped that the threat of secession, that familiar blackmail, would work once again. A certain few anticipated nothing save coercion from an outraged North and urged their brethren to make ready in dead earnest. Through the long and turbulent summer of 1860 the country writhed in uncertainty, sweltered in a miasma of political bombast, and drifted aimlessly toward the presidential election in November.

CHAPTER ONE

"The South, the Poor South . . ."

—JOHN C. CALHOUN

AMERICAN ELECTIONS ARE, to most foreign eyes, past understanding. A great country crumbles into dissident parts; confused voices chatter about hopes, aims, patriotism, destiny; a kind of recklessness deranges the national mind, and all semblance of purpose vanishes in warm personal enmity. But American elections are often a national cathartic; they unclog the system of a country gorged on plenty and bloated with power. The periodic immersion in venom and invective seems in some mystical way to cleanse the humors of the body politic and make it function again in compromise.

There was a chance that the election of 1860 might accomplish this magic for a rending nation. But to wise political eyes the chance looked slim. Too many things were out of joint that year; too many men had said too much; issues had hardened into dogmas, and the will to accommodate seemed worn beyond repair.

Why was this so? What latent differences gave such fateful portent to this particular election? Issues, as is so often the case, apparently had little influence. And yet leaders struggled to digest and make articulate those issues that cut sharply between two views of America, its purposes, its hopes, its future. On one side, holding to the constitution and to preservation of the Union under it, was a tall, raw-boned Illinois lawyer named Abraham Lincoln. Lincoln was the candidate of the new Republican Party. The party had selected Lincoln as a compromise—he had said little recently on such touchy issues as slavery and had the virtue of a certain obscurity. Opposed to the Republicans was the Democratic Party, the last truly national party left in the nation. This amorphously accommodating organization had absorbed many of the old Whigs who wandered from the wreckage of their party after the election of 1840 and mixed them with cotton oligarchs, conscience free-soilers, Jeffersonians, Polkites, and Buchanan do-nothings, in a potpourri of easy virtue. The party stood for compromise and adjustment of divisive quarrels and faced November 1860 full of confidence. Democrats could hardly lose, especially with the Little Giant, Stephen A. Douglas, as a leading candidate.[1]

New Ways of Southern Life

On the country's horizon lurked several lowering clouds. Biggest of all was slavery. This thorny provocation had disturbed the course of the Union since its beginning. Sage Jefferson himself had predicted that slavery was the rock upon which the nation would founder unless something removed it from the future. Nothing had. Slavery stayed in the South and grew through the 1830's, 1840's, and 1850's, until in 1860 it seemed bulwarked by the surgent prosperity of cotton. The South boasted some four million slaves, and they represented no less than a third of the section's wealth. The entire agricultural structure rested on the bondsman. More important, so did the social structure of the land below Mason and Dixon's line and the Ohio River. Slavery had grown through custom into an omnipotent solution to economic problems and race problems in a section of mixed colors and hot tempers. The stake of the South in slavery was total; anything threatening the system, the Peculiar Institution, called down the wrath of Southern patriots.[2]

Planters ranked at the top of the Southern social structure. Folk of lesser fortune accepted the tastes and prejudices of planters in the hope of reaching that lofty status in their turn. But planters' lives were not all leisure and fashion. Contrary to rumor, most owned fewer than fifty slaves; many worked their own land along with their bondsmen. Plantation routine demanded heavy capital outlays for land and slaves; management of vast acreage and slave gangs demanded attention and character.

Slave ownership brought peculiar challenges. Enslavement of blacks solved the race problem—one which could reach startling proportions in parts of Mississippi, Alabama, and Georgia, where blacks often outnumbered whites. But the solution rested on harsh slave codes imported from the West Indies, and on careful discipline. Owning Negroes either ennobled or debased the owners. "Good" masters took care of their property—it was sound business—and provided adequate housing, clothing, and food. "Bad" masters or overseers—those of the Legree sort—whipped and drove and wasted their slaves so cruelly that "land of the lash" almost became the South's sobriquet.

Southerners defended slavery as a necessity but often voiced qualms about its morality. These qualms were stilled by external threats in the years after 1831, and the South closed its mind to slavery's evils. It existed, it was a large part of the "Southern way of life," and it worked. If it was wrong, a substitute must be found, but until that time, Southerners would defend slavery passionately. They defended it by state laws that kept slaves in an inhuman chattel state; they defended it as vital to sectional economy; they defended it biblically, as allowed by Ham's curse.

To some with long memories, the new-found devotion of Southerners to slavery seemed strange. The South, after all, had nurtured Jefferson and his liberalism, had boasted James Madison and his gentle equalitarianism, had produced the nation's greatest devotees of individualism in David Crockett, Andrew Jackson, and Sam Houston. How could a section with such heroes defend slavery as a "positive good"? How could Southerners, passionate defenders of liberty, tolerate the bondsman's chains?

Until 1830–31, a fateful year in Southern history, antislavery societies flourished in Dixie. The evangelical religious sects had all begun by attacking slavery, and as late as the early 1830's continued to brood over it. More than a hundred of the one hundred and thirty abolition societies established before 1827 as reported by Benjamin Lundy, the predecessor of Garrison, were Southern-based.[3] Early 1830 had looked promising for freedom in the South. Thomas Jefferson Randolph, grandson of Monticello's squire, opened a long debate in the Virginia Assembly on the question

The Confederate States of America 1861~1865

WISCONSIN · Madison · Rockford · Chicago · Detroit · Cleveland · MICHIGAN · Lake Michigan · Lake Erie · NEW YORK · CONN. · New York · Trenton · Philadelphia · PENNSYLVANIA · Pittsburgh · Gettysburg · Baltimore · MD. · Annapolis · Washington · OHIO · Columbus · INDIANA · Indianapolis · ILLINOIS · Springfield · St. Louis · WEST VIRGINIA (1863) · Charleston · Fredericksburg · VA. · Richmond · Lynchburg · Petersburg · Norfolk · White Sulphur Springs · OHIO RIVER · Louisville · Frankfort · Lexington · KY. · Perryville · Paducah · Elizabethtown · Bacon Creek · Bowling Green · Mill Springs · CUMBERLAND R. · Saltville · Danville · NORTH CAROLINA · Durham Station · Albemarle Sd. · Roanoke Island · Cairo · Columbus · FORT DONELSON · FORT HENRY · TENN. · Nashville · Murfreesboro · Tullahoma · Jackson · Knoxville · Asheville · Salisbury · Charlotte · Raleigh · Goldsboro · Bentonville · Fayetteville · New Bern · MISSISSIPPI · Memphis · Shiloh · Pittsburg Ldg. · Chattanooga · TENNESSEE RIVER · Holly Springs · Corinth · Tupelo · Okolona · MISS. · SOUTH CAROLINA · Columbia · Wilmington · FORT FISHER · CHICKASAW BLUFFS · Vicksburg · Edward's Depot · Jackson · Champion's Hill · Brierfield · Natchez · Meridian · Selma · Montgomery · ALABAMA · Fayetteville · Five Points · Opelika · Columbus · Atlanta · Augusta · Macon · WESTERN AND ATLANTIC R.R. · Charleston · FORT SUMTER · Port Royal harbor · Hilton Head Island · Savannah · GEORGIA · Irwinville · OKEFENOKEE SWAMP · Baton Rouge · Port Hudson · Mobile · Pensacola · FORT PICKENS · New Orleans · FORT ST. PHILIP · FORT JACKSON · of Mexico · Lake City · Ocean Pond · St. Augustine · Fernandina · Jacksonville · FLORIDA · Atlantic Ocean · Bahama Islands · New Providence · Nassau · Havana · CUBA · Bahama Channel of ending involuntary servitude in the Old Dominion. And it seemed as though Virginia might free its slaves. Then, out of total obscurity there burst upon events a Messianic slave named Nat Turner. Convinced he acted on God's word, Turner led a small band of frenzied faithful on a rampage in southeast Virginia. His ill-starred "insurrection" lasted only two days, but its effects were to linger long beyond his time. His path was bathed in blood, his specter cast a shade of horror and fear wherever Southerners gathered. And, of course, he killed the debate for manumission. He killed perhaps far more than anyone knew. This strange fanatic had the same mettle of the other abolitionists, had their ardor, their zeal, their contempt for temporizing. He had no mind to match Theodore Weld's, no steadiness to match Garrison's, no guile to match John Brown's. But he had the directness and the will for freedom that made all abolitionists so dangerous to the South.

His followers died by the sword they raised; he finally surrendered and was hanged. His legacy? To Northerners his passion stood terrible proof of slavery's inhumanity. As for Southerners, Nat Turner's insurrection touched old currents of terror that ran hotly near the conscience. Fear of slave revolts and the prurient excesses they conjured were constants in white memory. Many Virginians felt Nat Turner's spasm had been good; it dampened the talk about freedom for blacks. And so old Nat, harking always for the voice of the Lord, served North and South in their own images and offered up his sacrifice as an earnest of retribution.[4]

Retribution seemed hardly the mood for the election of 1860, but there had been much talk of it in the thirty years since Turner died. Those were fitful and diseased decades for the democratic process, decades that marked the march of industrialization in the North, the steady growth of large urban centers in the East and Middle West, and the sameness of things Southern. Life in Dixie remained rural, decentralized, pastoral. And as the tide of the nineteenth century pulled North and South into different orbits, men and ideas changed apace.

American ideals were changing, all politicians' protests notwithstanding. The typical American, that fictional model men measure themselves against, no longer had the lean swagger, the squint-eyed, weatherworn look of the outdoorsman. The new hero wore a frock-coat with urbanity and was a cigar-smoking titan of brokerage or business. Roughhewn individualism was yielding to the inequality of money. Just as the images changed, so did the centers of power. Where once the strength of the Union marched with the advancing frontier, its strength now gathered behind the bastions of State Street and Wall Street, and a new kind of power altered the tempers of men.

Southerners boasted their resistance to this new order. Tradition, inheritance, and the protocols of chivalry held prominence in Dixie. There, for many, living remained an art. But in the Southland, the storied elegance and the festive leisure showed signs of wear. Certain trends of the times could not be turned back. As Northern economic life took on increased organization, some of the effects were felt in the South. The section supplied nine-tenths of the world's cotton; as population grew everywhere, as demand increased, old techniques of marketing and merchandizing had to change. Consequently, old cotton market centers expanded, middlemen multiplied, banking methods became more sophisticated. All of which meant that the lazy rurality of the Southern life gave some small way to larger cities and increased business.

Urban life hardly supplanted the back-country system. But such Southern towns as Atlanta, Charleston, Savannah, Mobile, Memphis, New Orleans, and Houston showed significant growth in people and power. Acute awareness of an alien North had made Southerners conscious of the need for sectional self-reliance in the three decades before the election of 1860. This awareness had transformed sectionalism into nationalism and produced an urge toward a South for Southerners, even an independent South.[5]

Those who doubted the wisdom of radical brethren who preached a kind of cotton irredentism had formidable evidence to show the weakness of the section, to show its incapacity for self-sufficiency, much less for independence. Most obvious among the deficiencies was lack of economic diversification. As the world more and more relied on Southern "white gold," the section had increased its arable acreage to the exclusion of many staple crops. More than that, the section boasted no adequate transportation network to tie it together. Its roads were poor, largely dirt traces; the few macadamized pikes were short and located mostly on the periphery of the South. Railroads below Mason and Dixon's line were multigauged affairs, disconnected, financially weak, and jealous of competition. Despite the surprising fact that more track was laid in the South during the 1850's than in the North, the South still counted only 9,000 usable miles to the North's 22,000 on the eve of the November confrontation at the polls.

The list of economic woes could have been extended almost indefinitely. Consider industrial growth, surely an index to self-sufficiency in any modern nation. Industries of a major kind were scarcer even than railroads. Some textile factories existed, notably the famed Graniteville, South Carolina, mills belonging to William Gregg, who was perhaps the strongest advocate of industrialization in the South. A series of "commercial conventions" held in various Southern cities through the 1850's duly recited the virtues of broadening the section's economic base, but the call of cotton rang too loudly.[6]

Voices beyond Gregg's were heard, harsh voices of cold truth. Hinton R. Helper, for instance, North Carolinian turned Yankee, penned a powerful indictment of Southern economics titled *The Impending Crisis of the South: How to Meet It*, a book which listed the items in common Southern use made in the North, which showed in figures that slavery was not really making money and would finally become a liability, and which preached that the whole Southern system imposed a moral decay on its people. Helper's hysteria disqualified him to all his former brethren. After all, anyone could see that his arguments were absurd: the South prospered in the late 1850's as never before; cotton receipts boomed; prices of all Southern exports held up; even slave prices rose. What omens could rational men see of the ruin Helper prophesied?

This reception had much validity—the book was wretchedly inaccurate and written in distemper. Still, the polemic had enough half-truths and partial insights to merit consideration in the South. Consideration it received, but in a full and hostile measure that revealed a growing and suffocating conformity of thought which would finally turn the section from reason to reaction.

Helper's economic attack came at a tender time. It seemed really an adjunct to the abolitionist offensive, which had gained momentum steadily since the appearance of William Lloyd Garrison's newspaper *The Liberator* in 1831. Garrison's intransigence, dating back to 1829, his devotion to abolition and abolitionists known by virtually all readers of newspapers, his call for instant, total, and uncompensated emancipation, fired all Southerners to defense of their property, moral qualms or no. True, Garrison represented only a small segment of abolitionist opinion (he finally gave his paper away on street corners to keep up circulation), but that segment was vocal and noxious.[7]

Abolitionism was a crusade for reform, one of many which seared the American conscience in the early nineteenth century. And as was often the case with reform movements, the abolition crusade gave an ideological refuge to devotees of all sorts—antislave extensionists, straight-outs, die-hards, fanatics like John Brown, moderates like James G. Birney (presidential candidate of the Liberty Party in 1840 and 1844) who favored political action, moral suasionists like the Quaker sisters Grimké of Charleston, and shrewd, rational reformers of the Charles Sumner stripe.[8]

Such dissident elements seemed unlikely to cling together for useful service, but the abolitionists did cling together and grow stronger. And their relentless push for change in the South finally succeeded, but not quite in the way they hoped. Constant pressure triggered a Southern—perhaps human—tropism for aggressive defense. Forced through the years to see itself eventually as a threatened minority section, the South erected defenses that went into action with real or fancied thrusts—witness, for instance, the state-rights propositions in the Virginia and Kentucky Resolutions, written by Madison and Jefferson in 1798, the nullification doctrine of the 1830's, the whole theory of rights reserved to the states that John Calhoun pronounced so fervently until his dying day.[9]

No defense matched the abolition campaign in intensity, and against it the South reacted with singular unanimity. As abolitionist propaganda increased, as hundreds and thousands of "freedom" letters, broadsides, and leaflets flooded the South, some states feared Turner-like uprisings and began to censor the mails. There were pretenses of legality, of course; the "police power" was erroneously cited, along with the right of state authorities to preserve law and order. But the effect was totalitarian and mentally stifling.

And the effect mushroomed. Soon ideas were censored, too, and most who expressed un-Southern sentiments on the main issue of the day were ostracized—some were even tarred and feathered.[10] No element in the population escaped the effects of imposed conformity. Unhappily not even the clergy lifted strong voices in opposition. So deep, indeed, went the current of fear for slavery that it finally rent Protestant churches along sectional lines; a Methodist Church, South, appeared, along with an intensely Southern Presbyterian Church. Although an attempt was made to maintain a façade of Roman serenity, Catholic parishes generally reflected the prejudices of time and place.[11]

Leaders of a Different Breed

As the Southern mind cowered at last behind a Cotton Curtain, creativity withered away. What few literary works appeared were largely panegyric, extolling the virtues of mother, home, and slavery; a whole subgenre denounced the image of the South presented in Harriet Beecher Stowe's *Uncle Tom's Cabin*. The rare voice of dissension which now and then could be heard in the South rings freshly through this dismal period. There were some hardy thinkers left who spoke their minds, men like strong nationalist James Petigru of Charleston, whose family and position ransomed his opinions. But in general the most influential citizens kept faith by defending the Southern Way of Life.[12]

Aggressive defense of the Southern position brought some new men to prominence, and in a way set the stage for the major transition promised by the election of 1860. The new Southern leaders were a different breed. Many of them had been initiated into politics at the lowest state of the art. Some few were gentlemen or descended from gentlemen and true heirs of the way of the South, but some were simply strident demagogues riding the crest of sectionalism.

Like abolitionism, Southern extremism collected its own strange adherents. And also like its Yankee cousin, Southern extremism had a voice far beyond its numbers. For the most part Southerners were moderate in politics; their long support of the Democratic Party pretty well proved the point. But the fire-eaters were vocal, and the loudest among them included rhetorician William L. Yancey, fire-eating secessionist editor Robert Barnwell Rhett, and politician Louis T. Wigfall.[13]

So loud did the extremists rant that even moderate Southern leaders of sound reputation were compelled to listen and to echo. And it is partly because of the radical element in the South that such reputable politicians as Mississippi's Jefferson Davis, Louisiana's John Slidell and Judah Benjamin, and Georgia's Howell Cobb seriously thought of secession as a last redress for Southern grievances.

Although secession is fashionably laid at the door of the South, a malformed political beast with dishonor its progenitor, secessionist theories spring from the earliest political alignments and had a prominent place in the founding of the United States. Nonetheless the South has been tarnished with the term to this day, not only because it did in fact secede, but also because of John C. Calhoun.

Once a nationalist, always an opportunist, Calhoun shifted his philosophy with his presidential fortunes. When, during Jackson's reign, he decided that he would never be President, the great Carolinian moved boldly to lead the state-righters of his section. Urbane, shrewd, a master rhetorician, he was a politician's politician. Apparent candor and simplicity masked a questing, incisive, original mind that translated guile into statecraft.

John C. Calhoun loomed over his times and his contemporaries not only because of his figure, not entirely because of his intellect, but also because of a prescience reserved rarely to politicians. He had an instinctive awareness of emerging trends and ideas, and he espoused or announced them first. As his capacity to discern the future developed, he grew famous for wisdom.

It must be said for him that it was not easy to discern South Carolina's future aims and ambitions. No state in the Union claimed quite such volatile folk as Carolina rice planters, aloof Charlestonians, and the hardy sand-hillers of the upcountry. Although an ancient and boastfully civilized state, Carolina still had some of the unruliness of the frontier. Gentlemen of the Palmetto

State had tenderer honor than most of their fellow Southerners and were quick with pistol, deft with foil. Leadership of their ilk was chancy, but Calhoun knew and led them. Better than most he understood the hotblooded resentment Carolinians and all Southerners felt for threats to Dixie, and he learned to use this resentment with frightening success.

Its use depended on approach. Calhoun rarely threatened; he persuaded. And he voiced often a passionate concern for liberty.

Perhaps his most far-reaching achievement, one which set him loftily above his contemporaries, was his triumph over the Southern dilemma of dual loyalties. Did a man owe life, fortune, and honor to his state or his nation? Most fiercely loyal of Carolinians, he nonetheless cherished a love of country to link him with his forebears. All his life, through all the convolutions of a fantastic career, he worked to realize a bifurcated hope: to exalt the state and save the Union. With this hope in his heart he elaborated—mainly in response to escalating protective tariffs—perhaps the most original political doctrine of the nineteenth century, the doctrine of nullification—the right of a state to suspend enforcement of an offending federal law—later transmuted into the theory of secession.

In fairness to Calhoun it should be remembered that nullification and secession were not, in his mind, devices for disrupting the Union; they were intended as accommodations to preserve minority rights in majority rule. The Senator did not contemplate using these doctrines lightly; during his last days in 1850, when the South appeared threatened from all quarters of the globe, he saw a bleak and sorrowful future for "the South, the poor South."[14]

A complex man, Calhoun represented complex constituents. The divided mind of the South plagued all leaders of the section from the Revolution to the election in November 1860. The majority were devoted to the Union but jealous of their rights and their "property," determined to preserve localism against a fancied Leviathan state, and intensely devoted to the reserved powers of the Constitution. And in that fateful winter there was no Calhoun left to know their minds and form their thoughts. In that crisis hour the South, the most political section of the Union, could find no greatness in its leaders and no caution in its councils.

This is not to say that there were no national leaders available—there were. A good many Southern Democrats hoped that Stephen A. Douglas could evade the Kansas-Nebraska slave-or-free-state dilemma and reach national leadership. He could if anyone could. No other public figure matched him in experience or in popular estimation. His rotund form was known to all, his rhetoric no less familiar.

In some ways this familiarity worked against him as a national candidate. Like so many public men, he had simply been around too long and had talked too much. But Douglas was a scrapper and intended a fight for the Democratic nomination.

As far as Southerners were concerned, Douglas might be "safe" enough on the slavery issue, but he hardly ranked as a crusader for the institution. Perhaps an outright advocate could not be expected to lead the Democrats, but the South felt it deserved some special consideration.

Especially did this seem essential when Lincoln and his party were examined closely. The country counselor who led the Republicans could not be as naive as he seemed. A rustic quaintness cloaked his actions and made it hard to see him clear. But his past career showed him to be much more than a cracker-barrel Socrates. He had served in the Black Hawk War—recalling it later with humorous nostalgia—and went on to represent his Illinois district in the national House of Representatives in the 1840's.

Some vital things about him could be learned from a glimpse at his congressional record. He had gone to Congress a Whig and stayed staunchly by the party until it disintegrated around him. He had opposed the Mexican War, and his support of Wilmot's proposition to keep all conquered territories free of slavery showed that he was a free-soiler at heart. But beyond a shading here and there it was hard to guess his true feelings. Like most politicians Lincoln talked a good deal, but unlike most he wrapped his meaning in allegory and obscured it with humor. Even when debating Douglas in their famous Senate race in 1858, Lincoln managed to avoid plain declarations. While maneuvering Douglas into statements of opinion and policy, Lincoln kept to a higher plane of principle. Cagey sphinx or artful dodger, Lincoln was truly a baffling man.

The Crisis of 1860

Rising from the ashes of Whiggery in the early 1850's, the Republican Party attracted dissident Free-Soilers, old Liberty loyalists, unhappy Democrats. Drawing most of its strength from the North and Middle West, the party boasted little following outside the old Conscience Whig and Free-Soil territory—and this alone branded it basically an abolition crowd. As if to prove its radicalism, the party had called on John C. Frémont to carry its standard in the 1856 campaign, and Frémont was the darling of the abolitionists everywhere.

True, most Republican leaders were eager to explain that the party's views on slavery were essentially conservative. Far from wanting to abolish slavery, the party stood only for restricting it to its present boundaries. No one in the hierarchy argued that Congress had any right to abolish slavery, but they did think restriction was constitutional. As for Lincoln, he took refuge behind the party's restrictionist platform and eluded direct questioning.

Slavery and its place in the nation could not be denied—this was the crux of the election, or so most people seemed to think. Southern extremists found the hesitant position of Republicans very useful. Restriction, they argued, amounted to disguised abolition; if the slave system could be denied growth, it could be denied life. And any fool could read between the Republican lines the real and insidious aim of the party. Republicans, according to Southern alarmists, wanted not only to abolish slavery but also to punish its devotees and to make the whole nation over in the image of the crassly mechanistic North. Abolition was, in other words, not enough; the Republicans wanted a total reconstruction of the Union on their own terms.[15]

Now, whether this was true or not, and the evidence scarcely supports it, increasing numbers of people below Mason and Dixon's line came to think it was. And as more and more of them believed it, chances for accommodation with Republicans eroded. This worked for the Democrats, of course, and for a time few national politicians caught the danger smoldering in Southern suspicion. A jubilant party hierarchy made ready for the Democratic national convention at Charleston in April. Douglas seemed a sure winner, and with some good balancer on the ticket, Democracy should trounce Lincoln and his hacks easily enough.

The effect of William Lowndes Yancey and a small coterie of followers was unsuspected by Douglas and his advocates, unsuspected by most beyond the bounds of Alabama. Yancey, an Alabamian, had been a Unionist during South Carolina's futile attempt to nullify the Tariff Act of 1832, which had imposed oppressively high protective tariffs on most manufactured goods (most other Southern regions were either inured to bleak times, were prosperous, or simply weren't so grieved by tariffs).[16] Thereafter, Yancey had moved to an extreme prosecessionist stand and had won some notoriety at a previous Democratic convention with his so-called Alabama Platform, a set of requisites for Southern support of the party. He had failed to win help from any but his own delegation in 1848. But his time had not really come.

It came in Charleston; there things were ripe for bombast and radicalism. And when Yancey rose during the first day of the gathering at the Institute Hall to declaim again the grievances of the South and list the guarantees the section needed to remain in the Democratic Party—perhaps even in the nation—a stunned convention began subtly to disintegrate.

The things he wanted were neither new nor especially startling. The South had often asked protection of slavery in the territories, honest enforcement of the Fugitive Slave Act of 1850—which called for the return from all states, slave or free, of runaway slaves—and some constitutional buttress for its minority rights. The difference this time was in the vigor of the demands and in the reaction to their refusal. After heated argument the Alabama Platform was rejected. Yancey rose slowly from his seat and began a long walk from the convention floor. For an agonized moment he walked alone—as he had in 1848—but finally others stood and began to walk out with him. In the final count the full delegations of five and partial delegations of two more Southern states took their stand with Yancey and with Alabama.

All thought of business vanished in the midst of sudden crisis. Nobody could win the nomination. Nobody could tell, for that matter, how much of the party was left to pick a nominee. Stalemated, the delegates adjourned to meet two months later in Baltimore after everyone had had time to cool off. In the weeks between the Charleston and Baltimore conventions a Southern Democratic Party appeared, dedicated to defense of the section's rights under the constitution. The new party's leaders again bolted the Baltimore gathering and held a rump convention of their own. And the mere existence of a rump party quickened talk across the South of secession as a rising possibility.[17]

A good many Southern moderates realized the dangers inherent in the breakup of the only remaining national party. Some scattered moderates, usually the great inarticulate mass, did their best to hold the Union together by creating the Constitutional Union Party in the South, designed to rally support from everyone who loved the Union regardless of political preference or of views on slavery.

After the fiery conventions ended, Douglas found himself at the head of a shattered National Democratic Party. John C. Breckinridge, incumbent Vice-President of the United States, led the Southern splinter group, and John Bell of Tennessee carried the Constitutional Union banner. It hardly mattered who led what; the wreckage of the great Democratic organism and the babel of confusion surrounding its descendants vastly enhanced Lincoln's chances. This was especially true because the Democratic eruption obscured most of the issues. Lincoln now could run the homiletical sort of campaign he most enjoyed.

Suddenly, as far as the South could see the future, the only important thing was the extreme likelihood of a Republican triumph on November 6, 1860. In that event the South must take counsel of its fears and make ready for the worst—and anyone could tell what the worst would be. Slavery would erode under grinding hostility from Washington (the Dred Scott decision, with the *obiter dicta* issued by the Supreme Court denying the right of Congress to prevent extension of slavery in the territories, would be only a temporary victory for slaveholders), cotton profits would vanish into the coffers of Northern industry, bureaucracy would stifle freedom everywhere. The last few rights left to the states and people under the constitution would vanish, and a mean egalitarianism would negate the fruits of birth and custom. The South, a last touchstone of fabled Greek democracy, would cease to be as it was; it would find itself yoked to crude modernity, a pale fief of the machine.

More and more the extremist press played the theme of Black Republican victory as the blight of the world, and people believed because they half believed already.[18] Finally, before the polls told their dread results, Southern opinion had crystallized into terror at the Republican threat and into conviction that secession was the only resort. No matter that a few preached delay and that others urged the possibility that a Lincoln victory might not really bring doom. As the election grew close, just weeks away, some special alchemy lulled the South into a spell of muffled fear. In this odd unreality truths became various and fancies absolute. A hope that fate would somehow prevent the future insulated the South for those last weeks.

The election came and the worst happened; news of Lincoln's victory rang a tocsin through the South. Reaction came swiftly and when it came it carried with it most of the fence-sitters. The fire-eaters, the hotheads, all pointed to the truth of their prophecies. Time for temporizing had run out. The South must save itself by departing the Union.

Not unexpectedly South Carolina acted first. The legislature immediately called a state convention to meet at Charleston on December 17. Delegates duly elected by popular vote arrived in a violently secessionist mood, and on December 20, 1860, they adopted unanimously an Ordinance of Secession, which proclaimed to the world that "the union now subsisting between South Carolina and other States under the name of the United States of America is hereby dissolved."[19]

Events followed swiftly in wake of Carolina's boldness. As other states seceded (Mississippi, January 9; Florida, January 10; Alabama, January 11; Georgia, January 19; Louisiana, January 26; Texas, February 1) emissaries from the Palmetto State appeared armed with plans for a Southern Confederacy. South Carolina vividly recalled being left alone by her sisters during the nullification crisis of the 1830's; this time sentiment for secession ran strong across the

South, but South Carolina was not leaving anything to chance. Her heralds of disunion preached the need for cooperation in independence and sought a convention of seceded states to form a new government for mutual protection. There was some antisecession backlash. Strong cooperator, or delay, groups almost stalled the withdrawal of Alabama and Georgia, but lost out narrowly to the radicals.

Moderation at Montgomery

Alabama invited the new Southern sovereignties to meet at Montgomery in February 1861 for the purpose of organizing a new and better nation. Six seceded states—South Carolina, Georgia, Alabama, Florida, Mississippi, Louisiana—cloaked their delegates with government-forming powers and sent them off to the Montgomery convention with jubilant enthusiasm. The Texas delegates arrived after proceedings were under way. On February 4, 1861, the delegates gathered for their first session, and things were never again the same with the South.

There was much of interest in this convention. It was a conglomerate of political tones, reflecting the whole spectrum of opinion from radical secessionists to cooperationists. The cooperationists, who wanted to wait for cooperators in disunion, were a forlorn remnant of conservatism, and most were men who had clung desperately to the Union until that old patriotism became un-Southern and unsafe. Each delegate knew why he had come, and all were eager to form a new government for the South, a government to reflect traditional views of democracy, liberty, and the sanctity of property. From a number of willing candidates the convention selected Howell Cobb of Georgia as its president and proceeded to the important tasks of constitution making and election of national officers.

History has generally ignored Cobb's elevation to the presidency of the Montgomery convention—it has tended to get lost in the whelm of portentous deeds. But Cobb's position was the key to the tenor of events—the key, in fact, to the future of the South. Howell Cobb, of illustrious Georgia lineage, commanded the high regard of most Southern politicians. They knew him to be a sane, somewhat silent man of sense and placid judgment. They knew, too, that he quietly coveted the post of Chief Executive in whatever new government emerged. But Cobb's deficiencies denied him the greater role. Too taciturn, too moderate—too bland, in fact—he seemed to lack the drive needed in a Southern President. He knew his own disabilities, and it measures his sagacity and his weakness to say that he chose to accept leadership of the convention rather than risk the larger race.

But there were impressive things about this mild man. His calm exterior hid real determination; his reason bridled daring; his moderation tempered passion. Moderation had become with him a sort of guiding principle. Neither a fire-eater nor a lingering Unionist, Cobb believed utterly in the soundness of the Southern cause; he accepted hesitantly the need for secession, but once it was accomplished he supported it earnestly. In his view, the South remained the real defender of ancient and revered principles of American constitutionalism. The South, not the North, hewed hard to the ideals of the Founding Fathers.

With that conviction it is not surprising that he conceived the work of the Montgomery convention as evolutionary, not revolutionary. Many contemporaries, and legions of later students of the Confederacy, argued that the convention should have confessed its inherent revolutionary quality by adopting revolutionary measures. This idea never seriously disturbed the constitutional deliberations of the convention, for Cobb and his political brethren were products of a legalistic South, a South steeped in the constitutionality of Calhoun. They did not believe there was any revolution in what they did; revolution was anathema to them all.[20] As patriots they sought to preserve the best of the old Union by evolution toward a new order. Under Cobb's easy hand the convention proceeded to erect around itself and its actions a bulwark of legality to show plainly the moderation of the emerging nation.

Cobb put his confreres early to the business of drafting a constitution for the South. With a shrewd guess at his man he put the constitution committee in the charge of his friend Alexander Stephens. At first glance this was an absurd choice, for the wizened little Georgia Senator had lagged far behind in secessionist zeal and was one of the latest comers to the Southern cause. And yet no man in the South was a better constitutional lawyer, none enjoyed higher repute for honor and patriotism. Stephens's presence as a delegate lent a good deal of respectability; his authorship of the constitution would confer a kind of imprimatur.

While Stephens and his committee worked on the Southern charter, Cobb began to gather opinions on the national officers. Since the South conceived itself the successor government to an older, more legitimate United States, it was obvious that the government and its machinery would be similar, if not the same.

What kind of man should be president of the new Confederate States of America? Ideas were as numerous as delegates. But slowly a consensus developed. As it did, something very interesting came clear: the secessionists, the fire-eaters, those impetuous hotbloods who strode Montgomery almost as conquerors, were losing control of their own creation. The convention and the new government were simply not going radical. The man the convention began to see as Chief Executive must be Southern, of course, "safe" on the Peculiar Institution, experienced in government at national and local levels, and a man whose fame transcended opposition.

This composite criterion ruled out several willing candidates from the race. Robert Barnwell Rhett, of the fulminating Charleston *Mercury,* lacked some of the requisites. Robert Toombs of Georgia, heavy with political honors, portents, and ambitions, had too long harangued for Southern independence to carry the image of moderation now necessary for the world. William Lowndes Yancey, Alabama's favorite son, was disqualified by the simple test of verbiage. One man only seemed to meet all the requirements, one man with the capacity for statecraft. On February 8, 1861, the Montgomery convention unanimously chose Jefferson Davis to be President of the Confederate States of America.

There were few doubts about the wisdom of the choice. No other Southern spokesman had Davis's repute for political acumen, for devotion to his section, for administrative ability, for personal courage, for integrity and honor. In the days after Calhoun passed from the scene, various politicians had hoped to inherit the Carolinian's mantle of leadership, but Davis ran ahead of all candidates.

Crittenden of Kentucky shared some of the luster, as did Bell of Tennessee, but none could match Davis's stature.

A glance at his record showed his rightness for the Confederate presidency. Kentucky born, Mississippi raised, Davis had attended Transylvania University, had been graduated from West Point, had served with real distinction as Colonel of the Mississippi Rifles and earned credit for victory at Buena Vista in the Mexican War,[21] had done a stint in the House of Representatives, then performed brilliantly as Secretary of War in Franklin Pierce's cabinet, and his long career in the Senate was distinguished for compelling oratory and trenchant thought on the major issues of concern to the South and the nation. By all standards Davis ranked as one of the principal leaders in the old Union. He ranked certainly as one of three or four principal leaders of the South. The new country knew him; the old country knew him; his name would be recognized around the world.

Man and Hour

Varina Howell Davis remembered always the way the message came. From the long veranda of Brierfield House she saw the dust cloud behind a galloping horse. Her husband looked up from the rose garden and watched the rider speed toward the house. The courier reined in, swung from the saddle, and gave Jefferson Davis a dispatch. Varina looked for some clue to the contents in his expression. She had been worried about him ever since he departed the United States Senate after his state quit the Union. His solemn farewell speech on January 21, 1861, had measured his foreboding for the fate of the Republic, a foreboding that became deep melancholy in the few weeks since. He had cautioned all who would listen on the horrors of a brother's war, had preached moderation and forbearance, but found only emotionalism seething through the South as he had traveled home to Mississippi.[22]

Mississippi seceded on January 9, 1861. Her people were caught in an orgy of independence, and military preparations captured the public's fancy. This martial craze had so far progressed that by the time Davis reached Jackson the state convention had already created a Mississippi Army and appointed him its commander. The job suited a West Pointer and Mexican War hero, but the prospect it conjured reinforced his gloom. He tarried briefly in the state capital, then left for a plantation visit—necessary, he said, "to repair my fences." Once home with Varina and his four children fears of war faded in the warmth of friends and fireside.

The rider who brought the fateful message on February 10, 1861, revived the fears, but Davis kept a stoic calm, and Varina could tell nothing of the news. Finally he spoke to the messenger and then turned to the veranda and to her. As he walked to the familiar porch, she saw the long lines of anxiety deepen in his face and some look of distant dread. Then she read the message and knew that their lives were changed forever.

She knew her husband sufficiently to realize that he would have preferred to stay with Mississippi's troops; but she knew his character, too, and understood that he would do his duty.

And duty called urgently—there was little time for packing, even for goodbyes. Davis decided to go ahead alone and arrange for the family to follow. He took time for fond farewells to faithful servants, for special moments with the children and with Varina. He went, then, and she watched him off on the road to Jackson and the future.

Davis departed filled with anxiety, uncertain of his tasks, and dubious about a South cut off from the Union and cast on the seas of independence; the trip to Montgomery did much to change his attitude. Everywhere his train stopped on the long route to the Confederate capital (a roundabout series of rail connections testified to the weakness of Southern transportation), everywhere throngs of new Confederates cheered and applauded and called for their President. The crowds were concerned for the wages of secession, and they looked to him for some kind of consolation. At each stop he had to appear, talk, reassure his countrymen. And he enjoyed it.

As the presidential train progressed the trip took on all the aspects of a triumph—the crowds swelled and Davis waxed warmer in his oratory. By the time his entourage reached Atlanta many of the Chief Executive's misgivings about the Southern future were charmed away in a spell of enthusiasm.[23]

Montgomery proved no different from other towns en route. The train pulled into the station late at night, but a great and cheering mob waited to escort President Davis to the Exchange Hotel; once there, the mob roared on until a much fatigued traveler appeared on a balcony and William L. Yancey introduced him: "The man and the hour have met." Davis spoke briefly and went to bed.[24]

With morning the President settled down to serious business. Among his first discoveries was the changed nature of the Southern capital. He knew it before, everyone knew it, as a sedate and genteel city of some four thousand, a state capital accustomed to seasonal population swells when the legislature met in the stately columned building crowning the hill at the head of Dexter Avenue. Never in its long history, though, had Montgomery known such agonies of importance. People—people from all over the South, the North, from foreign parts—paraded in the streets and clogged the halls of the convention; people clamored everywhere until the sedentary pace of Montgomery crumbled in the rush of independence.[25]

That rush swept the convention with it in the days after Davis's election. While awaiting their new leader, the convention's delegates had installed the Vice-President, accepted a provisional constitution, and evolved under it into a unicameral Congress, which would continue until a permanent constitution and government were created.

Constitutionalist Davis admired the provisional Confederate charter for its theme of continuity. Despite the unicameral legislative feature, which allowed the Montgomery convention to continue as the Confederate Congress, the new document preserved the spirit, and most of the letter, handed down by the Philadelphia convention. The Confederate government would be federal and representative; the constitution remained the keystone of the national structure and the supreme law; the time-honored separation of powers remained intact. A few improvements on the United States constitution were included: the item veto, for instance, and a Bill of Rights written into the heart of the constitution. Some few things purely Southern could be glimpsed in the new document—strict enforcement of the fugitive-slave acts and prohibition of the slave trade.

Overall, the provisional constitution of the Confederacy smacked strongly of nationalism. Nothing in it recalled the Articles of Confederation of the 1770's; the history of that loose and confused compact, which made the United States weaker than its components, lingered fresh in Southern memory. The provisional constitution provided the framework of strong government if its officers would make it so. And Congress had begun by adopting for the South all laws of the Union not in conflict with the new constitution—and by giving the vice-presidency to Alexander H. Stephens.[26]

Stephens was no less than the author of the government's strength, and his presence in the administration augured well for its power. No one could have guessed differently. So distinguished and full of prestige was Georgia's brilliant and diminutive senator that only his reluctant Southern patriotism denied him the presidency. And by all rights he belonged in the government; his great experience and boundless craft would be invaluable to Jefferson Davis. Stephens had all the portents of greatness.

But somewhere in the long labyrinths of a precise and nimble brain, Stephens nursed an ambition as twisted as his body. In time, frustration and a growing devotion to state rights would turn him from Davis and the government. Part of his problem lay in an unaccustomed role of subordination, a role which thwarted his prowess. The vice-presidency might be an honor, but it was an empty one that crowned his career too soon.

In his confining sinecure Stephens's brilliance corroded into resentment, and at last all his great potential seeped away in a shabby feud with Davis. The feud began almost immediately, began with Stephen's assuming to himself the role of proclaimer of Southern purpose. At Savannah, Georgia, on March 21, 1861, the Vice-President dealt a heavy blow to the moderate posture struck by every other Confederate. Warming to a good audience in that especially Southern city, Stephens proudly recited the merits of the provisional constitution, recalled that the South stood firmly by old American principles, but went on relentlessly to make a shocking point:

"The new constitution [he said] has put to rest *forever* all agitating questions relating to our peculiar institutions. . . . *Our new government is founded . . . its foundations are laid, its cornerstone rests, upon the great truth that the negro is not equal to the white man;* that slavery, subordination to the superior race, is his natural and normal condition."[27]

However truly this bold statement reflected Southern opinion, Stephens had talked out of turn and surely out of time. Davis had not been consulted about the speech, and the image he had been molding suddenly became flawed.

But by March the new President had grown accustomed to assistance unbidden and problems unexpected. Six weeks in the Chief Executive's chair had almost inured him to surprise. Not to say that he began with many illusions. Almost a decade in the halls of Congress had burnished a healthy cynicism and lowered his view of Olympus. Still, the shocks had been heavy and persistent.

Fortunately for him and his country he knew how to begin. First among his myriad tasks he put the welding of public support behind the new government. Achieving this would solve such other problems as private loyalty, state-federal relations, financing, possibly even recruiting. Achieving a popular base of power depended to a large extent on the administration, and Davis knew it well enough.

Nothing would be more vital to the administration than the men who ran it. So, while he fashioned his Inaugural Address, Davis considered carefully the matter of cabinet appointments. Experience taught him the usefulness of able aides and he forced himself to consider even total strangers if strongly recommended. As with all presidents, he found himself pushed to other considerations than those of ability alone: one state proffered a favorite son; Democratic leaders in another state urged reward to the faithful; Texas, last to join the Confederacy, expected representation in the cabinet. As things worked out Davis selected his men on the basis of geography, party loyalty, support of the Southern cause, and then on the basis of ability.

In picking the various ministers Davis did his best to soothe feathers ruffled by disappointment. He wanted to honor friend Robert Barnwell with the State Portfolio, but when the South Carolinian who followed Calhoun in the Senate declined, Davis used the office to mend political fences. Would Robert Toombs, Georgia's blighted presidential hopeful, accept? Davis had wanted him in the Treasury, but his acceptance of the State Department would bring prestige to the office and help heal the wounds of election. Hurt and nursing petulance, Toombs had gone back to Georgia to ponder the whims of justice. In his mood a cabinet post seemed small enough sop, but he rose above frustration and joined the government.

For Secretary of the Treasury, Davis selected Barnwell's personal choice—Christopher G. Memminger of South Carolina.[28] Stately, white-haired Memminger brought human talents to a superhuman task. But his service in the South Carolina legislature as chairman of the Committee on Finance boded well.

An old acquaintance from the Senate became Secretary of the Navy. Stephen R. Mallory of Florida, formerly chairman of the Senate Committee on Naval Affairs, accepted the assignment in better faith than it was offered. Despite the obvious need for ocean commerce, there seemed little likelihood that a nation poor in manufactories could support much of a navy. But Mallory determined to do his best. Gifted with originality, he proposed and carried out a program of ironclad construction. Poor workmanship and feeble engines hampered the effectiveness of Rebel iron ships, but the *Virginia (Merrimac)*, the *Tallahassee*, the *Albemarle*, and the *Arkansas* did remarkable duty against overwhelming foes. In the realm of naval strategy, Mallory showed shrewd grasp of necessity. Since the South could not match the Union ship for ship, could not hope to protect all the coastline or all the rivers and harbors, Mallory schemed to make selective use of inferior strength. In time he devised a program of commerce raiding which so hurt the North that many merchantmen sought protection under neutral flags. Sleek raiders like the *Sumter*, the *Alabama*, and the *Florida* attacked sea lanes in order to draw Union warships from blockading stations and to hit Yankee businessmen in the pocketbooks. Their efforts were felt. Mallory's navy was never formidable but rarely ignored.

Usually the forgotten man of the cabinet, cast back in the corners of history, Mallory brought shrewdness and conciliation to an often turbulent group. And he did one thing better than most of his colleagues—he got along with a precise and zealous President.[29]

None of the cabinet got along better with Davis than the Attorney

General, Judah P. Benjamin of Louisiana. Benjamin shines from the Confederacy as one of its lasting lights. A gifted lawyer, sometime planter, polished politician, he combined the art of persuasion with the craft of power. Born on the British Island of St. Thomas, he had been adopted by a wealthy New Orleanian and trained in the law. Suitable marriage brought him a lovely wife and personal grief at a later prolonged estrangement. But with his combined base of law and land he fashioned a career in politics which took him to the United States Senate and made him a man of mark.

Like his colleague John Slidell, Louisiana's other Senator when the state left the Union, Benjamin had grace of manner. A few carpers said in envy that his features were too often twisted in an unctuous smirk and that he was as crooked as he was fat.

It is hard to see him clear. From accusations against his honesty at Yale, he had learned not to trust all his friends; from countless courtroom encounters, the harsh realities of conflict; from years of planter life, the humiliation of failure. These lessons he learned well, and they made him by 1861 a complex and special man. Because he was himself complex he had a knack for comprehending others like him. And so it was that he understood Jefferson Davis. They were unlike in every obvious way: Benjamin outgoing, jovial; Davis wrapped in some inner turmoil, aloof—but beneath their different poses they shared a passion for the South which made them more than friends. Consequently Benjamin soon became the most trusted of ministers and earned the jealousy of many. But Davis needed him and used him in various roles.

Texas, the seventh Confederate state, had submitted secession to popular referendum and received the Postmaster Generalship as a reward for joining the Confederacy. The portfolio went to John H. Reagan, regarded by Davis as a "sturdy, honest" man with a knowledge of "the territory included in the Confederate States . . . both extensive and accurate."[30] Reagan had no easy task, for the post routes of the Union were in disarray, Southern roads and railroads unreliable at best, and the Confederate constitution would require his department to pay its own way by March 1863. But the Postmaster General met his problems successfully enough to win the respect of the people and the admiration of the cabinet.

The President considered long before appointing a Secretary of War. And it was natural; after all, he prided himself on his record as War Secretary in Franklin Pierce's cabinet. Martial matters were close to the President's heart; West Point and the Mexican War had had a lasting effect on his self-esteem, and deep down he thought himself more soldier than statesman. Whoever served him in his own best role must follow cherished practice, which meant, of course, that whoever got the job would function always under Davis's special eye. It was a role that could not be filled—and certainly not by the man who first assumed it. Leroy P. Walker, prominent Alabama lawyer and politician, came highly recommended by his delegation and he got the job. Doubtless he merited all kinds of regard, but hardly as a military man. Practically all he knew of war he had gleaned from somewhat honorific service as a militia general and from passing acquaintance with soldiers.

Sadly enough, he seems to have had few compensating virtues. Doleful and sententious, he hated administration and distrusted activity. Around him in the war office he generated chaos like a great malevolent sloth. Decisions were delayed until they were unnecessary, routine wallowed in a swamp of detail, and Walker himself shirked all responsibility. Such dreary incompetence earned him a nation's derision and the nickname "Slow Coach." Finally, both he and the President agreed he should resign. He bequeathed to his successors a legacy of disorganization and presidential supervision that boded nothing but trouble.[31]

There were already troubles enough, a major one being that nobody seemed willing to recognize any. And that pointed up a special strain in Southern character—the strain of romantic optimism that shrouded the present in hope and the future in whimsey. The quirk left realism to the President; he must tell the hard truths to his countrymen.

It was scarcely a task he relished, but neither did he relish the presidency. Duty, nonetheless, must be done; someone had to inject a dose of sense into the country, or else it would collapse at the first stroke of tribulation. How best to do it? No way would be palatable, but the upcoming Inaugural Address offered the most obvious chance to be cautious as well as hopeful. Davis seized his opportunity.

Because of long and prominent government service, the new President knew better than most the high import of a President's maiden speech. And he could guess the special impact his own would carry, not only across the Southland, but in the North and around the world. He labored over the Inaugural diligently, and when finished, it bore indelible marks of his logic and his stilted cadence.

Monday, February 18, 1861, dawned cloudless and balmy; gay crowds eddied up Montgomery's Dexter Avenue at the approach of high noon. An elegant coach and six[32] took Davis in regal state to the capitol. An inaugural committee of Congress met him, escorted him to an ovation of the membership, and, at one o'clock, led him out on a sun-bathed portico. There, framed by the white columns, he took the oath of office and stepped forward to speak.

Now the curious throng on the capitol grounds could glimpse something of the manner of their man. Tall, straight, and dignified, immaculate in formal frock coat, Jefferson Davis looked the perfect model of a President. His high forehead framed in wispy curls, his ascetic face lined by tension, his tapered hands expressive and alive, his voice strong and pleasant, he had a force about him which gave truth to what he said. But, when he started speaking, none in the audience could guess that he proclaimed a different history for them and for the world.

Certainly he blurred the impact of his moment with recollections of the past and seemed at pains to recite for all Southerners their course to independence. For a few minutes his talk sounded a little like a declaration of the reasons for secession, and it was. This part was for foreign and Northern consumption and lingered on constitutional matters and the legitimacy of the Confederate government. The Provisional Congress had adhered strongly to hallowed American tradition in all its actions; what was done in Montgomery was more evolution than revolution. If the old Union had been broken, Northern industrialism had broken it; the South departed to preserve the promise of American democracy.

"We have changed the constituent parts, but not the system of government," said the President, and added that "the impartial and enlightened verdict of mankind will vindicate the rectitude of our conduct; and He who knows the hearts of men will judge of the sincerity with which we have labored to preserve the Government of our fathers in its spirit."

By no stretch of the imagination, he said, could the Confederacy be considered an aggressive or vindictive nation. Lest foreign nations fear economic repercussions from Southern independence, Davis spoke soothingly of commerce and pledged a free-trade policy. And, lest the North read weakness in a plea for foreign trade, Davis pledged, too, the course of liberty. "We have entered upon the career of independence," he reminded, "and it must be inflexibly pursued." Peacefully pursued, he devoutly hoped, but "if . . . passion or lust of dominion should cloud the judgment or inflame the ambition of those [Northern] States, we must prepare to meet the emergency and maintain, by the final arbitrament of the sword, the position which we have assumed among the nations of the earth."

And so saying, he tolled for Confederates some of the costs of reality. As he went on, he indicated to any who listened carefully an intent for strong central government, an intent perhaps at considerable variance with Southern expectation.

"For purposes of defense," he announced, "the Confederate States may, under ordinary circumstances, rely mainly upon the militia; but it is deemed advisable, in the present condition of affairs, that there should be a well-instructed and disciplined army, more numerous than would usually be required on a peace establishment. . . . To increase the power, develop the resources, and promote the happiness of the Confederacy, it is requisite that there should be so much of homogeneity that the welfare of every portion shall be the aim of the whole."

Clearly the President expected a hard future for the Confederacy and was not deluding his countrymen; but he did soften reality with a ringing call to hope.

"It is joyous in the midst of perilous times to look around upon a people united in heart, where one purpose of high resolve animates and actuates the whole; where the sacrifices to be made are not weighed in the balance against honor and right and liberty and equality. Obstacles may retard, but they can not long prevent, the progress of a movement sanctified by its justice and sustained by a virtuous people."[33]

Odds Against Phantoms

The whole problem for the South came down to a matter of time. Given enough time, Davis could finish creating his administration, could consolidate it, and could put his program for Southern unity into effect. Unity must be the South's pose to the world; there must be no show of weakness, no hint of indecision. Regardless of the appalling inferiority of the South in every natural resource, regardless of the bickering already rife among governors and legislatures, among vying favor seekers, among factions in the Congress, the President had to show none of it, had to be calm and hopeful and certain of his course.

Statistics that came to Davis daily told a harrowing story. Seven Confederate states with a population close to nine million (of which three and a half million were slaves) stood in opposition to twenty-two Northern states and twenty-two million people. Worse yet, no less than nine-tenths of the old nation's money rested in Yankee banks; in all the coffers below Mason and Dixon's line only $27 million worth of specie could be counted; beyond that lay nothing save the dubious expedients of credit and confidence. More statistics gave less comfort: In all of the seven seceded states there was not a single factory of consequence, no foundry to cast cannon or roll heavy iron plate, no furnaces, no significant powder works. The few manufactories that stood exceptions to Southern worship of King Cotton were either textile plants or tiny shops incapable of vast production.[34]

Even if arsenals to rival the North's Raritan and Picatinny, if industrial centers to match Pittsburgh and Altoona, had dotted the entire Southland, the future would still be bleak. Where was the coal, iron, lead, all the raw materials needed to sustain an industrial economy? Optimists might argue that the Confederacy had more resources than industries, that coal and iron abounded in Alabama, that lead could be gleaned by diligent search, that mineral surveys would show untapped riches lurking near the Southern surface. But the hard facts were inescapable—until other states seceded, precious little could be taken from the ground. The Montgomery government recognized that even if resources were as plentiful as fancies, the nation had neither the talent nor the tools for their development. Virginia, if she would cast her lot with her separated sisters, would bring to the cause Richmond's industrial complex and bountiful lead mines in the southwestern corner of the state. Missouri, should she follow the hearts of her people, could contribute important lead mines in the southeastern section of her domain as well as the vital rail and boatyards of St. Louis.

Anyone struggling to count the credits of the Confederacy would be hard pressed. The country boasted more coastline than the North; some 3,000 miles of it dotted by small harbors, cut by inlets, estuaries, rivers, and roadsteads. But there were few large ships, not even many commercial boats, and no large facilities to build them. Without adequate shipping the glorious Southern coastline might well become a liability, a tempting platform of invasion. The coast might be dubious, but surely the vast lands of the Confederacy, the endless acres of cotton and tobacco, were solid advantages. They were, of course, if things remained as they had been. Land had value in direct relation to its role as a national resource. If cotton kept its world market, all would be well. If, though, by some awful accident cotton lost its sway, the land would suffer and so would the country.

Nothing save the people, then, could be counted on the Confederate side. Were the people safe? None could deny the impact of a sudden exultant nationalism, but how deep did it run? How many in the South were Southerners but not Confederates? Until their loyalties transcended their states, the people were a chancy resource.

Strange Patterns for a President

Appearances to the contrary, Davis had qualities to cope with his chimeric land. True, he had no touch of magic to make men more than mortal, to lead them against history and somehow charm their fate. But he had formidable compensations. When he took his oath of office he gave himself wholly to the cause, became first and last the foremost Confederate. Devotion, dogged determination, and a will of iron were some qualities he brought to his task. More than that, he brought an unexpected capacity to grow with the presidency. This is not uncommon in men elevated to that high place, but Davis seemed more the sort to exalt than be exalted. Still, despite his romantic heritage, despite his rigid molding in the postulates of Calhoun, Davis had a grasp of progress. He was touched by change. And the problems of his office gave him a perspective on reality which wrenched romance to pragmatism and made him finally a modern chief executive.

Like it or not, he forced himself to the alien task of making rapid decisions on a vast variety of questions. Congress had instructed the Chief Executive to contract for arms and munitions, and since these could be had only from Northern factories, Davis sent Commodore Raphael Semmes to Yankee country to buy what weapons could be found.[35] Nor did he neglect other foreign markets. In collaboration with the Chief of Ordnance, the President dispatched Major Caleb Huse, an energetic munitions expert, to Europe with the hope that Confederate credit might work some miracle of finance and produce a stream of guns and ammunition.[36]

The constitution and various statutes impelled the Chief Executive to supervise the organization and administration of the Confederate armed forces. Working through his secretaries when he thought them competent, with others when urgency demanded, the President built a rudimentary military system in outline and made progress in reducing the number of recruiting and supply puzzles.

Nothing intrigued old soldier Davis as much as military matters, and during the history of his country he lavished especial attention on the army. Contemporaries and later critics would say he wasted time on military details better left to his service secretaries, but the record of the war belies the charge. In some military details he stood on familiar ground and took confidence for less familiar tasks.

Among the most important responsibilities of the President is control and direction of foreign relations. In the intricate realm of foreign affairs Davis groped with atypical uncertainty. Nothing in his background lent precedence for diplomacy; here he must be taught by circumstances. Certainly the circumstances of the South's world position were peculiar enough to challenge the deftest diplomat. Chief among confounding factors was the condition of the

Union. Everything concerning the United States became the special province of the Executive. No Confederate state could continue in direct relation with the Union. All contact between the North and South must follow careful diplomacy. The same was obviously true for other foreign nations.

The world's view of the Confederacy was Davis's inescapable burden. With Secretary Toombs, the President had to project a fair view of the South, showing a pastoral, peaceful country questing only for liberty. And the ultimate achievement of that liberty might well rest on the success of Davis as a diplomat.

Ultimate is a concept in future tense; the South had no time for concern with long-range visions. The immediate future loomed too heavily and rested too clearly on relations with the United States. None could deny this overriding fact, and so the Confederacy awaited the coming of Abraham Lincoln with bated curiosity.

Few people below Mason and Dixon's line knew much about the Illinois lawyer who now led the Republicans. Most Southerners considered him a political freak, a misfit who blundered onto the stage in a great tragicomedy, a buffoon. Even Lincoln's Inaugural Address did little to dispel the image of a back-country bumpkin. Confederates were not the only ones to see Lincoln in this light—many of his own party shared the impression, as did most foreigners. And the impression lingered. As late as April 1861, the British Ambassador in Washington would write to Victoria's Foreign Secretary, Lord John Russell: "Mr. Lincoln has not hitherto given proof of his possessing any natural talents to compensate for his ignorance of everything but Illinois village politics. He seems to be well meaning and conscientious, in the measure of his understanding, but not much more."[37]

Even friends of Lincoln's had to admit that his inactivity during the first weeks of his administration smacked of spinelessness or vacillation. Every passing day surely lent aid and comfort to the Confederacy. All those stern pronouncements of solemn oaths in heaven, or intent to collect taxes and execute the laws, that rang bravely in the Inaugural Address lapsed into bombast. All neophyte Lincoln seemed to do was follow veteran Buchanan's path to paralysis.

From Montgomery, Davis watched his Yankee counterpart in mortal fascination. Common problems forged a curious bond between them, a bond which would grow finally into the respect of worthy foes. They never really knew each other and were opposites without personal congruents. Davis looked like a statesman; Lincoln did not. Lincoln had height on Davis, but not much more. And even his height worked against him—it gave him a long-shanked looseness that cast his plain face into ungainly caricature.

But Lincoln had charm and a warm, bubbling humor that brightened his drab appearance. And because he had an earthy humanness he had also a special affection for people. War confirmed this affection, enlarged it, made it almost unbearable for him. All the terrible suffering of so many must have a dignity beyond mere victories and defeats. Finally Lincoln would glimpse the deeper meaning of sacrifice—glimpse it dimly shrouded in an endless battle smoke. What he saw was a vision of the triumph of man, and the vision grew with the horrors of war. As it grew it seemed to sustain him, buoy him, justify him, but it would not come wholly clear. He fought to compel it, to see it, grasp it. Still, for almost three years the full meaning eluded him. At last, at a memorial service in Gettysburg, something would touch a poetry in his soul and he would speak democracy's lasting promise for the future.

Far to the South, Jefferson Davis wrestled with a tortured affection of his own. He loved the Confederacy as Lincoln loved the Union. And he felt that the conflict between North and South cut deeper than slavery, state rights, or secession—that it was a kind of "crack in time itself," a moment of confrontation between past and future. This knowledge brought Davis a special agony; he yearned to tell it eloquently, to summon his country to a final battle for tradition and sustain it with some lasting language. But eloquence is a product of emotion, and emotion had been quenched by stoicism and by a crippling shyness which banked his passion, parched his fluency in stilted phrase, and left him forever a strangely muffled man.

Beneath the careful symmetry of his exterior lurked a different Jefferson Davis, a surprising one of churning, boundless ambition, of high pride and tender feeling, a calculating man of measured brilliance. If he lacked the easy guile of a practiced office seeker, he had the shrewdness of a statesman. More than that, he had a facile mind that was at its best in crisis. Predictably stubborn, he nonetheless could learn from experience and from observation.

He learned something about Lincoln from experience and observation. The first lesson involved policy. Experience reminded the Confederate President that policy does not always involve action. And as he watched Lincoln's inactivity in the weeks after he took office, Davis could hardly escape the conclusion that inactivity might well prove the best of all possible Yankee policies. For none knew better than Davis the fragile nature of Southern unity. All his new countrymen were loudly patriotic, but few could nerve themselves yet to selfless devotion over a long period of calm. Time became a subtle Southern enemy. An unfanned crisis loses impact rapidly. As weeks stretched on without overt trouble, Confederate unity showed signs of strain.

Lincoln cannily guarded the mystery of his plans. Even after his inauguration no one really knew his intent, and none could guess it. That very uncertainty put special pressure on the Confederate States and forced a pause in plans that shifted initiative from Montgomery to Washington.

Davis did try to shift it back. Acting under a congressional mandate to send a three-man commission to Washington "for the purpose of negotiating friendly relations between that government and the Confederate States of America, and for the settlement of all questions of disagreement between the two governments, upon principles of right, justice, equity and good faith,"[38] Davis took his first steps toward diplomatic disillusion.

Any calm survey of the Southern situation would confirm his own later opinion that a "peace commission" ranked above most things in importance. Two issues had to be settled as a prelude to peaceful separation of North and South. First was the matter of such public property as forts and arsenals; second, the question of free navigation of the Mississippi. Freedom of navigation and the famed "right of deposit" had been vital to the growth of the American West; they had loomed largely in the acquisition of Louisiana and the expansion of the nation. Now the mere threat of a blocked Father of

Waters wracked the Mississippi Valley in a spasm of the pocketbook. Part of the task to be done by Confederate emissaries in Washington certainly was to allay fears about the river.[39]

The men who went to the Union capital needed to be wise, discreet, and soothing, models of Southern moderation. On February 25, 1861, Alfred Roman of Louisiana, Martin Crawford of Georgia, and John Forsyth of Alabama were approved by Congress as commissioners. Davis's reasons for selecting this particular trio are revealing. "These gentlemen," he explained later, "represented the three great parties which had ineffectually opposed the sectionalism of the so-called 'Republicans.' Ex-Governor Roman had been a Whig in former years, and one of the 'Constitutional Union' . . . party in the canvass of 1860. Mr. Crawford, as a State-rights Democrat, had supported Mr. Breckinridge; and Mr. Forsyth had been a zealous advocate of the candidacy of Mr. Douglas. The composition of the commission was therefore such as should have conciliated the sympathy and cooperation of every element of conservatism with which they might have occasion to deal."[40]

By all rational lights the commissioners should have done well; they were, after all, veteran politicians. Unfortunately, diplomacy was not politics. Too soon they found that in the diplomatist's murky realm truth was delusion, logic a snare.

In a way their problem was the South's in microcosm—they were agents of an older order caught in a fundamental shift of history. In the world crisis that had been rending all kinds of institutions for a dozen years, norms were warped, traditions uprooted, values forgotten, standards changed. As the crisis grew, even language lost its structure and gained new meanings. Society suffers this kind of fierce remolding now and then, and the people caught up in the process are always somehow out of pace. Not surprisingly, in times of abrupt reformation new breeds of people rise up to shape the change, breeds without courtesies, without honor for what has gone before, crude breeds ungraced by tradition. These mutants, though, are usually brokers of the future and in time will become its victims.

Sadly for them, the three Southern gentlemen in Washington

37

stood for much more than the simple independence of their country; they stood with the rear guard of their age and were the first sacrifices to its going.

Like some earlier colleagues representing South Carolina, Roman, Crawford, and Forsyth arrived in Washington hoping to present their credentials to Lincoln and get on with negotiations. With any luck at all they felt they could succeed. Instructions from Davis left them wide latitude; they could do almost anything, accept almost any conditions, were to be generous on every issue save one: Fort Sumter.

Fort Sumter, athwart Charleston harbor, counted as a vital Southern symbol. The fact that symbols had entered the situation told something important about the gathering crisis: the conflict between North and South had moved from an amorphous argument in abstractions to focus harshly on something tangible. The whole confrontation had grown dangerously rigid. There is always an encouraging flexibility in arguments over principle; the ground shifts easily with prejudice. But there is no flexibility in arguments over symbols. They become talismans of honor, charged with awful sanctity.

So it was with Fort Sumter. Fort Pickens in Pensacola harbor had less impact on world opinion because the port was less vital. And though sovereignty was a factor in Pensacola, Fort Sumter in Charleston harbor was the major problem. If Sumter went to the Rebels, so would Pickens. Sumter was a decrepit thing with virtually no military value. It had, since December 1860, sheltered a small Federal garrison commanded by Major Robert Anderson, and hence became the test of sovereignty for Carolina and the South. As long as the Stars and Stripes flew over Sumter, Southerners were not dictators of their own destiny. Virtually everything else might be conceded, not Sumter. That single proviso laid a shadow on the commissioners' task but did not dim their hope.

Washington and its denizens also clung to hope, or something like hope. The city lay in the grip of fierce cold in early March; stragglers from the bootless Washington Peace Conference lingered in some of the hotels,[41] Congress continued in fitful session, and the pages of the *Globe* bulged daily with fusty monologues on disunion.

A curious kind of suspense hung over everything; people on street corners, eddying in crowded stores and theaters, clustering in Willard's lobby or the foyers of the House and Senate, talked in oddly muted tones, as if through some chemistry of silence they might deny the trends.

The three Confederate emissaries encountered this silence almost immediately. Their presence in the city was no secret, but no sooner did they set about making themselves officially known to President Lincoln than they ran into a baffling conspiracy of isolation. Polite but firm blocks intruded between them and the President; so careful were these blocks, in fact, that the envoys could never be sure that Lincoln really knew of their presence in the capital.

Inexperienced as they were at diplomatic hedging, they quickly saw their problem: no one in the Yankee administration dared receive them as accredited representatives of a rebel nation. As far as Northern officialdom was concerned, the Confederacy simply did not exist, secession had never happened. Clearly any contact with Lincoln's government would have to be unofficial and off the record. This situation presented serious and touchy questions. Could the Confederacy afford to become involved in clandestine negotiations? Could it tolerate being ignored?

The automatic Southern response to those questions was, naturally, no. Nothing riled the prideful folk of Dixie quite as much as studied insults. The commissioners were irked, but curbed their anger long enough to seek instructions from Montgomery. Davis, Toombs, the whole Confederate cabinet shared fully the ire of the commissioners, but responsibility tempered rage with caution. Stay, the three emissaries were told, stay and see what indirect contacts through friends of the South might accomplish.

Two friends offered themselves as go-betweens. Both were Associate Justices of the United States Supreme Court, both men of integrity who sincerely hoped to keep the peace. Justices John A. Campbell and Samuel Nelson were highly regarded and seemed the finest possible allies. In full good faith they approached the new Secretary of State, William H. Seward, put the Confederate case as clearly as possible, and requested an appointment with the President so that the Southern three could present their credentials.

In all that happened later Seward played a curiously impenetrable role. He is not easy to fathom. Few men held such high office in such turmoil of ambition. Formerly Governor of New York and Senator from his native state, Seward's every act, every statement, every gesture, appeared to serve some personal purpose, so much so that he seems lost in his guises and a creature of expediency.

Many contemporaries doubted his honor; not a few suspected his motives; some even questioned his balance. Seward stands surely as the most positive personage on the stage of the Union; a man as impossible to know as to ignore. Perhaps the completest product of his changing time, Seward was a strange and cynical idealist driven by great emotions and uncertain scruples.

Negotiation with Seward's sort required a guile unknown to Roman, Crawford, and Forsyth. They came armed with the techniques of a more formal time. So they were in for trouble, especially since their two go-betweens also lacked the duplicity for their job.

Honest and artless, Campbell and Nelson accepted Seward's courtesy as evidence of good will and were eager to believe his assurances that nothing overt would be done in Charleston. He promised to influence Lincoln toward evacuating Sumter and implied evacuation would come soon. When the commissioners heard this news they were vastly encouraged and reported gleefully to Montgomery. Davis, having known Seward well in the Senate, had his doubts and urged caution. What did Lincoln think?

That, the commissioners could not say. Seward talked glibly of his sway at the White House, but the Union President had said nothing to Campbell or Nelson. Still, the commissioners could not imagine Seward would deliberately dupe the two judges. And it seems that Seward at first intended to be fair with them. He had hopes of settling the Sumter issue without war, and he did seriously consider giving up the fort. So, for that matter, did a majority of Lincoln's cabinet.[42] But Seward had no intention of recognizing Confederate independence; reunion remained his goal. So firm was his purpose that the British minister became convinced Seward would foment a foreign war to repair the Union.[43]

A serious miscalculation led Seward to temporary alliance with the South on the Sumter issue. He believed firmly—and Lincoln seems to have shared this delusion—that a groundswell of Union sentiment would sweep the South if trouble could be averted through the summer. In fact, he counted heavily on "counterrevolution" starting in Sam Houston's Texas and spreading eastward.[44] As long as that hope bemused him he willingly connived to prolong the Charleston status quo.

Events finally outran his schemes. Delay was practical only so long as Northern public opinion remained ambivalent about secession. But gradually the North began to harden its views toward the South: businessmen shifted to a no-compromise stand, idealistic patriots talked the sanctity of the Union. The cabinet finally sensed the altered sentiment, and by the end of March a majority supported a hard line at Charleston.[45] Seeing himself alone Seward suggested a wild plan of foreign bullying which Lincoln rejected, and by April 1 Seward had almost no voice on the Sumter issue—the final decision would come from Lincoln.

Davis had anticipated Lincoln's decision. The Confederate leader accepted Lincoln's Inaugural Address in the same light as his own—a pledge to the people. In his Inaugural Lincoln had promised that "the power confided to me will be used to hold, occupy, and possess the property and places belonging to the Government and to collect the duties and imposts." He promised no invasion of the South save to fulfill that pledge.[46]

As Lincoln saw the situation, his promise would be kept if Fort Sumter and the lesser Fort Pickens in the harbor of Pensacola, Florida, remained Federal. To ensure their retention he ordered two relief expeditions sent South. Why? Surely he knew the result of this act? Seward had not kept him totally unaware of Montgomery's views on reinforcing or provisioning Sumter and Pickens. Certainly he weighed his action carefully. But he could do no less than he promised and still keep the respect of his country. In the final analysis he could argue that the outcome really depended on the Confederates.

As a matter of fact Lincoln took pains to explain to Southerners that he intended nothing more than a preservation of the status quo.

To South Carolina's Governor Pickens he sent a personal messenger with a carefully worded statement of purpose: "I am directed by the President of the United States to notify you to expect an attempt will be made to supply Fort-Sumter [*sic*], with provisions only; and that, if such attempt be not resisted, no effort to throw in men, arms, or ammunition, will be made, without further notice, or in case of an attack upon the Fort."[47]

This bold announcement would have appalled the Confederate delegates in Washington if they had not been appalled already. Seward's treatment of Campbell and Nelson, his promises and insinuations, threats and bombast, had at last made cynics of them all. The two judges suffered most the tarnish to integrity, since they faithfully reported Seward's bland assertions that he had no plans for Charleston up until almost the moment the Sumter relief expedition sailed. Lincoln's warning to Governor Pickens merely confirmed deceit and spurred the commissioners' departure for Montgomery on April 1.

Davis learned from Lincoln and Seward. But he had no time to wallow in outrage. Word of the coming expedition put the next move squarely up to the Confederates, and they knew it. Events had left them almost no maneuvering room. Two choices seemed to be theirs: attack and capture the fort or confess a lack of sovereignty. Neither alternative had much charm. The Confederate cabinet weighed the possibilities at several urgent meetings in early April. Some members urged no action, and yet no action meant accepting defeat. What could be done?

Dilemma and Decision

By the morning of April 10 the crisis had accelerated almost beyond control. The Carolinians verged on frenzy and were likely to take the decision away from the cabinet at any moment; rumblings from around the country indicated mounting tension. Late in the morning Davis's harried ministers gathered at Montgomery in one of the Exchange Hotel's large conference rooms. They grouped around a huge table, the President presiding, everyone present save Robert Toombs. After some nervous conversation, Davis called for order. No hopeful news came from Charleston, but General P. G. T.

Beauregard reported thorough preparations to take the fort, should the order come.

As with all great moments there was much trivial talk and hesitation. Davis listened to the nervous gabble with aloof attention and said little. Sentiment ran for taking the fort, but with a kind of face-saving: Beauregard should give Anderson a chance to surrender. If he did, the issue of the first shot might be delayed. Suddenly, in the midst of anguish, the door opened and in strode Toombs. Locks afly he paced the room, listened to the timorous trend toward action, stopped, faced his confreres, and told them in measured phrases the portent of their plans:

"The firing upon that fort will inaugurate a civil war greater than any the world has yet seen. . . . Mr. President, at this time, it is suicide, murder, and will lose us every friend at the North. You will wantonly strike a hornet's nest which extends from mountains to ocean, and legions, now quiet, will swarm out and sting us to death. It is unnecessary; it puts us in the wrong; it is fatal."[48]

Who doubted he was right? But what else could be done? Everything had narrowed down to the symbol of Fort Sumter. True, an attack on it might start a civil war, but in war the South had a chance. Failure to take a stand denied any chance at all. None of the men at the table wanted to vote. Still, for the record . . . Past and present fused for an instant in that room. And with the decision, past and present faded and the future had been cast.

Secretary Walker put the decision in a telegram to General Beauregard. Demand surrender of the fort; if refused, reduce it.

The general pushed his preparations hard on April 10, and by noon on the 11th he was ready. Two officers went out to Anderson with a surrender request. They returned with the major's admission of short provisions and intent to quit the fort in a few days. Interested in Anderson's comments, Beauregard entered into lengthy negotiations.[49] In Montgomery the cabinet seized on any pretext to delay and authorized Beauregard to withhold bombardment if Anderson would state a specific departure date and promise no hostile action on his part.

After careful consideration Anderson found himself unable to meet the exact provisos of the Confederate government. He would leave, he said, by noon on the 15th if not relieved sooner, and he would not attack unless attacked—or ordered to do so. These qualifications were unacceptable to Montgomery.

Beauregard's aides respectfully informed Major Anderson at 3:30 A.M. on April 12 that firing would start in an hour. When they left, the fort's big doors closed behind them and shut away forever something of America.

Promptly at 4:30 A.M. venerable Edmund Ruffin, a famous old Virginia firebrand enlisted in the ranks of the elite Palmetto Guard, strode to a Southern cannon, touched match to fuse, and watched a fiery shell arc over the water toward Fort Sumter. It was a moment the world never forgot.[50]

CHAPTER TWO

"Cast upon the Winds and Waves"

—THOMAS BRAGG

Crisis on the Middle Border

Seldom had two hostile camps approached combat so timidly. With a few hotheaded exceptions on either side of Mason and Dixon's line, almost nobody confessed to wanting war. But spilled blood attracts emotion the way an insulted flag attracts heroes.

Northward in the Union capital, fate rested on the decision of Abraham Lincoln. Respect for humanity required cool reckoning on his part; yet concern for his country made action imperative. If he waited he might lose the cohesion Sumter had suddenly brought the North. Until the moment when Major Anderson's little band marched forlornly from their smoking fort, countless Northerners doubted the wisdom of coercion. Why not let the erring sisters depart, and good riddance to them? Years of niggling complaint about rights and constitutions had worn thin the fabric of union anyway. Shut off in their own cotton kingdom Southerners could rant and rave to the limit of their pocketbooks and the North could get on with progress. But once the Stars and Stripes was sullied and the power of the Union challenged, patriotic fervor swept inertia aside. For one burnished moment the North rose united in wrath. At that moment Lincoln moved. On April 15, 1861, he called on the states for 75,000 volunteers to put down "combinations too powerful to be suppressed by the ordinary course of judicial proceedings, or by the powers vested in the Marshals by law."[1]

His proclamation calling for troops is worthy of attention not

45

only because it set a policy and tone for whatever happened next but also because it denied Southern interpretations of the conflict between the sections.

Lincoln clearly knew the Southern conviction that secession had legal sanction and was inherent in the federal compact. He also knew that the constitutional issue so dear to Southerners might win converts in Europe, especially in England. At the same time he knew that the constitutional argument about the nature of union had less impact in the North. Possible foreign entanglements and Northern apathy made his initial moves in the conflict especially important. A confusing problem in statecraft faced him, a problem which he met squarely with his proclamation. In that document he announced insurrection existing below Mason and Dixon's line and hence neatly denied the existence of the Confederate States. Secession was not an issue, according to his view of things; the Southern states had not really departed the Union, they were merely out of proper relationship to it. And as long as he could maintain that interpretation, the Confederates would have to plead their case unsupported in the capitals of the world.

Some embarrassments might follow the proclamation. A complete political realist, Lincoln understood clearly that his call for volunteers to compel peace in Dixie would provoke various reactions in the border areas. He understood, too, perhaps more clearly than anyone else save Jefferson Davis, the importance of the border zone stretching between North and South from western Virginia along the Tennessee-Kentucky line on beyond the Mississippi to the Missouri-Arkansas boundary—a zone which insulated the Northern and Southern heartlands from one another. Kentucky and Missouri appeared Southern in sympathy and might conceivably join the Confederacy with any sort of shove; Tennessee and Arkansas were committed to the South but divided in sentiment. Careful statecraft might deny at least two of these states to the Rebels.

Whatever the possibilities, Lincoln determined to secure for the Union as much of the vital middle border as possible. His proclamation could well inflame Southern passions in Virginia and North Carolina, could even drive the prestigious Old Dominion and its lesser satellite into Rebel concert, could conceivably weld Tennessee and Arkansas into the Confederacy; but if it thwarted rebellious actions in Kentucky and Missouri, if in any way it kept those vital anchors of national communication west and south, the proclamation would succeed.

With the nation solid from the Hudson to the Missouri, with all the rich farmlands of the new west still in reach, with the population and industrial centers of the Mississippi Valley safely in the fold, prospects were high for the Union. Peace could conceivably be preserved by those prospects alone.

So Lincoln issued his proclamation with hope, much more hope than the situation justified. He gambled, as did Seward, on a vast silent tide of pro-Union sentiment in the South which would swell to save the nation.

No such Union tide ran in the Confederacy. Not to say that a glacial unity locked the Southern republic together—certainly not. But the currents of Unionism that could be seen before the Montgomery convention had slowed with the paralysis of the Washington Peace Conference and stalled almost completely in an overwash of martial patriotism, as thousands upon thousands of young Southerners marched to drums and calls of glory. Such fervent enthusiasm offered temporary strength to the South, and President Davis worked to make it last.

Like Lincoln, Davis grasped the importance of the border and hoped earnestly to win it for the Confederacy. More clearly than his Yankee counterpart Davis knew the divided border mind. In Missouri, where Southern sentiment ran strong, he realized that local frenzy might well counterbalance reason and actually hurt the cause. Missouri stayed in conflict for months. Pro-Confederate Governor Claiborne Jackson believed that Missouri beyond St. Louis was staunchly Southern, and that the Unionist Germans of the state's metropolis represented an element without real significance.

New realities are hard to see when they first intrude on history; they are especially murky in the midst of great crises. So Governor Jackson did what experience taught him to do. To his legislature he recommended caution and advised a pro-Southern line and the general isolation and eventual seizure of Unionist St. Louis. When his call for secession and attachment to the Confederacy went largely unheeded, he successfully avoided outright Union allegiance, called out the state militia, and sought a hazy neutrality while rallying his people to final Southern alliance.

St. Louis foiled his plans. Despite the fringes of plantation aristocracy which marked Southern approaches to the city, the preponderant population was German and Union and determined. These loyalists were delivered into Lincoln's hands by an unheralded Yankee soldier, Brigadier General Nathaniel Lyon. Lyon spied out a camp of Jacksonian militia in the city, surrounded and captured the whole establishment, and so smashed the governor's hope of seizing the city and its invaluable arsenal.

Failure of Jackson's projected coup pretty well doomed the Southern cause in Missouri. St. Louis provided a fulcrum of power for Federal control and relegated the governor and his henchmen to that southern portion of the state called "Little Dixie."[2]

Kentucky had no particular Dixie zone—the whole state might qualify under that heading. Some members of the legislature were straight-outs, the fieriest of secessionists. Certain officers of the militia, particularly the ranking general Simon Bolivar Buckner, were of like views, and throughout the state were other Confederates. But Unionists were about equally spread the length and breadth of Kentucky, with Governor Beriah Magoffin at their head.

Shrewd and tough, the governor guessed the diffuse strength of secessionists and sought to thwart them by maneuver. He proposed neutrality for his state, and despite the bizarre sound of his proposal its merits could hardly be denied. Kentucky's geography gave her rich prospects for profit in a civil war. And if Magoffin's proposition lacked patriotic zeal from Lincoln's standpoint, it had at least a proper respect for Kentucky's sundered spirit. More than that it reflected the hedging propensities of Magoffin, whose quest for policy followed the scent of success.

Neutrality had no reality in the fluid crisis of 1861, but briefly both Washington and Montgomery found an open avenue to the enemy's country useful and permitted Magoffin's conceit.

Neutrality ended with military necessity at the reluctant hands of the Confederates. In late September 1861, Major General Leonidas Polk (a unique West Pointer who took the cloth and then again the sword) led a small garrison into Paducah. He intended to deny the Yankees a convenient route to the South, but Southern aggression merely opened the doors of Kentucky to a large Union army of occupation.

Still, there was some consolation for Jefferson Davis and his government. No sooner did the bluecoats pour into Kentucky than thousands of Rebel sympathizers trekked southward. Virtually all of the state militia decamped with Buckner, and so loud were cries of tyranny that a kind of Rebel state-in-exile came into being. On the hopes confessed by so many exiled sons of the Bluegrass, the Confederacy fashioned another star in the flag of the new republic. On November 20, Kentucky took its place as one of the Confederate States of America.[3]

Something like the Kentucky charade finally occurred in Missouri; a government-in-exile received token sanction by Confederate authorities, and representatives of Missouri took seats in the Southern Congress.[4] If such gestures struck many as empty, even absurd, they had a purpose for the moment.

President Davis, like Lincoln, was new in the game of international deceit, but he was not unintelligent. He understood the basic requirements of statecraft. World opinion about the Confederacy would be shaped—rightly or not—by its size. People everywhere tend to measure power by dimensions, so the boundaries of the nation were vital to its future. Obviously the Confederacy's eastern and southern limits were soundly fixed by the Atlantic and the Gulf of Mexico. On western fringes lay the Great American Desert, a wasteland stretching beyond Texas through Apache country and the badlands of New Mexico and Arizona. Only the northern border was questionable, and hence much care was lavished on its proper demarcation.

Quibblers might argue that Kentucky and Missouri scarcely offered natural barriers to the United States, that Tennessee and Arkansas with their river skeins were really better bastions for an outward wall, that Indian Territory, where most tribes were Southern allies, stood solidly on the left flank of the west.[5] But these are purely geographical arguments, and by late 1861 geopolitical factors were coming into meaning. Geography reinforced by political potential meant a double base of power; if Missouri south of its own river and Kentucky south of the Ohio could be made truly Confederate, the water lines would give pause to intruders and so would the sentiments of proud people. These, then, were the realities of a murky problem in diplomacy. Davis tried to turn them to advantage.

One to Make Ready

Southern preparations to meet the obvious martial consequences of Fort Sumter lagged alarmingly. Once the initial burst of energy that produced a heavy concentration of guns and men at Charleston waned a bit, enthusiasm for such tedious matters as mobilization and logistics faded. Southern history seemed to teach the same lesson as American history: a minuteman force would rise when needed, find the weapons of war from assorted manorial mantles, and sweep away any foe who dared tread on Dixie's ground.

And so it might have been in a Walter Scott novel. But things were not as simple in the war that developed in April and May of 1861. Lincoln's call for a huge army generated an equal need in the South, a need which Jefferson Davis did his best to meet.

Taking the initiative in the absence of Congress, Davis issued his own call for twelve months' men. Each of the Confederate states was asked for a quota for national service, a quota which would ensure an army of at least 100,000 men. This was the time-honored way to raise an army; states would ask for volunteer regiments, presumably equip them (thus solving a touchy problem), and send them off under state-appointed officers. The sanctity of the states would be preserved.[6] Davis had no intention of invading state prerogatives in raising troops, for he knew more clearly than most the easy pique of his governors. At the same time he could not permit this easy pique to ensnarl the whole Confederate war effort in a petty quarrel over state rights. Davis decided to meet the explosive issue head on in his call for troops. According to the terms of the President's request, the various states would contribute their men to Confederate service; once mustered, they would be state forces in name and federal force in fact.[7]

Small as this distinction may sound, it marks a basic policy of the

Confederate government. Errors of the Confederation would not be repeated by the new nation—control of the war would stay firmly in the hands of the central administration. This principle could be glimpsed on every hand. The Montgomery government, acting under sanction of the constitution, did everything necessary for making war.[8]

These details were myriad and they involved Davis and his cabinet in ever-widening activity. Tiny as the Charleston confrontation had been, it confirmed what General Beauregard and other professional soldiers had told the government: preparations had to be pushed desperately for a war of vast scope. Earlier American experience was misleading; the kind of conflict likely between North and South would dwarf everything known before. Larger war required larger dimensions in strategic and political thought.

Larger dimensions fortunately harmonized with the spirit of Montgomery. Experimentation was in the air, and Davis found the climate favorable for pursuing a hard war policy.

From a military standpoint the achievements of the Confederacy in the early months were essential to the country's future. The successful mustering and equipping of almost 200,000 men, together with their organization into regiments and brigades and armies, procurement from both North and South of at least 200,000 arms and 500 cannon (with enough powder for initial battles), the selection and assignment of competent field commanders—all these achievements provided a vital military foundation.[9]

None of it came easily. There is some doubt that the army and navy would ever have amounted to much without the martial acumen of the President. Davis pushed for intelligent military legislation. His wise leadership gave a direction to congressional action, which provided a Regular and Provisional Confederate Army and offered a grade promotion to United States officers who took commissions in either. The President also urged enough money to sustain the country's forces and supervised closely the initial regulations and orders that put the army and navy in service.

There were some who argued then and later that Davis devoted too much time to petty organization. Doubtless Secretary of War Leroy P. Walker would have agreed, for Davis virtually ran the War

Department.[10] Administratively he should have delegated the War Department to Walker and let him run it. But could Davis have kept his hands off? Probably not, for the War Department was his own; it was known and dear to him. He was good at the job and could not let a politician of dubious experience do it for him. Walker was only one of six secretaries of war to suffer the stewardship of Davis. It was a presidential flaw that time and advice never smoothed.

As his own War Secretary, Davis appointed the first chiefs of the War Department bureaus. Important in themselves, these initial selections are also important for what they reveal about Jefferson Davis.

Rising above American rules of patronage, Davis cast around for men of ability to head the supply services of the Confederate Army. Many of his selections he had known when he served officially as Secretary of War; many others were warmly proffered by trusted friends. It is certain that the War Department comprised a strangely homogeneous group of men whose general attitudes and styles were very like their complex leader's.

American custom divided the War Department into several supply and housekeeping bureaus, each under a ranking army officer and each charged with providing specific army needs. Most important among these logistical agencies were the ordnance, commissary, and quartermaster services—respectively responsible for arming, feeding, and furnishing clothes, shelter, transport, and pay to the troops. Such essential functions could not be left to inexperienced and incompetent men; each of the services demanded able and resourceful chiefs.

Surely administrative talent abounded in the South? Not so, and the reason is readily seen: Dixie's crop of administrators shrank in direct ratio to the expanse of the plantation system. Overseers and owners formed only a small segment of Southern society; entrepreneurs, bankers, and businessmen were scarce, for a nascent urban middle class lacked cohesion and repute. War would propel the Confederacy into a managerial revolution to rival that of the North. Supervisors would be essential to all phases of the war, and the South must find them.

Finding them appeared deceptively easy at the start. Numbers of experienced army administrators resigned from United States service and sought Southern commissions; others with martial pasts departed civilian life and joined the new army. There would not be enough of them for the tests of attrition, but these early comers were indispensable to the Southern cause.

Perhaps the finest of the lot was Josiah Gorgas, a dumpy, unimpressive man from Running Pumps, Pennsylvania, who bore his biblical name with solemn dignity. He came to the Confederacy from Frankford Arsenal in Philadelphia. Fifteen years' service in the Ordnance Department brought an unspectacular captaincy and a reputation for competence coupled with thorny independence. Blunted ambition and an Alabama-born wife pushed this artless genius of technology into Confederate allegiance. When Gorgas offered his help to the South, President Davis harked to the glowing recommendations of such friends as General Beauregard, commissioned the stray Yankee a major, and put him in charge of the Ordnance Bureau. Gorgas would distinguish himself and his cause by a burning drive that overcame shortages and provided arms, munitions, and cannon to the utter limit of resources.

Gorgas's appointment stands to the lasting credit of the President, for Davis made it without personal acquaintance with Gorgas. Professional competence alone directed the choice. On that basis the President often selected well; on other, more subjective bases, he often blundered.

Rarely did he blunder as abysmally as in appointing the head of the Commissary Bureau. Here of all places, tact, patience, business sense, and a saving gift of legerdemain were essential. To this critical post Davis called South Carolinian Lucius Bellinger Northrop, a wizened cripple thwarted by life into a petty, malicious curmudgeon. To an office of scope he brought limitation, to a task of vision he brought myopia, and to the army he brought hunger. Why did he get the job? Surely others less misanthropic were available, others with hope in their hearts? They were, but they were not friends of the President.

Friendship had less to do with Davis's selection of the Quartermaster General. Because of its traditional importance, the Quartermaster Department enjoyed the largest popular support of any logistical bureau; almost everyone knew something about its functions. And that complicated the bureau's tasks immeasurably, for there is nothing as confounding as relentless enthusiasm. Since so many knew smatterings of his job, the Quartermaster General became an object of special attention. What kind of man was the bureau chief? Did he know his business?

It was hard to say. Abraham Charles Myers, son of a prominent Charleston attorney and descendant of Moses Cohen, first rabbi of the city, boasted West Point training and a solid army career. He carried his fifty years easily, exuded competence, and obviously knew military routine. All of which surely boded well; and yet there was a question about him, a caveat born in the routine of his previous army life. Things he had done were done according to the rules and ramifications of the quartermaster manual. Where was the artful gesture, the daring innovation, the saving grace of irreverence to transform competence to conjury? Never in his army years had Myers departed from the comfort of the regulations.

"And Here's to Brave Virginia"

Men, money, supplies, international position—all focused public attention on how little the South had with which to face the future. Few in those optimistic early days doubted that all had been done that could be done by a harried government. Was it enough? Within the confines of the Confederacy were there resources sufficient to the challenge of nationhood? For the immediate present, possibly; for the long run, no. More of everything had to come from somewhere. That urgent necessity fixed the Confederate gaze firmly on Virginia and North Carolina. These two states lagged behind the tide of secession, clung resolutely to peace hopes, took a border view of conflict between the industrial North and the cotton South. Lincoln's call for men to suppress insurrection tipped the balance of uncertainty in both the Tarheel State and the august Old Dominion. They both were reluctant to quit the Union but more reluctant still to join in coercion of sister states. On April 17, 1861, Virginia concluded a curious alliance with the Confederacy, which permitted mutual assistance and paved the way for eventual secession. North Carolina departed the old compact for the new on May 20, 1861.

In numbers alone these two additions were vital to the Confederacy; Virginia brought 1,047,411 new white Rebels to the fold and North Carolina brought 631,100. But statistics told only part of the impact these new states had on the balance of power between North and South. Virginia's tradition as a haven of patriots, as a producer of presidents, gave the Old Dominion influence and power beyond numbers. When she cast her future with the Confederacy, Virginia lent the new cause formidable prestige.

Prestige was especially valuable among those intangibles known to statesmen. Simply in terms of power, though, Virginia's coming meant much to the Confederacy. In the rugged western mountain areas were mines and mineral deposits vital to a war effort; east of the lofty Alleghenies, in the sheltered valley of the Shenandoah River, rich farmlands offered bumper crops of foodstuffs; farther to the east, across the peaks of the stately Blue Ridge, the prosperous counties of northern Virginia promised horses and fodder and meat for legions.

Position also gave special importance to Virginia. Her northern border ran along the Potomac westward to the Ohio, making possible river communication with the Mississippi country. Alexandria sat across from Washington and was virtually a suburb of the Northern capital. Jutting sharply into enemy country, Virginia might be a springboard of aggression for either side.

But Virginia's greatest value to the Confederacy probably was Richmond. Most of the state was as rural as the rest of the South. But the capital stood apart from the state, apart from almost all of Dixie: Richmond was a modern city in the fullest American sense.

Down by the banks of the James long rows of warehouses stored the commerce that pulsed through Richmond's streets. Nearby were the long black buildings of Joseph R. Anderson's storied Tredegar Iron Works, which alone among the South's manufactories could roll and cast big cannon; its ample mills and shops cut nails, turned locomotive wheels, and rolled boiler plate, rails, and sheet iron.[11] Out in the historic James River lay Belle Isle, with its small but important government arsenal. It was not the only ordnance establishment in Richmond, for the city had long been an important center for the United States Ordnance Department. Richmond Armory, a state installation helped along by federal aid from time to time, boasted scant equipment but proudly claimed James H. Burton as its master armorer, an Englishman of Yankee experience who cherished both his craft and a set of plans for Britain's peerless Enfield rifle.

In the city's heart the terminus of the Richmond, Fredericksburg and Potomac Railroad marked a curious break in a major artery of trade. Across town, just far enough to make good mileage for the city's organized draymen, lay another terminus of the same line. A similar hiatus disconnected the track of the Virginia Central as it came in from northwestern Virginia heading for Petersburg. Why these breaks? Some engineering vagary, some designer's whimsey? The reason was a difference in gauge on the same rail lines. This anomaly was common to most Confederate carriers.

As the state drew closer to the Southern crisis, lines of men and wagons moved through Richmond in a rush of preparation. Clearly the city's influence reached beyond the Old Dominion. Roads and rail lines and canals fanned its interests and ideas in all directions; it was the focus of the upper South. And because it was, it worked a vast attraction across the whole Confederacy.[12]

Nowhere was this attraction more strongly felt than in Montgomery. This was natural enough. Since Virginia had joined up, most of the Confederate government's attention had turned toward the new northern boundary along the Potomac. Suddenly now the limits of the South reached a scant river's breadth from Washington and the heart of the Union. And no matter how hard the President, the cabinet, and the Congress tried to avoid it, each suddenly saw Virginia much larger than any other Confederate state.

Whatever Lincoln and his government did about the war would likely be done first in Virginia. Sheer accessibility made her vulnerable, and that posed a special problem for the government. To lose Virginia's people, her money, her industry, and her place in world opinion would simply undo the Confederate States. Nothing must be left undone to convince Virginia and every other state, North and South, that the Confederacy would defend its borders and honor its commitments.

It happened that this necessity became clear at a time when various pressures were combining to force a change of capitals on the Southern government. Montgomery had grown too cramped for the burgeoning bureaucracy; its hotels and rooming houses bulged with visitors and office seekers, its streets thronged with the flotsam of unrest. Discomfort became a real problem. The capital would have to move to some larger place simply to survive, and what more likely place offered itself than Richmond? It was a question which spurred a Virginia delegation to Montgomery with an invitation to accept Richmond hospitality. There were reasons aplenty to accept. A shift of the capital to Virginia would surely prove the South's determination to protect the Old Dominion; Richmond lay in the path of several vital communication routes north, south, and west, was well seated for contact with the troubled border, and had the size and capacity to expand with emergency.

True, there were some Confederates who doubted the wisdom of departing Montgomery. Colonel James Chesnut, redoubtable South Carolina firebrand who had carried Beauregard's messages to Fort Sumter, argued for staying put. Mary, his witty wife, mixed his objections in the gossip of her *Diary*. "Mr. Chesnut," she recorded, "opposes it violently because this is so central a position for our government. . . . He wants our troops sent into Maryland to make our fight on the border, and to encompass Washington." Such solid reasoning found scant credence from Mary, who caught well enough the real motivations of men: "I think these uncomfortable hotels will move the Congress. Our statesmen love their ease. And it will be so hot here in the summer."[13] Mrs. Davis, no mean realist herself, is reputed to have commented that "the Yankees will make it hot for us, go where we will." And she was right.

Whatever the wisdom on both sides of the move, it came. The President considered and finally took the opportunity offered by a congressional resolution and scheduled the hegira of his government for May 27, 1861.[14]

"Natives to the Soil"

No special panoply marked the government's departure. Bits and pieces of furniture went, desks, chests of documents, an occasional cabinet member, clerks and secretaries mixed together. Trains northward through Opelika, Five Points, Atlanta, thence onward into Tarheel country, at length into the Old Dominion, all trains northward for several days, even weeks, carried some component of Confederate administration. Ordinarily there would have been ceremonies signifying so large a departure, but the President was simply not up to it. Wracked for years with torturing facial neuralgia—the pain worked up into an eye and throbbed with migraine fervor—he had learned to temper his illness with rest. But rest had been virtually unknown during his hectic weeks in Montgomery, and worrisome labors took their toll of his strength. No gathering, then, at the depot to draw out the departure, no bands and trumpets to signal a chieftain marching closer to the foe, no pomp and circumstance for a tired President. A small coterie made its way to the railroad station Sunday evening, boarded the cars, and rolled slowly from the ex-capital of the Confederate States. It was a quiet beginning for a trip to punctuate history.

Still, any who conceived something slinking about this strange leave-taking would have been wrong. For President Davis the parting broke no continuities, closed no books; the northward shift meant simply a shift in emphasis.

With him went an aide and three close friends: Senator and Mrs. Louis Trezevant Wigfall, South Carolinians transmigrated to Texas, and Georgia's Robert Toombs. For a tired Chief Executive no more exhausting companions could have been chosen,[15] but the presidential party traveled in a good comradeship made easier by the excitements of their journey. Travel, after all, is instructive, and as the train rocked slowly northeastward toward Atlanta, Davis and his small coterie began to learn more about their country.

Land is a sadly neglected teacher. Geographers plot it, poets praise it, painters capture some finite piece of it, farmers scar it; while it sustains these varied shards of human life it mutely shapes humanity. Particularly is this true of the South. Southerners are not landlocked; a long and accessible coastline opens the world to Southern quest. And yet Southerners have always behaved as though they were welded to the soil, as if they were children of the ground. As they measured quality by kinship so they measured life by land. In all of them the rolling loamy soil of the Black Belt, the bounteous Mississippi Delta, the grass prairies of the west, Virginia's fruitful Shenandoah Valley, even the sandy pine barrens of the Georgia and Florida coasts, touched deep currents in the blood and lent some mystic strength.

Such tools of modern times as highways and miles of shining iron might cut the surface of the land, might infringe on nature's span, but the earth returned to itself in some predestined power. For the South it had ever been so. From earliest times men had given themselves to the land. Cotton's march etched the edges of westward migration; behind the cotton frontier Southern society prospered. From the northern boundaries of cotton's domain along the Potomac to the western reaches in Texas, the land yielded its reward to the plantation system which it nurtured.

Evidence of the land's importance rolled past the windows of the presidential train. Up from Montgomery through the red hills of Alabama the wide-stacked locomotive took its cars, up through Atlanta; eastward then, through the rich acres around Augusta, the almost lush savannas of South Carolina; northward at last through the upland cotton stands into the curiously different timber country near Wilmington, North Carolina; sharply north-northwest the rails turned to the tobacco patches of Goldsboro and on into the hard-scrabble farm country of southside Virginia, that verged on the tobacco acres of the Tidewater. Every mile told a tale of people born of the soil, a tale of work and dedication and frustration and sweat and love and life. An ancient conjurer could witch from those miles the real history of the South, a history told in emotion as a man looked upon the ground that kept him, told in blood as he drove away the Indian to keep his ground his own, told in pride as his children grew and took the land in trust.

For President Davis and his friends, though, no conjurer's magic was needed; Southerners, they knew within themselves the mystery of ground. It is a mystery perhaps best revealed to the poet's wider

eye. South Carolinian Henry Timrod caught a touch of the spirit
of the soil in "The Cotton Boll":

> Ye Stars, which, though unseen, yet with me gaze
> Upon this loveliest fragment of the earth!
> Thou Sun, that kindlest all thy gentlest rays
> Above it, as to light a favorite hearth!
> Ye Clouds, that in your temples in the West
> See nothing brighter than its humblest flowers!
> And you, ye Winds, that on the ocean's breast
> Are kissed to coolness ere ye reach its bowers!
> Bear witness with me in my song of praise,
> And tell the world that, since the world began,
> No fairer land hath fired a poet's lays,
> Or given a home to man![16]

It was no poetic fancy Timrod indulged in calling the Southland
"home." He understood a special facet of Southern emotion: well-
being came with a sense of place, with a certainty of belonging.
Genealogy and geography were inseparable touchstones of identity,
touchstones revealed in such talismans as "The Lees of Virginia,"
"The Hamptons of South Carolina," "The Bregniers of Louisiana."
Ground proved birth, gave nurture, and lent strength. To some extent, too, it shaped character, which is to say that the character of
the Confederate people would be as diverse as the land of Dixie.
But there was a subtle unity in this diversity, a unity strong and
lasting, a thing greater than the sum of segments.

Jefferson Davis and his traveling companions innately knew the
diverse solidity of the South; in a way, they reflected it. Together
they showed the new purpose of an angered nation; apart, the
disparateness of Southern society.

Elevated to the highest echelon of administration, wrapped in a
hauteur born of shyness, Jefferson Davis looms a figure to himself.
But to many he typified the South. He was almost the perfect
Southern prototype; a planter, a man of grace and refined charm,
with ambition modulated in service to his section.

There were many like him in the new Confederacy. Planters had
for years dominated life in the South. If mythology later would

soften some of the harder realities of life in Dixie, would recall the slave as faithful servant, and the starveling, ignorant cropper as hardy yeoman, if Southern womanhood would loom forever in finery from an unsullied pedestal, if mythology would remember only the moonlight and magnolias, there was some truth to the remembrance. Planters made part of that truth.

Men like Davis, such men as Duff Green of Georgia, Wade Hampton of South Carolina, Clement Clay of Alabama, Hill Carter of "Shirley" on the James River in Virginia, James F. Perry of "Peach Point," Brazoria County, Texas, all shared the planter's mystique. Wealth, often measured in slaveholdings, came to these men in varying amounts—troubles, too, in plenty—but they shared an outlook and a way of living. During a Southern visit in 1849, young Rutherford Hayes described all of them in describing one: "He is a real gentleman, holds his honor dear, respects the wishes and feelings of others, is a warm and constant friend."[17]

Planters in earlier years had really controlled not only the social but also the political life of their section; time and increasing business concerns eroded part of their political prominence but enhanced their personal prestige. Prestige and wealth and peculiar control over fellow human beings brought high responsibilities, which decent men accepted in a spirit of *noblesse oblige.*

And all across Dixie, especially in the large towns, an entirely new class began to take a hand in shaping events. Generally well connected and entrenched in the society of their section, members of this new class comprised the professional element in Southern life —they were lawyers, bankers, businessmen, doctors. This type was epitomized by Robert Toombs. Big, loose-jointed, with a heavy, shambling gait which added subtly to his dignity, the well-known Georgia politician had fierce brows, and jowls which dropped in tandem with bags under his disturbing eyes. Heavy features showed nothing slow in him; tension, ceaseless drive, native talent marked the man. He was a man of power, of raw personal force. Toombs, Gazaway Bugg Lamar of Georgia, Arthur Colyar of Tennessee, Daniel Pratt of Prattville, Alabama, William Marsh Rice of Houston, Ashbel Smith of Texas—men such as these did much of the modern work of the South.

Perhaps the most interesting fact about the new professional class was the imperceptibility of its coming. So slowly had old patterns of business evolved in the Deep South, so slightly were methods modified, that the almost complete revolution of business techniques represented by commercial agriculture, by capitalistic expansion of plantations and slavery, went almost unseen. Nonetheless, a revolution in commerce and business had happened, and new men were essential to make it work. Most of these new professionals had two things in common—they specialized in getting things done and they supported the slave economy. They grasped the growing impact of urban development in the South and to some degree worked to shape it to fit old traditions. Because they did they were more essential than they knew. Without them the Confederacy could scarcely hope to last.

When the Davis train pulled into the cities, into places like Atlanta, Augusta, Wilmington, and Goldsboro, some portents of these new men could be glimpsed. But beyond the confines of towns, out in Georgia's rolling countryside, along Carolina's marshy coasts, older things fell back in place; older perspective came with space and solitude.

President Davis and Toombs both shared this older perspective. Fellow traveler Wigfall shared it, but with a zealot's special sense.

Wigfall belonged to the "fire-eater" element in Southern society. The fire-eaters were colorful, strident, persuasive folk of uncompromising bent. Politicians for the most part, these men—among them such notables as Robert Barnwell Rhett of South Carolina, William Lowndes Yancey of Alabama, and Edmund Ruffin of Virginia—had for years been viewing the Southern position in the Union with dissatisfaction. Almost all of them boasted allegiance to an idealized image of John Calhoun; his old rhetoric echoed in their shrill cries for retribution, his life itself promised absolution to any who stood for the South. And so the fire-eaters acted as they thought he would approve, and believed they used him truly.[18]

Perhaps they did. At any rate Calhoun was the deity of Wigfall and his breed, and success had surely crowned their campaign for secession. Fire-eaters had a large hand in making the Southern Confederacy; fate could hardly be so cruel as to deny them all the fruits of their labor. Still, Wigfall and the others might have some legitimate doubts about the equity of fate. As he rode northward out of accustomed country into the harsher climes of North Carolina, as he watched the President and the Secretary of State, the restless Texas Senator might have wondered about a revolutionary state which put a conservative at its helm and an oddly professional legalist in charge of its foreign relations. But he could take comfort in his own presence in the official train; he would stanchly uphold the radicals in a cause they understood best.

Perhaps the only true perception of Southern circumstances in that uncertain May came from emotions, was felt rather than known. To the extent that this was true, one among the President's party may have grasped the new South and glimpsed the way events were pointing—Charlotte Maria Wigfall.

Charlotte Wigfall was a true and tender lady, product of proud lineage and replete with connections proper and secure. Demure and slightly proportioned as befitted her station, she had strong eyes to twinkle when needed, a coy humor to turn away wrath, and charm to bend wills to her way. She knew her Louis in all senses and she cleverly urged his advancement.

More than merely pushing him ahead in the world—a thing he did fairly well himself—Charlotte gave some direction to his hope, sharpened some of his prejudices, and kept fervid his love for the South. She was the perfect conscience for a fire-eater. She was also the perfect conscience for a man of action; dainty as she was, Charlotte Wigfall had a hard passion for politics and a forged anger for Yankees. Moderation had no place in her presence; the times were past for doubters. A small bundle of cold steel, this was Charlotte Wigfall. And this was much of Southern womanhood.

Men are often creatures of passing fancy; their passions cool sometimes in proportion to sobriety or time. And although most Southern men in 1861 were true to the quest for independence, many who flocked eagerly to the colors in those heady days of excitement might have been less jaunty, less fervent, without feminine encouragement. Southern women were the Confederate Army's best recruiters, the South's firmest pillars. Some might argue that petticoat patriotism came easily from the safety of noncombatancy, but this shabby accusation is unfounded. Southern ladies loved their country.

The new nation appeared to be generating love in large measure. The crowds flocking to each station on the presidential route seemed full of affection for their cause. That small clutch of people in the President's car learned much about the body social of their country at each wood stop, each way station, each depot. News of the train went ahead and people drifted down to the railroad, crowds of new Confederates—some just curious, some eager to glimpse their leader. Time and again the scene repeated—the train wheezed to a stop and cheers would start. "Where is President Davis?" some called; others, friendlier and more personal, called for "Jeff Davis," or "the old Hero!" Flags and banners and kerchiefs fluttered always; a special gaiety touched every stop. Each time Davis grew more eloquent, his musical voice rang stronger, his charm mounted. When he finished, the crowds called usually for Wigfall and then for Toombs, each in his turn vying for affection.

Those crowds were cross sections of the Confederate populace. Each in its way showed the varied strands of a hardy social order, many of them not represented in the close confines of the President's carriage. Out among the revelers and among the worried and concerned who mixed with them were the plain people of the Confederacy: the hard-working little farmers, the steadfast womenfolk who tended the families and held the South together, the solid city dwellers of the rising middle class who were doing much that never had been needed before, the black faces of curious slaves and freemen, and always and everywhere children, children of all ages, running, yelling, waving banners, many of them far more devoted and rabid Confederates than their parents.[19]

If crowds were measures of sentiments and hopes and fears, President Davis had reason to take heart. Certainly the fearful were present, the timid and the anxious, those who had known the Union and were adrift since it had gone. But they were there, in the crowds awaiting words of certitude from the one selected to guide them. And there, too, were the blissfully happy, the patriots of excitement, those who basked in danger for its own sake; and they listened, too, to their serious President. And each time there were the sober folk, more of them than others, the solid citizenry, quiet and anonymous, watchful, willing, and devoted. Separately the people were proud, mercurial, passionate, dilatory, romantic, devout, dogged. One thing about them was clear by the time Davis's train reached Richmond on May 29—together they could be mighty.

E Pluribus . . .

Out of a deep cut in a riverbank the presidential train came, weaving slowly across a great trestle bridge over the James. The passengers, suspended for a moment above the water, saw the panorama of Richmond spread before them. Romantics of the South often considered the "Queen City" as an American Rome. There was some truth to this, for Richmond rambled over its own seven hills, had its high temples of angular severity, its spires, its avenues, its Capitoline elegance.

It was early when the special train rocked into view, just a little after seven on the morning of May 29, but the early hour dimmed no spirits, and a huge, enthusiastic crowd awaited the President and the official party that had gone to greet him in Petersburg. When at last the engine slowed for the Richmond depot and the cars rolled to a halt, a steady cannonade began, a measured, pounding salute of eleven guns—a gun for each state of the Confederacy.

Excited by the warmth of public welcome, President Davis waved at the multitudes and joined Virginia's Governor John Letcher in gracious acceptance of homage. Finally the Chief Executive escaped to the care of Thomas W. Hoeninger, of the Spotswood Hotel, who escorted him to a waiting carriage for the procession to Richmond's new and sumptuous hostelry on the corner of Main and Eighth.

Everywhere on the way gay crowds saluted their leader; the whole city appeared wrapped in a kind of ecstasy. After fighting through the hordes, a handsome set of bays delivered carriage and passengers at the hotel, and the wearied President took refuge in a parlor specially decorated with a huge coat of arms and a flag of the Confederate States.[20]

Governor Letcher, Richmond's Mayor Joseph Mayo, the City Council, and random citizens all laid claim to some of the presidential time. Eager discussions of the moment and the future stretched on through most of the morning. In the first rushes of optimism, Richmonders exuded togetherness.[21]

And there was something comforting in their optimism. If the size and decibels of crowds signified anything at all, the new Confederate capital burned with a Southern fervor hotter than that of many parts of the country. Such zeal could be tedious. But while it lasted it must be courted and acknowledged; from this kind of eagerness the new country would unite.

Uniting the nation had been largely behind the government's move to Richmond. Davis himself had supported Richmond's invitation to the exclusion of other cities, and the wisdom of the move was apparent everywhere. Richmond's wharves bustled with sail and canal boats, testimony to the harbor's contact with the sea and with the interior. The same wharves were burdened with tobacco cargoes, forage, salt, food, dry goods, all the trappings of modern life. Warehouses lining the riverbanks bulged with goods, and Richmond's big factories—the Crenshaw Woolen Mills, the Tredegar Iron Works, the Old Dominion Iron and Nail Works, and others—produced to virtual capacity. Up on capitol hill the Virginia Assembly toiled to gear all counties for war, before its halls were given over to the Provisional Congress of the Confederate States. People of all types and classes—city dandies, dockhands, beggars, patrolmen, frock-coated lawyers and merchants, ladies in finery and in homespun, boys and girls running the streets—offered a confidence to the nation which enthralled and sobered.[22]

They were confident, most of them, that the serried legions gathering across Dixie were equal to any challenge and certain that the government lately come to Richmond had the power and wisdom for independence. Eagerness made them rash and almost comically troublesome.

In every sizable place in the South military units surged into being; governors lavished commissions on almost anyone who boasted enough money to "raise a company": that is, finance the equipping of one. Ordinarily this kind of patriotic activity would have been wholly commendable, but the process became complicated. No sooner did a man get a colonel's commission than he considered himself endowed with supernatural military prowess and yearned to rush for the decisive field, which his superior strategy would conquer.

The governors were convinced that each plan hatched, each warrior sworn to state fealty, each "traitor" cast in dungeon deep, struck a blow for Southern rights—no matter that the plans usually ignored constitutionally authorized Confederate efforts, that each militiaman pinned within the borders of his state diminished the Confederacy's field forces, that most of the "traitors" found in the early days of strained excitement were true and friendly Southerners outraged by eroding civil liberties.

Only by the hardest effort had Governor Pickens kept his sons of Carolina in leash until Beauregard fired on Fort Sumter; and now, when the government was in the act of moving, Florida authorities fumed at the lack of effort in Pensacola harbor, where the Yankees held Fort Pickens. Roughly at the same time word flashed on the telegraphs concerning a New Orleans dentist. Dr. Metcalf, a New Englander, with the outspoken tendencies of the breed, had "uttered seditious language against the Government, making use of the expressions, that 'Lincoln was a second Jackson, and that if he was in Lincoln's place, he would lay Charleston in ashes. . . .' " Righteously wrathful listeners swore affidavits against him, and the loose-mouthed extractor was arrested for treason.[23]

Everybody was being helpful in a headlong rush to run the country, and a besieged President approved the motive but feared the consequences.

From the day of arrival in Richmond this spasm of relentless good will bore in on Jefferson Davis. He enjoyed Richmond's welcome, but he could be pardoned a lurking doubt as to whether all Virginians were wholly loyal. The Old Dominion had come late to the cause and seemed to make up in anger what it lacked in speed. Mobilization worked apace across the state; regiments and troops and batteries gathered in hasty response to the governor's call, and they were organized by General Robert E. Lee.[24] But there was an insistent Virginia refrain to all these preparations.

Even while the President settled in new offices, minor trouble arose between him and Governor Letcher over rifle-making machinery. Some distance from Richmond, at Harpers Ferry on the

Potomac, a well-stocked United States armory had fallen into Virginia hands. The famous armory of John Brown's raid had been partially damaged by fire, but most of the machinery had escaped unscathed. Colonel Charles Dimmock, Virginia's Chief of Ordnance, coveted the machinery and urged its hasty removal to Richmond Armory. There, Colonel James H. Burton would combine it with the machines already at hand to create the finest rifle factory in the South—with which surely no one could argue, since machinery of any kind was scarce in the Confederacy. Richmond was the logical place for anything scavenged in Virginia, perhaps in the South.

But this was Virginia logic. Confederate ordnance authorities had other ideas. Richmond was fine for some purposes, but factors other than industrial concentration entered the picture. There was, for example, the matter of transportation. Richmond, while admirably situated to supply the upper South's industrial needs, lay far above the Confederate heartland. Distribution over the rail lines coming to the capital might be a problem, especially as military activity accelerated. Rifle fabrication should be concentrated somewhere more central, and the Ordnance Department fixed its attention on a small arsenal in Fayetteville, North Carolina. Virginia's Dimmock did not want to lose control of Harpers Ferry's vital machines; neither did Confederate Chief of Ordnance Josiah Gorgas. National orders went unheeded by state authorities; the governor was asked to protect the rights of his state; the President, the rights of his country. In the end the issue went the way as most such collisions of desire—it was compromised. Richmond Armory got some machines; the bulk went to Fayetteville. All of this tempestuous absurdity consumed vast amounts of time; both the President and the governor wasted endless hours in attempts to persuade each other without offense.[25]

And virtually every time any state fell heir to public property the whole seriocomic charade was repeated. Arsenals and armories and other public buildings, arms, munitions, commissary and quartermaster stores, money, men, even prestige, were contested hotly by state officials. The President found himself enmeshed in internal diplomacy when his energies were necessary elsewhere.

"We Are a Band of Brothers . . ."

Sound administrative practice dictated immediate attention to emergencies, but which? They were everywhere. Morale and the matter of unity certainly stood high on the list of immediacies, but what of things like the Harpers Ferry squabble, the army, the navy, the finances, the railroads, diplomacy, politics, civil law? What of Harpers Ferry itself? Harpers Ferry had strategic importance because of its railroad bridge, its armory, and its status as a Union spearhead south of the Potomac. As long as the Federals possessed it, they guarded the Chesapeake and Ohio Canal and kept the vital Baltimore and Ohio Railroad open. When the Virginia state forces took it over they instantly threatened Union communications with the Middle West and forced special attention on the town. In Confederate hands, Harpers Ferry would protect the lower (northern) Shenandoah Valley, possibly the richest granary in the South. To both sides, then, the drowsy little settlement was worth a good deal of concern.

Confederate concern continued steadily after the rifle-machinery incident. To guard the town and its environs, Virginia's governor had dispatched a small state force commanded by Colonel Thomas J. Jackson, quirky professor of artillery tactics at Virginia Military Institute. A thin force and orders restricting him to defensive action on Virginia soil irked Jackson, but he eased frustration by smartening his command into a semblance of military order. By the time the Confederate government moved to Richmond the dour colonel boasted a small army of 8,000 men.[26]

With the coming of the government there arrived also a new commander at Harpers Ferry. He, like Jackson, was a Virginian of long service in the "Old Army." Joseph E. Johnston had risen to Brigadier General and Quartermaster General in Federal service, and when he reached the northern frontier of Virginia on May 24, 1861, he wore a Confederate brigadier's wreath. Colonel Jackson, though, with iron devotion to the regulations, refused to acknowledge Confederate rank higher than state. Until Johnston could get authority from the governor to take command, Old Jack would hold his own. This amusing minuet of precedence had its lighter side, but showed that clashes between federal and state officials were continuing despite tact and patience.

Johnston's ideas for defense of the lower Shenandoah were not Jackson's—the professor would have been bolder and seized the high ground around Harpers Ferry even if it were north of the Potomac.[27] But Johnston was himself a stickler for obedience to orders, and he did what the War Department asked. He worked on defense, plotted battery positions, and soon reported the town indefensible. Useless, he said, to try to retain a position dominated by hostile heights and exposed to plunging artillery fire that could scourge his lines relentlessly. Fall back, Johnston counseled, to better ground for maneuvers. What Johnston wanted to do would, for the moment, be done. He untangled his men from the Harpers Ferry coils and pulled them back to positions covering all approaches to the lower valley. Correct in this instance, Johnston would suffer for his advice. Richmond leaders could not accept the idea of yielding ground for tactical purposes, not when ground held such high political portent. In the future official eyebrows would rise in knowing smirk when Johnston urged Fabian retreat.[28]

The kind of trouble Johnston had at Harpers Ferry would be duplicated endless times. There was a kind of chaos to Confederate high command which never really vanished, a chaos born of *politesse,* of a penchant for personal accommodation to entirely official situations. This was the Southern way, of course, the way of tradition, but it was a poor way to run an army.

Johnston knew better. No one in the service had more experience in tighter places to tell him the proper way. He is an appealing figure in the Confederate coterie, a dapper little dandy of a man, short, bewhiskered, with a fine head, quick eyes, and the bearing of Mars, full of spunk and bravery—a "gamecock," his men called him—a soldier's soldier who used his men well, spared them wisely, remembered the things which turned men into armies. And yet, was there something missing? Was there in all that dazzling energy and zest some unfinished cast of character, some haunting lack in him? Possibly.

Johnston's luck and skill were questions for the future. When sent to Harpers Ferry, he owned a distinguished record and the high opinion of most of his peers. The President had no reason to hesitate in giving the hottest assignment of the moment to Johnston, no reason lest there was substance to a rumored breach[29] between them in their West Point days. But apparently it had been forgotten or buried, for the President sent him.

Personal troubles and brambly questions of protocol and demeanor were so much a part of martial affairs that they seemed likely to consume a good portion of the President's time. And there were those who hinted that human relations scarcely were a strong point with Davis—much less human relations en masse. It seemed unlikely, though, that Davis lacked the touch for suasion; years in the army, in politics, and the stint as Secretary of War taught him surely the vagaries of people. He passed a fairly rough test in personnel management when he organized the army.

Mobilization and organization of the army continued during the busy weeks of moving the government. The center of military gravity was shifting to Richmond. Troops coming in great numbers added to the hectic pace of capital affairs, swelled the bars, jails, and bawdyhouses, and poured money into merchant tills. Soldiers were often a rowdy lot, unwholesome many of them, uncouth and wild.

To any who watched the depots daily and studied the Confederate Army as it gathered, Southern soldiers gave a graphic index to their country. From early days in February, from the first military laws passed by the Provisional Congress, troops had mustered as an essentially federal force. Those regiments gathering the length and breadth of Dixie were the army of the nation. True, they boasted—sometimes suffered—elected company and line officers, and their higher commanders often held state commissions, but the men who entrained for Richmond were under national colors.[30]

And as the trains disgorged them by the thousands, they were already different men. Perhaps this was because the crucible of comradeship forged a strange and uncertain alloy. Whether it would break apart in battle tempers or would fuse into a weapon—these were unknowns for the moment. Admittedly the chances for annealing looked thin; there was little precedent in Southern history for a cohesive society. Why should the army be other than the people?

The army's future depended on how it was led. If experience, zeal, verve, and devotion counted at all, the officers appointed over the new national army were likely to do spectacularly. Gossip had it that the Confederacy gleaned the richest crop of West Point graduates, and even a casual glance at the roll of Rebel brass seemed to prove the point.[31] Southern men more often than their Yankee brethren chose the military life, and military education became virtually a caste mark of the landed gentry. After all, the noblesse tradition of plantation life demanded responsible service to state or nation, and outdoorsmen were naturally cut for the field or the saddle. Not surprising then that Lees and Stuarts and Hamptons and Johnstons, Manigaults and Hugers, and Magruders and Taylors formed a kind of Southern martial nobility.[32]

Tradition and calling and disposition—all these things made Southern men likely soldiers and promised success in the field. Whatever qualities the army possessed, it would be showing them soon enough. Concentration of so many at Richmond indicated clearly that serious business loomed in Virginia, possibly near the capital itself. And if those daily trainloads were not yet proof enough, there was more.

There was, for particular instance, General Pierre Gustave Toutant Beauregard, who also arrived by train. As befitted the first true hero of the new nation, the short Creole general weighted with Sumter's laurels arrived a day later than the President and was offered the same becoached splendor to the Spotswood House. With typically ostentatious modesty he declined such pomp and proceeded with his staff in another carriage. It was a good beginning—the great man's humility went noticed.[33]

As for why he was in Richmond, even Beauregard did not know. He did know that the President beckoned him from an assignment which would have given him a huge command along the Mississippi. Whatever the President wanted, it certainly loomed urgent and likely would take Beauregard to war. And that suited him. No career officer needed to be told that glory came with combat, that fame went to the takers. Glory and the trappings of heroism were part and parcel of Beauregard's volatile Gallic nature.

Some who knew him found him pompous; some, merely vain;

others saw him goaded to extremes of braggadocio by his desire for rank and fame. All of these images were partly true—and partly false. On casual meeting the Louisiana soldier could be impressive; his flamboyant martial air, his hauteur, his infectious zest for war combined to give him stature larger than his five feet seven inches. In moments of public enthusiasm his rhetoric rang Demosthenic periods and his self-confidence ran beyond decency. At such times he bordered on self-caricature. At his best he sometimes approached his own self-estimate. But never quite sure of what he wanted, he could never quite win against himself.

Beauregard's dreams could remain a problem for the future. When the President met him on May 31, the important issue was beating the enemy. Reports from Virginia's Potomac frontier indicated frenzied Federal activity in Washington. Spies—a term that included such fair Southern damsels as Rose Greenhow and Belle Boyd[34]—as well as Washington newspapers told of a great army building in the Yankee capital and of plans for an invasion of the Confederacy. Discounting the exaggeration of neophyte agents, the reports were alarming enough. Federal General Irvin McDowell commanded a force of over 30,000, and his intentions were easily guessed. With war a reality, Lincoln was pushing for swift subjugation of the Rebel states, and it was common Washington gossip that he favored a drive on Richmond. There was a chance that Richmond's fall might finish the South.

Southerners argued that for reasons of political prestige and industry the loss of Richmond could not be tolerated. McDowell must be stopped and Beauregard must do the stopping. This was the assignment Davis gave him. Beauregard had no moment of qualm or doubt, no hesitancy, just exultation at the chance to save his country once again. And more exciting yet, he would have charge of the Confederacy's biggest army! At last he had the legions and the stage sufficient; greatness lay northward with his troops.

Northward meant Manassas Junction, where the Manassas Gap and Orange and Alexandria railroads met. There, south of a small stream called Bull Run, Confederate troops now numbered something over 6,000. Fortunately for the new commander, his initial orders were defensive and directed him to hold the line along Bull

Run.[35] Defense would be almost all so few grayclads could manage, and as Beauregard surveyed the positions his men occupied, a great uneasiness quenched some of his ardor. The lines entrusted to him were so long that no continuous line could be drawn. Two days after he reached Manassas he asked for help and in such a characteristically positive way that his request sounded more like a proclamation of grand strategy. "I must . . . be reinforced at once," he wrote the President, ". . . or I must be prepared to retire (upon the approach of the enemy) in the direction of Richmond, with the intention of arresting him whenever and wherever the opportunity presents itself; or I must march to meet him at one of . . . [the] fords, to sell our lives as dearly as practicable."[36] With his special flair for public relations, Beauregard summoned the people near his army and in all Virginia to rise against the foe. The people, of course, could do little, but the general sounded as though he counted on them and they liked him for it.

His troops liked him, too, for he paid attention to details and was seen frequently. With almost demonic devotion to preparation he worried and fussed with positions and drills and orderlies until his army became hideously over-organized. Orders cascaded from headquarters, each a miracle of complexity; officers galloped hither and yon bearing these missives along with notes, maps, letters, and reports. Out of confusion came finally a kind of system.

Badgering and fulminating brought more troops to the Bull Run line. Beauregard placed real and "Quaker" guns along his extended front, kept an active cavalry screen forward in search of any scrap of intelligence, and by mid-June could boast an army well in hand. By the end of the month he had about 15,000 men, organized into six brigades. Strength fanned his boldness, and he led his army north of Bull Run to protect an advanced base at Centreville and to hit Irvin McDowell in flank should he advance.[37]

This sound bit of audacity was dashed by two hard facts: McDowell was going to advance with some 40,000 men, and he would not move against the point Beauregard expected. For the Creole, the early weeks of July were filled with vacillation. Optimistic and gloomy in dizzying succession, Beauregard baffled the President and the War Department as to his intentions and seems almost to have confused himself. Into his weltering uncertainty came one certain piece of news on the night of July 16—Mrs. Greenhow reported that McDowell was starting![38]

"The Bonnie Blue Flag . . ."

Everything assumed a different perspective in the Confederacy now that McDowell was moving. A Federal advance into Virginia quickly drew blood in an unfortunate encounter at Alexandria.[39] Colonel Elmer Ellsworth, a Zouave officer, walked into the Marshall House Tavern on May 24, removed a "large secession flag" from the staff, and was shot dead by James Jackson, proprietor, who was himself instantly killed. The incident prompted new attitudes toward the conflict with the North. McDowell's men had stalled for a time not far beyond Alexandria, but their ultimate purpose remained unaltered.

Beauregard's activities were conditioned by enemy presence in Virginia; the activities of General Johnston in the Shenandoah Valley were similarly affected; all plans for military organization and supply, for national preparation and civil administration, felt the same pressure. Beauregard was doing what he could to meet the threat; Johnston's cagey retirement from Harpers Ferry and his concentration near Winchester put him in position to deal with another Federal probe in the Valley area or to cooperate with Beauregard if need be.[40]

For its part, the government was doing its best to prepare the whole Confederacy for combat. Unity still ranked as the biggest imponderable; perhaps the threat of battle would generate a fierce Confederate spirit. If that happened the government would see to it that all other facets of war were ready. Some important steps had already been taken in military organization.

Before departing for Richmond, the Confederate Congress recognized the existence of war between the United States and the Confederacy and authorized the President to use all national resources to wage it.[41] Thousands of men had quit homes to defend their new nation; money was raised with bonds and loans and some hesitant taxes;[42] arms and munitions were donated, bought, made, and ordered. Camp supplies—tents, canteens, kitchens, utensils, spades, picks, axes, all the tools of field existence—were sought and partially provided; garrison equipage—uniforms, shoes, bedding, "gum blankets," soap, socks, tobacco, the small essentials of civilization—was carried to war by every soldier.[43] And at first there was almost too much of everything. Generosity swept the Southland; everyone left at home joined in a national compulsion to provide for the "boys" who marched northward with hope and honor on their pennons.

And who could argue with patriotic giving? Surely it showed morale? It showed morale well enough, but, like the relentless good will which enmeshed President Davis when he first reached the capital, quenchless philanthropy had its inconveniences. None appreciated this embarrassing fact more clearly than the President, General Beauregard, and certain officers charged with supplying the Confederate Army gathering at Bull Run. Men and munitions were going forward daily from Richmond. Their transportation from the capital seemed simple enough; after all, for years people had been traveling easily northward to Washington. The Virginia Central Railroad ran to Hanover Court House where it crossed the Richmond, Fredericksburg and Potomac tracks, and from there the line continued to Gordonsville, where the Orange and Alexandria joined, to run on to Alexandria. Obviously the army near Manassas Junction was well located to receive supplies. And so it should have been.[44]

Near Manassas Junction Beauregard's officers established a railhead. There all supplies were to be received and distributed; there regimental and brigade wagons would congregate to collect rations and munitions and equipment; forage masters would get daily allotments of fodder; mail, packages, and baggage would detrain. No depot yet devised was equal to the task. Efficient organization disappeared in a milling mass of men, equipment, horses, trunks, cases, carpetbags, mail sacks, boxes, guns, and people. Other depots were established and with each came a little more chaos.

Newness was the problem. No tactical or supply manual, no tradition, not even veteran sergeants—those guardians of army lore —could tell the needs of such thousands. As demand and supply developed, organization crumbled. Old ways of supply were hopelessly outdated.[45] This lent special menace to the news of Mc-Dowell's advance from Alexandria.

There were several dimensions to the menace of McDowell. His advance posed purely tactical problems for Confederate leaders along Bull Run; it also posed problems in strategy for the Richmond administration. Now that a substantial invasion was under way, the President and the Secretary of War had to come to some hard conclusions about concentration or dispersal of force.

To any student of war in the 1860's there was really no question of what had to be done. Napoleon, Henri Jomini, Johnston, and even Robert Lee, Davis's personal military adviser,[46] agreed on the basic point: concentrate maximum Confederate force on the battlefield. Nothing else made sense. Troops might protect the rail lines, garrison towns, and guard bridges, but when battle loomed, every available soldier must be rushed to the field.

Strategy, then, made the gathering of Confederate clans at Manassas mandatory. Troops in North and South Carolina, Georgia, Alabama, in every spot within reach of Bull Run, received orders to come.[47]

Beauregard received news of these hastening reinforcements with gratitude, but fixed his main reliance beyond the Blue Ridge Mountains. Out in the Shenandoah Valley Joe Johnston's 8,500-man army confronted a hesitant Union force under General Robert Patterson. A scant sixty miles separated the two Confederate armies; no other organized and trained force was closer. Discussions between the two Rebel generals had already explored possibilities of co-operation; Johnston expected to come if emergency demanded. Success rested on his ability to slip unnoticed from Patterson's front, cross the Blue Ridge, and march to Manassas.

Time proved to be the unknown quantity. No one knew how long it would take the Army of the Shenandoah to reach Manassas. How much warning did Johnston need? When should he be ordered eastward? Everything depended on McDowell.

For his part, McDowell was less concerned with time than circumstances. Secure in the conviction that he need not expect Johnston (Patterson would keep him pinned down), and that Beauregard's army suffered limited mobility, the Union commander developed

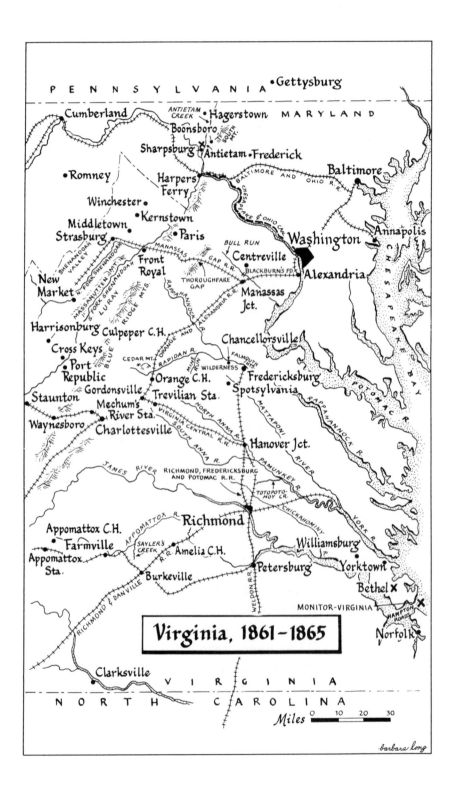

Virginia, 1861–1865

Miles 0 10 20 30

PENNSYLVANIA • Gettysburg

Cumberland ANTIETAM CREEK • Hagerstown MARYLAND

Boonsboro

Sharpsburg ✗ Antietam • Frederick

• Romney Harpers Ferry

Winchester •

Middletown • Kernstown

Strasburg

Paris BULL RUN Washington • Annapolis

Centreville

New Market Front Royal THOROUGHFARE GAP BLACKBURN'S FD. • Alexandria

Manassas Jct.

Harrisonburg Culpeper C.H.

Cross Keys Chancellorsville

• Port Republic CEDAR MT. WILDERNESS Fredericksburg

Orange C.H. Spotsylvania

Staunton Gordonsville Trevilian Sta.

Mechum's River Sta.

Waynesboro Charlottesville

Hanover Jct.

RICHMOND, FREDERICKSBURG AND POTOMAC R.R.

TOTOPOTOMOY CR.

Appomattox C.H. APPOMATTOX R. Richmond

• Farmville SAYLER'S CREEK • Amelia C.H. Williamsburg

Appomattox Sta. Burkeville Petersburg Yorktown

Bethel ✗

MONITOR-VIRGINIA HAMPTON ROADS ✗

Norfolk

Clarksville VIRGINIA

NORTH CAROLINA

CHESAPEAKE BAY

POTOMAC R.

RAPPAHANNOCK R.

MATTAPONI RIVER

PAMUNKEY R.

YORK R.

CHICKAHOMINY

JAMES RIVER

RICHMOND & DANVILLE

WELDON R.R.

barbara long

a careful plan of battle. As he understood the situation, Rebels were strewn along Bull Run at various fords and bridges; if Beauregard had any concentration at all it seemed to be well toward the Union left. This suited McDowell—he planned a feint toward the enemy strength and a flank attack around and behind the Rebel left.

Everything about McDowell's plan looked right. It fitted the latest military theories of mobility and objective; it seemed simple and clear enough for green troops to execute; it fixed heavy force on weak enemy positions; and if successful, it promised decisive victory. The first part of it went into operation late on the night of July 16, when advanced Federal units probed toward Bull Run and a Confederate outpost at Blackburn's Ford.[48]

Alarmed and alert, Beauregard telegraphed the War Department late on the 17th news of increased Federal activity and urged instant orders to Johnston. He got results. Close to one o'clock in the morning of July 18, General Johnston was awakened to read a message from Adjutant General Samuel Cooper: "General Beauregard is attacked. To strike the enemy a decisive blow a junction of all your effective force will be needed. If practicable, make the movement, sending your sick and baggage to Culpeper Court-House. . . . In all the arrangements exercise your discretion."[49]

A rare piece of luck accompanied this summons. General Patterson, who had been keeping Johnston's army under close observation, suddenly pulled away and lost contact with the Rebels. Johnston took swift advantage of his freedom. He made arrangements for his wounded at Winchester, left a militia garrison temporarily aided by Jeb Stuart's cavalry, and put the rest of his army on the march. As it turned out, Johnston made a clean getaway—so tight was Stuart's security screen that Patterson was fooled for a whole day.

For a while, though, Johnston wondered whether the stolen hours would count. Everything about the march went awry—stragglers dawdled along the column, and no rhythm could be kept among the green recruits who walked in casual pace to war. Not until two in the morning of July 19 did Johnston's lead brigade under General Thomas J. Jackson reach a bivouac area at Paris, Virginia, a long forty miles from Manassas Junction. To speed the march Johnston put his infantry on trains at Piedmont Station on the

Manassas Gap Railroad. At seven o'clock on the morning of the 19th Jackson's men began boarding; by four in the afternoon most had reached Beauregard's camps. Johnston's remaining brigades would come as fast as the trains were provided—wagons, guns, and cavalry went by road. More arrived during the 20th, but not all, despite promises from railroad officers.

From the Confederate standpoint there were several other things missing. Cohesion certainly seemed absent everywhere on Beauregard's eight-mile line. And to even a casual observer something was wrong with Beauregard's troop dispositions. He had about six and a half brigades of infantry available to hold a front which meandered along the southern banks of Bull Run. There were not enough men at hand for the job, yet Beauregard appeared to compound this deficiency by skewing his army in great bulk on his right flank. If McDowell crossed Bull Run upstream, far on the Rebel left, he would meet feeble resistance and likely flank the whole Confederate position.

The matter of dispositions took on peculiarly Confederate importance, an importance forced by protocol. As it happened Johnston ranked Beauregard, and military custom gave command to the senior officer. Johnston understood this and normally would have insisted on it, but he knew his impetuous colleague. Sensitive himself to the anxieties of ambition, he recognized the symptoms in Beauregard and knew the Creole's verve would vanish in subordination. Johnston waived rank and left Beauregard in command.

Beauregard's plan, as explained to Johnston, was simple enough. Four Confederate brigades were to strike McDowell's army almost frontally at Centreville; six other brigades would smash the Union left rear. With any kind of luck the Federals would be caught in a vise. There were two things wrong with this plan: its conception and its execution!

First indication that something was wrong came to Johnston early in the morning of July 21. Beauregard brought his battle order to Johnston's headquarters at 4:30 and asked for final approval. Johnston was dismayed. Beauregard's paragraphs were models of obfuscation; inherent confusion, shifting intent, and Byzantine complexity permeated the entire document. Brigades were reconstituted, divisions designated, corps created, all without warning; no time for advance was set; lines of authority were blurred or cut. Only a highly disturbed man could have produced such a monstrosity. Only a desperate man could have approved it—but Johnston had no choice. Everything depended on speed. A swift and unexpected thrust offered the only chance for any army outnumbered by almost 20,000 on the field.[50] There was no time for clarification, and so Johnston endorsed the order.

As it happened, a merciful fate intervened to wreck Beauregard's plan before it could be carried out. Even while couriers were carrying his baffling order to some of the advanced brigades, McDowell attacked. The Yankee commander had arrived at almost a mirror image of Beauregard's plan—with clarity as an added ingredient. By five o'clock in the morning his flanking force was in action.

News of firing far to the left began the longest day in Beauregard's career. Thin and scattered Confederate forces on that flank could hardly be expected to stand off a major part of McDowell's army. Was the attack on that neglected quarter a feint? Or was it a major drive that would wreck all Beauregard's planning? For anxious minutes he writhed in indecisiveness, torn between devotion to his scheme and dread for the safety of his army. At last he made a compromise decision which almost cost him the day. One brigade, Jackson's, of the Army of the Shenandoah would be sent to the threatened flank. If the front there could be held, Beauregard still intended to deliver his own attack.

As it turned out the front could not be held and was, in fact, crumbling. As Jackson's men marched toward the swelling sound of musketry and cannon, they encountered the first backwash of disaster. Stunned soldiers, jaded mounts, and empty caissons were eddying to the rear. No one knew anything save that thousands of Federals had crossed Bull Run, had finally pushed aside a heroic little force under General Shanks Evans, and were rolling up the whole Confederate line of battle. News of the mounting debacle went back to Army Headquarters, and Jackson marched on to the fighting.

About midmorning Beauregard accepted reality, scrapped his hopeless plan, and began to get hold of himself. There is no doubt that he had verged on hysteria most of the early hours—a dizzying array of orders and counterorders, plans and counterplans, misplaced and castaway units were ample proof of his demoralization. With crisis came a kind of calm. If he lacked strategic gifts, he had a soldier's greatest asset—battle sense. Once convinced of what had happpened, Beauregard shifted his front with the flow of action. But until the main Rebel strength could reach the left, everything depended on small units under Evans, Barnard E. Bee, Francis Bartow, and Thomas J. Jackson.

By late morning everything depended on Jackson. Bee, Bartow, and Evans had done well. With scarcely 2,800 men they had stalled McDowell's 13,000-man assault force until almost noon. But they were finished at last; increasing numbers of bluecoats extended the enemy line until the Confederates were flanked. Bee watched in horror as his South Carolinians cracked and streamed backward, as cohesion disappeared and the whole Confederate line became a milling rabble. In wild disarray they raced for high ground at the Henry House Hill. Bee rode ahead of the stampede, tried to turn it, to coax a mob into an army. At the height of his despair and at the top of the hill he rode into a Confederate line of battle. Jackson's brigade was in position along the eastern edge of a small plateau. Guns dotted Jackson's front, an air of expectancy hung over his line, and a fiery determination lighted his eye.

Frenzied, Bee shouted to him, "General, they are beating us back." Jackson, with a hard stare, replied, "Sir, we'll give them the bayonet." Suddenly Bee believed, reined his horse, rode among his fleeing troops, and shouted his immortal last words: "There is Jackson standing like a stone wall. Let us determine to die here, and we will conquer. Follow me."[51]

And so it happened that when McDowell's men assaulted the Widow Henry's hill they ran into fierce artillery fire and were thrown back by the bayonets of "Stonewall" Jackson's men.

While the drama of Stonewall Jackson was played on Henry House Hill, Johnston and Beauregard reached the heart of their battle. Galloping in front of Jackson's line, Old Borey assumed charge of the field. As Johnston urged more units forward, Beauregard put them in line, encouraged, harangued, led them in charge after charge, until at last there was a subtle change in things.

Close to three-thirty a column of dust appeared off to the southwest. Beauregard could make out a line of men through his glasses, could even see a flag, but it drooped baffling around the staff. It was the decisive moment—one brigade to either side and the battle was over. Friend or foe, blue or gray? A breeze, a fluttering pennant—the South's "Bonnie Blue Flag!" Jubal Early's vagrant brigade from Johnston's Army had come at last. He joined in a sweeping bayonet charge against the Federals, who broke and fled in panic across bloody Bull Run.

It was a great and costly day, far costlier than the victors guessed.

CHAPTER THREE

"*A Knack of Hoping*"

—MARY CHESNUT

Easy Victory?

Richmond's Spotswood House sheltered a new social class—anguished officers' wives. A group of them, all sisters in adversity, stayed in that famous hotel and awaited news from Manassas. Mrs. Davis, as the First Lady and as a friend, presided over this inner circle of ladies of quality.

She got the first word and spread it quickly. "A great battle has been fought," she announced to her charming South Carolina cohort Mary Chesnut. "Jeff Davis led the center, Joe Johnston the right wing, Beauregard the left wing of the Army. Your husband is all right."[1] That wildly wrong and wonderful story marked the sudden tone of Richmond. Victory became a kind of opiate to ease fears and frustrations, to sanction death, and to crown heroes.

Richmond's finer ladies, those of quality who enjoyed Mrs. Davis's approval, found heroes abounding. To that patriotic claque every wearer of the gray at Manassas was "*sans peur et sans reproche.*"[2] And the feeling seemed general. Exultation mixed with nervous relief lent an almost carnival spirit to the city. The wounded were all but deified. The hastily organized hospitals were overstaffed with novice nurses, basking in reflected glory. Ladies brought fancy food and plain, bandages cut from dainty linens, cooking utensils and soap and candy and cake, adoration and brimming zeal. Recovery midst their teeming tenderness was precarious but not dull.[3]

Even without Richmond's ladies of mercy, dying became familiar enough. Reversed boots in polished stirrups, parades pacing cadence to the "Dead March" dimmed some of victory's joy. There was an oddly filial quality about these Manassas deaths, at least among the higher officers. It is a quality worth remarking, since it tells something interesting about Southern society.

Consider the case of Colonel Francis S. Bartow, killed leading an advance. A Georgian, former mayor of Savannah, Bartow led a regiment from his state and achieved considerable popularity as a promising soldier. News of his death stunned most of Richmond's gentry and hit the coterie of ladies around Mrs. Davis especially hard. They all knew the worthy Bartow and had ushered his wife into their Spotswood House inner circle for obvious reasons. She was Mrs. Bartow of Georgia and "a charming person, witty and wise," daughter of Judge Berrien.[4] She belonged. And because she did, she deserved special treatment; Mrs. Davis was the first to tell her that her soldier had fallen. The Bartow case was repeated with almost every prominent casualty; quality knew its own.

Easy victory is not a primer for hard war. But there were a few people in the happy capital who saw behind the glitter of Manassas to certain disquieting truths. The blue invaders had come in brimming confidence, numbers of Yankee Congressmen and their ladies journeyed with picnic baskets to the "Bull Run Races" with full intent to follow their army to Richmond, the North had not really taken the Confederates seriously; now events of July 21 changed everything. They changed things for the South, too, and there was the problem. Southerners were already wallowing in confidence, many had boasted gleefully that one Confederate could handle ten Yankees, and who now could dispute these claims? In the wake of success who could halt this certitude?

Victory at Manassas, welcome and retrospectively anticipated, turned out on close examination not to be enough. After Richmond salons dissected the battle to its most minute parts, certain glaring deficiencies came clear. Victory without fruits seemed barren indeed. Even though the Yankees were put to flight across Bull Run, questions were raised about the aftermath. Could the Confederates perhaps have captured Washington? Surprising as the question might seem in the early blush of deliverance, it had a serious point.

85

Many Manassas veterans, and more who had not been in the battle, argued that nothing could have stopped a Confederate dash for the enemy capital. A beaten horde of bluecoats streaming backward midst the wreckage of defeat would have offered no obstacle; Washington's defenses were alleged to be weak and undermanned. Instead of pursuing the foe, the Confederates had simply stopped. A feeble cavalry chase hastened the enemy retreat slightly, but nothing more was tried. Why? Was there, perhaps, a mysterious plot afoot? Were Southern leaders suddenly timid? Or did Jeff Davis's arrival on the field just at the moment of victory spread some strange lethargy?

The whole issue was blown up into a full-scale controversy, with people passionately taking sides. A few said that there were sound logistical reasons for merely holding the battlefield; rations, wagons, ammunition, everything necessary for an advance was lacking. Others—among them such influential officers as Stonewall Jackson —brushed aside reasons for caution and claimed momentum would have made its own possibilities.[5]

And thus began the first great quarrel among Confederates. It would rage throughout the war with bitterness increasing in direct ratio to later lost chances. Sadly enough the President became the focus of the fury, an unwitting and largely guiltless party to it all. There was no escape for him, since everything that happened in the country in some degree touched the chieftain. Davis could have borne his proper share of venom, but as it happened he received a good deal more than his share and in a form especially galling to a man of military bent. Rumors—later direct accusations—had it that during a council of war after the battle he listened to arguments for and against an advance on Washington, and decided against it.

A good deal that happened on that confused day became muddled and distorted, some events were happily forgotten, others magnified enormously. But one thing Jefferson Davis remembered always and with icy clarity: he did not forbid an advance. He considered pursuit "a matter of importance"[6] and in the battle's twilight asked both Beauregard and Johnston their views. They were in favor of pressing the enemy but convinced that circumstances, especially supply shortages, made it impractical. In retrospect the issue is as academic as it was at the time. One overriding factor made advance impossible—the condition of Rebel troops at the moment of victory. Victory had come suddenly to a wildly jumbled field. During the long afternoon's fighting on the Confederate left, myriad units had been shoved into combat wherever they appeared. Companies and battalions shifted with emergencies until at last a sprawling inchoate mass comprised the Confederate line of battle. And when fighting stopped, when men could breathe again, when the rage of war receded, a strange sort of wanderlust touched the Rebel army. Men ranged over the battlefield seeking comrades or units, seeking water or food, or merely walking in search of nothing save life itself. Pursuit was ruled out by human endurance.

Later generations would know the symptoms, would label the malady "shell shock" or "battle fatigue," but in 1861 there was no name for it, no real understanding of battle stress. No one yet knew the price of bravery. From a comfortable distance victory without decision seemed unacceptable, and somebody must be blamed for that failure.[7]

Still, there was enough of victory to make most Rebels happy. More than that, Manassas had a positive effect. If it did breed more contempt for Yankees, if it seemed to prove Southern superiority, it also helped make a nation. Manassas was a victory bought by common blood. Those amorphous legions so recently detrained at Richmond had fused into the semblance of an army and had won a national victory. The pride of it was felt everywhere.

"Our Better Policy Would Be to Invade . . ."

Nations are creations of human yearning; they give focus to hope and substance to ambition and they persist in ratio to patriotism. Great nations are maintained by great devotion. American history to 1861 made the point. Would Confederate history prove it?

In the weeks after Manassas the answer seemed an obvious yes. But patriotism comes easily with success. Whether Rebel enthusiasm would linger in times of waiting and defeat, whether the South was tough enough to win, depended on a good many intangibles. The most important of these intangibles was the way the war was run.

Running the war depended, in turn, on national strategy, on

some kind of over-all plan for success. Responsibility for providing such a plan rested squarely on the Chief Executive, and it was a task Davis gladly assumed. He had considerable understanding of strategy, had studied principles of war at West Point, and had learned something about applying these principles during his spectacular service in the Mexican War.

According to accepted military theory—especially according to the revered Henri Jomini, whose *Principles of War* transmitted the wisdom of Napoleonic planning to generations of soldiers—strategy was almost an exact science of victory. But strategy is never a matter of such stark simplicity. The idea of strategy expounded by Jomini, and by virtually all other students of war in the 1860's, was seriously distorted. Most military theorists at the outset of the Civil War were talking in tactical terms, were planning maneuvers and battles and evolutions of the line, were mired in the notion that wars are won by troops in the field.[8]

Modern times had gone past mere battlefield heroics, had progressed even beyond the battle as the final decision, and had reached the era of mobilization, communications, and logistics. By 1860 war was almost total. Total war dictates total strategy. Neither North nor South could make adequate preparation for waging modern war with antique ideas; whatever worked in the Mexican War simply was irrelevant.[9]

Almost every participant in war planning in 1861 missed one fact: strategy is indivisible. A nation's strategy must consider every facet of life; everything impinges on war. Those few who had studied the theories of Karl von Clausewitz, that relatively unknown Prussian military philosopher, understood a little of the new realities. Clausewitz postulated that a country's military system will parallel its social system, since war is, after all, merely an extension of politics. The situation of the Confederacy in the post-Manassas months seemed to prove Clausewitz's theories.

By midsummer Confederate leaders could agree that circumstances dictated strategy. Most high officials realized that victory went to the bold and agreed with the President that "our better policy would be to invade rather than . . . stand on the defensive."[10] But there seemed no freedom of choice. The Confederacy appeared trapped by circumstances in a strategy of defense, although one facet of defense needed consideration: like the patriots in the American Revolution, the Confederates might win by simply not losing.

To some degree the circumstances were self-inflicted. Consider the field of diplomacy, an area with large impact on strategy. From the earliest Montgomery days Southern leaders had sought to project a world image of a Southland seeking only peace and freedom. Any sudden shift to aggression would shatter this idyllic pose and probably wreck any chance for foreign recognition. No one understood this better than the President, who worked diligently to charm England and Europe through public pronouncement and direct negotiation. Uninitiated into the subtleties of international politics, Davis entered the diplomatic arena with disarming directness. Honesty would beget honesty, and there was virtue among nations. Armored by this whimsey he supported in April 1862 a straightforward deal to France and to Europe: Confederate cotton for recognition of the Confederacy.

There was much to commend this proposal, beyond its startling candor. Cotton was the one tangible asset possessed by the South which the industrial nations of Europe desperately needed. Without it countless mills in England and France would close down and thousands of workers go unemployed. Hence Europe had a direct stake in lifting the blockade proclaimed by Lincoln on April 19, 1861. Recognition of Confederate independence appeared the surest way to end the blockade. Once the Confederacy was acknowledged, Lincoln's paper barrier would vanish in a crush of international commerce. The assumption that cotton was king, a sure fulcrum of power, formed the initial basis of Southern diplomacy.[11]

Success of this diplomacy depended in large degree on deft presentation. Skillful, suave, and canny men were needed to carry the message abroad. The Confederacy's first diplomats had none of these qualities. Picked by Davis with Secretary Toombs's approval for reasons happily beyond historical analysis, they were envoys of odd ineptitude. William L. Yancey's vocal attributes and his enchantment with slavery suited him to the Sublime Porte but hardly to Whitehall; Pierre Rost's French heritage made him comfortable in the language but hardly in the salon; A. Dudley Mann's verbosity pre-empted conversation and his ego limited his European welcome; his credulity and fascination for commercial enterprise limited his scope in negotiations.

This miscast trio descended on Europe in April 1861 as spokesmen for the new Confederacy. Luckily for them, their timing was right. Shortly after they arrived and before they could infuse idiocy into international relations, Britain and France proclaimed their neutrality in the war and then granted the Confederacy belligerent rights—a great boon that gave Confederate ships and soldiers international acceptance. The Yancey-Rost-Mann mission had nothing to do with this early Rebel encouragement. The extraordinary envoys' efforts were fruitless—no commercial treaty was signed and recognition was in abeyance—and they were replaced in January 1862. Britain and all of Europe waited to see the way the war trended, waited to measure the profits of neutrality, waited to determine whether the Confederacy could hold off the Yankees and maintain itself.[12]

As far as maintenance of independence was concerned, most of the process was going to hinge on the strange and baffling business of logistics. This high-sounding branch of military science, devoted to procuring, distributing, and sustaining men, munitions, food, and communications, had always been at the heart of martial affairs. Until a modern war of mass and movement occurred, however, the science of supply had remained a simple process handled mainly by the Quartermaster General, the Chief of Ordnance, the Commissary General, and their naval counterparts. By the time opposing armies groped toward each other in northern Virginia, matters of supply were no longer simple.

Problems of mobilizing, supplying, and transporting thousands of troops distorted every facet of national economy. Normal patterns of wages, workers, profits, production, and consumption were sharply altered. Armies were parasitical: they took producers from factories, farms, and firesides; they scavenged the country around their camps and left blight where they had been. Money, material, food, munitions, clothes, everything flowed to them without end; they became the focus, the object, the purpose of total national effort.

The armed forces were gigantic consumers and a peculiar type of big business. Peculiar business techniques were required to gear the country to sustain the military, to arrange a new economy, and these new techniques were embraced in the science of logistics.[13]

No coherent supply planning had been done in the South. Ignorance of the enormity of the problem was not the only reason; hope hindered preparations. Despite scant munitions, minerals, and shipbuilding facilities, the vast acreage of the South, the limitless stocks of cotton, the gusty enthusiasm of Rebels everywhere made supply problems appear solvable. John Slidell, a prominent Louisiana politician, put the hope of the South clearly in a letter to a New York friend:

> When we move our cotton crop, I think that our finances will be in a better condition than yours. We have now between 18 & 20,000 men in the field from our little State; three more regiments having been called for. The question is not who shall go but who shall stay at home— When we meet in Virginia—you will largely outnumber us in men, but ours in general are of much better quality than yours & we shall have the enormous advantage of fighting . . . for our very existence.[14]

Slidell's opinion was echoed widely. After all, optimism clouds doubts and beggars statistics.

There are limits even to the most outrageous optimism. In the post-Manassas period these limits began to quench some Confederate ambitions. Even though diligent recruiting had persuaded almost 200,000 men to the colors, even though victory created a veneer of strength, by midsummer 1861 the Confederacy was in trouble. Short-term enlistments were expiring, arms were in short supply, the blockade pinched already.[15] Serious defects became apparent in the South's transportation system.

Nothing revealed these defects more strikingly than the pressure of getting supplies from the Deep South to Johnston's and Beauregard's men along the Bull Run line. Coordination between the various railroad companies was imperative, and absent. With rare exceptions the rail companies of the South had each followed individual policies and had cooperated with each other as little as the traffic allowed. Rates differed between companies, equipment varied, and tragically for the war effort, rail gauges did not always match in the larger rail centers.

There was, consequently, no true rail network to sustain logistics. Railroads had not been vital to the prewar South. Small companies vied for the cotton trade to coastal cities and resisted a common building scheme. The South's 9,000 miles of track was a patchwork of short lines and hybrid rolling stock. Trainmen knew where the money was, and they built short lines designed to connect interior cotton lands with seaports. Schemes for a trunk track running from Virginia to Texas remained shimmering speculations. It was possible to take a train from the Mississippi River to Richmond, but only a devotee of discomfort would take it.

As the immensity of war touched everywhere, the importance of transportation became obvious. All facets of life now depended on rapid and sufficient communications. Transportation lines were the arteries of war. Railroads, weak and spasmodic, were, nonetheless, the largest arteries, and weakness or coagulation in the arteries meant rapid ruin. Unless sense and order could be insinuated into rail lines, all other phases of transportation would atrophy. There was no substitute circulatory system adequate to the burdens of mass and distance.[16]

True, a veinlike skein of roads covered the South. But Southern roads were dismally unsuited to conflict. Most were dirt traces with here and there a modern, macadamized pike to point the way of the future. Under stress of guns, horses, and marching men, the roads became avenues of torture—in summer, shrouded in dust or steeped in slime; in winter, the ruts rimed red with the blood of men and mounts.

Even good highways could not have compensated for bad railroads. Effective use of roads depended on such intangibles as livestock production. How many horses would be available for cavalry and artillery use, for army wagons and ambulances, for the hundred and one things needed in a day's war? How many mules could be found for harder work? These were puzzling questions, particularly at a time of unsettled boundaries. Answers hinged on how many animals could be brought from Texas, filched from Kentucky, and obtained in Virginia. According to popular rumor every Southerner was somehow a horseman, raised—perhaps born—to the saddle. Statistics dispelled the rumor. Future supplies were going to depend on what states remained Confederate.[17] Would ample horse population solve the transportation problem? Not unless there were enough wagons, caissons, ambulances, and other conveyances to keep military and civilian commerce moving. And these were all in short supply. Wagon factories existed in the South, a rural section spawns them naturally, but total war overreached normal capacity. The emergency was complicated, too, by shortages of iron for tires, of leather for harness, even of cut lumber for beds and tongues.[18]

Waterways were not going to be especially helpful. This might seem odd, since Southern commerce in prewar days followed most navigable streams to market and port towns. But that changed when Lincoln proclaimed his blockade of the Confederate coastline in April 1861. The blockaders were present more in fear than fact, but the mere proclamation of blockade frightened off some ships. Chronic shortages of small vessels, barges, and riverboats sharpened the problem.

Many in the Confederate hierarchy caught the import of the transportation crisis; none felt it more poignantly than the Chief of Ordnance, the Quartermaster General, and the Commissary General. Gorgas, Myers, and Northrop recognized the symptoms of economic paralysis sooner than anyone else. Their constant efforts to find supplies within boundaries likely to shrink, their efforts to expand and modernize Lilliputian industries, to locate talented subordinates, to develop dormant natural resources, their efforts simply to do their jobs were infinitely complicated by unpredictable conveyance.

There were those in the War Department and in the Confederate Congress who argued that money would make everything right. Gold would banish all evil. They were wrong. There was simply not enough of anything—a reality beyond even the alchemy of money.

This reality the President understood, and it dictated much of his strategic thinking. He grasped the obvious advantages of concentration so loudly proclaimed by Generals Johnston and Beauregard.

But unlike his generals, Davis had to see beyond the field. And all the evidence coming to him in ominous plentitude indicated that the South would have to compromise between the hopes of strategy and the limits of logistics. Davis met this necessity with a bold and original war policy, which he called the "offensive-defensive." Designed to defend all the resources of the Confederacy and stockpile its strength, the offensive-defensive would enable the country to maintain its armies and to counterthrust when chances and supplies permitted.[19] Such a plan would prolong the war. Later, in the bitterness of recollection, Davis would be condemned for this policy, would be castigated as a man of ice and calm and caution who lacked a gambler's soul and had no spark for revolution. Perhaps. And yet, who dares more desperately than the man who parries strength with time?[20]

"We Are Resting on Our Oars . . ."

Civilians are the most involved and least informed ingredients of modern war. Part of the trouble lies in the waiting. Actually total war is nothing save activity, but not all of it spectacular. The people of the Confederacy knew from the firing of the first Sumter gun that they were at war. Excitement crackled across Dixie, lingered after Fort Sumter and the uncertainties of preparing and shifting the capital, lingered happily longer than the President dared hope.

Excitement is the child of danger, and danger the surest bond of unity. Danger abounded for the infant nation and helped it stick together.

Technical matters of mobilization, logistics, the intricacies of martial preparation were dimly grasped by many new Rebels, despite their loud devotion to Mars. Some measures made essential by struggle never were really understood. Loyal Confederates grasped the need for taxation, but the mysteries of public finance, the strange devices of the Treasury Department to glean the last small change in every hamlet, the machinations of a remote Secretary Memminger, were simply baffling.

No special financial knowledge was needed to realize the limits of money raising. Free-enterprise Southerners bitterly opposed high taxes, and a sensitive government sought other ways of finding revenue. Loans were sensible and expected. The $15 million loan of February 28, 1861, proved a success, and even the May and August loans, seeking another $100 million, were not unpopular.[21] A few bankers and businessmen shared doubts about the Confederate Congress's quick reliance upon paper notes instead of hard money. The need was obvious enough, but the practice dubious. Once printing presses began to roll sheets of notes, the process would be easy to continue until cascades of money stifled commerce.

Paper, however, makes good sense to most people. It is a cheap form of money since it stimulates inflation. Debts contracted in tighter times are more easily discharged. Which is charming enough to everyone except government financiers.

Unfortunately Secretary Memminger botched the issuance of paper money. The notes he so cavalierly printed looked good but lacked one essential for public confidence: they were not legal tender. Which meant, simply, that debts were not necessarily discharged by the bills. Why print them save to benefit investors?

There were other mysterious things to question about Memminger's policies. Although it seemed a boon to numbers of planters stuck with an unsalable cotton crop in 1861, the "produce loan" provisions of the early bond issues were puzzling. If farmers and planters could subscribe to the Confederate loans by mortgaging produce, where did that leave the unlanded gentry and plain folk? Such schemes smacked of class favoritism. And as it happened, dismal ill luck dogged the produce loans throughout most of the Confederacy's history. In time the planters and farmers, who were the designed beneficiaries, turned against the loans for fear of being victimized by low prices.[22]

Produce loans and legal-tender problems were fairly esoteric things to most people. But Confederates caught the meaning of more direct actions, actions like suspension by Southern banks of payments in hard money. Savings and other accounts were not confiscated, and there were few interruptions in banking activities; it just became suddenly impossible in most of the Confederacy to get anything but paper from the banks. Reasons for this were fairly clear. As the Treasury Office of Virginia put it in a circular to state banks, suspension was authorized "to provide for the defense and honor of the state." Large cash demands would be made by Virginia on her banks; the banks should be warned so "that you may prepare to meet the demands, which we flatter ourselves from your past loyalty, and liberality, will be cheerfully and promptly responded to."[23] A good many irate citizens missed the advantages of suspension until various states enacted "stay laws" permitting delays in debt settlement, laws essential in an economy almost bereft of legal currency.[24]

Despite all grousing, and the South seemed peopled with raucous grousers, early financial policies were relatively kind. The first direct war tax of August 1861 scarcely touched hearth and home.[25] As it worked out the various states pledged quotas and tried to meet them by state loans and bonds. So cumbersome were these fragmented efforts that much of the desired revenue never came. Why? Many astute observers offered opinions. Some said that the Secretary of the Treasury lacked energy; worse, a simple grasp of his job. Others argued that the Confederate government should scorn state feelings and reach directly into everyone's pocket through its own agents and collectors.

Whatever the proper policy might be, something stringent would have to be done to avoid bankruptcy. Clearly the President and the administration needed a firmer grasp of financial problems.

Stability was really the main concern throughout the country. Governors and Congressmen caught disturbing hints of unrest in each day's mail. From the far-western edges of the Confederacy came plaints of Indian troubles, Unionist depredations, unsettled political conditions. Kentuckians who journeyed eastward to plead the sad state of things on "the dark and bloody ground" urged swift Confederate measures to protect sympathetic fellow Southerners. Arkansans told of disarray throughout their remote domain, of haphazard defense measures, of wandering bands of Missouri militia under the independent General Sterling Price, and of confusion among Confederate generals on the scene.[26] Texas had a serious Unionist problem among German settlers (which was to be met awkwardly by a massacre of Germans at the Nueces River) and a feudal State Military Board. Citizens who were scattered beyond the Balcones Escarpment out on the semiarid plains complained of Indian raiders;

border patrols reported rising antagonism across the Rio Grande.[27]

Up from Texas beyond Indian Territory into Arkansas and across the Mississippi in Kentucky and Tennessee came a strange and new cry, the cry of the dispossessed. Faint at first, the cry rose until at last it reached a crescendo in the halls of Congress, rattled the doors of the Executive Mansion, and touched the conscience of each Confederate—the cry for help and sustenance from those tragic nomads of war, the refugees. They came in a trickle in the beginning from border places; as the enemy inexorably pressed the Confederacy upon itself they came in steady streams and then at last in torrents; they brought the things they could carry, some the practical tools of survival, some the Bible to prove a family and not much more, some the touching, pretty things that give a shred of dignity to wandering, some just shock and terror and hate. All of them had one great possession they shared together: hope.[28]

Hope was a commodity in great Confederate store. It cloaked a multitude of realities, made light of scarcities brought on by even a thin blockade. With hope people could laugh at the dwindling stocks of shoes and clothes, at the sudden popularity of homespun and the crudity of boots. Perhaps there was a saving grace in Southerners, a grace of humor in adversity, or as Mary Chesnut put it, "a knack of hoping."

Excitement still prevailed in a troubled land, but it was tinged with uncertainty. While the enemy made great preparations and the North rang with pride in the Union, what was being done for the good of the Confederacy? What did President Davis and his colleagues plan for the next campaign? A churlish and articulate War Office clerk caught the prevailing winds of doubt when he said "we are resting on our oars after the victory at Manassas."[29] With the general drift of spirit, how chill would be the winter?

The Eagle at the Feet of the Lion

U.S.S. *San Jacinto* looked mournful as she kept station in Bahama Channel between Cuba and New Providence. Dingy, her planking begrimed by heavy seas, she lay waiting for a strange rendezvous. Up until that day, November 8, 1861, the *San Jacinto* had made a dubious record in the war. Much of her lackluster history could be blamed on her master, Commander Charles Wilkes, a captain in quest of glory. So far he had missed, but on this day he would have his moment.

About midmorning, a smudge of black marked the horizon; as the day wore on the smudge became a plume, then a little after 1:00 P.M. clearly ship's smoke. The Royal Mail packet *Trent* was beating eastward toward Nassau. The *San Jacinto's* hands stood to, orders were snapped, speed came up. Slowly the two vessels made a collision course. At last, when closed to range, the *San Jacinto* put two shots across the *Trent's* bow, and Wilkes hailed the British vessel to heave to and receive boarders.

Wilkes had no interest in Her Britannic Majesty's mail or her ship; he demanded custody of two Southern passengers—Louisiana's John Slidell and Virginia's James Mason. These two, recently designated Confederate Commissioners to the courts of St. James's and the Tuileries, had accepted Britain's offer of passage on the mail ship to Europe. Wilkes had learned of their presence on the *Trent* from his executive officer, Lieutenant D. M. Fairfax. Fairfax, a Virginian, had spotted Mason in Havana's Hotel Cubana and had picked up local gossip about Mason and Slidell's sailing plans. Wilkes brushed formal protests from the British captain aside, took his prisoners, and steamed away. The whole episode ended with astonishing abruptness. Too little time was taken by an event that could shape history.[30]

The enormity of the event worried Wilkes's second in command, but not the arrant captain. He had neatly plucked two Rebels from a possibly troublesome mission; an act of considerable value to his cause. When word of what he had done reached the United States, public reaction seemed to confirm his expectations. Hurrahs and cheers filled Northern newspapers and Wilkes became the hero of the moment.[31]

There was a good deal of cheering in Richmond, too. John B. Jones, the garrulous war clerk, confided happily to his diary that "it would bring the Eagle cowering to the feet of the Lion." Judah Benjamin, newly appointed to the post of War Secretary, admitted that "it was, perhaps the best thing that could have happened."[32]

In Whitehall, in the British Embassy in Washington, in most

world capitals, outrage and disbelief mixed with hatred for the Yankees. Lord John Russell, Lord Palmerston, and a large majority of Her Majesty's cabinet pondered the price of Britain's forgiveness. Honor had been infringed, a royal vessel had been accosted on the high seas, and reckless American sailors had done what their own country had so loudly rejected in 1812. British public opinion ran hotly for redress. Talk of war against insolent Yankeedom echoed across England. Mason and Slidell seemed likely to accomplish more by incarceration than they could by negotiation.

Everything depended on the British government, on the nature of its reaction. Palmerston and Russell wanted no war with the United States, but neither did they wish to settle the affair with a gentle wrist slapping. British statesmen knew that Seward had long cherished hopes for a foreign war as a possible way to re-cement the Union. Even though the moment might appear late for such a gambit, Seward could be mad enough to try. Lord Lyons, the British Ambassador in Washington, received extremely careful instructions: he must keep M. Henri Mercier, the French Ambassador, fully informed of all dealings with the Americans; he must take a firm tone with Seward, and he must put plainly certain essentials. The government of the United States faced an ultimatum: within seven days from December 19, 1861, an official apology must be given Her Majesty's government and Mason and Slidell must be returned to British protection, or Great Britain would declare war.

Lyons did deft and firm duty, and he was aided considerably by Mercier. The French Ambassador glimpsed in Seward's manner a suspicion that Napoleon III might welcome war between France's old enemy and revolutionary friend, might even fan it with support for the Yankees. In an informal meeting Mercier put France's position clearly. "He begged Mr. Seward to dismiss all idea of assistance from France; & not to be led away by the vulgar notion that the Emp: w[oul]d gladly see England embroiled with the U.S. in order to pursue his own plans in Europe without opposition."[33]

Seward and Lincoln debated, estimated cost, and finally gave back the Confederate commissioners. A foreign war, though often threatened by Seward, was for the time beyond capacity, especially one which would confirm secession rather than deny it. And so the great crisis passed. For the moment, at least, Confederates must still help themselves.[34]

As President Davis put the South's position bravely to a visitor: "I am far from complaining of the conduct towards us of European Governments. It is better for us that we should work out our own Independence and the rest will come in good Time."[35]

Mason and Slidell, once they reached England and France, worked toward persuading Europe that the Federal blockade leaked like a sieve and hence failed to rank as a blockade according to the Declaration of Paris. Such an argument had the sterling ring of truth and was strongly appealing to commercially bent nations. It was a good argument, one bound to win attention, but it lacked drama. It also lacked demonstrable reward. Would lifting the Federal blockade be worth the trouble to England and France? Reward often makes policy and sometimes makes diplomacy.

There was an incident trailing swiftly in wake of the *Trent* affair that had much drama and perhaps enough obvious reward to secure recognition. When the Federals sank a "stone fleet" at the entrance to Charleston harbor, Britain's interest in free commerce was involved. With a bit more care, Confederate diplomacy might have fanned this interest into anger, for British leaders were stunned by such Yankee brashness. Closing the port of Charleston might be militarily expedient to the North but internationally disastrous.

Foreigners see with a different eye, and trends and changes and portents focus more sharply at a distance. What was happening in America had much to do with anger, with the abrasive nature of long war. Things had not so degenerated by mid-1861, but already there were warnings even beyond Charleston of a possible turn in the war.

Lord Palmerston could scarcely believe the Charleston blunder. Early in 1862 he wondered if Britain and France might join "in an official Remonstrance against a Proceeding more worthy of the barbarous ages than of the present time and which is an Injury to all the commercial nations of the world having intercourse with the North American Continent." He felt that such an enterprise might make hate the result of the American conflict. "This . . . Proceeding deprives war of its legitimate object, by stripping Peace of its

Natural Fruits. The present contest between the North and South must end either in the Conquest of the South by the North or by a Separation by Mutual Agreement. In the first case this operation is suicidal by taking away from what will in that case be a Part of the Territory of the union advantages which the Bounty of Heaven has bestowed; in the latter case this Proceeding will have implanted undying Hatred in the Breasts of those who being close neighbors ought to be also firm friends."[36]

Cotton, Ships, and High Reward

Cotton crops in 1859 and 1860 had approached bumper size but consumption abroad seemed to keep pace with Southern production. Schoolboys could recite cotton statistics, for they ranked high in the Confederate catechism. The 1860 harvest was 3,656,086 bales, the yield a year before a million higher,[37] but England and France called for more cotton to help sustain textile production. It required no great intelligence to grasp the obvious. A sudden drop in cotton exports from the South would ruin Europe's economy; ergo, the blockade must be broken.

All of which rang true enough, but cotton was not king. The South was finding that the bumper crops of 1859 and 1860 had created an oversupply. Just for a time in 1861 cotton glutted the foreign market. If there seemed a poignance to this, it was missed by most Confederates. Not entirely untutored in the nostrum of colored statistics, Southerners had long since accepted David Christy's argument in his popular *Cotton Is King: Or Slavery in the Light of Political Economy,* a persuasive treatise published in 1855. Christy's title gave the South a slogan and his tables and arguments proved it.

Realities contend weakly against slogans and more weakly against hope. Most of the early diplomatic policies of 1861 and 1862 were based on the King Cotton theory. Davis and Toombs and later Hunter and Benjamin played a constant game of suasion, holding cotton as bait.[38]

But despite a natural yearning to get at the acres of cotton in the South, Europe held aloof; the Confederacy had not quite proved a safe risk. Faced with a stalemate in the recognition game, Rebel diplomats shifted ground. They were learning that diplomacy is a good deal like war, and like war, it can be waged at various levels. For the embattled Confederate States there was a distinct possibility that the first diplomatic level—that of direct negotiations—offered the least chance of speedy success. On the secondary level of commercial relations, chances looked considerably better.

Success in establishing commercial ties abroad came slowly and as the outgrowth of logistical need. Confederate supply officials gradually conceived a passionate interest in the importation of everything—scarcity sometimes fashions a special clarity of insight. Adjuncts to domestic supplies were essential, and imports were the obvious source.[39]

Imports were obvious but practically and theoretically difficult. The practical complication was clear enough, the theoretical was not. It required, in fact, an eye for legalities to see it at all. Not that it was nonexistent; it was real enough to Jefferson Davis and his diplomats. Part of the problem was national image. The administration had been eagerly constructing a world view of a law-loving Confederacy locked in mortal combat with Yankee usurpers. The law of nations held that blockades must be effective to be recognized, and statistics collected almost daily at every Rebel port proved that the North maintained nothing more than a paper blockade. From April 29 through August 20, 1861, four hundred ships had entered and cleared Southern ports, and sheer numbers proved that there was no legal interdiction of commerce.[40] This was the official Confederate position, and there was good reason for holding to it.

With so much evidence laid before them, who could doubt that English and French leaders would honor the Declaration of Paris of 1856, which abolished privateering, announced that a neutral flag covered all enemy goods save contraband and that neutral goods are not subject to capture, and accepted the usual legal requirement of effectiveness as the basis for recognition of a blockade. Once Britain and France acknowledged that the Federal blockade did not exist, they would doubtless encourage trade with Confederate ports.

Doubtless, that is, in other times and other crises. But Southern leaders were yet to learn how their world had changed. Rulers abroad watched the conflict from varying viewpoints; Britain's cab-

inet, for instance, was intrigued by Northern insistence on the
legality of a paper blockade. Anyone could tell that the thin cordon
of ships cruising the Southern coast barely troubled commerce. As
a blockade the Federal patrol made an admirable sieve. But Yankee
statesmen insisted on its sanctity. Britain took counsel of the future
and pondered the possibility that in time this Northern precedent
could be most useful.[41] For reasons of potential self-interest, Europe
accepted the blockade.

If such cynicism baffled Jefferson Davis and men of the Confederate State Department, their naïveté irked some of their own com-
patriots. To such logistical realists as Chief of Ordnance Gorgas,
Southern reliance on legalistic argument was a bemusing whimsey
which paralyzed action. Instead of wasting time denying its existence, Gorgas thought the blockade should be systematically ex-
ploited. The Confederate government should enter the business of
eluding blockaders on a grand scale.

There was precedent aplenty behind this scheme. Private enter-
prises had done amazingly well. Corporations formed for the purpose of buying specially designed, light-draft ships capable of speed
and deception had already proved that two successful runs to Bermuda, Nassau, Cuba, Barbados, or Jamaica repaid all costs—everything later was sheer profit.[42]

These private ventures also proved the necessity of diverting the
big freighters to island depots. Large ships were easy prey to blockading vessels. Once deposited in the islands, merchandise—luxuries,
most of it, things like women's fashions, fine cloths, champagne, good
cheroots, gourmet foods—could be exchanged for cotton sent from
the South, put aboard the little ships, and run to the Confederacy.

There was a kind of gentlemen's recklessness about a voyage to
the South. It had everything a sporting man could want—a taste of
the hunt while running under Northern guns, a sense of daring
death, the rectitude of gallantry in helping the oppressed. And so
there came a host of young gentry to this enticing game. Among
them were such foreign naval officers as Lieutenant (later Admiral)
Charles Murray-Aynsley, R.N., known to the trade as Captain Mur-
ray of the blockade runner *Venus;* and Augustus Charles Hobart-

Hampden, V.C., late commander of the Royal yacht *Victoria and Albert,* hero of the Crimea, younger son of the Earl of Buckinghamshire, famous among Yankee blockaders as "Captain Roberts" of the uncatchable runner *Don.*[43]

Listed, too, among foreign participants were young entrepreneurs seeking a stake. Chief among these was Tom Taylor, a twenty-one-year-old Liverpool clerk, whose firm shipped him to Nassau and put him in charge of a fleet of blockade runners. He reaped profits beyond belief. By title "Supercargo," young Tom was far more than a desk man; he was a seagoing manager and soon a veteran Rebel visitor.

Taylor's career deserves a close look. His position gave him a broad view of blockade running, knowledge of every phase of the business, and contact with all kinds of people. Intricacies of finance were a daily part of his job; his employers trusted to him all matters of purchasing cargoes of cotton, of choosing loads for the South, of hiring and firing crews and captains. He did everything well. If he had a special talent, it was picking good captains.

Taylor had a seaman's love for a fine ship. Trim lines, good fittings and rigging, sound engines, all these things were splendid, but a sailor feels something from the keel, a nimble grace in running that gives life to a vessel. Taylor was lucky, he found a ship with lines and grace and life. It was called the *Banshee,* a 217-ton, iron-hulled beauty from Merseyside. She came from England early in 1863 to end the era of wooden runners and change the tempo of the blockade. Strength and response were her marks, and she deserved a proper captain. Taylor gave her to Captain J. W. Steele, a man of wisdom and daring and style to strike the spirit of his craft. Together they wrote records.

Steele and Taylor never forgot the first of the *Banshee*'s runs to Wilmington. She cleared Nassau at night, kept close to the British coastline as long as possible to avoid roaming Yankee cruisers, struck for the open sea, and steamed for two days. A noon sighting on the third day confirmed that the *Banshee* was almost close enough to run into Wilmington before daybreak next day. She had some trouble with her engines, and Taylor, who stood with Steele on the bridge on this and most voyages, cautioned against risks. The

Banshee steamed on in the darkness. Details of that night were fresh to Tom Taylor when he recalled them thirty years later:

> The night proved dark, but dangerously clear and calm. No lights were allowed—not even a cigar; the engine-room hatchways were covered with tarpaulins, at the risk of suffocating the unfortunate engineers and stokers in the almost insufferable atmosphere below. But it was absolutely imperative that not a glimmer of light should appear. Even the binnacle was covered, and the steersman had to see as much of the compass as he could through a conical aperture carried almost up to his eyes. . . . We steamed on in silence except for the stroke of the engines and the beat of the paddle-floats, which in the calm of the night seemed distressingly loud; all hands were on deck, crouching behind the bulwarks; and we on the bridge, namely, the captain, the pilot, and I, were straining our eyes into the darkness.

After running awhile in uneasy silence, the *Banshee* hove to for a sounding—sixteen fathoms, bottom sandy—and everyone listened for a sudden hiss of steam from the resting engines. There was no betraying sound, and a new course was plotted to carry the ship farther north. Another sounding an hour later indicated a true approach; speed dropped, again that pulsing silence, and then the pilot's sudden whisper:

> "There's one of them, Mr. Taylor on the starboard bow."
> In vain I strained my eyes to where he pointed [Taylor wrote], not a thing could I see; but presently I heard Steele say beneath his breath, "All right . . . I see her. Starboard a little, steady!" was the order passed aft.
> A moment afterwards I could make out a long low black object on our starboard side, lying perfectly still. Would she see us? that was the question: but no, though we passed within a hundred yards of her we were not discovered, and I breathed again. Not very long after we had dropped her [the pilot] whispered.—
> "Steamer on the port bow."
> And another cruiser was made out close to us. "Hard-a-port," said Steele, and round she swung, bringing our friend upon our beam. Still unobserved we crept quietly on, when all at once a third cruiser shaped herself out of the gloom right ahead and steaming slowly across our bows.
> "Stop her," said Steele in a moment, and as we lay like dead our

enemy went on and disappeared in the darkness. . . . "Ahead slow" we went again, until the low-lying coast and the surf line became dimly visible. . . . It was a great relief when we suddenly heard [the pilot] say, "It's all right, I see the 'Big Hill.'" . . .

And fortunate it was for us we were so near. Daylight was already breaking, and before we were opposite the fort [Fisher] we could make out six or seven gunboats, which steamed rapidly towards us and angrily opened fire. Their shots were soon dropping close around us; an unpleasant sensation when you know you have several tons of gunpowder under your feet. . . . It began to look ugly for us, when all at once there was a flash from the shore followed by a sound that came like music to our ears—that of a shell whirring over our heads. It was Fort Fisher, wide awake and warning gunboats to keep their distance. With a parting broadside they steamed sulkily out of range, and in half an hour we were safely over the bar.[44]

Taylor and the rest who dared the trip soon learned that excitement and peril were part of the pay—no trip was made in dead calm. Yet few runners stopped trying. Some did much better than others, for some had the luck that came with care. Steele was one of the lucky ones. He kept careful rein on his ship and crew and attended to such matters as looks and seamanship. With her dull white finish, her rigging stripped to two crosstreed masts, her boats lowered level with the rails, an almost invisible *Banshee* made eight safe trips before losing a race to a blockader, and those trips brought her owners 700 percent on their investment![45]

Success stories like the *Banshee*'s were common to the business. If the system worked for such fabulous private profits, why not for government necessities?

There was at least one large argument against the government's participation in the trade. Participation would confess the blockade, a confession the administration could ill afford. But Confedreate supply men were desperate; they knew that blockade running offered the best chance of augmenting the South's dwindling resources. Desperation inspires audacity, and official approval was ignored. Chief of Ordnance Gorgas and some colleagues in other supply agencies went ahead with planning and constructing a system of breaking the Yankee hold on commerce.

The whole thing was done with remarkable inventiveness. Certain prerequisites were quickly found: cotton was purchased or impressed in the normal course of bureau activities; once in hand it was shipped to Southern financial agents in Europe who converted it into ships and munitions and myriad materials. While European purchasing was under way, officers went out to Bermuda, Nassau, and Cuba; there local merchants and businessmen were employed to handle Confederate freight as they handled civilian cargoes.

People in the islands cooperated easily. Why not? Places like St. George's and Hamilton, Bermuda, Nassau on New Providence, Bridgetown, Barbados, Kingston, Jamaica, even Havana, Cuba, had for years lazed away on the fringes of progress, forgotten haunts of history. Suddenly came the war and the blockade, and a boom to touch again old buccaneer strains of greed.[46] All monied comers were welcome in the new marts of the Indies.

Later the entire enterprise would take on a romantic gloss; novelists, reminiscers, and historians would paint blockade runners in dashing strokes, give their derring-do heroic verve and size. But on the islands, in the Confederate seaports, in those places where such mundane matters as cotton pressing, warehousing, and lading took everyone's time, blockade running was fairly drab.

In Wilmington, North Carolina, the best of the blockade ports outside of Bagdad, Mexico, things settled early into a pattern of hard work. Most citizens decamped in fear of invasion or of pestilence from foreign ships, or because the town became little more than a military depot.[47]

In Bermuda, particularly in St. George's, things were different. By the time Mason and Slidell resumed passage to England and stopped en route at St. George's, in January 1862, Confederate affairs flourished. An eager denizen, John Tory Bourne, served as commission agent to the South and ran a growing warehousing and transshipping business. He made all blockade-running crews welcome in his home, introduced visiting Rebel dignitaries to Bermudian society, and generally worked for future reward.[48]

A few Bermudians shared United States Consul Charles Allen's sullen resentment of war prosperity. Rowdy gangs of sailors roamed the streets of picturesque St. George's looking for places to spend quick money. Places could be found. There was, for instance, the infamous Shinbone Alley with its varieties of diversion; its dives and girls drained much of the blockade's profits into Bermudian hands.[49]

Long Winter

Virginia winters can be hard. Richmond suffers especially; its stately public buildings seem to add some phantom chill of stone. Winds buffet the city's hills, race along the avenues, knife through the thickest coats. By late November 1861, winter laid close seige to the Confederacy's capital. People huddled in their mufflers, drew into themselves, scudded quickly to their work. The air attacked with an icy clarity and edge. Thomas Bragg felt it in his Alabama blood as he journeyed to dinner at the Confederate White House.

The White House, a scant three city blocks from the capitol, at the corner of Clay and Twelfth Streets, was the old Brockenbrough mansion, a familiar Richmond landmark that commanded a fine view over the lower town. Now spruced and renovated, it had been home to President Davis and his family since July.[50] On close scrutiny, the house fitted the purpose. There was an angular, severe dignity about it, a quiet aloofness to set it apart from its neighborhood. It seemed to reflect something of its occupants.

Inside, Bragg found things warm and to his liking. The President and Mrs. Davis entertained a great deal, often with receptions and large levees, but preferred small gatherings. At the moment, Mrs. Davis was "confined" and not "seeing company," so the dinner was a stag affair. Bragg was a guest because he was the Confederacy's Attorney General and also a friend of the President's. Two other men filled the table.

There was nothing ornate about dinner. "It was plain and unpretending," Bragg recalled, "but enjoyable." With ladies absent, conversation settled pretty much on business and had some dismal overtones. Davis, normally an affable, outgoing host, was sober and drawn, his cheeks sunken, the ravages of neuralgia obvious in one blurry eye.[51] And as the talk focused on the coming spring, on all the crises likely then, Davis grew more somber still.

Dinner finished, the President led his guests "to his 'own room'— a sort of 'snuggery,' " and passed out cigars. In a way the room was a surprise. With tables piled with books, desk awash with papers, an air of unordered comfort everywhere, it was personal refuge for a public man. Here, away from the need for pose, Davis settled easily into relaxed conversation. And in private converse he was an artist —animated, full of gesture, a close listener, with a gift of ingratiating. In those personal moments, too, he had a dangerous power of persuasion.

Bragg fell quick victim to the Davis charm. A flattering declamation by Davis that his guest's brother, Braxton, was "the only General in command of an Army who had shown himself equal to the management of volunteers and at the same time commanded their love and respect" won the Attorney General to lasting devotion. But Davis was serious. Administration of troops was close to his attention, and he developed the theme at length. It tied in with his concern about enlistments. The basic problem with the army was how to keep it in the field. A good many twelve months' regiments would go home next spring and might not come back. Morale was poor and growing poorer; lax discipline and incompetent officers were partly to blame. Real danger would come when the men started home.

But there was danger already, there had been danger ever since Manassas. Bragg knew it, Davis knew it, everyone close to the South's high councils knew it. The chill winds gusting round the White House carried the cold dread of the country. Defeats had come to Rebel forces with dismaying regularity in the wake of the great Manassas success. General Robert E. Lee had suffered a galling loss to General George McClellan in western Virginia during September.[52]

Lincoln was making significant changes in his management of military affairs. After Bull Run he had shelved the luckless McDowell and given the Army of the Potomac to the rising western hero George Brinton McClellan. Little Mac, as his men would fondly call him, had every obvious quality of leadership. Groomed always in immaculate braid, well-seated on a prancing charger, a poser gifted with bombast, he stirred some schoolboy yearning in his troops and they took him to their hearts. McClellan paraded and drilled, cajoled, persuaded, and molded at last the finest, biggest army that had ever served the Union. Thousands gathered in camps near Washington; and as the gigantic amalgam took on form, as "awkward squads" became soldiers, soldiers blended into legions, as horses and guns and gargantuan depots dotted the environs of the Federal capital, a new war cry rose in the North: "On to Richmond." McClellan surely would take it, if not immediately, certainly when the Federal Navy completed commissioning huge fleets of wooden ships of the line, when numerous ironclads slid from the ways, when the blockade grew tight and every Southern river became an avenue of death.

In November Port Royal harbor in South Carolina fell, and the Yankees established a south Atlantic base on Hilton Head; that same month Rebels were repulsed in an attempt to seize Fort Pickens in Pensacola harbor.[53] While McClellan blustered an army out of green recruits, other blue commanders were mustering other legions in the west. Away in St. Louis, John Frémont, the famed "pathfinder" who would lose his way in war, sought to organize a department and an army. Under him labored a slightly tarnished soldier who had recently been forgiven old charges of drunkenness and reinstated in command of an Illinois regiment, Colonel Ulysses S. Grant. In that part of the hinterland, too, another tarnished soldier also led some volunteers. Colonel William Tecumseh Sherman, he of the angry bristles and fiery temper, had to fight two wars, one against Rebels, another against nerves.

This far-flung activity contrasted sharply with the steady pace of preparation, while Lincoln left the war to Winfield Scott. That old hero of 1812 and the Mexican War had little to give his country save knowledge won on fields from Lundy's Lane to Chapultepec. He was scheming to build a new strategy, the Anaconda Plan, which would apply pressure on all borders of Rebeldom and so squeeze the South to death. He would have done it, but he was too slow, and *had* to go, for Lincoln knew that action of almost any kind was essential. McClellan at least had purpose; Frémont gyrated with energetic frenzy; and two new naval officers, David G. Farragut and David D. Porter, promised operations suited to an ironclad revolution on the sea.

North from Richmond, all along the line from Virginia to Indian

Territory, pressure mounted. Deep in Florida, around the harbor of Pensacola, General Braxton Bragg worked to mold his men as McClellan molded his. The men who came to Bragg from neighboring states, untrained, high-strung, rustic, made good soldiers, but not easily. The peculiar nature of the Confederate Army worked against quick discipline and almost nullified good order. From Bragg's camps, from the mustering places above Chattanooga along the phantom "Tennessee Line" so dear to Bishop General Polk and to General Gideon Pillow, from Little Rock and Houston, San Antonio and New Orleans, especially from Virginia camps, Confederate commanders all echoed one serious plaint—an army liberally sprinkled with individualists would not stoop to labor.

Choruses from such sober soldiers as Virginia's able General Robert E. Lee, involved in strengthening Charleston's defenses,[54] and General Joseph E. Johnston repeated this aversion to work. Johnston was also amazed at the amount of baggage his troops contrived to collect near the Manassas railhead.[55] Baggage was symptomatic of an attitude of comfort, which many Rebels brought with them to the field. Comforts took various forms, not just trunks and portmanteaus, but wine casks, food packages, tobacco and cigars, fine linens. There were many in the ranks who enjoyed little luxury, and who found the pomp of richer comrades often vexing. Certain dandies from the great landed estates brought faithful slaves—and there were many who stayed faithful to their "whitefolks" and the South—to care for their "massas" on campaign as at home.[56] Those who boasted such comforts found war an occasional chore, enjoyed the excitement of marches and parades and young ladies' favor, but shied like balky thoroughbreds at work, especially at digging latrines and trenches.

Trenches were a special consideration. They were the concern of menial folk, hardly of the free and especially the wellborn. Cavalier allergy to labor certainly lay partly behind this attitude, but there was another vital cause: many Southerners believed that only cowards and Yankees skulked behind earthworks and stone walls and other sops to bravery, while good men stood in the open and shot it out.

Whatever the cause, this antidigging passion plagued Southern officers throughout most of the war. Slaves were the best available solution to this delicate social problem; they were impressed from their owners when necessary and employed for work on fortifications, usually performing ably and loyally for the cause. But resort to the bondsman's brawn often proved unsatisfactory. As campaigns developed, who could predict when an army must entrench? Hence, who could procure Negroes on schedule? It worked out pretty much as class differences do in armies; rich men tried to buy the work of poor men, and officers berated everybody. In the end, trenches were dug and labor was done, but the problem engaged attention from the ranks right up to the Confederate Congress.

Patriots might boast that good men would stoop to anything for the South, that nothing for the war was beneath a true Confederate, but events belied the oratory. Hard work eroded morale. By late summer, when heat and awful boredom of army life sapped the ardor of the hardiest Rebels, in the dog days, resentment against plying pick and shovel boiled over. When enlistments finally lapsed, why should men return to such a sordid life? Why, indeed? Officers could have offered answers and examples (good ones did), but Confederate law provided for election of company and some field officers, and most military politicians echoed the anger of their constituents.[57]

Anger disturbed the body martial. Work was only one irritant. Confederate Congressmen and Senators, state governors, the Secretary of War, and President Davis had come to know that summer how low morale had sunk. Pay and allowances dimmed some patriotism—paymasters were slow, money was scarce, and troops grew restive. Not that infantry privates could do much with $11 Confederate a month, but there was a certain principle involved.[58]

Armies all complain about food; it is a sign of hardihood. But Confederate food seemed astonishingly worse than the worst imaginable. For one thing, Southern soldiers were terrible cooks. For another, field kitchens were scarce, mobile bakeries almost unknown, and rations ran to monotonous reliance on fatback and corn meal. Herds of cattle sometimes accompanied armies on the march, but beef soon became a missing grace of Rebel menus. Green vegetables and fruits were abundant at first, when the armies ranged through growing country. But as they scavenged with a special Rebel gusto, the land went bare and commissary agents were hard pressed to prevent scurvy.[59] Few in the ranks bothered to consider Commissary Department problems, few understood the impact of constricting borders on food procurement—such things were technical excuses for a program of mean starvation. If anyone had bothered to check statistics during the early fall, reasons for shortages would have looked thin indeed. Commissary General Lucius B. Northrop, an increasingly unpopular bureaucrat, counted over 3 million pounds of bacon available for winter rations and 23 million pounds potentially available from live hogs. But most hogs came from Kentucky and Tennessee; Kentucky was gone and Tennessee going. Beef was already scarce.[60]

No doubt that a commendable and cautious parsimony caused much of the commissary trouble in the summer and fall of 1861. Commissary agents worried about the winter and tried to stockpile everything at hand. They overworked a large meat-packing plant at Thoroughfare Gap near Johnston's army[61] so that meat might be salted and cured for later issue. Looking ahead was good logistics but poor army relations. Napoleon's maxim about an army's marching on its stomach was already part of folklore, and it was one of his truer sayings. Short rations in the midst of stockpiles defied reason. What answer could Confederate leaders make to complaints?

President Davis urged generals in the field to give food their special attention. To one he wrote: "Frequent complaints have been made to me of improper food. . . . I most respectfully invite your attention to . . . [this subject], and hope that abuses may be promptly corrected."[62] But lofty admonitions brought small reward to hollow stomachs.

Hard work, no pay, and short rations—what better destroyers of morale? There was another, wrapped in an aura of dread: medical care. Armies throughout history have depended heavily on men of medicine to keep hospitals bare and ranks full, but historically military doctors have been a shabby crew of butchers wallowing in ignorance and necromancy. In the 1860's much of the mystery had been pulled from medicine's machinations; what was left was a small body of dubious treatment and a limited store of herbs and chemicals. Together with a doctor's touch, if light enough, these could promote healing, or at least not retard it. As for military medicine, too many remembered too well the agonies of the Crimea.

Field techniques were crude, sanitation was suspect. An arm or leg wound would almost always mean amputation. Gruesome as this was, it made sense; the fetid promise of gas gangrene lurked always in the dark corners of field surgeries. Antisepsis had yet to win wide medical approval.

Nor were prospects for getting well much better for soldiers stricken with such age-old army scourges as flux, measles, diphtheria, or scarlet fever. Epidemics ran through camps like quicksilver; frequently whole regiments, brigades, divisions even, were riddled by disease, with more men in bed than at muster.

Nothing brought greater anger from parents than bad medical care. Countless letters to Congress and the Executive proved the point.[63] What could be done? Doctors were a scarce commodity in the Confederacy. Often practitioners of questionable gift or learning were employed on army contract. Medicines were scant and daily dwindling. Anesthetics were urgently needed in field hospitals, but the Yankees early resorted to the practice of declaring all medicines, especially morphine and chloroform, contraband of war. There was one great boon left to the Confederate infirm: whiskey. That miracle of human concoction offered balm, solace, and bravery to thousands. There was a chance, though, that even spirits would become scarce.

The Medical Corps under Samuel Preston Moore, a compassionate and gifted physician, found stores of grain, bargained with state governors to restrict certain acreages for wheat and barley, impressed private stills, and kept a partly filled Rebel flask for the war. It was one of the compensations offered to wearers of the gray.[64]

Moore and his officers achieved far beyond the medical resources of their country. Like every other supply agency, the Medical Department was pressed for money, trained men, and transportation, hampered by few laboratories or chemical factories capable of mass-producing medicines. But with energy and ingenuity to rival Ordnance Department miracles, Moore's subordinates created makeshift laboratories across the Confederacy. So well did they succeed that in time there was hope that certain essentials like blue mass, tincture of cinchona, spirits of ammonia, and castor oil, that bane of armies immemorial, would be produced in plenty.[65]

All such achievements were spectacular since the South had so little. And all these things were essential to civilian medical care. But as for Johnny Rebs, the thing most important to them was hospital service. Hospitals conjured nightmares of vermin and maggots and bloody sputum, visions of yellow fever's black vomit, of wracking coughs and dying spasms. Tragically these visions came too often true. Some of the better hospitals, like the rapidly expanding Chimborazo establishment in Richmond, offered all the care the Confederacy could lavish. Well run and efficiently managed, Chimborazo, with 8,000 beds, would become the largest military hospital on the American continent.[66] But there were others less savory in the same enlightened city. Let diarist Mary Chesnut describe a pesthouse called the St. Charles: "Horrors upon horrors. . . . Want of organization, long rows of men dead and dying; awful smiles and awful sights. A boy from home [South Carolina] had sent for me. He was lying on a cot, ill of fever. Next to him a man died of convulsions while we stood there. . . . I do not remember any more, for I fainted."[67]

Men who had to be moved to base hospitals in large cities suffered unspeakably. Davis could scarcely believe one tale told him. In October 1861 he had written General Beauregard that "complaints are made to me of shocking neglect of the sick who are sent down in the trains [to Richmond]; such as being put in burden cars which have been used to transport horses or provisions, and into which the sick were thrust, without previously cleansing the cars, and there left without water, food or attention." The result of such stories was clear enough: "These representations have been spread among the people, and served to chill the ardor which has filled our ranks with the best men of the land."[68]

Horror piled on starveling soldier-laborers, and the dismal prospect ensured that only the foolish would go again to the ranks; those lucky enough to survive the ennui, the vermin, the "trots," Yankees, and doctors, those hardy souls who lasted their twelve months, could go home and regain human dignity. The feeling insinuated into letters home and worked insidious harm to the army.

Consider the example of Private E. J. Lee of Union Parish, Louisiana, who enlisted early and suffered much. In late 1861 and early 1862, he put his philosophy of army life in two letters to a brother-in-law. In the first, he said: "I advise you to stay at home. You could not stand the fairs [fare] and hardships of a Soldier. Tell Rufe and Henry [brothers] to stay at home until I come back. . . ." In the second letter, he put it this way: "I dont want you and Henry to leave home if there is any other chance."[69]

And so came the specter of thousands, with the veteran's wary wisdom, leaving not to return. It was a real possibility.

There was a political slant to the enlistment crisis, too, a slant soon ominously magnified. As dissatisfaction sapped morale in the ranks, voters at home would complain. Politicians would listen and would turn the complaints to advantage. Governors in close touch with their people would engage in open argument with federal authorities. Governors of states with exposed coastlines finally called for the return of their troops; at home they could perform useful service and avoid the worst of field existence. These calls had the ring of necessity. Fateful Yankee operations around Hatteras, incursions along the Georgia and North Carolina coasts, all pointed to amphibious invasion. Increasing numbers of letters with demands for the return of state levies, letters from such governors as Joseph Brown of Georgia, John Ellis of North Carolina, and Thomas O. Moore of Louisiana, alerted Davis to growing gubernatorial restiveness.[70] To those whose complaints were reasonable, Davis explained the relentless need for soldiers everywhere and remarked on the strategy of concentration as the reason why regiments in Confederate service could not be detached for service in their states. To those whose demands reflected nothing save selfish concern, Davis was curt—which was doubtless a mistake, since it fanned smoldering resentment against him. But patriots of convenience vastly irritated a devoted President. He once confided to a friend his opinion of state-conscious politicians and confessed that "if such [interference] was to be the course of the States toward the Gov't, carrying on the war was an impossibility. . . . We . . . better make terms . . . soon."[71]

Coastal defense loomed an issue without solution. As long as the Federals extended amphibious operations and used their superior sea power to land troops at exposed Rebel positions, some kind of counteraction had to be taken. Confederate land and naval forces were used when the point attacked was sufficiently vital, state forces when it was not. States left to their own defense sulked; those aided by government troops screamed loudly at every Yankee success. And there were too many Yankee successes. Hatteras fell to a combined attack on August 29, 1861. Some said that rudimentary caution on the part of Rebel commanders would have prevented this strategic disaster. Not long after came word of an attack building against Roanoke Island, where vital Confederate batteries guarded Albemarle Sound.[72]

Roanoke Island soon became a symbol much like Sumter. To lose it would confess virtual Southern impotence. But increasing numbers in the country expected it would fall. Some even considered it a deliberate sacrifice on the altar of military professionalism. Why? War Clerk Jones explained it in January 1862:

> The department leaves Gen. [Henry A.] Wise to his superior officer, Gen. [Benjamin] Huger, at Norfolk, who has 15,000 men. But I understand that Huger says Wise has ample means for the defense of the island, and refuses to let him have more men. This looks like a man-trap of the 'Redtapers' to get rid of a popular leader.[73]

Public attitude toward Roanoke Island reflected low morale and indicated a civilian spirit to match the army's apathy. A kind of hopelessness seeped across the Confederacy, a hopelessness which sapped energies and stalled action.

Little wonder, then, that the visible sloughing of the armies riveted the attention of the guests that November night in the President's "snuggery." Attorney General Bragg summed up the South's situation with the observation that "dangers thicken around us."[74] They did. To keep the ranks intact loomed suddenly as the real test of Southern statecraft. It was a test of peculiar concern to Davis, since his administration had just been returned to office in an unopposed election November 6. That election supposedly constructed the government under the permanent constitution. But the new government's permanence hinged entirely on the armies. As long as they kept the field, the Confederacy persisted.

CHAPTER FOUR

God and the Weakest Battalions

"Confront the Enemy Without Reserves"

When the President took his oath of office as head of the "permanent government" on February 22, about the only credit the South could count was the "permanent constitution." This document, written in February 1861 by Alec Stephens's committee in Montgomery, was virtually a copy of the United States Charter. It differed from the old in preamble (states were declared sovereign), in length of executive terms (six years for President and Vice-President with the President ineligible to succeed himself), in granting the Executive an item veto, in forbidding the reopening of the slave trade, in admitting the Bill of Rights to the main body of the law. Among the similarities between both constitutions, one stood out: they both were "the supreme law of the land." Both preserved the honored division of powers between two legislative houses and both provided for strong judiciaries. In practice, the Confederacy failed to follow tradition in creating a Supreme Court. The Congress never authorized one. But the permanent constitution was a sound basis for efficient administration—like its provisional predecessor, it gave large powers to the Confederate government. Sadly, delegated power hardly appeared sufficient in early February 1862. The Confederacy was seriously imperiled.

There was, for instance, the peculiar position of Professor-General Stonewall Jackson, the hero of Manassas, whose laurels had withered somewhat because of a bootless expedition to Romney, in

January 1862. It was an expedition buffeted by snow and sleet and wrapped in endless controversy. Troops unaccustomed to cold campaigning, unwilling to sacrifice for strategy, misunderstood the reasons for their discomfort, sought relief, and found it in the personal nature of the Confederate hierarchy. Their complaints followed direct routes to Richmond, caught the ear of Secretary of War Benjamin and of the President, and did some damage to Jackson's reputation. Davis decided that the erstwhile stone wall was "incompetent,"[1] and Benjamin ordered Jackson's little Army of the Valley to regroup near Winchester.

Jackson construed this intervention by the War Department as an indication of no confidence in him and did the thing expected of a professional soldier: he tendered his resignation through Joseph E. Johnston. This was according to protocol, and very much like the punctilious "deacon" so wrapped in shyness and regulations. Johnston was department commander, and if Richmond might ignore protocol, Jackson would not. Johnston shared Jackson's outrage at lax military administration, protested it, and at the same time urged Jackson to reconsider. Virginia Military Institute's Professor of Natural Philosophy and Artillery Tactics would not reconsider. Appeals by friends to Governor Letcher, applications by high state authorities and distinguished clergymen, and a general sentiment in Jackson's favor brought second thoughts from the President and Benjamin. Jackson stayed.[2]

A sense of duty surely was the only reason. Certainly there was nothing appealing in the valley situation during the winter, nothing to entice an ambitious soldier to keep the field. Once the Romney venture was wrecked, Jackson found his army ensconced in the lower (northern) Shenandoah Valley, his 4,500 men ill clothed and badly fed, arms and munitions scarce, and Federal opponents gathering in great strength. His task remained the same as it had been from the moment he first arrived in the valley in November 1861: guard Virginia's granary against all comers, without substantial reinforcement.

If this frankly superhuman assignment gave Jackson pause, he showed only stoic calm. He would do his best with the men the government could spare. That determination had led him to unusual activity during the winter. He considered his Romney plan to have been right, wasted no anguish on lost chances, and worked to prepare for spring.

Altogether it proved a fairly thankless task. While a force under General Nathaniel Prentiss Banks gathered as one prong of a Yankee pincers, a pincers aimed at clearing the Shenandoah and flanking Joe Johnston from his Manassas lines, Confederate attention remained fixed in northern Virginia. Jackson's stray army, tiny and suspect, seemed destined for little more than observation.

Serious activity continued in the first month of 1862. On the 19th and 20th of January an important Confederate force under Generals George B. Crittenden and Felix K. Zollicoffer attempted to secure control of the middle border by attacking a Union army near Mill Springs, Kentucky—result: Rebel defeat, Zollicoffer dead.[3] In February 1862 an amphibious Union expedition under General U. S. Grant tested Rebel defenses on the Tennessee and Cumberland rivers, defenses hinged on Forts Henry and Donelson. Of these forts Henry was the weaker, went awash in high water, and was passed abeam by Yankee monitors; Donelson, a more imposing bastion designed to stand siege, endured a tragicomic defense led by that martial miscreant Gideon J. Pillow, of Mexican War ineptitude, and fell on February 16, 1862. With both rivers open to enemy incursions, the heartland of the Deep South lay virtually helpless and exposed. General Albert Sidney Johnston would have to shore up the center with forces weak beyond Southern belief. The last important Rebel victory had come six months back at Wilson's Creek on August 10.[4]

Roanoke Island joined the list of Rebel losses on February 8.[5] Initiative had passed to the enemy. Omens for the South were so bad that President Davis tried to negate them in his Inaugural Address—a speech of partial candor, which admitted the troubles at hand and ahead but avoided confessions of true weakness. By the time Davis stepped before a sodden crowd on the capitol grounds that rainy inauguration day to pledge himself anew to the cause, there were many who wondered if he was the man for the job. Loud hue and cry against his policy of strict defense touched one of his tenderest nerves. In a curiously confessional letter to a Mississippi friend he admitted certain military errors but explained his problems with stark clarity:

I acknowledge the error of my attempt to defend all the frontier, seaboard and inland; but will say in justification that if we had received the arms and munitions which we had good reason to expect, that the attempt would have been successful and the battlefields would have been on the enemy's soil. You seem to have fallen into the not uncommon mistake of supposing that I have chosen to carry on the war upon a 'purely defensive' system. The advantage of selecting the time and place of attack was too apparent to have been overlooked, but the means might have been wanting. Without military stores, without the workshops to create them, without the power to import them, necessity not choice has compelled us to occupy strong positions and everywhere to confront the enemy without reserves. The country has supposed our armies more numerous than they were and our munitions of war more extensive than they have been.[6]

Spreading Rebel forces thinly along sea and inland borders spelled trouble from the start, and yet the states, the condition of transport, and the chaotic nature of logistics all demanded it. While compelled to follow circumstantial dictates, the President worked to apply the principle mentioned in his letter: to find a time and place for attack. The offensive defense seemed the only true course for the inferior side. Manassas showed the virtue of taking good ground and holding it, of turning defense to offense. The lesson surely could be applied elsewhere. With that hope in mind, Davis approved a bold plan of veteran General Henry H. Sibley to carry the war to the enemy in New Mexico and Arizona in February.

A successful expedition from Texas might well add a vast western domain to the Confederacy and hence win diplomatic as well as military advantage. Sibley did his best, fought well at Valverde and Glorieta Pass, New Mexico, in February and March 1862, but lost and came pell-mell back to Texas with nothing but casualties and dead dreams.[7]

One defeat did not invalidate the strategy. Davis waited for another chance. It came at last in a strange form, in wake of loud plaints from representatives of Missouri and Arkansas that their states were sacrificed to Virginia concern.[8] To salve the sensibilities of western advocates Davis dispatched a dashing soldier across the Mississippi to bring order from martial chaos. General Earl Van Dorn, a man of grace, charm, boldness, and competence, took no troops with him but nonetheless accomplished much. He forced cooperation on bickering bands of Missourians, Texans, and Arkansans and at last launched a campaign toward Missouri.

If all went as hoped, he would defeat Union forces under General S. R. Curtis, cross the Mississippi, and join Sidney Johnston in a crusher offensive against Grant. It was an audacious scheme, but it came to grief at a place called Elkhorn Tavern in far-western Arkansas. A confused, almost ludicrous, drawn battle, Elkhorn Tavern had flanking maneuvers, gallant frontal assaults, and heavy casualties. Texas hero Ben McCulloch and James McQueen McIntosh, two stalwart Rebel leaders, were killed, Confederate Indian allies participated in awed amazement at white men's stand-up, point-blank folly, and Van Dorn lost his chance to help Johnston east of the river.[9]

While Van Dorn and his army toiled away in Arkansas, Albert Sidney Johnston toiled at the ruin of Ulysses S. Grant. An old and practiced soldier, veteran of the Army of the Texas Republic, commander of the Utah Expedition against the Mormons in the 1850's, Johnston understood his responsibilities for the spring of 1862.

With the central Confederate front breached, with the Deep South threatened, with the Confederate fabric unraveling everywhere, he had to win a decisive victory. If Grant's army could be smashed and driven northward, initiative along the Mississippi would pass to the Rebels; Tennessee would be safe, Kentucky possibly liberated, Ohio threatened. Victory for Johnston's army might change the course of the war.

Victory would not come with waiting. Johnston knew he must attack Grant and beat him, and he planned battle with care. Davis sent every available man. Even beleaguered Virginia spared help— General Beauregard went west in triumphant procession. Did he go as a talisman of western hope or a bird of ill omen?

By March 1862 everyone admitted that the Confederacy's future rested heavily on Sidney Johnston. Davis had no doubt of his man.

In fact, his faith in the Western commander led him to say that "if Sidney Johnston is not a general, I have none."

Johnston had no doubts of himself. With an army larger than any he had commanded, a force close to 35,000 men, he looked for a place to aim it. When, at last, he got word that Grant's army had debarked from transports at Pittsburg Landing, on the western bank of the Tennessee, he guessed his chance had come. The Union position was a scant thirty miles from Johnston's base at Corinth, Mississippi, an easy two days' march. His subordinate commanders, Beauregard, Braxton Bragg, Leonidas Polk, and John Breckinridge, received orders: move forward on April 3.

Time is the one certain inconstant in war; nothing ever really goes according to schedule. Johnston's advance was cumbered with confusion, mixed units, balky mules, raw recruits, and conflicting orders, and it took a good deal longer than he hoped. When he finally got in position on April 5, most of the day was gone and, as far as he could tell, so was the vital element of surprise. Surely no half-awake enemy could miss the raucous sounds of thousands gathering for attack. Indiscipline plagued Rebel ranks; men shot at rabbits and yelled at one another; cavalry thundered everywhere; guns and caissons rumbled through the dense woodland; pickets wandered around in gay abandon. The whole situation would have unnerved most veterans, but Johnston was determined to attack, no matter the odds or alarms.

As it happened, fortune was with him. A special bafflement hung over Grant's camps on the morning of April 6; noises had been heard, reports of gray masses were made, but nobody believed their eyes or ears. Federal officers remained sure that Johnston's army lay at Corinth; nothing could shake their faith.

First breaks in their certainty came at dawn, with the scattered popping of skirmish fire, the cracking, rolling volleys, the cadenced pounding of cannon. All illusions went at last when the eerie, high-pitched Rebel yell echoed through the woods. Among the first to suffer the Confederate attack was General William T. Sherman's division, camped on the fringes of Grant's perimeter. Quickly smashed, Sherman's men streamed back through other camps and spread chaos and terror. Almost before anyone knew what happened, confusion gripped the whole Yankee army from Lick Creek on the left to Owl Creek on the right. On came the Rebels, in three awesome lines of battle, on, running, yelling, firing as they came. Bits and pieces of resistance built here and there, only to be smothered by the pace of the charge. Slowly the Union left flank withered back toward the Tennessee, back until it seemed the Rebs might catch the whole Yankee army in a huge sack.

Johnston ranged the field through the morning, placing brigades, spotting batteries, urging his horde forward. He noticed at last a line of Yankees holding in a copse; storms of shell scourged their cover, line after gray line rolled at them only to recoil under determined fire. There, at the Hornets' Nest on the blue left center, the battle stalled for precious hours; there Yankees endured beyond the reach of humans and held the field for Grant. And there, near that fulcrum of the battle, Johnston lost his life. As he rode recklessly in search of men to storm Benjamin Prentiss's position, he paid no heed to a bullet in his right knee and kept on till he fell from the saddle, dead from loss of blood. Command passed to Beauregard, and the Rebels kept pushing ahead.

Grant missed all this; he was downriver on other business. But battle brought him back to a sight beyond imagination. As his staff boat drew near Pittsburg Landing he saw the riverbank thick with bluecoats, many of them skulking unashamedly for cover, others vainly looking for a place to fight. Wreckage of defeat was scattered everywhere, his army was a shambles. One final Rebel push, and an entire Union Army would wallow in the Tennessee. A disaster beyond any ever suffered by an American force haunted Grant's eye.

Like Johnston, Grant could fight. Clamping his frayed cigar firmly in his jaw, he looked for help. General Don Carlos Buell with a fresh army was not far away; he must speed to the field. Meanwhile, units at hand must rally and take position on a final fringe of hills covering the landing; gunboats must come to lend firepower to the line of cannon Grant sought to build along his front. Nerve alone goaded him on; the chances were all but gone.

They were not entirely gone, for the Confederates were fought to a frazzle. Loosely organized to begin with, the Rebel army had been held together through a long and wearing day by the impetus of victory. Time and attrition and looting and death slowed the attack until at last the hills Grant worked to hold loomed in front, an impossible barrier. The Rebels were hungry, weary, lost, and dazed; they had to rest, and Beauregard ordered a halt. It was probably the most fateful order of his life; one final charge might have won the battle.

During the night Buell's army came in strength; Union regiments and divisions regrouped, and the next day they attacked, carried positions they had held the day before, and drove Beauregard's spent forces slowly back. When April 7 waned the Battle of Shiloh was over. It had been an awful cataclysm of death. Twenty thousand were slain on the fields near Shiloh Church, about evenly divided between blue and gray. Of the outcome there would be much to claim and little to prove. That such a bath of blood could mean so little could hardly be borne, but it was so. Back to Corinth went the Rebels, and into temporary eclipse went U. S. Grant.[10]

To those who sought solace for the Confederates, this could be said: for a while, at least, the Yankee penetration of the middle border stopped. Fear of the Rebels remained high. Perhaps this was worth the flower ·of an army. Perhaps, too, this was all a weaker force could win.

Wages of weakness were being paid everywhere across the Confederacy—New Mexico, Missouri, Virginia, the Carolinas, and Shiloh were enough. But there was more, there was New Orleans.

From a small French settlement in the seventeenth century, New Orleans had spread slowly along the eastern bank of the Mississippi until at last it was the largest, lustiest, wealthiest port south of New York. The Crescent City lived up to its legends, boasted graceful French Colonial houses, public buildings nobly cast in Grecian mold, stately monuments, burghers, merchants, and high-toned gentry. It also boasted the French Quarter, possibly the finest district of ill fame in the Western Hemisphere. Time and mythology finally would make the Quarter and its practitioners synonymous with the city. But there were other good reasons for fame.

For all the years since Jefferson stretched his conscience and the constitution to purchase Louisiana for the Union, New Orleans had been the hub of Southern and Western trade. River boats laden with grain, timber, pelts, and outlandish boatmen came downriver to New Orleans. From the wharves these boats took cargoes of manufactured goods, luxuries, medicines, all the needs of the back country, and toiled upstream to Natchez, St. Louis, Cairo, on into the Ohio. There were signs of change in the 1850's with the spread of railroads westward, but the Mississippi still ran southward and New Orleans remained the metropolis of the Gulf. Its banking houses were the richest in the South—they held most of the specie in the Confederacy—its citizens almost the proudest Southerners.

War brought New Orleans new importance. It became the Confederacy's greatest port. To lose it would endanger foreign confidence and increase the internal weakness of the Confederacy. The city was not only a financial and trade center, it was also an industrial and manufacturing focus; especially important was the Leeds Foundry Works, possibly the best in the South.[11] No one understood New Orleans's importance better than the city's military commander, Major General Mansfield Lovell.

Lovell, a conscientious if luckless leader, soon suffered the hazards of most post commanders—his force withered away in small detachments to the active fronts. Sidney Johnston and Beauregard had demanded aid and Lovell sent it; coast operations hither and yon claimed bits and dribbles of the New Orleans army.[12] And so it was that when a large Yankee force under David G. Farragut and General Benjamin Butler gathered to run the Rebel forts near the mouth of the Mississippi, Lovell found himself commanding phantom legions and paper brigades. When Forts Jackson and St. Phillip were passed by the Yankee fleet on April 24 and 15,000 men hovered on ships near the Crescent City, defenders were too few to stop them. New Orleans fell on April 29, 1862. With it went control of the southern end of the Mississippi and a good portion of south Louisiana. Although the specie was saved from the banks, the price of defeat was high. The harshest cost was in spirit; New Orleans seemed to many the essence of the South. Now it was gone and with it part of the hopes of yesterday.[13]

"Cease This Child's Play"

Everyone with the smallest knowledge of Confederate affairs understood the odds. Everything had turned sour for the South; the road shifted suddenly downhill and energy, blood, treasure, potentials all were giving out. Armies melted away or went forfeit as prisoners of war. Even the vaunted Rebel answer to the Union Navy, the remarkable ironclad C.S.S. *Virginia,* cruised victorious for only a day in March; then the U.S.S. *Monitor* fought her to a draw in a famous duel in Chesapeake Bay on March 8, a duel that ended the era of wooden ships.[14] The moral was clear enough: Confederates lacked for no ideas, just for reserves of men and materiel.

This scarcity would be chronic, there was not and would not be enough, penury would stalk the South. Many knew this binding truth but could not admit that there was absolute dearth. Dearth offered no hope for salvation, and there must be salvation. If impersonal causes for the South's plight could not be accepted, personal ones could. Human error lay at the root of the Confederacy's decline and human error could be rectified. People are, after all, replaceable.

Resentment at the steady lists of reverses fixed at last on an obvious target: the Secretary of War. Judah Benjamin proved a nimble target, one apt to evade a scapegoat's role. Quick to admit his wrongs, open in accepting responsibilities more rightly the Chief Executive's, Benjamin turned public wrath from the President to himself. It was a hard service for his country, but one with just reward. Davis knew loyalty when given, and his friendship for his Louisiana cohort deepened enough to generate envious carping. Yet Benjamin had hardly compiled a distinguished record in the War Office. True, chaos and clutter came with the job, and he did untangle reams of red tape. But administrative success is no substitute for sound policy making, and Benjamin made few changes in policy. More than that, he apparently blundered in the Roanoke Island mess by paying too little attention to command problems. Certainly he helped confuse national internal security measures by signing passports through the lines for almost anyone who asked, and he took little trouble to charm Congressmen.[15]

Congressmen are a naturally touchy lot, a fact Benjamin must have known from personal experience. Confederate Congressmen were no different from their Yankee counterparts in jealous preservation of status. People of privilege resent it for others, and Benjamin enjoyed a relationship with the President denied to lesser mortals. To some among the lawmakers the unctuously smiling Jew seemed an alien proconsul whispering sedition in Caesar's ear.

All of which made Benjamin an efficient cause of trouble. Congressional ire fastened on him, investigations of his department were plotted in the capitol halls; muttered cabals against him eddied throughout Richmond and found their way to the President. Davis hated amateur intrigues, especially intrigues based on error; and he knew the charges against Benjamin to be false. Still, the outcry proclaimed sufficient discontent for notice. And Davis took notice.[16]

Loath to bend to criticism, or sacrifice a trusted ally to slander, he refused to fire Benjamin, elevated him instead to the State Portfolio. It was deft but dangerous parry that accepted congressional censure while it flouted congressional wish. On March 22, 1862, George W. Randolph of Virginia accepted the War post in Davis's cabinet. Randolph proved a man of sense and vision and wisdom. The challenges facing him upon taking office would have dismayed lesser men; they inspired this quiet gentleman of banked aspirations.

The new War Secretary was a veteran of the Battle of Bethel, had been promoted to Brigadier General in February, and hence already realized the pressing need to fill the Rebel ranks. Manpower was the first and constant concern. Back in February the President had confessed to Congress terrible confusion arising from misguided furlough policies. Haphazard attempts to win re-enlistment had induced the government to dissolve the ranks with liberal leaves and demoralize them with bounties. Men went home, some to recruit friends, some to mend homes, fences, and families, some never to return. This vast hegira did damage beyond imagination; regiments dwindled to companies, armies to corps. Confederate military organization wallowed in awful disarray. The President guessed—and things were so confused he could do no more than guess—that the armies counted some 400 regiments, or about 300,000 men. He hoped that at least that many would stand muster when the furloughs were finished.[17] In the period of confusion only one advantage seemed clear: Congress accepted Davis's constant urging and abandoned the policy of short-term enlistment. Finally men had to sign on for the war, which was fine as far as the volunteers went—but were there enough of them?

Secretary Randolph, Generals Joseph E. Johnston and Robert E. Lee, and several distinguished Congressmen joined in telling the commander in chief of the army and navy that volunteering ought to be abandoned. It was failing.[18] Zealous patriotism waned with reality. War lost its glory in dank and dirty camps, in the endless ennui of waiting, in the timeless ills of armies. Most who served and won discharge shunned return, and their reluctance influenced others until enlistments slowed to a trickle. Conscription was the only alternative.

Davis agreed that there was no other means of saving the army. Later students of the subject would say that Lee's prestige convinced the President; Lee's greatest biographer would claim for his hero the prime role in achieving conscription. No doubt the magisterial Virginian did help the cause.[19] But Jefferson Davis needed little propulsion. Experience shaped his conviction. Late in March 1862 Congress received from him a surprising document, one which showed the President to be an advocate of radical change, and pointed out the hard path of the war.

> Executive Department,
> March 28, 1862

To the Senate and House of Representatives of the Confederate States:

The operation of the various laws now in force for raising armies has exhibited the necessity for reform. The frequent changes and amendments which have been made have rendered the system so complicated as to make it often quite difficult to determine what the law really is. . . .

The right of the State to demand, and the duty of each citizen to render military service, need only to be stated to be admitted. It is not, however, wise or judicious policy to place in active service that portion of the force of a people which experience has shown to be necessary as a reserve. Youths under the age of 18 years require further instruction—men of matured experience are needed for maintaining order and good government at home, and in supervising preparations for rendering efficient the armies in the field. These two classes constitute the proper reserve for home defense. . . . But in order to maintain this reserve intact, it is necessary that . . . all persons of intermediate age not legally exempt for good cause should pay their debt of military service to the country, that the burthens should not fall exclusively on the most ardent and patriotic.

I therefore recommend the passage of a law declaring that all persons residing within the Confederate States, between the ages of 18 and 35 years . . . shall be held to be in the military service of the Confederate States, and that some plain and simple method be adopted for their prompt enrollment and organization, repealing all the legislation heretofore enacted which would conflict with the system proposed.

JEFFERSON DAVIS[20]

This proposal could hardly have come from Davis a year before. Conscription was a response to crisis, the kind of response possible only from a man who grew with experience. Davis learned the changing nature of the war and realized more clearly than others that traditions and values were fast diminishing in the battle smoke. To persist at all the government must mobilize and use every resource according to rigid national plan. It was not pleasant for a natural state-righter, not easy for a man appalled by centralization. But centralization was vital to survival, and the President worked diligently to build a powerful central government. Conscription was the first essential—it would give the administration control over manpower. "Cousin Sam" could reach over state boundaries and touch every man in the South.

Initial reaction to the draft ran favorably. Richmond newspapers copied the President's message, and even editor Edward A. Pollard of the *Examiner,* who often attacked administration policies, praised it. Alabama's fiery Lowndes Yancey raised his voice in support.[21] Happily, Congress seemed well disposed. One Senator confessed that the administration "evinced energy of purpose . . . not . . . exhibited heretofore." Another accepted conscription "cordially" and added that he "respected the doctrine of the sovereignty of the States, but in times like these the sovereignty of the States must be secondary to the sovereignty of the people." Davis's stormy Texas friend Louis Wigfall took the floor to urge that his colleagues "cease this child's play" and hasten passage of a draft law. He had no doubts of the constitutionality of conscription. "No State government has the right to make war, raise armies, or conclude treaties of peace. These rights," he said, were "expressly conferred upon the Confederate Government." Far from the draft being unconstitutional, he felt that "the volunteering system . . . was extra-constitutional, if not unconstitutional." Now was the time for realism. "The enemy are in some portions of almost every State in the Confederacy; they are upon the borders of Texas; Virginia is enveloped by them. We need a large army. How are you going to get it? Take these conscript soldiers and put them into the old regiments. . . . No man has any individual rights, which come in conflict with the welfare of the country."[22] Scattered opposition appeared in both chambers, but Congress largely accepted the idea of a national draft and all the changes it implied.

On April 16, 1862, Congress passed and sent to Davis a law calling to the colors all white men between eighteen and thirty-five.[23] Five days later the lawmakers rectified an oversight and passed a liberal class-exemption law.[24] Exemption would be a lasting problem. But for the moment, at least, the gray legions were saved.

Once enacted, conscription met stubborn resistance from certain governors. Those like Georgia's Joseph E. Brown, of fiercely ambitious bent, correctly saw the draft as a blow to their authority and rummaged among political expedients to raise again the standard of state rights. The Confederacy's Attorney General might approve conscription,[25] but surely the courts would void so drastic an invasion of personal and state liberty. There seemed a chance the courts might do exactly that, especially since Congress had failed to create a Supreme Court and left appeals to state tribunals.

But this time state rights went begging for support. Across the Confederacy when conscription cases were tried decisions, in almost every case, went for the government. Most State Supreme Court judges based pro-Confederate opinions on Article I, Section 8 of the Confederate States Constitution: "Congress shall have power to raise . . . armies." This, they agreed, was authority untarnished by prescribed methods. These opinions were important victories for the first draft law in American history.[26]

They were also important victories for the administration's hard-war policy. Conscription dealt severe blows to the compact theory of the federal system—blows with lasting import to the future. Militias would parade still, governors would brandish hordes of "colonels" yet, but armies would be tools of the nation. Lessons learned in beleaguered Richmond were not lost in Washington; Lincoln applied them within a year.

"God Blessed Our Arms with Victory"

Stonewall Jackson, the iron-willed Presbyterian deacon who had come from heroic deeds at Manassas to the Army of the Valley, was reputed to be in direct communication with heaven; certainly in battle after battle he stretched an arm high in gesture much like supplication. Some of his soldiers suspected, even, that he prayed constantly midst the bullets; a few devoutly hoped so, for he took them places and summoned them to deeds beyond mortal competence. Take, for instance, the matter of marching. Jackson's men had to do more than march; they had to sustain a steady gait mile after mile, to continue on with only ten minutes' rest per hour until miles and days and trails stretched into a continuum of strain. Ten, twenty miles a day were too light for Jackson's "foot cavalry"; they could and did slog steadily for thirty, sometimes forty miles, deploy, and charge bayonets, all as a matter of duty. With them when they formed for action, somewhere close to the line of battle, their begrimed general slumped astride an improbable war horse named Little Sorrel. Critics painted horse and rider in caricature—"Fool Tom" Jackson and his tanglefoot. Bad humor, this, for it had no tangent to fact. Rider and mount bore little resemblance to champion and charger, but together they changed war. Rumpled Old Jack, long legs almost dragging the ground as he sat ungainly on the sorrel, fixed paces to make iron men of mortals, and kept the paces himself with rare self-discipline. Jackson and Little Sorrel were made of a coarse-grained fiber without style or grace, but somehow they touched men and lent them grandeur. Those men who marched alongside the horse and rider would recall it always, if they lived, with the stubborn pride of heroes. Most of Jackson's landed troopers hardly looked like heroes; their rise to that state came slowly and began unpromisingly.

In a rare lapse of caution, Jackson took his small Valley Army down the Shenandoah to Kernstown, not far from Winchester, with intention to do battle. Provocation for a Confederate attack was intense. As Lincoln's new Union savior George McClellan moved his huge army to the Virginia Peninsula below the Confederate capital and began his "On to Richmond" campaign, other enemy units in Virginia poised to swoop on Richmond from the north, hitch on to McClellan's extended right flank, and tighten a noose round the heart of rebellion. These moves had caused Joseph E. Johnston to abandon his Manassas line and fall back to the peninsula.

In the Shenandoah, Federal troops under James Shields were among those preparing to swing eastward to Richmond for the showdown of the war. Shields outnumbered Jackson heavily in the valley; it seemed, though, that at Kernstown a small detachment of his army had been left behind to guard Jackson and was simply not strong enough to do it. Turner Ashby, that peerless horse soldier with a gift for reconnaissance, told Jackson that the enemy was weak; careful scouting in and through the rolling hills near the Union camps revealed no more than four regiments of infantry. A swift, crushing blow might force Shields to call his departing brigades back from their Richmond journey to deal with the Army of the Valley, and great strategic harm would be done to Little Mac.[27] If the Rebel ranks were thin, the stakes were fat enough.

With few qualms for Sunday fighting, Old Jack hurled his army into battle on March 23, 1862. First advantage went to his valley soldiers, who charged with zest and yelled madly as they went. Incipient panic ran among the bluecoats suffering the brunt of Jackson's attack; Federal units broke and retired. But back behind those hapless victims, behind hills which baffled the perception of Ashby, lurked more than 6,000 reserves, who came swiftly into action. Rolling volleys echoed ahead of the unsuspected enemy, volleys countered for stubborn minutes here and there along the Rebel line, but inexorably fresh men and more firepower prevailed. At last a tired, battered, and bested Valley Army broke off the fight and retreated. It was the only real defeat Jackson was to know.

Defeats, though, have a way of lingering. People recall them when commands and promotions are handed out. There were those in Richmond who cherished memories still of Jackson's luckless campaign to Romney; Kernstown seemed confirmation of the deacon's fecklessness. Little could be expected from him, and that was just as well; little could be expected from anybody in the cast-away Valley District. Great events were looming around Richmond and in time Jackson might render his best service by coming east-ward to help defend the capital.

Not everyone thought ill of the former stone wall of Manassas. His men, for instance, were growing accustomed to him, were com-ing to a slow appreciation of his careful administration, his drive, his sense of urgency about war. He knew the things that matter to soldiers, worked to provide shoes when there were none to give, to produce dry socks, to see that worn uniforms were exchanged or patched, and took special pains to find food and forage. What small comforts hard campaigning and a poor country could offer, Jackson won for his faithful. Slowly in the weeks after Kernstown he nursed his tattered force, recruited diligently in the valley counties, per-suaded, cajoled, threatened, dealt harshly with slackers and deserters, and forged an army with a spirit of its own.

In March Jefferson Davis created the official position of military adviser to the President and appointed Robert E. Lee to fill it.[28] Lee was scarcely acquainted with Jackson—their paths had rarely crossed in Old Army days—but he admired a general who would fight. And Jackson, from the valley, soon revealed the germ of a campaign plan to Lee, a plan so daring and uncertain as to frighten lesser generals. But there was a streak of gambler in the unruffled Robert Lee. He knew that the tiny force with Jackson could do little near Richmond, but used the way Jackson began to think it should be used, the Army of the Valley might be the lever to move McClellan. Davis gave Lee authority to devise and execute strategy, and Lee liked Deacon Jackson's plan.

What Jackson wanted to do was to pin all the Yankee forces west of the Blue Ridge, even west of the Alleghenies, firmly to the mountain theater, keep them from concentrating against Richmond, and perhaps beat them one by one. Finding and fixing enemy units is elementary tactics, beating them in detail fine art. Jackson's genius lay in the scope of his imagination.

Lee knew the odds; they were prohibitive. In the post-Kernstown weeks, the valley had been saturated with Union troops. Most of Shields's men were kept there; a large force under General Nathaniel P. Banks entered the lower end of the valley and settled near Winchester; beyond the Alleghenies in the fastness of Lincoln's so-called Mountain Department, John Frémont led another army. Against Jackson's small army—not larger than 16,000 men—the enemy could gather almost 50,000 men. The trick was to keep them from gathering. Old Jack conceived that he just might do it by speed, deception, and desperate marching. He would trust God to sustain the weaker battalions.

With a zeal becoming customary, Jackson called for all the men Lee could spare him from northern Virginia, took his own small force splashing headlong through recently drenched paths in the southern end of the Shenandoah, crossed the Blue Ridge in an obvious move toward Richmond, caught the "cars" at Mechum River Station on the Virginia Central track, and rode impatiently westward away from the capital. Surprised villagers in Staunton saw the mud-flecked Valley Army move through en route to the Allegheny Mountains. Out in the lands westward, atop one of the ridges guarding Staunton's left approaches, General Edward (Allegheny) Johnson pitted his 2,000 men against attack from Indiana's General Robert Milroy and his 4,000 bluecoats. Milroy threatened Johnson's position near McDowell, Virginia, and thence Jackson took his army.[29]

It was a strange tactic. General Richard S. Ewell conceived the venture as some aberrant chase for wagons, dubbed his new chieftain "wagon hunter," and expected naught save madness from his doings. Madness they seemed also to Milroy and to his fuddled commander, Frémont. A swift stroke at McDowell on May 8, along with confusion in Union ranks, brought an abrupt Yankee retreat northward in the South Branch Valley—madness turned to mastery.

Attention to threats beyond the Shenandoah showed Jackson was aware of protecting his flanks. As Milroy fled northward, Rebel engineers closed the passes behind him into the Shenandoah and so bottled Frémont tightly in his department.

Once safe on the left, Jackson turned, darted quickly back toward Staunton, and lavished care on the discomfiture of Major General Nathaniel Banks. Banks had some daring, the kind born of ignorance, and he assumed his strength sufficient to deal with Jackson and at the same time reinforce McDowell's attempt to aid McClellan by joining in an attack on Richmond. Federal forces inched up the Shenandoah to Strasburg, outposts went to Front Royal on the far side of the oddly shaped Massanutten Mountain, and Banks ordered James Shields once more to go east toward Fredericksburg. It all seemed safe enough. Jackson lurked somewhere in the hinterlands; Ewell kept an anxious vigil atop the Blue Ridge Mountains; the valley lay tranquil in Yankee yoke.

On the morning of May 23, the absent Jackson hit the Union outpost at Front Royal, smashed it, and led his men swiftly to intercept Banks's certain retreat toward Winchester. Jackson's maps were poor, his men became lost, the victors moved slower than necessary, and the Rebel advance struck the center of Banks's fleeing column. A running engagement continued from Middletown to the environs of Winchester, where Banks took refuge behind fortifications. On the 25th the implacable Jackson stormed the works and carried Winchester. Banks's remnants streamed away toward the Potomac and suddenly the Shenandoah Valley was clear of invaders.

If there had been skeptics before, few in the North now denied that the Shenandoah Valley pointed like a rifle barrel at the heart of the Union—and Stonewall Jackson lurked in that barrel as a virtually unstoppable charge. President Lincoln, showing greater strategic grasp of the valley situation than most of his generals, realized that Rebel positions near Harpers Ferry were ideally suited to capture and ordered a gigantic pincers formed to close behind Jackson and bag his whole force. Military advisers who told the Union Chief Executive that Jackson's army was too large for bagging were admonished about phantom legions. The sage veteran of Black Hawk maneuvers guessed rightly about Jackson; no more than 16,000 Confederates were in the valley. Rumored Southern reinforcements had not swelled Old Jack's ranks to respectable army size, but with few men he dared the impossible. Washington was indeed threatened. Lee and Jackson and Jefferson Davis believed that Washington's safety counted for more in the Yankee view of the firmament than sound strategy, and they were right.

President Lincoln knew the folly of denying help to McClellan, whose plan to capture Richmond by advancing up the peninsula between the York and James rivers languished in the doldrums of the general's caution. McClellan counted on McDowell's force to join from upper Virginia and hence partially encircle the Rebel capital; until that help came caution ruled the Union commander's plans. Even a small diminution of force would sanctify Little Mac's hesitation, but politics sometimes overrides preferences. Washington had to be held inviolate. If it fell to some wayward band of Rebels, Europe would probably rush to recognize the South; northern Democrats with little heart for the war would raise the standard of peace. The Union might flounder in a backwash of derision.

Frémont must come out of his mountains; McDowell must detach men to pierce the Blue Ridge at Front Royal; these two forces must strive to meet below Strasburg and cut Jackson's escape route. Who could doubt the soundness of the plan? None save old martial hands. Such experienced folk recalled the age-old difficulty of joining separated forces in the face of the enemy. Emergencies, though, often beg precedents. The try must be made.

It was, and it failed—just barely. As Frémont eased tentatively into the Shenandoah abeam Jackson's road to safety he could almost see the Federal column sent from McDowell. He could see Jackson's column, strung out long on the road, burdened with seemingly endless wagon trains, a column marching cadence southward. Flank guards were out; some engaged Frémont and soon chastened him severely enough to quench his taste for glory. He waited for signs of help, and as he waited Jackson escaped. It was a classic tableau of war, the hunter confounded and hunted.

By the end of May the Army of the Valley knew it had slipped Lincoln's toils and was loose. It had picked up few men, but its supplies were unlimited. Wagons, horses, food, munitions, all the tools of armies went to Richmond in bounty from the Shenandoah.

Old Jack was a wagon hunter with a sense of logistics. He had strategic sense, too, a fact no one now could deny. Richmond sang his praises from the White House to the halls of Congress. General Lee basked in the reflected daring of his taciturn lieutenant in the valley. And General Lee had plans for him. Could he now come eastward to help repel McClellan? Or was there still some damage he could do to Banks and Frémont and James Shields? The choice was Jackson's.

He decided to do damage first and then to go east. At the southern tip of Massanutten, near the confluence of the Shenandoah's branches, he indulged in a piece of military flamming heretofore unknown in American history. On June 8 he hurled his army at Frémont west of the river near Cross Keys, drove him back, and thoroughly cowed him; on the 9th he crossed and struck Shields's advance near Port Republic and smashed the whole Union front. Regular blue infantry under General E. B. Tyler streamed back down the Luray Valley east of Massanutten, leaving vast stores behind. So ended Jackson's famous campaign in the Shenandoah. It would be studied for generations as a model of getting the most from the least. The gentle man in the rumpled tunic, who solemnly and persistently sucked a lemon and surveyed the valley he had made forever his own, saw before him the work of the Lord. To Lee he reported that "God blessed our arms with victory."

A Man "So Cold, Quiet and Grand"

Probably no one in service carried more lead in his body than Joseph E. Johnston. He collected bullets in Indian wars, in the Utah campaign, in Mexico, on almost every hostile field he knew. On the peninsula below Richmond during the afternoon of May 31, 1862, Johnston's luck ran typically. At the height of the Battle of Seven Pines—a battle Johnston designed to thwart McClellan's Peninsular Campaign against Richmond's exposed southeastern approaches—Old Joe was hit and unhorsed. Badly wounded, unable to keep the field, he was sent to the rear under the saddened eye of Jefferson Davis. Who would now command the army standing between Little Mac and Richmond?[30]

Johnston had brought that army to fighting trim, had kept it from useless combat until it numbered almost as many as its adversary, the Union Army of the Potomac; he had pulled it slowly back up the peninsula until patience strained with fear in the Rebel capital and people began to think the city would fall from "Retreating Joe's" inertia. But Old Joe's retreating was no product of cowardice. Some generals prefer to counterthrust, to await a chance for menace.[31] Johnston was one of those Fabian folk whose waiting boded ill for his enemies. At last came the moment he had expected: McClellan divided his army across the swollen Chickahominy River. Quickly Johnston plotted the wreckage of the stray Yankee divisions, isolated below the river, but his plan was too ambitious for a green staff and untried troops. A confused melee at Seven Pines a scant five miles below Richmond did drive the enemy back in disorder but failed to smash him. Still, Seven Pines was a Confederate victory, with chances for more to come if leadership continued. But would it, with Johnston gone?[32]

Jefferson Davis cast around for a successor and fixed on his military adviser, Robert E. Lee. What reason for the choice? Surely not Lee's record in western Virginia; there Confederate units under his coordination were lucky to escape annihilation at the hands of a force under General William S. Rosecrans. Not, certainly, for his engineering feats in South Carolina, where his insistence on digging branded him the "King of Spades." What, then, led Davis to link a man with destiny?

Recalling the appointment years later, Davis mustered sound reasons for his choice. "Laborious and exact in details, as he was vigilant and comprehensive in grand strategy, [he had] a power, with which the public had not credited him, [which] soon became manifest in all that makes an army a rapid, accurate, compact machine, with responsive motion in all its parts." These were qualities that endeared Lee to the President.[33] But there were others.

Consider the general and the commander in chief. History recalls them as opposites; it holds Lee high as a model soldier without flaw, as the paragon of such virtues as the South could claim; it grudges Davis even a loser's mite, and consigns him to the limbo of flawed mortals. And yet they were alike, those two, in ways more real than obvious. They shared a devotion to the cause beyond mere declaration; both were wrapped in unaffected dignity; both were ambitious and cloaked it in good manners; each man had prodigious talent and saw it in the other. They made a powerful team.

In some inner quality of life these two were most unlike. Davis's personality trapped him in a prison of quenched affection; Lee was lofty and still loved.

Lee is a riddle always. No human weakness breaks his character, only rarely does emotion disquiet his serenity. Perfect men are sometimes irksome to lesser folk, and there were a few who sniped bitterly at "Bully Bob" Lee, a few who found his symmetry cloying, and a few who hoped his stoicism simply hid stupidity.

But he had a power that was felt by all who knew him; those who could not quite love, admired. There was, of course, his bearing and carriage and grace. He attracted notice. Socialite Mary Chesnut could not quite forget the first time she met Lee in July 1861.

> I had heard of him, strange to say, in this wise. . . . Last summer at the White Sulphur [Springs], I met Roony Lee and his wife . . . and I spoke of Roony with great praise. Mrs. Izard said: "Don't waste your admiration on him. Wait till you see his father! He is the nearest to a perfect man I ever saw." "How?" "Every way. Handsome, clever, agreeable, high bred!" Now, here in Richmond, Mrs. Standard came for Mrs. Preston and me, to drive to . . . camp. She was in an open carriage. A man riding a beautiful horse joined us. He wore a hat with somehow a military look to it. He sat his horse gracefully, and he was so distinguished at all points that I very much regretted not catching the name as Mrs. Stanard gave it to us. He, however, heard ours, and bowed as gracefully as he rode; and the few remarks he made to each of us showed he knew all about us. . . . I felt she [Mrs. Stanard] had bagged a big fish, since just then they abounded in Richmond. We chatted lightly and I enjoyed it, since the man and horse and everything about them was perfection. As he left us, I said eagerly: "Who is he?" "You did not know? Why, that was Robert E. Lee, the first gentleman of Virginia."[34]

Mary, with a qualm or two, or maybe a touch of spite, added a qualifying paragraph.

All the same, I like Smith Lee better; and I like his looks too. Besides, I know him well. Can anyone say they know his brother? I doubt it! He looks so cold, quiet and grand.[35]

Behind the unruffled tunic, behind the placid face with its steady eyes, behind the pose of order, what was there? Could some message be glimpsed in the honest gray eyes? Was some hidden, restless quality waiting the call of battle? Davis thought so, and he was right.

Robert E. Lee was a creature of battle. When he took command of the Confederate Army near Richmond on June 1, 1862, he found another self. The terrible threat of McClellan's legions almost within cannon shot of Richmond touched a current of daring in the cool, smooth soldier. He began to plan a campaign to save the capital, which, if successful, would brand him forever one of history's great captains.

Information about the enemy proved the most urgent necessity. What were the positions held by McClellan's army across the Chickahominy River? Was the Federal right flank "in the air," and hence turnable? To headquarters near Richmond General Lee called a freshly made brigadier of cavalry, James Ewell Brown Stuart. Stuart, a Virginian, in his late twenties, had flowing locks, a reddish-brown, heavy beard, and brilliant blue eyes, stood square and not particularly tall, and had a look of boundless energy. There was brusqueness and jingle to him to match his plumed hat. His performance at Manassas had won praise from prickly Joe Johnston; he had all the qualities for leadership of light cavalry. Lee asked him to reconnoiter the Federal positions north of the Chickahominy and report on the feasibility of a flanking attack that might roll up the enemy right and pin part of the blue army to the river. It was a great assignment, one that sparked Stuart's smoldering enthusiasm. "Jeb" knew he could count on his men, accepted the orders, and then extended them in his mind.

By 2:00 A.M. on June 12, 1862, he had a long column moving away from Richmond, toward Stonewall Jackson's valley. In the morning of Friday the 13th, the column shifted direction eastward and the men knew they were going around the enemy's flank. For the next two days Stuart's men rode all the way around McClellan's army. There were skirmishes, feared battles, excitements of sufficient kind to inspire the most daring troopers, but the ride continued until the Confederate horsemen returned to Lee's army. Information was plentiful. The enemy's right could be turned, his rearward security was badly disorganized, and his cavalry put to shame! Stuart's fame spread across the land. And Lee was ready to try a daring scheme. The first necessity was Stonewall Jackson.

Partners in Daring

Perhaps Lee learned something from Jackson, some element of gambling. More likely, though, Jackson ignited Lee's smoldering audacity. A look at Lee's career gave scant hint of audacity. An honor graduate of the Military Academy, he had served with distinction in the cavalry and had earned an enviable reputation as an extremely competent soldier, one with great potential for leadership. But the kind of leadership he seemed to typify was that of calmness and deliberation. He would study, plan strategy, and watch his operations unfold according to pattern. More than that, he was likely to "organize" men, mounts, plans, operations, supplies with skill. He seemed more competent than brilliant. But his success as a staff officer with Winfield Scott in Mexico had caught the eye of that doughty old soldier, and when the Civil War loomed Scott offered Lee the command of United States forces. Lee had turned down the honor to remain loyal to Virginia—it was a decision that ran in the blood.

With Virginia's secession he had commanded the state's army with consummate administrative ability and had served well for a time as a sort of military secretary to President Davis. The sad history of his western Virginia defeats did not really dim his potential, though it cast him further into public obscurity. A stint as engineering inspector in South Carolina had taught him interesting lessons in entrenchment that might help him later.

Now that he was in command of Johnston's old army there was considerable speculation about him. What kind of strategy would he plot? Would he wait behind earthworks? Would he attack? He had watched Stonewall Jackson's brilliant maneuvering with growing admiration. Speed, mobility, audacity, these were the requisites of the weaker side. Lee planned with these necessities in mind. At any rate, Lee assumed from the moment he took command of the Confederate forces defending Richmond that he would hit McClellan. If the Rebels waited behind the far-stretched fortifications covering the city, McClellan could fight the kind of engineering campaign he knew best. Regular approaches, digging, transverse trenches, battery bombproofs, and siege tactics all would inexorably capture the capital. So Lee would not wait.

Now Jackson must come from the pacified Shenandoah, bring with him his small force, plus the reinforcements just sent him as a ruse, and fall upon McClellan's right flank north of the Chickahominy. Jackson agreed and quit the Shenandoah Valley on June 17, 1862.

While valley troops slogged toward the capital over sodden and hampering pikes, Jackson journeyed for a conference with Lee at his headquarters near Richmond. In addition to the commanding general and Jackson, bluff James Longstreet, taciturn A. P. Hill, and bristly D. H. Hill attended. Lee told his hopes: Jackson was to swing beyond Little Mac's exposed right, hit the Union forces north of the Chickahominy, and drive them into the still swollen river; when the Army of the Valley opened the battle, succeeding Rebel units stretched north of the river would join the wheeling turn and increase pressure on McClellan's right wing. With luck, no less than half the Federal army would be rolled into a cul-de-sac with Rebels on three sides and an unfordable torrent behind.[36]

There was a weakness. Suppose McClellan left his right to take care of itself, seized the moment of Rebel concentration north of the Chickahominy, and made a dash with much of his force straight for Richmond? What chance did the few divisions left in the capital's defenses have against a determined Yankee thrust? It was a point. But Lee took the first of many risks in deciding to ignore it. He knew McClellan, admired his meticulous kind of fighting, but thought caution would smother his boldness. If the guess went wrong, Lee could cope with the problems when the time came.

A glance at maps of the peninsula below Richmond showed Lee's strategy to be daring indeed. Roads were soggy and streams roaring from rain, but McClellan was admirably placed for ruination. He had come out of the closer confines of the peninsula; now only his left was guarded by gunboats; his right was exposed. If the plan worked, Lee might be able to cross the Chickahominy below McClellan's ruined divisions and snare the rest of the blue army in a giant double envelopment.

It was a good plan for several reasons. It capitalized on surprise, since Jackson's army was rumored once more en route toward Washington; it wrenched initiative to the Confederates; it concentrated superior force on the enemy's weakest point. All of it hinged on timing and coordinated staff work. Lee's staff and the staffs of the other commanders present at the headquarters conference were hardly experienced enough to count cadence on a routine march. But the commanding general decided to try.

The result of daring scheming at Army Headquarters were the famous Seven Days' Battles around Richmond. Beginning late because Stonewall had unexpected trouble reaching the field, the battles sputtered badly at first with heavy Federal resistance against A. P. Hill and Longstreet; they were replete with almost everything possible in fighting. Jackson was delayed by confused orders; he was late again at White Oak Swamp because of fatigue and unfamiliar ground; Longstreet got into a stand-up fight with stubborn Yankees that cost too many grayclads; McClellan saw the ruination piling around him and achieved a brilliant change of base to the James in mid-campaign; at the end Lee threw his legions piecemeal against impregnable Union lines on Malvern Hill. And yet, if much less than Lee had hoped was achieved after Mechanicsville, Gaines's Mill, Savage Station, Frayser's Farm, and Malvern, one thing was clear: McClellan would not take Richmond. In the week-long fighting he had been superb in defense, but all aggression was beaten out of him. When the firing died away on Malvern's slopes, the Army of the Potomac slunk quietly southward along the James to the full protection of Union gunboats. The Union's first Richmond campaign had failed in a welter of blood—9,474 Rebel casualties against 14,462 Federal casualties.

Civilians are a sorry lot. Craven and obsequious when theatened

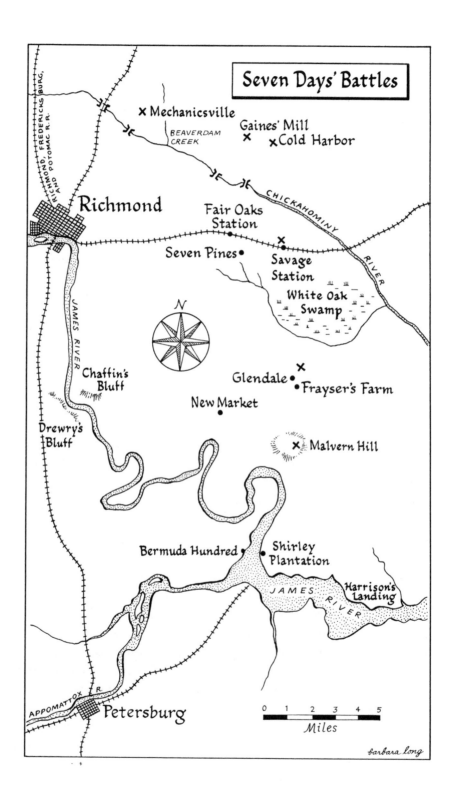

with defeat, they are truculent and scornful in success. Richmond newspapers were fairly accurate reflectors of civilian vagaries. In the weeks before the Seven Days' Battles they wailed for deliverance of any sort; in the backwash of the century's greatest series of battles, they carped about things undone.[37] The fickleness of civil ignorance scarcely bothered General Lee.

If he lamented the failure to crush McClellan and the loss of so many men, he hid his feelings well. He had praise for most subordinates, even the strangely tardy Jackson. From the Seven Days' Lee learned that staffs were collections of human beings and had to be trained to duties; that Confederate soldiers were tough, devoted men who were hard to stop; that the aggregation under his command was beginning to act like an army. Shortly after he took command Lee had changed the name of Johnston's force to the Army of Northern Virginia. It described the theater of operations accurately, it looked well on paper, and now it had a special meaning.

Lee took no time to cherish laurels. McClellan for the moment was forgotten. Another Yankee general occupied attention. John Pope, late hero of the west, had been called eastward by Washington to take charge of Banks's remnants and other scattered units in upper Virginia. Obviously Pope would aim at Richmond in hopes of relieving pressure on McClellan. Before he got fairly set, Lee decided to wreck him. How?

There was a chance that Stonewall Jackson, still bothered by some odd inertia, might be used better in detachment than in subordination. Possibly he was more leader than follower. In the valley, as his own man, he had made martial history. Again alone he might do as well. Orders went to Stonewall: take more than half the army, march to central Virginia, find Pope, and fight him.

To anyone interested in army organization, Lee's action made sense. Jackson, in effect, was a wing commander operating under over-all directions from Lee. Details were his to work out. Away toward Gordonsville went Old Jack, and once his men were on the road, something of the old *élan* returned. Pope's advanced units under Banks were found near Cedar Mountain. On August 9, Jackson attacked; the battle seesawed for a time, the issue hung in balance, but Old Jack himself led the deciding charge. Cedar Mountain restored Stonewall's confidence, and justified Lee's.

Leaving a small force to observe McClellan, Lee took the rest of his army northward to join Jackson. Together with Longstreet, who took charge of Lee's other wing, Jackson and Lee devised a brilliant, if dangerous, plan of encirclement for Pope. Jackson marched far off around Pope's right, got behind him, and burned his supply base at Bristoe Station. On August 29 Pope—who had received some units from McClellan's army, which was clearing the peninsula—at last found Jackson's force entrenched near the old Manassas battlefield. That day and the next Pope threw line after serried line against Jackson's position, and they were beaten back each time. The Federals were rallied for the one last effort which might have succeeded (Stonewall's men were fought out and low on ammunition), but as the charge began it was hit in left flank by Longstreet, whose men had reached the field secretly. The second Manassas proved as woeful to the Union as the first[38]—15,849 bluecoats were killed, wounded, or captured against 9,749 Rebel casualties.

A few days later, following some harsh mop-up fighting, Lee could reflect on certain miracles. In a scant two months the valley was saved, Richmond snatched from capture, enemy troops cleared from Virginia.

How had it happened? Jackson had had a lot to do with it. His Valley Campaign inspired Confederates everywhere, and after the Seven Days', freed again from close rein, he had outshone himself. Learning to trust each other, he and Lee became model partners. Second Manassas was a triumph of their joint daring: find the enemy, fool him, flank him, ruin him. Longstreet, too, and the division commanders all deserved a share of renown—the summer campaign was an army effort. But the real glory went to the Confederate soldiers. One of their enemies caught their greatness and dubbed them "that incomparable infantry."

Gaily the battle-thinned gray veterans—now barely 50,000 strong —sloshed through shallow Potomac waters on September 5 and carried the war to the enemy. Across the river was independence.

CHAPTER FIVE

"They Have Made a Nation"
—WILLIAM GLADSTONE

The Hesitant Lion

There was a vague incestuousness to British foreign relations in the 1860's. Leopold, King of the Belgians, was Victoria's uncle; German princes from Gotha to Mecklenburg boasted blood kinship to the Queen; her beloved consort, Albert, was Prince of Saxe-Coburg. If there was a taint of paternalism in Crown attitudes toward other nations, it was hardly surprising. From Osbourne House or Whitehall, the world glistened as a family bauble.

Her Britannic Majesty's emissaries traveled the globe on personal missions. Troubles in Italy, Denmark, Prussia, Austria, Russia, in dimly known Latin America, or deep in Africa—troubles anywhere —disturbed family humors and roused a motherly concern. Or so it often must have seemed to those foreigners suffering the beneficence of a lingering Pax Britannica. And while there was a tenuous sort of peace suffusing Britain's global family, it was a peace of odd dimensions. Where local unrest bubbled to the surface, where lesser royalties plotted war, where revolution threatened an end to tranquillity, there gunboats appeared, British commissioners read proclamations of the Queen's displeasure, and all became as it had been.

A close look at the world revealed this family bauble as nothing more than costume jewelry. Most British politicians, Victoria herself, certainly Prince Albert, knew the complexities of British sway. The world had grown beyond London, beyond the long arms of the throne; restive peoples raised new flags unbidden by the British and uncaring. Asia pursued destinies inscrutable; the Near East chafed under zealous English yoke. America had long ignored its family ties and stood in curiously affectionate disrepute. And yet the Atlantic, wide reaches of the Pacific, the Caribbean, the Mediterranean still were strewn with British sail; the Royal Navy held together the loose-limbed corpus of empire.

On this uneasy scene of English calm came the American war and the Confederacy. War cut harshly into British aplomb; the Confederacy thrust itself urgently into the balance of power. So Britain took a considerable time to react to both war and Confederacy. Beyond the quick recognition of the South as a belligerent, beyond a broad claim of neutrality, Victoria's government did no more than watch American events. Why? Self-interest, some Britons cried; inept leadership, others said; still more saw the usual guile of Perfidious Albion behind inaction.

Causes of inaction lay far deeper than these guesses, lay in Anglo-Saxon temperament, in economic possibilities, in national policies, in longings, hopes, and secret fears, in weaknesses undreamed beyond Whitehall, in relations with Canada and with Europe, in the nature of the mercurial third Bonaparte, and in the natural caution of public men.[1] And the causes are really unimportant. As long as England stayed her hand in the war, the United States rejoiced, the South yearned—but both traded. Britain really did not want to war with either side, but Prime Minister Palmerston and Foreign Secretary Russell saw involvement as almost inevitable. Both sides abused England's neutrality; the Yankees more than the Rebels, since they were stronger and had voices in the seats of world power.

Southern leaders shrewdly won attention to their country through two virtually unassailable claims: one, the Union blockade leaked ludicrously; two, recognition of the Confederacy had been earned by stout defense.[2] This last point piqued British concern for *de facto* legitimacy, and as gray legions turned back blue legions throughout the summer of 1861 and the spring and summer of 1862, recognition became almost undeniable. Sentiments in the British cabinet were divided on the war. Palmerston weighed the trends and deeds in America, the political currents at home, and the temper of his ministers. When, at last, Lee pushed the Yankees from Virginia, the Prime Minister felt action must come. Russell agreed, and set the question of recognizing the Confederate government on a late September agenda for cabinet discussion.[3]

It was all extremely delicate. Any public comment, any sudden shift in the fortunes of war could anger either or both belligerents, and the British people as well. At this critical moment a member of Her Majesty's government left London to keep a speaking date in Newcastle—a date almost fateful for the world.

William Gladstone, Chancellor of the Exchequer, confronted his Newcastle audience on October 7, 1862, with his own views of the American Civil War. "Jefferson Davis and other leaders of the South," he said, "have made an army; they are making . . . a navy; and they have made what is more than either—they have made a nation."[4] Bold words, indeed, from a cabinet minister at so tender a time. But Gladstone was a radical; it was a facet of his make-up tolerated with some anxiety by his conservative colleagues. He wanted change at a time when change could only be dangerous, and there was a good deal of potential danger in his Newcastle pronouncement. Mistaken for official British policy, his remarks might enrage the United States, inflate the status of the Confederates, and embarrass the Crown. Too much interest in the American question had lingered too long for any public statement by a member of the government to go unnoted.

Quickly Gladstone realized—reaction in the press and in his mail made it abundantly clear—that some felt he had said too much. In letters to Russell he admitted indiscretion, but took some consolation in the knowledge that his views reflected much cabinet sentiment.[5]

Gladstone had breached etiquette, which was embarrassing enough, but his timing added to the discomfort of the government. American events were crowding hard on the British stage. Ever since the *Trent* crisis pro-Confederate elements in Britain had been urging action. Voices for the South were heard among all classes of English society. Rich parvenus who held romantic attachment to the Southern landed gentry, factory workers who saw freedmen as tough competition for their Southern working brethren, merchants with an eye for peaceful Dixie markets, all these harangued the government to recognize Davis's regime and bring an end to the war.[6] Much of this pro-Rebel feeling had been generated by the canny manipulations of perhaps the most effective Confederate ever sent abroad—Henry Hotze, propagandist. In May 1862 Hotze began publication of the London *Index,* a newspaper financed by the Davis government and dedicated to the truth through Rebel eyes. A brilliant editor, Hotze purveyed his point of view with good-humored candor, and beyond his editorials offered readers a lively, balanced paper. During its four-year life, the *Index* won many converts to its cause.[7]

Partly because of the *Index,* partly because of sentiment and selfishness and altruism, many Britons supported the Rebels—there were enough of them at length to force attention in Parliament. In those somber halls W. H. Gregory, William Lindsay, and other pro-Southerners had already tried to win approval of the Confederate government. Now that gray columns thronged beyond the Potomac, the call for recognition was bound to rise anew. Gladstone's remarks seemed likely to excite a fresh attack in Parliament; they might even end Napoleon's quest for British support and propel him to recognition on his own.[8] The cabinet might have to act simply to keep up with events.

History intruded into this apparent chain of logic. Two unexpected events shifted the trends in Britain's higher councils. On September 16–17, 1862, General George B. McClellan checked General Lee's Maryland invasion at the Battle of Antietam; and on September 22, President Lincoln issued his Preliminary Emancipation Proclamation.

Federal victory, even a defensive victory, indicated a strength unseen for some months, and the Proclamation indicated a fundamental change in the nature of the American war. These new considerations brought into clear focus the uncertainties plaguing part of the English cabinet. Some of Victoria's ministers were concerned at the apparent reversal of roles by Yankees and Confederates. Lord Granville observed after the Second Manassas that "we know that the Federals have been defeated in their attempt to conquer the South. But we also know that the two parties have changed parts in the great tragedy.— The Southerns instead of being invaded are become the invaders."[9]

And hence, presumably, the South abdicated its pose of an aggrieved innocent holding barbarians at bay. It seemed like a small point, but it embarrassed many pro-Confederate Britons.

Britons with pro-Yankee proclivities felt mixed reaction to the Lincoln Proclamation. It was true that antislavery sentiment ran high among Britain's ruling class; true, too, that many textile workers who endured harsh privation because of the cotton shortage felt ennobled in their sacrifice by the Proclamation. Their stoic acceptance of hunger as a price of freedom gave dignity to workers everywhere and brought them nobly to the notice of a grateful Queen and cabinet. But a few cabinet members caught the flaws in Lincoln's Proclamation, knew its inconsistencies, its political expediency. Some of them knew, too, its strange inevitability. The Duke of Argyll, always steadfast for the North, put the feeling aptly:

> It is very easy to point out the logical inconsistency of the Proclamation with an abstract principle on the question of Slavery. But the North has never professed to fight for the abolition of Slavery. I have always looked to the irresistible tendency of events, rather than to the *intentions* of the North, for the Anti Slavery effects of the War.
>
> Of that tendency—and of its irresistible character—the President's Proclamation is a signal proof—crowning many other proofs which have been accumulating rapidly as the war went on. . . .
>
> Halting, imperfect, and inconsistent as the Proclamation is—interpreted strictly—it has nevertheless been hailed by the Abolitionist Party as a great—irrevocable step—towards their "Platform."[10]

Lord Russell canceled the prospective cabinet discussion of Confederate independence. Once again safe in indecision, Palmerston commented piously that "the Slavery Question was from the Beginning an obvious Difficulty in our way. . . ."[11] England would await a more decisive moment to acknowledge Southern freedom. It was a decision that affected France, since the Emperor hesitated to act alone; it affected tiny Belgium with its own starving textile millers; Russia, too, whose aid was contemplated by all who sought intervention; and Austria, with its anti-Seward ministry.[12]

Was the government's retreat to neutrality the act of abolitionist rectitude it seemed? Or was the government scared of a blustering Brother Jonathan and an unstable American Secretary of State? Some concern beyond fright surely dictated the counsels of the most respected nation in the world. What of an economic concern scarcely mentioned, a concern to balance cotton against corn? Historians would later advance the corn thesis as a reason for English neutrality, would urge the importance of Northern corn exports to the continuance of English nourishment. A word for the corn thesis remains to be said by the Duke of Argyll: "If America has deprived . . . [us] of cotton, it is at least pouring forth its corn in wonderful abundance; and if any action of the Govt sh[oul]d endanger this supply, the responsibility w[oul]d be great indeed."[13]

No cabinet member believed the American issue settled, but most were willing to dodge it for a time. The decision to delay a move for either mediation or recognition—the two issues were complex and inseparable—set a fatal precedent.

Motives for delay were of only passing concern to the South. The important fact was the result. Out of all the great opportunities of late 1862, out of the smashing chain of victories from Front Royal to Second Manassas, was the South to reap no more than foreign good will? Was the Confederacy perhaps the victim of historical inevitability? Was there some inscrutable purpose to be worked out in the war, some purpose that lent fortune to Lincoln and somehow let him reshape the course of America? If so, there must be a secret balance to the scales of justice, a balance tipped by fate. No matter, the South defied fate in the beginning and would defy it to the end.

Of Divers Paths to Happiness

Stonewall Jackson's men rested in cornfields and woods near the Dunkard Church, on the left of the Confederate line. During the late afternoon and early evening of September 16, 1862, heavy Yankee cannon raked the Rebel left, and Fighting Joe Hooker's men probed the front held by General John B. Hood's division. Nightfall ended the skirmishing, cannonading ceased, and the vague restlessness of approaching battle disturbed opposing armies.

Jackson had no illusions about his situation, nor did General Lee.

The Confederates were in trouble, trouble caused by one of those impossible flukes of circumstance. Several days before, some wayward grayclad had dropped a packet of cigars in the road near Frederick, Maryland, where Lee's army rested after crossing the Potomac. Fantastic as it seemed, a copy of General Order No. 191, Army of Northern Virginia, was wrapped around the cigars. The order gave details of Lee's plan to split his army into several parts for strategic and logistical reasons, then to regroup near Hagerstown. Once in the hands of General George B. McClellan, newly reunited with the Army of the Potomac, the order induced him to move with unseemly haste against Lee's diverging columns near South Mountain.

Lee had fragmented the Army of Northern Virginia. Stonewall Jackson had been sent to besiege the 11,000-man garrison at Harpers Ferry; some of James Longstreet's men were cooperating with Jackson, others were guarding passes through South Mountain, still others were ranging the country near Hagerstown for supplies and information. Only Lee would have dared this danger, and he would scarcely have dared it against anyone but McClellan. McClellan was dependable; he would not act. But he had acted; his columns had moved steadily on South Mountain, and during the wild and battle-seared night of September 14–15, he all but forced passage of South Mountain. Lee had to abandon the mountain passes and find new defensive positions.

Lee called every unit to concentrate near Sharpsburg, a small hamlet boasting little save a range of rolling hills between shallow Antietam Creek and the Potomac, a few houses and a cemetery; it was chiefly important as a stop on the road from Boonsboro to Virginia's Shenandoah Valley.

Lee's men came slowly, in dribbles, and the general grew tense with waiting. As September 16 stretched its endless hours, Lee and Longstreet and D. H. Hill, the ranking Rebel officers present, watched the gathering host in blue. Sprawling columns came down from South Mountain, from Boonsboro; once near the Antietam the columns broke and spread along the hills; guns came and rolled into batteries; troopers rode along the lines: there were 80,000 or 90,000 bluecoats spread before the Rebels. On other hills beyond Antietam, from the Stone Bridge on the right of the Confederate line all the way along Longstreet's front in the Sharpsburg cemetery, along Hill's lines near a sunken road left of Longstreet's guns, on beyond the cornfields around the Dunkard Church, the Union ranks arrayed.

Lee disposed a shadow force—no more than 40,000 men—behind the Antietam; men came in during the day, and finally, late in the morning of September 16, Jackson's wing of Lee's army arrived victorious from Harpers Ferry, missing A. P. Hill's famed Light Division. Out to the left Lee sent Jackson's jaded marchers, and once in position they stayed.

All through the night of September 16–17, Lee waited for reinforcements. With dawn the Yankees came. They hit Jackson's position first, tried to turn the Confederate left away from the Potomac and roll the Confederate Army into a gigantic sack. They came in steady, compact lines and moved from their woodland positions into the cornfields on Jackson's front; they came behind a storm of shell. They smashed the first opponents, staggered others, but Jackson stood once more like a stone wall—and the Yankees were caught in a crossfire and finally stopped. The bluecoats were closer to success than they knew. Had they tried one more charge against Jackson's fought-out brigades, they might have won the day. But they, too, were fought-out and dazed by a volume of fire and noise beyond belief, and they did not come again.

Instead the battle shifted to the Rebel center, rose again in weird cacophony, rolled against the sunken road to be known forever as Bloody Lane, ebbed in the face of dauntless defense, and at last washed forward for a final venture against the Confederate right near the Stone Bridge. This last ground was south of the cemetery where Longstreet's guns had held position all day, south almost of Sharpsburg, and if the Yankees prevailed here they would be between the Potomac and Lee's army. Federal General Ambrose Burnside's thrust at the Stone Bridge could hardly fail. Scarcely 5,000 Rebels opposed his 13,000 men. Everything in that sector came down to a matter of time; the time of final Northern attack, of last-ditch Southern defense, the time of A. P. Hill.

Hill with his division came from Harpers Ferry late in the afternoon of the 17th, but in time to fan his men hastily into lines of battle and hurl them at Burnside's flank. Hill beat Burnside back and hence beat McClellan. Little Mac surveyed the smoldering four-mile battlefield, saw at least 10,000 bluecoats strewn on all the slopes before him, and was sated with blood. He could not charge again.

Lee certainly could not charge; he had scarcely enough men left to form a skirmish line. And so the Battle of Sharpsburg ended. Warm night breezes carried the restless sounds of carnage: doctors and litter bearers scurried between the armies, piteous calls from the wounded came, and finally the survivors slept. With that slumber went the last chance for quick Northern victory.[14]

Casualties totaled some 20,000 men, blue and gray. Surely there was purpose in their dying? Lee knew rightly the purpose of his stand: he had stopped McClellan cold, had taken the best that the North could give, and had withstood. True, he had not beaten the enemy, he had to retreat to Virginia without vast treasure or many recruits, but he had prolonged the war. McClellan could boast equally: he had stopped the Army of Northern Virginia, driven it from Northern soil, and ended Lee's spell of success.

If Little Mac missed his chance to annihilate Lee's army, he did achieve a kind of victory. A kind of victory was something for which Abraham Lincoln had waited in mounting despair, and on the threadbare coattails of McClellan's "success" he issued his Preliminary Emancipation Proclamation. For Lincoln, then, Antietam gave new meaning to life and liberty. For Britain and the world, Antietam marked a moment of appraisal.

For Jefferson Davis, Sharpsburg had an especially mournful impact. It marked not only a military and diplomatic reverse, but also a reverse in statecraft. To understand Davis's peculiar reaction it is important to see Sharpsburg in full perspective. It is important, too, to understand the reasons for the invasion of Maryland, and to look at the venture beyond the Potomac as both a military campaign in itself and as part of the biggest, most comprehensive political campaign attempted by the Confederate government.

Consider first the state of the Confederacy by late summer 1862. Largely because of the armies, the internal structure of the country had solidified. As Jackson's columns had cleared the Shenandoah and as Lee's battles near Richmond had released the capital from McClellan's thrall, Southerners everywhere had taken new faith in success. That faith brought easy obedience to Confederate laws, acceptance of Confederate promissory notes, affection for soldiers and administrators. By late summer, the Confederacy existed in its armies, in its emissaries, and in the hearts of its people—there was a Confederate "nation."

Securing this nation in fact was Davis's constant concern. Daily military emergencies had absorbed him for months, forced his attention almost entirely on the armies to the neglect of other facets of the war. Respite from military crisis gave Davis time to think of politics and statecraft as weapons of war. With Confederate arms triumphant, proper diplomacy and blandishment might sway Northern political sentiment. There might be a chance, even, to detach a Yankee state or two from the Union. Wild as this might sound to some Yankee politicians, the Confederates had some reason for thinking about separate state action. For months rumors persisted in Northern and Southern papers[15] of an obscure peace plan, one that seemed to hinge on activities in some northwestern states, on activities of such Northern Peace Democrats as C. L. Vallandigham and those pro-Southern Copperheads who unctuously preached sedition and hoped for conspiratorial aid from Confederates in Canada. Cloaked in secrecy, the movement grew in report until it reached the status of a "conspiracy." The precise aims of the "conspiracy" remained mysterious, but some said it looked toward a new nation made up of the present Confederacy plus some northwestern states.

Rumor is often a basis for statecraft, sometimes the only basis. And Davis took notice of the lingering tales of the Northwest Conspiracy. He could hardly accept the idea of another nation; he could accept the idea of adding certain northwestern states to the Confederacy. His task was obvious enough, but exploiting the rumors to Southern advantage looked to be a chancy business. Open wooing of the northwest might fasten attention on pro-Confederates before they were ready to act, might attract Lafayette Baker's Secret Service. Whatever was done must be done deftly. Davis acted deftly enough. He devised a scheme to blend military reality with political hope in a special appeal for liberty.

His plan hinged on the old military maxim that prolonged in-action after victory breeds sloth and conceit. Now that Virginia had been purged of invaders, Lee's men were free for further success, and what they had achieved in the eastern theater of war gave special opportunity to the western forces of the Confederacy. The South must take advantage of a hard-won opportunity for a strategic offensive, must preserve military momentum and seize political initiative. Hence, Davis urged a gigantic Confederate drive in both east and west. Lee would continue with his plan to invade Maryland; Braxton Bragg, who had succeeded Beauregard in command after the abortive Corinth campaign, and who had now based the Army of Tennessee on Chattanooga, would march for Kentucky; and General Edmund Kirby Smith, commanding an army in Knoxville, would join Bragg's advance. Other units would join in this attempt to push Federal General Don Carlos Buell out of Tennessee and to wrest Kentucky from the Union. A combined attack on the Yankee right and left fronts in the east and west would prevent shuttling of troops and hence tend to equalize numbers. If the offensive succeeded, there might well be interesting dividends.

Be it said for Jefferson Davis that he caught the possibilities of his great offensive in fuller perspective than his generals and sought from the outset to wring every advantage from so large a risk. And risk this offensive certainly was, for it put past Confederate success in the jeopardy of combat, committed every reserve of men and supplies to invasion of the North. Defeat in the west would expose the entire Mississippi Basin to Federal depredations; failure in the east would expose Richmond. But possibilities offset risks. The offensive might touch off the Northwest Conspiracy, might win Kentucky and other key states, might earn recruits by the thousands, might defeat important enemy forces. Bragg could conceivably invade Ohio and cut the North's vital communications link between east and west. After that . . .

To emphasize the special importance of the campaign, the President sent each of his field commanders draft proclamations, which he expected them to issue upon reaching enemy soil. No other state document issued by Davis reveals him so thoroughly aware of politico-military power, and it is worth close study:

September 7, 1862 [?]

To Genl. R. E. Lee, Comdg &c., Genl. B. Bragg,
   Comdg. &c, Genl. E. K. Smith, Comdg. &c.

SIRS:

It is deemed proper that you should in accordance with established usage announce by proclamation to the people of _____ the motives and purposes of your presence among them at the head of an invading army, and you are instructed in such proclamation to make known,

That the Confederate Government is waging this war solely for self-defence, that it has no design of conquest or any other purpose than to secure peace and the abandonment by the United States of its pretensions to govern a people who have never been their subjects and who prefer self-government to a Union with them. . . .

That among the pretexts urged for continuance of the War is the assertion that the Confederate Government desires to deprive the United States of the free navigation of the Western Rivers although the truth is that the Confederate Congress by public act, prior to the commencement of the War, enacted that "the peaceful navigation of the Mississippi River is hereby declared free to the citizens of the States upon its borders, or upon the borders of its navigable tributaries" —a declaration to which this Government has always been and is still ready to adhere.

That now at a juncture when our arms have been successful, we restrict ourselves to the same just and moderate demand, that we made at the darkest period of our reverses, the simple demand that the people of the United States should cease to war upon us and permit us to pursue our own path to happiness, while they in peace pursue theirs.

That we are debarred from the renewal of formal proposals for peace by having no reason to expect that they would be received with the respect mutually due by nations in their intercourse, whether in peace or in war. . . .

That the Confederate army therefore comes to occupy the territory of their enemies and to make it the theatre of hostilities. That with the people of _____ themselves rests the power to put an end to this invasion of their homes, for if unable to prevail on the Government of the United States to conclude a general peace, their own State Government in the exercise of its sovereignty can secure immunity from the desolating effects of warfare on the soil of the State by a separate treaty of peace which this government will ever be ready to conclude on the most just and liberal basis.

That the responsibility thus rests on the people of _____ of continuing an unjust and aggressive warfare upon the Confederate States, a

warfare which can never end in any other manner than that now proposed. With them is the option of preserving the blessings of peace, by
the simple abandonment of the design of subjugating a people over
whom no right of dominion has been ever conferred either by God or
man.

JEFFN. DAVIS[16]

As a statement of faith in free trade and freedom, as a license for
invasion, the proclamation had dignity, purpose, and style and was
suffused with Davis's sense of truth. But it had a greater importance:
if all went well with the offensive, the proclamation would be the
South's platform for peace.

In the beginning things looked good for Davis's strategy. Lee's
invasion of Maryland caught Federal forces in post–Second Manassas
demoralization. Bragg's troops had marched northward from Chattanooga in late August, well covered by ranges of mountains, and
Federal troops under Buell were confused and finally flanked out of
Tennessee. There seemed to be some truth in one of Bragg's
aphorisms: "This campaign must be won by marching, not
fighting."[17]

Everywhere Union forces were thrown on the defensive. The
Army of the Potomac huddled near Washington in the throes of
reorganization; Buell's forces retreated in confusion toward central
Kentucky and soon found themselves in a losing race with Bragg
and Kirby Smith for Louisville. If Louisville went to the Rebels, all
of Indiana and Ohio would be open to them, the vital Baltimore and
Ohio rail link would break, and the Stars and Bars might wave over
the Great Lakes; if McClellan failed to halt Lee, results could well
be fatal for the Union—Washington might fall. McClellan or Buell
could lose the war.

Lee or Bragg could win it. Davis trusted them. He had put his
largest armies in the hands of the two generals he thought best. Lee,
everyone acclaimed. There were a few in the halls of Congress, in
the army, among veteran politicians, who sniped at Bragg; some
dared to suggest his incompetence at anything save fault finding, to
accuse him of a strange blindness to military realities that made him
a prisoner of his wishes. There was also a rumor that Davis kept
him in command more from friendship than from judgment—a

harsh thrust at an executive wrapped in rectitude. Bragg had experience from Old Army days, had won laurels with grapeshot in the Mexican War, and had commanded ably at Pensacola and at Shiloh. Stiff, formal, and cold, he was nonetheless a soldier of relentless polish. No general left to the South kept better discipline, achieved better organization, ran a better army. Braxton Bragg scarcely needed special pleading. Perhaps he was all charms, virtues, and perfections. Certainly he looked to be these things. A high forehead, graying hair and beard, angular cheeks, firm jaws, and strong lips accentuated hereditary grace; heavy brows and large, dark eyes hinted at a brooding, restless force. And yet there was some small lack in him to baffle biographers, some vital spark that fled and left the face a façade. Well-set, not fleshy, a manly figure in Rebel gray, Bragg passed as model soldier, the delight of ladies and photgraphers.

At moments he could be a model soldier, could gather shattered, wasted regiments spent from battle and remold them into armies. In the summer of 1862 Bragg was at his best.[18]

Taking Beauregard's place at the head of the Army of Tennessee, Bragg forced respect for rules, put spirit in disspirited men, rebuilt the character that seemed beaten out and lost somewhere between Shiloh and Iuka. The army had come to think like an army, to believe in itself and its generals, to march northward sure of victory. This large achievement Davis perceived as final proof of Bragg's ability.[19] But Bragg had one fatal weakness—he would not fight.

That absent strength cost him the fruits of an otherwise brilliant campaign. After maneuvering Buell from Tennessee, Bragg feinted toward Louisville (which he should have taken), darted eastward toward Frankfort, and presided over the installation of Richard Hawes as Confederate governor of Kentucky. Admirable concern for politics almost brought military ruin, since the ceremonies were interrupted by unexpected Union troops. Governor and general decamped in haste. Bragg had been badly fooled by the enemy and by his ally, General Kirby Smith.

Troubles with Smith can be cited in partial excuse for Bragg's results in Kentucky. Had Smith cooperated heartily, Bragg's plans for concentration between separated elements of the Federal Army might have succeeded. But Smith helped when it suited him, a caprice that illustrated a glaring weakness in Davis's command system.

In an attempt to solve a vexing equation of three variables—size, communications, and logistics—the President had adopted the geographical command system. Various geographical areas were designated military departments and put in charge of a general who had virtually dictatorial powers over resources within his area. This sound design was still new by mid-1862 and needed time for testing and adjustment. Bragg's campaign strained the system at the point of most rigidity—no accommodation had yet been made for cooperation between separate departmental forces. Davis and his generals appreciated the problem of divided command, yet this was exactly the absurdity confronting Bragg and Smith. Who was really in charge? Bragg thought he was, but was not certain. Smith feared Bragg was, and guarded his prerogatives. Result: Bragg could request Smith's aid but could not order it; Smith was free to follow pride's dictates.

All these considerations bore directly on the crisis of the campaign at the Battle of Perryville, Kentucky, October 8, 1862. This battle resembled Bragg's campaign and Buell's countercampaign in microcosm. Bragg led his army to battle in pieces. Bishop Leonidas Polk's corps furiously attacked Buell's army, drove part of it, and would have carried the field save for the determined stand of the Union center. When the fighting ended, Buell, who learned of the battle hours after it started, had yet to get his whole army on the scene, and Bragg failed to press the advantage earned by surprise. Casualties were heavy, the outcome slightly against the Rebels, and Bragg began a withdrawal to Tennessee.[20]

Was the Kentucky campaign a success? It can be rationalized into success by stressing the advantage of Southern initiative, the importance of keeping the North pinned to Rebel plans for months, by harping on the fear struck in the North, by pointing to the wagons, supplies, and livestock captured. But direct results were negative. Buell went undefeated, Governor Hawes fled Kentucky, and perhaps most significantly, few recruits came to join Bragg's columns. Where were those rumored Rebel thousands in Tennessee and Kentucky who waited only for a chance to join the cause? If there was no pro-Southern enthusiasm in the border states, there was scant hope for a northwestern conspiracy.

And so the Great Offensive failed, east and west. Costs were high in men and morale, especially high in expectations. A bitter lesson could be read in the wreckage of Sharpsburg and Perryville: the South must pursue its "own path to happiness" unaided at home or abroad.

"I Build My House on Shiftin' Sand...."

Lincoln had waited for a kind of sign, for some indication that all the blood and sacrifice of the North had hope and meaning. For long months the signs were all Confederate. Since the heady days of early summer, since the weeks when Little Mac oozed up the Virginia Peninsula to threaten the capital of treason, all portents had gone bad. Lee's quick career matched the North's woe, and when the gray hordes crossed the Potomac, doom came close for the Union. And then Antietam and an almost miraculous respite from Rebel victory—the sign at last was given. That Lee escaped annihilation might be regrettable, but enough for glory had been done. The world could see anew the North's strength and purpose. Now was the time to take from limbo the draft Preliminary Emancipation Proclamation, to issue it, and to change the nature of the war.

On September 22, 1862, Lincoln published the proclamation. At first reading it seemed an innocuous sort of political document, one couched in terms sufficiently vague for utility. If, said the Union President, states in rebellion did not lay down arms by January 1, 1863, he would then declare all slaves in rebellious areas thenceforth free. This promise to liberate slaves in Rebel hands rang hollowly to some abolitionists, who glimpsed immediately the impotency of Lincoln's plan. Many Southerners, too, jeered at Abe's idle boasting. But there were those in the North who saw the fundamental and inescapable fact of the Proclamation. The President of the United States had put his nation on record for freedom; the world would see and notice, the South would see and fear, the North would see and rejoice. With every step toward victory, abolition came closer to reality. There was now a trend to encourage the Argylls, the

Welds and Garrisons, and to redeem the promise of the Declaration of Independence.

Many in the North derided this trend, and saw another, wilder one, which might yet wreck the country. General McClellan put this fear clearly in a post-Antietam letter to one of his New York friends:

> I am very anxious to hear how you and men like you regard the recent Proclamations [*sic*] of the Presdt inaugurating servile war, emancipating the slaves, & at one stroke of the pen changing our free institutions into a despotism—for such I regard as the natural effect. . . .[21]

Northern Democrats feared the consequences of the Proclamation in Union country still sustaining slavery—in such places as Missouri, Kentucky, Maryland, and Delaware. Some doubted the constitutionality of an Executive edict which changed the social structure of the country.[22]

Among Southerners were many who also doubted the constitutionality of the proclamation, and who held it final proof of Lincoln's perfidy. All his pre-election and preinauguration pledges to the contrary were now proved lies; he was an abolitionist in abolitionist guise.[23] Others in the South knew instantly the finality of Lincoln's move. Whatever the war's conclusion, slavery would have to go. If the North prevailed, go it would by victory's fiat; if the South triumphed, go it would by evolution. The Duke of Argyll's faith in "the irresistible tendency of events" toward abolition was justified.

In the South were many, too, who saw only the "horror" of the thing Lincoln had done. His proclamation was not a charter of humanity but a license to crime. Northern confiscation acts, those odious laws that wiped out whole segments of Rebel property, already jeopardized slaves, but Lincoln's document did more than that—it raised servile insurrection to the level of war, made anyone who helped slave uprisings an ally of the Union.[24] Streets of the South might run with Haiti's awful gore. When word of freedom—Jubilo, in Negro parlance—spread across Dixie, how many slaves would remain loyal, how many would revolt? Thousands of Southern white men were in the army; at home, wives and sisters, mothers, many dauntless Southern ladies, relied on faithful Negroes to sustain plantations, farms, and homes. Alone and unprotected, the women of the South might fall victim to the vilest vengeance ever wrung from war.

There was rhetoric to this feeling, of course, a conscious appeal to the horror of the world, but there was sincerity, too, a sincerity carried for generations in Southern thought. Beneath the Southern conscience ran the fear of black terror; visions of white women falling prey to unfettered blacks, of murderous bands roaming and burning, were a part of the South's inheritance.[25] This is not to say that there was no trust, no genuine bond between white and black; there was love and honor and respect, a bond to defy reason, to grow from some strange partnership in fate. Where that bond existed it was strong and met the test of war and temptation.

But fear ran even in the fondest hearts. The idea of emancipation raised horrid specters of unchecked insurrection. So the idea produced a certain distrust of Southern Negroes—a distrust that reduced the usefulness of one of the South's great manpower sources and so hurt the war effort.

And the Confederate war effort was damaged, too, by emancipation's effect abroad. Lincoln had achieved a change in the nature of the war.

World opinion counted heavily in the South. President Davis and his Secretary of State, Judah P. Benjamin, understood clearly the impact abroad of emancipation, did their best through Hotze's *Index* and Southern friends to counteract its effect, and failed. There was a good chance that attempts to negate emancipation's effects behind the Confederate lines might also fail.

An old slave song seemed to describe the South's dilemma:

> I build my house on shiftin' sand,
> De first wind come he blow him down.[26]

Now came emancipation, the first wind blowing.

Cold-Water Christmas

A melancholy gaiety hung over Confederate festivities during late December 1862. In cities and the larger towns something of the old hospitality could be seen. Parties, galas, "hops" were common, all enlivened by the presence of Rebel troops on leave. Southern belles doffed briefly the homespun cottons patriotism had forced upon them; there was a welcome respite from revolutionary austerity. Where good food could be produced, it was, along with such spirits as survived from peacetime or filtered the blockade. But menus mostly were thin, cellars almost bare. Despite the optimism of the season, two war years worked a drabness across the South impossible to hide.

Survival had become about the whole of life. War industries burgeoning in every large community provided jobs and attracted hordes. But the quick industrialization of an agrarian society, the hasty expansion of every governmental level, added new dimensions to inflation. Rising price levels hurt everyone's buying power, especially the salaried groups, and dimmed the glitter of hospitality. High prices directly affected Christmas.

Richmond more than any other Rebel city suffered the vagaries of prices. Part of the problem stemmed from numbers of citizens, of troops, and especially of refugees. These tragic nomads of the Virginia war zone came to the capital in search of shelter and work. Work they could find aplenty in government offices and shops; shelter was another matter. Hotels, rooming houses, and private residences were soon filled and space evaporated. Outlying communities took Richmond's overload and became commuter suburbs. But Richmond remained the food source for its satellite towns. By deep winter 1862 warehouses and stores counted scant inventories, and with scarcity came privation. Some people said that food, luxuries even, could be had by those with money. There may have been some truth to this rumor.

Mary Chesnut, indomitable sybarite, left all household buying to a resourceful servant and did well.

> Lawrence [she wrote] has simple ideas, but effective. "You give me the money, I'll find everything you want. . . . There ain't nothing to eat in Richmond, not a bit of it; but you give me the money."[27]

Poorer folk fared poorly. People with incomes adequate in 1860 now teetered near to starvation. Consider some comparative costs.

In 1860 Richmonders bought thirty pounds of flour for $1.50; in December 1862 they paid $3.75 for the same amount. Four pounds of coffee two years before sold for fifty cents; now the price was $20. Soap brought ten cents per pound in 1860 and now brought $1. Tea, never a vital necessity before the war, had cost only fifty cents per half pound; now that same half pound went for $8.[28] The list could be extended in every area of human consumption, and the comparison tells a hard truth: scarcity and inflation had come in earnest.[29]

But optimism frequently can offset privation, and optimism ran high that Christmas season. Shabby gowns and raveled shirts and fraying coats of gray set new tones of style and taste. Beauty burnished shab and bravery banished tatters. The joy of the season would have been complete save for one annoying scarcity: spirits. Southerners, accustomed as they were to generous libations, viewed with disdain the petty attention of commissary and quartermaster functionaries to barley, corn, and all other grains. Bulk breadstuffs had seemed always uneconomical in the cotton kingdom; everyone preferred liquidity of assets. Now, though, pious preachments could be heard about saving oats and wheat for hard rations. And this was hard indeed, especially when rationed distillations were given to hospitals.[30] At a time of merrymaking enforced teetotaling parched humors and whetted angers. How low had come a Southland without whiskey? What chance for graceful leisure now remained? How could Christmas be properly observed?

There was an awful simplicity in the answer: with water. "Coldwater" parties were suddenly the rage. Around punch bowls brimming with this newfound delicacy Confederates wallowed in fellowship, cheer, and a certain sober satisfaction. Even in refined Charleston, that bastion of society, the craze caught on and enlivened an otherwise "dull" Christmas. "I gave a grand party Xmas night," one dapper Carolina gentleman reported, "on 'cold water' and it answered admirably. We danced until 2 o'clock. There were plenty of young ladies in town. . . ."[31] Water and young ladies— what, after all, could whiskey add?

As with all wartime Christmases, the spirit of the season reflected the course of the contest. Good news buoyed the South and soothed the pangs of want. Despite Lee's drawn fight at Sharpsburg, his army had recruited handsomely and almost wrecked the reconstituted Army of the Potomac at Fredericksburg, Virginia, on December 13, 1862. On that long, red day for the North, General Ambrose Burnside watched in mounting horror as his blue lines sallied up from the Rappahannock banks, stormed against Jackson's and Longstreet's fronts, stalled, bled, and recoiled—and when at last the slaughter ended 12,500 bluecoats lay dead or dying on the field. Costs to Lee were comparatively light and the fruits of victory were important: the Virginia front was stable once again.

No less heartening news came from the west. And in the somber wake of Bragg's dismal Tennessee and Kentucky campaign, good news from his theater brought great relief. It seemed that there was in that area of war at least one Rebel soldier capable of the sort of derring-do to snatch profit from loss. This new gallant was a recent comer to the Confederacy's pantheon of greats, a bearded, sad-eyed horse soldier who rode with a kind of rakish confidence and longed to hurt the enemy. He was John Hunt Morgan, perhaps the finest independent commander in the western army—with the exception of another newcomer, Nathan Bedford Forrest.

True and honest Southern heroes ran pretty much to pattern. Straight from Walter Scott romances, they were bold, tough soldiers with a flair, but gentle, too, with courtly care for ladies. Morgan proved no exception. In mid-December, as General William ("Rosy") Rosecrans gathered his army near Nashville and made menacing probes toward Bragg's camps at Murfreesboro, Morgan issued invitations to a wedding. His charming fiancée, Martha Ready, had consented to marry him before he departed on one of the hardest campaigns assigned a trooper, and he intended that the nuptials be well remembered. They were. The guest list alone ensured remembrance. First, on that December Sunday—Morgan's lucky day—came the President, visiting Bragg's army on a "swing around the Confederacy"; then Braxton Bragg, immaculate in gray tunic with the gold swirls of a full general; then such lesser luminaries as General William J. Hardee and the former vice-president of the United States, General John C. Breckinridge. Once this glittering company gathered at the Ready home in Murfreesboro, the minister prepared to officiate, and he, too, was a Rebel general: the Right Reverend Leonidas Polk, Episcopal Bishop of Louisiana. While the rites were read, Morgan's men thronged outside for a look at the general's lady. Sentimental tunes were played by regimental bands. It was a wedding and a spectacle for a disappearing age.[32]

In keeping with romantic tradition, Morgan tarried briefly with his wife and then led his brigade for the heart of the enemy's country. His idyl had every poignant ingredient; his assignment had real danger. Just below Louisville, near Muldraugh's Hill on the Louisville and Nashville main track, were two trestles, each about five hundred feet long and one hundred high. Burn them, Bragg told Morgan, and Rosecrans's supply line would be severed for most of the winter. It had to be done, and on December 22 Morgan began the campaign known as the "Christmas Raid." Northward rode his men, into Kentucky; they skirmished and fought at Green's Chapel, Bacon Creek, and Elizabethtown; on December 28 the trestles were reached, their defenders beaten, and the spans burned. Fittingly enough, Morgan escaped and wrote a new page in American folklore. Songs and mother's threats celebrated the raid. A poem caught the fright it caused:

> Morgan, Morgan, the raider, and Morgan's
> terrible men,
> With Bowie knives and pistols are galloping
> up the glen.[33]

The raid was daring, brilliant, effective, and a dash foolhardy—and when Morgan tried the same thing again in Ohio during June and July 1863, his luck ran out.[34]

Nathan Bedford Forrest was the man of constant luck. An unlikely Great Captain, untutored in much save direct English, unlearned in martial matters, Forrest suffered no prejudices or certainties about war. Reputed to have once put his military theory in a pithy sentence—"get there first with the most"—he had a superior grasp of logistics and terrain and the knack of command. Tall and almost wispy-looking, Forrest had a practiced horseman's grace of movement, and his wild hair, heavy brows, and hollow cheeks lent a fierceness to his patriotism. In that hard winter of 1862 he was still making his fame, and when the year ended, it was made. While Morgan raced to burn his trestles, Forrest received orders from Bragg to range into western Tennessee and clog the supply lines of another Yankee army threatening Vicksburg and the whole left flank of the Confederacy—an army commanded by General U. S. Grant.

Forrest did his duty better than Bragg could have hoped. By December 19, 1862, Forrest's command had reached Grant's main rail supply line at Jackson, Tennessee. By Christmas Day his troopers had worked their way northward almost to Columbus, Kentucky; they tore up track and burned bridges, trestles, shops, and stations in the most thorough destruction of a railroad during the war. The line north from Jackson was a complete ruin. And when the task was done, Forrest fought his way back to Bragg. In tandem with Earl Van Dorn's dashing attack on Grant's base at Holly Springs,[35] Mississippi, Forrest's venture finished Grant's overland approach to Vicksburg. The only threat remaining to the Confederacy's middle-western frontier was Rosecrans's hungry army. On Friday, the day after Christmas, Rosecrans put that threat in motion toward Bragg's camps at Murfreesboro.

As battles go, the encounter at Murfreesboro between Bragg's Army of Tennessee and Rosecrans's Army of the Cumberland ranks as one of the bloodiest ever. The forces were of almost equal strength, Bragg's a bit the smaller; they engaged on the last day of the year, and the day went to Bragg. So hot the fight, so terrible the carnage, so full the measure of Rebel success that Bragg believed the New Year would dawn on the greatest Southern victory of the war.

New Year's dawn came to a quiet field, to the hostile armies resting in lines of battle. Morning of January 2, 1863, revealed no change, and Bragg decided that day to end speculation and confirm success. Breckinridge's men attacked the Union left late in the day, swept to the crest of a hill where they were supposed to halt, but rushed on beyond safety in the excitement of victory. A thunderous, roaring volley from hidden Federal guns withered the exposed Confederate ranks, stalled them, and finally drove them back. Night found enemies in old positions, still waiting for decision. All through January 3 the armies waited, each hurt and licking wounds, unable to attack. That night Bragg took his own decision and retreated thirty-five miles to winter quarters near Tullahoma, Tennessee.

Bragg gave up the field, so technically he lost. But Rosecrans could not press an advantage. So badly had Bragg's men hurt the Army of the Cumberland that it lay inert for six months. No stalemate ever took such toll in men. Of 37,000 engaged, the Rebels lost 10,000; of 44,000 engaged, the Federals lost 13,000.[36]

There was this consolation for the Southern New Year: Bragg had blunted the last Yankee threat and propped the central border; Lee held firm in Virginia, and the Yankees were still at bay.

How comforting this peculiar consolation? What hope could be wrung from the past six months, months that offered such a glittering chance for independence when Lee invaded Maryland and Bragg thrust through Tennessee? All the high expectations faded as early victories were followed by new disasters. Southern realists understood the chilling portents of drawn battles, of military stalemates. Inflation, dwindling resources, and exhaustible manpower set limits to attrition. Once again on the defensive, how long could the South stave off those limits? Would Jefferson Davis's new nation know another Christmas?

CHAPTER SIX

A Look over Jordan

"Congress Shall Have Power . . ."

Pressure reveals the flaws in nations and societies. War, the fiercest pressure, found the rents in a Confederacy scarcely knit, reworked a way of life already in decay, and imposed at last a strange and alien modernity. These changes began with secession and by 1863 were deep and harsh. No man saw them in clearer focus than the President of the Confederate States.

His snuggery window looked out on a world vastly changed, a world gone from lazy Southern grace to hectic patterns of industrialism. Close in view was Richmond, grimy with a war effort, bulging with a transient populace, sober with a tension of survival. Beyond Richmond's confines was a country yoked in desperate cause and suffering. Cities were newly powerful,. all filled with soldiers, civil servants, profiteers, businessmen, and a migrant flotsam from combat zones. In the back country, in smaller towns and hamlets, a forlorn society of boys, older men, and Negro slaves did much of the nation's work. Out from the hamlets, out in the heart of the South, life had altered drastically. On the plantations and farms a kind of matriarchy prevailed, with women working in fields with slaves, tending the shops and keeping accounts. A few able-bodied men remained, spawn of the hated twenty-slave law (which exempted one white man—owner or overseer—for every twenty slaves), and these became the symbol of a dangerous and spreading slogan: "This is a Rich Man's War and poor Man's Fight."[1]

A look at rural life seemed to confirm the slogan. Families of soldiers, especially families of enlisted men, felt the hard pinch of inflation. By 1863 an infantryman's $11 a month would scarcely feed two people for one day. Where crops were poor or harvesters absent, starvation stalked the country.

Even the wealthy knew privation, for the South suffered far more than inflation. An imbalance of distribution, special shortages, and artificial markets all combined to drain away necessities. Salt, for instance, could not be had in some areas for any price. It was an absurd, almost laughable, shortage. Everyone had salt; it was a part of life. What would life be without it, especially in the sunny, humid South? How could meat be preserved for storage or shipment? These questions told the urgency of the matter and dictated an almost fanatical search for every saline source in the Confederacy. Speculators and profiteers grabbed much of the total salt output off the market, created artificial scarcity, and drove prices up. States gradually took over salt wells and licks within their borders and established a kind of rationing. Any salt lick or spring became a national treasure. The great wells at Saltville, Virginia, the fabulous works on Lake Bisteneau, Louisiana, were seen as leases on life.[2]

Salt is but one example of a general commodity shortage. Almost everything was scarce everywhere in the South. Food should have been abundant in an agricultural country, but droughts and army scavengers almost brought famine. Clothes became expensive beyond common reach, since the army consumed most of the production from the big mills in North Carolina and lesser ones across the land.[3] And so the old arts of carding, spinning, and weaving took renewed vigor.

Leather, essential for cavalry and artillery accouterments, for army footgear, and for wagon harness everywhere, became a critical war necessity. The leather supply dwindled in proportion to herds of hogs, cattle, and horses.[4] This dearth drove up the price of civilian boots and shoes and made home cobbling respectable.

Nothing hit the civilian population more harshly than the shortage of medicine. Yankees put medicine on the contraband list. Anesthetics, bandages, splints, surgeon's instruments, anything to advance healing, was to be denied the South. The army suffered cruelly enough, but people at home were simply forgotten. Everything went to army doctors and hospitals, and civilians struggled almost unaided against diphtheria, the poxes, measles, flux, ague, or yellow fever. Some city folk enjoyed formal medical attention, albeit with scant medication; rural folk did their best with home remedies. In mid-1863 the Surgeon General's office published for public and army use a unique herbal giving recipes for many domestic and Indian remedies. Dr. Francis P. Porcher's *Resources of the Southern Fields and Forests* (1863) offered substitutes for essential medicines (even for coffee!) and gave health to thousands otherwise doomed.[5]

Porcher's efforts reflected a trend. He found medicines where there were none. As 1863 wore on, Confederates found substitutes for virtually every need, even for men in the ranks. Where traditional foods were scarce, new weeds and berries were cooked and tasted and found nourishing. Where clothes were rags, Osnaburg sacks and gray homespun became milady's fashions. Where leather could not be had, multiple layers of cotton cloth stitched together and soaked in linseed oil served instead. When shoes faded from the memories of the Rebel infantry, the Quartermaster General devised the supreme hoax of the war: wooden-soled, canvas-topped brogans, said to have satisfied everyone but the wearers.[6] Such massive legerdemain shows healthy national morale; people capable of turning sacrifice to substance are devoted to their cause.

In a new year of contest, it was essential that Southern devotion increase, for the enemy showed no sign of weakening. Southern magic must continue until sham became reality and resources evolved from nothing.

Jefferson Davis had some doubts about magic. The changes he could see in his country gave him small comfort. Southern genius at seeming, at making something from nothing, would fail when, at last, everything was gone. What could gallantry, devotion, and selfless courage win when the soldiers all were dead?

Conservation became Davis's constant worry, conservation of money, resources, men, even of the Southern spirit. He worked earnestly to include methods of hoarding every kind of strength in his war plan for the Confederacy: witness national strategy, conscription, concern for military and naval innovations (ironclads and commerce raiders), and the parsimonious national budget. Now that the war had begun sobering the vain and winnowing the foolish, the time seemed right for a change in tempo. Congressmen and Senators were drifting into Richmond through early January 1863 for the opening of the Permanent Congress's third session. Fresh from the "grass roots," full of the public view of war and privation, the members might be ready to do some of the unpopular things needed for victory. At least the President could point the way and hope for cooperation.

A good deal depended on executive leadership, for Congress lacked outstanding leaders of its own—with the sordid exception of Henry S. Foote of Mississippi and Tennessee, who championed good causes for bad reasons and whose raucous voice rose in anger constantly in the House. Thomas S. Bocock, Virginian and House Speaker, had a popular following in the membership but lacked a convincing manner. His fellow representatives were mostly men of substance, often of high legal capacity, but few rated statesman's rank.

Senators, by definition deliberative, freighted with wisdom, and ever responsible, presented impressive fronts and scarcely more. Vice-President Alexander H. Stephens, who presided over the solons with increasing infrequency, lurked in Georgia as a churlish critic, and left the chair to Virginia's distinguished Robert Mercer Taliaferro Hunter.[7] As president pro tempore, Hunter showed commendable impartiality, even skill, in parliamentary management, but left leadership to others. And there were precious few others with depth for the task. Among the more distinguished Senators were Alabama's William Yancey, Georgia's Benjamin Hill, Louisiana's Thomas Semmes, South Carolina's Robert Barnwell, and Texas's special firebrand, Louis Wigfall. All bore high honors and good repute, were able and loyal in fashions peculiar to them, and shared an important debility—powerful personalities. Members of both houses brandished their own prejudices and demands with typical Southern zeal.

The new Congress convened on January 12, 1863. There were brains and hearts and courage in abundance when the halls were filled—all ingredients for greatness. But ingredients alone were not enough. They needed to be mixed by a master hand into a society of power. Was the President strong enough?

Despite Sharpsburgs, Perryvilles, Elkhorns, despite even Joe Browns, Henry Footes, and Edward Pollards, a policy of conservation had made good Gladstone's boast: Jefferson Davis had made a nation. The Confederacy was more truly his creation than many guessed; his spirit compelled it, his devotion gave it purpose. He built his country largely by changing himself, by making himself think, believe, and do things alien to his nature. None of it was easy for a deeply private person. There was no respite for a symbol. All the horrors of war focused somehow on the President. Calmness, an essential in his make-up, vanished with crisis; there came instead a pervading tension that stretched tender nerves, made endless agony of neuralgia and a shambles of digestion, and forged finally an awesome self-control. Davis forced himself to think nationally, to cajole factious governors, flatter silly Congressmen, endure ignorant critics, to find dignity in service. He was ready for the congressional session.

Since returning from his trip to the west, Davis had lavished many hours on an address to the lawmakers. This time there was a difference in the way he wrote. He sought cabinet advice on certain points, but the writing was his own. Freed from deadening consensus, Davis in his finest address talked to Congress plainly and with force.[8]

Davis gave due space to history, and the South's record for the last two years rang proudly in his opening paragraphs. But history was a lasting teacher. No more would the South believe foreign proclamations of neutrality or assume honor among diplomats. Intervention had been expected and been denied. Craven self-interest marked international relations; self-interest would dictate future Confederate diplomacy. Now realities of war dictated that the South expect no foreign assistance. Rebels must fight alone. It would not be easy. The enemy showed a desperate change in temper with Lincoln's emancipation program and Butler's odious "Woman Order," which branded New Orleans ladies who showed disrespect for United States troops as "women of the town." Confederates must meet desperation with patience and strength.

Three essentials, then, formed the heart of the President's legislative program for 1863: money through stringent tax laws; men through better organization of the army and better management of conscription and exemption; supplies through impressment. Success or failure of the program was squarely up to Congress. "The fate of the Confederacy," Davis told the members, "especially devolves on you . . . to sustain in the people a just confidence in the Government of their choice."

Legislators have a natural fear of radical change, and caution shaped early debate on the President's proposals. In the House, bickering grew bitter, petty, and frequently irrelevant.[9] But there was progress. Senators proved more responsible than their insecure brethren, and did the real business of the session.

Congressmen offered various financial plans, all aimed at curbing inflation and all bad. No matter the rising clamor for sound monetary measures, no matter the chilling effect of soaring prices and eroding currency, representatives still rummaged in illusions for salvation. Three fundaments in the Confederate economy set standards of value: land, cotton, and slaves. These, especially land and slaves, comprised the real wealth of the South. Sound legislation would levy hard on all three, especially on the profits of the planters. Planters would object, and they were powers in the electorate—which meant that every other source of money must be sought before planters felt the burden. Congressmen looked elsewhere in a kind of cowardice.

By April Congress had written a great, cumbersome tax law that spilled across endless pages, levied boldly on personal salaries, incomes, and profits, exacted a surcharge on occupations, and contained a unique provision for a tithe tax in kind on agricultural products.[10] At first glance the law seemed effective—bulk often brings reverence—but closer scrutiny showed it weak, temporizing, and slanted to soothe planters. Land, slaves, and cotton were virtually untaxed.[11]

Davis tried for a stronger law, but Congress balked. The tax law of 1863 failed finally in the onrush of inflation, in the strangle of commerce, the dwindle of confidence. There would be a tardy lesson in the failure.

Elsewhere Congress showed more courage. Both houses faced the scarcity and maldistribution of supplies with uncommon force. All deplored starvation in the ranks, and on March 26 Congress passed an "Act to Regulate Impressments."[12] The law was popular, and public acceptance ensured its success. That fact should have convinced even the most timid of Congressmen that Confederates had fortitude. Impressment of private property—livestock, produce, machinery, cotton, tobacco, sugar, wagons, myriad equipments— touched the tenderest nerve of state-righters, yet objections were mild. People submitted to impressment as they did to conscription because the necessity was clear. There were objections, but they reflected resentment against emergency commandeering—the informal, unregulated, and often spurious impressment by often spurious army supply officers. The new law made the odious practice subject to national standards of appraisal and compensation. The impressment act pointed to a possible path for war legislation: if Congress set strict balance between public needs and private rights, the people would submit.

Conscription was another proof of the point. Certain problems in the draft had been faced during the last session of Congress. The initial levy on the white male population, although reasonably well received by the people, had failed to produce expected reinforcements. Reasons were obscure, but obviously the coexistence of volunteering branded draftees as laggards at least, and the system of substitutes put the rich beyond the burdens of patriotism. At any rate, forced enrollment had done scarcely more than preserve the twelve months' regiments.[13] In September Congress faced reality and did what had to be done; on the 27th, the second draft law went into effect. Men between thirty-five and forty-five were made eligible and substitutions in that age group were canceled. This last proviso brought loud protests from those who employed stand-ins; cries of breached contracts rang in courts throughout the land. A few state-rights jurists held the drafting of principals (those who had purchased substitutes) unconstitutional, but for the most part the courts held that there was nothing in the supreme law of the land to prevent the government from impairing contracts.[14]

Nothing about conscription proved more irritating to the people than the iniquitous system of exemption, a system which lost the armies whole classes of professional, clerical, skilled, and semiskilled men. Complaints of fraud multiplied and raucous anger at the "twenty-slave" exemption clause mounted. Governors raised fierce objection to the numbers of state officials dragged from "essential" jobs. Obviously the entire system needed overhauling.

Shortly after the January 1863 session began, Congressmen took up the matter of recruiting reforms. There were various suggestions, but all met sullen resentment. After weeks of wrangling, Congress passed a new exemption law in May. On the surface it "satisfied" many objections. The twenty-slave clause was repealed, all state officials classed as essential by governors were made untouchable, and the President received wide authority to exempt men in areas already hard hit by the draft. Closer reading of the law shows it a poor compromise with crisis. On farms or plantations owned by minors, the feeble-minded, women alone, or soldiers in the field, one exemption still was allowed for every twenty slaves. Few in the insurrection-conscious Confederacy denied the need for slave policing; provision for patrols and protection of isolated farms was essential. With most able-bodied white men off in the armies, slaves at home were virtually untethered. Special watches seemed necessary, although events proved the loyalty of most Negroes to their masters. But Congress blundered badly in the new law by referring to twenty slaves and by apparently offering overseer exemptions for sale. "For every person exempted [on farms or plantations] . . . there shall be paid annually into the public treasury, by the owners of such slaves, the sum of five hundred dollars."[15]

After all the words and anger lavished on draft reform the country expected more than relaxed exemptions. Beyond the insulated halls of Congress, Confederates understood the price of liberty. What fear robbed lawmakers of the courage common to the country?

It was a question that cut to the heart of the war effort. Good men sat in the Congress, men of sufficient wisdom for managing a war. They were well advised now; the President had shed his own timidity

in power and offered skillful leadership. Energy, devotion, and
sacrifice abounded in the nation—the people could do the deeds of
victory. Congress had simply to do its duty bravely and the country
would respond. But there seemed to be some chemistry in Congress
that made the whole lesser than its parts. It was perhaps predictable,
for there is always caution in consensus, but it was tragic and it
marked a path to ruin.

Satrapy à Trois

Mountains ringed it, the Tennessee River ran by it on the west,
the town itself struggled mightily to live up to its location. By
appearances Chattanooga looked to be one of the most vital cities in
the Confederacy. A case could be made for holding on to it at all
costs—its strategical and logistical possibilities were unmatched.

No one doubted the import of the place in the dawn of a new
year, a year complicated by steady erosion of Southern positions
west of the Appalachians, a general dissolution checked finally by
the desperate gambles of Bragg. Now Chattanooga was more than a
town of opportunity; it was a frontier. Better suited to its traditional
role as a hub of Southern commerce, it sat now on the rim of the
Confederacy, a gateway to North or South.

The wide Tennessee River had a deceptive depth and current, was
navigable from the Ohio almost to Knoxville, and lay open to the
side with the most ships. Confederate vessels, nascent ironclads, in-
congruous cottonclads, small steamers, and skiffs had plied the
Tennessee and taken trips to the forts and stations which earlier
formed Albert Sidney Johnston's outer lines. These assorted boats
were gone now, along with the forts and stations they had served.
Along the snaking channels of the river came the iron monitors of
the Federal Navy, which made possible combined activities of armies
and fleets, even in the heartland of the South.

Chattanooga covered the heartland, or exposed it. From the foot-
hills of the Appalachians to the Mississippi, and from the Gulf to
Tennessee, lay a vast span of land essential to the Confederacy.
Much of it ranged hilly, sometimes breaking up to small mountains;
much, too, was the rolling, rich farmland that for years had yielded
a bounty of cotton; some, in Alabama especially, had the coarse

redness of mineral dirt and promised iron, copper, other precious metals. A part of this great basin had no value save history. Here were men and resources to sustain the country if Virginia and the rest of the northern borderland was lost. This heartland might last until the enemy simply wasted and stopped.

But if the Yankees broke through the mountains near Chattanooga, then the heartland would open to capture. As long as Chattanooga remained Confederate, the best, most usable passes were safe, and invasion of the Deep South remained speculation. To defend the city, Bragg's Army of Tennessee pitched winter camps nearby.

Some Southerners had doubts of the Army of Tennessee. No other Rebel army had so long a scroll of ignominy, no other nursed memories of so many moments of near victory. It was an army cursed with bad luck, bad weather, and bad generals. If analogies are useful, it was the South's match for the Army of the Potomac.

There are, sometimes, armies that lose but go on against the enemy, their own doubts, their leaders, until they wear out such words as victory and defeat, and fashion a new glossary of bravery. So it was with the Army of Tennessee. Defeat had made the army tough. Lose it might, but its will was sound.[16]

The army needed a new commander. Bragg might be an extraordinary organizer, adept at the exact chess game of war, but he was no leader. There was no life in him to inspire hope for life in others—but instead some aura of falseness, some scent of doom soon coming. The men wanted him gone. It was a deep-seated want, spilling upward from companies to regiments and brigades, to divisions and corps, hanging darkly in the air over headquarters.

Word of discontent had started after Perryville and finally reached Richmond and the President. Lapsing faith in a field commander boded ill for the future, and Jefferson Davis put the condition of the Army of Tennessee high on the agenda for his western swing late in 1862. He had visited Chattanooga, glimpsed the general morale of the ranks, went to the wedding of Miss Ready and General Morgan, and considered the state of things. Appearances were good, as was likely to be the case, for Bragg tolerated no sloven in his camps. Satisfied, the President quit the army and left the general in command. On the heels of the visit had come Murfreesboro and new degradation. Would Bragg have to go after all?

This question was one facet of a huge problem bothering the President—the problem of the west. There were those in Congress, especially representatives of Trans-Mississippi states, who felt Jefferson Davis paid scant attention to the situation west of the river, who felt that his soul and mind were occupied with northern Virginia.[17] This is a difficult charge to refute, for much of the President's concern did go to Virginia. Reasons were obvious and hardly needed justification.

None could doubt his quickening concern with western matters when he approved the great combined offensive in the late summer of 1862. And his eye had remained fixed westward even after Bragg's Kentucky venture fizzled. This new awareness seems largely the doing of Secretary of War George Randolph, grandson of Thomas Jefferson. Randolph, a Virginian, had a refreshing breadth of vision on the war. He had some field experience as commander of the Richmond Howitzers, and shortly after he assumed the difficult role of Davis's alter ego in the War Office, Randolph began a careful campaign of western emphasis. In October 1862 he felt confident that the President now fully appreciated the need for coordination of military effort in the area between the Ozarks and the Appalachians. Because he was sure of his ground he issued orders to General Theophilus Holmes to bring his army east of the Mississippi for combined operations with Bragg. Sound as the order was, Davis balked at it, decided that it infringed his constitutional prerogatives as commander in chief, and suspended its execution. With that suspension he cost himself Randolph's astute services—the Secretary refused to continue in the role of errand clerk.[18]

Randolph's going did not relieve western pressures on the President. Randolph's permanent successor in the War Department was also a Virginian, who inherited and continued Randolph's advocacy of western importance. James A. Seddon, law graduate of the University of Virginia, former Congressman, adviser of John Calhoun, lacked a quality of energy, but behind his rheumy confusion he had steely nerve and unswerving devotion to the cause. And he possessed one rare ingredient, a good ear. In the frequent cabinet meetings—

those tests of auditory endurance—he would absorb great freshets of words with courteous calm and when the verbiage halted would make cogent and persuasive argument.

He assumed office on November 22, 1862, at a difficult moment when the President watched fascinated as Congress faced the issues of survival. Just at this moment solidarity in the administration was essential to bolster presidential influence in the capital. Seddon was in a dealing position; in return for accepting the War Portfolio, he doubtless received some concessions. He certainly won a reciprocal presidential ear. And into that ear Seddon steadily preached the value of the west.

Davis had already adopted the sound departmental command system and also devised a blend of army and geographical commands which had produced spectacular success in Virginia, where Lee commanded the department as well as the Army of Northern Virginia. The President thought a simple enlargement of the geographical scheme should suffice in the west.

But Seddon was extending a pet project of Randolph's that might produce one of the most intrepid innovations of the war: a new concept of high command. With martial vision surprising in a sedentary man, he realized that the war had grown beyond old methods, even beyond the newer ideas of geographical command.[19] Davis, too, recognized the challenge and together with Seddon worked out the Confederate response. A deputy war leader was needed in the west, a military man of experience adequate to broad authority. Such a man would take charge of the Confederacy's heartland and rule it as a personal satrapy.

There were multiple possibilities in the theater command scheme. If the commander rose to his opportunity he could coordinate operations of all Confederate forces within his domain and all logistical efforts on land and water, and could insinuate his authority into state and local politics to the advantage of the army. It was a great idea, one that showed the President and the War Department capable of original contributions to military theory.

There was, however, one imponderable to the theater system— the commander. Everything depended on having the right man in control of the new Department of the West. And the right man would be hard to find. How many generals were qualified for the most important assignment of the war?

Robert E. Lee stood at the top of the list, but he could hardly be spared from his army. Bragg was marred by defeat. P. G. T. Beauregard, the first Rebel hero, might be the man, but he had found a niche for the moment in Charleston; he loved the city and its people, was loved in return, and was defending it handsomely. By careful management of land and naval forces, by his own brand of bluff, Beauregard kept a besieging fleet and army at bay. So competent men were already engaged, all save one, and he was the one lurking always in Seddon's mind as the ideal candidate.

By every external, Joseph E. Johnston (almost recovered from his Seven Pines wounds) was marvelously suited to the Department of the West. Although a Virginian, he had the whole war in view, and urged always the need to combine scattered Rebel forces at decisive points. No one in the South was an abler advocate of combination, cooperation, and coordination. As commander of the Department of the West he could use his considerable strategic skill in countering Yankee plans to chip away segments of the South.

Davis had some doubts about him. Competent and fiery he might be, but was he a winner? In Johnston's case that question immediately became tangled in qualification and semantics. The answer depended on the quality of victory. If outright, smashing repulse of the enemy was the issue, then the answer was clearly no. If bafflement and confusion in the enemy ranks was the measure, or defense done so deftly as to be offense, the answer was clearly yes. A general is often measured by another question: will he fight? Many thought Johnston would shirk committing his men to battle, but they were wrong. Old Joe, as his men called him, would fight when he had properly set the odds.

Davis had qualms—and so, possibly, did Johnston. Yet the offer was made and accepted, and the General journeyed westward to Chattanooga to assume his post.[20] His first task concerned the Army of Tennessee. The President wondered about the army's morale, thought Johnston should inspect the camps, report on Bragg's fitness to retain command, and if necessary, take charge himself. This was a perfectly logical initial task for the theater commander, but it nettled General Johnston. He could not escape the feeling that he had been sent to spy on friend Bragg, and this seemed somehow to compromise a soldier's honor. When direct orders to relieve Bragg came, he found a way to evade them—Mrs. Bragg became ill, and could not leave Chattanooga. So Bragg kept his army.[21]

There were overtones to this episode that must have worried Secretary Seddon. Did Johnston really understand the true freedom of his choices? Did he grasp the fact that everything happening in his department was his responsibility and hence his direct concern? If so, how could he quibble about taking command of an army which was already in his charge?

Soon there were other questions raised by deeds of the new commander. He made a lengthy survey of his satrapy, found it contained three armies—Bragg's, John Pemberton's in Mississippi, and Simon Buckner's at Mobile—plus numerous small organizations, and that its logistical support systems were complicated by external lines of communication, weak railroads, poor highways, and captious state supply officers. Obviously, coordination of effort in the midst of such chaos was hopeless. Presumably Johnston was expected to coordinate the operations of Bragg's and Pemberton's armies, but he reported this to be impossible. "Pemberton's troops are farther from Bragg's than Lee's are," he wrote in March 1863, and added, "It takes about six days now to come from Jackson to Chattanooga, four from Richmond. But to move troops, so long a time is required that any emergency for which they might be needed would certainly have passed long before their arrival."[22]

Something more sinister than logistics worked against the President's military viceroy in the west—competition. Bragg and Pemberton both commanded armies in the new theater; army commanders had an autonomy akin to kings, and they would hardly yield it to a mere department coordinator. Johnston believed fervently in the sanctity of armies and assumed the inferiority of any general not directly leading troops. Because he did, he totally missed the point of his job and wasted its chances.

Shuttling around his vast acreage, he moved brigades and divisions from Tennessee to Mississippi and back, tended to details of food and munitions and clothing, and watched as Bragg fought at Murfreesboro and Pemberton stalled Sherman at Chickasaw Bluffs in late December 1862. As theater commander his presence with either army in action would have been expected, but he stayed away. His rationalization was good: had he been with either army he would have embarrassed its general and risked the confusion of dual command.[23] A general's job is to lead troops. That was why he so envied Bragg and Pemberton and felt them the real commanders in the west—they led armies and he led nothing. He put this sentiment in a revealing confession to his friend Louis Wigfall: "I should much prefer the *command* of fifty men."[24]

This feeling left Johnston at some disadvantage in dealing with his supposed subordinates. Bragg and Pemberton he treated as equals, never ordered or directed them, merely suggested and hinted. This meant that Davis's scheme for western coordination went awry. The new theater idea produced confusion, wrangling, and general dissatisfaction. Was the system workable?

Davis kept faith in his plan but lost faith in his general. Why had Old Joe failed his opportunity? Perhaps because the chance came too late, when his vision was fixed, his daring worn; perhaps because he distrusted Davis and so could never quite believe his power. Happily for him he never knew the awful dimensions of his failure, nor did he know the supreme irony of his life—that fame was almost thrust upon him.

He continued in his self-imposed role of observer, or "inspector general," until summer. He would find himself later, when the glory time was gone. At the end, in the war's final grinding down, he would be magnificent and history would remember.

"Kirbysmithdom"

Rumors about the hard life on the western frontier looked to be pretty accurate. An arid flatness broken by an occasional mesquite, a stray arroyo, some forlorn cactus, this was the lay of the land from Matamoros in the Mexican State of Nuevo Leon to Brownsville, Texas. Flat as the country seemed, the road was rough and Lieutenant Colonel Arthur James Lyon Fremantle, H.M. Coldstream Guards, felt it sharply in a light buggy.

This unlikely traveler had recently arrived in Mexico by Royal

Mail packet and worked his way into Texas. Evidence of war was everywhere; irregular troops rode hither and yon, and every man in sight carried a six-shooter which Fremantle happily discovered "it is very seldom necessary to use."[25] The wilderness of land and people were disquieting enough. Not long after taking the road northward from the Rio Grande, Fremantle got his first look at a lynching—or the remains of a lynching. The victim "had been slightly buried, but his head and arms were above the ground, his arms tied together, the rope still around his neck, but part of it still dangling from quite a small mesquite tree. Dogs or wolves had probably scraped the earth from the body, and there was no flesh on the bones." Such violence would have daunted many, but not sightseer Fremantle. He had a flair for places and a knack for people —all kinds: plain, rough, great—and a grace that made him welcome. He liked the Confederates who greeted him, accepted their oddly assorted uniforms, and found "nothing ridiculous or contemptible in the appearance of these men, who all looked thoroughly like 'business.' " One starlit evening Fremantle shared fire and supper with a regiment of Texas Rangers. It was an odd interlude for a British officer—the fire, the circle of dusty men—an interlude touched with some strange kinship of nature. When the fire lowered and the food was gone and pipes were smoking, the rangers moved the visitor deeply with "God Save the Queen!"

There seemed to be a good deal of singing in Texas. Even elegant General John Bankhead Magruder, Confederate commander in the state, tried his voice with his staff; it happened the evening Fremantle met the general. There were other cherished memories of that meeting. It was April 1863, and Magruder basked in the fame of liberating Galveston and capturing the U.S.S. *Harriet Lane* in January. He had a glittering and convivial entourage, including beautiful damsels, and everyone accepted the visiting guardsman as friend. And the general proved a useful friend; letters from the Texas commander opened many doors for Fremantle, ensured that at least the first phase of his trans-Confederacy trek would be comfortable.

Comforts were scarce in the west. Fremantle noted the rising food prices and showed proper shock in San Antonio when told coffee brought $7 a pound. Clothing had all but vanished from sale, and Texans were now a homespun lot. Hotel space was scant, and beds, to Fremantle's revulsion, were always double-sold—a circumstance that taught him how to sleep fully clothed and booted.

Everywhere there were hard marks of war. Cities and towns were populous but drab. San Antonio had been obviously on the way to prosperity before the fighting started, but now this ancient settlement looked forlorn. "Trade," noted Fremantle, "is now almost at a complete standstill." Stagnation forced the manager of the famous Menger Hotel, host to such as Robert Lee, J. E. B. Stuart, and David Crockett, to ponder the wisdom of closing.[26] Houston struck the English tourist as "a much better place than I expected," largely because of animation. But a scant fifty miles to the South was harsh evidence of combat.

Galveston, which was fascinating to Fremantle because of its recent recapture by Magruder and his minions, offered a pleasing view at first glance. Wide, straight, shady streets were in handsome contrast to the dusty traces of most Texas towns; well-built, stately houses showed the inroads of comfort—and yet decay was here and growing. "The city was now desolate, blockaded, and under military law. Most of the houses were empty, and bore many marks of the ill-directed fire of the Federal ships. . . ."[27] Once a thriving port, Galveston was now a place of troops, guns, and forts; the broad bayfront looked out on hostile cruisers.[28] Fremantle found Galveston's garrison-like atmosphere uncommon.

Despite war's drabness, Fremantle noted the bubbling hospitality of Texans; people were outgoing, friendly, eager to have news from an unblockaded world. These, of course, were Western folk, and everyone knew they were heroic braggarts and liars. Tales of martial exploits by Texans could scarcely be matched. Some of them claimed that a mere handful (no more than forty), had checked an entire Federal invasion fleet at Sabine Pass, Texas, in January, disabled several ships attempting to put men ashore, and repulsed a large landing party. It was a stand worthy of Thermopylae, the Alamo even, to hear Texans tell it, and it prevented occupation. Oddly enough the story was true. Forty-five Texas troops under Oscar Watkins and Dick Dowling did hold a scruffy sand fort at the mouth of the Sabine and stand off a Yankee invasion fleet. If anyone doubted it, there was a congressional resolution of thanks on record.[29]

As the Queen's soldier journeyed northeastward from the Gulf coast toward Louisiana and a crossing of the Mississippi, evidence of the enemy increased. In Texas the slaves scarcely knew of emancipation and ignored it when they did hear the news; in western Louisiana, though, masters fled Federal incursions to escape roaming Yankee "liberators" who confiscated slaves as contraband. Stories were told of faithful retainers decamping to Federal asylum, horror stories that pronounced sentence on a way of life.[30]

A wash of refugees from western Louisiana crowded into Texas as Federal raids increased along the Mississippi. With these uprooted came a great unrest and disintegration. And as Fremantle trekked eastward toward the river, he saw evidence of strain in all conditions of travel. From Houston he sampled Texas trains (one class), stage lines (thin springs), and survived in moderate spirits a constant diet of bacon, corn bread, buttermilk, or some gagging substitute for coffee. By the time he reached Shreveport, Louisiana, none could beat him at snatching corner seats and first helpings.

That city, swollen to some 3,000 people, sprawled along the Red River in budding discomfort. Sudden elevation to prominence had ended an old and easy languor. A brief stay encouraged Fremantle to seek a quick crossing of the Mississippi. Such a venture was dangerous and required conniving, careful timing of Yankee gunboat patrols, and immoderate luck, but Fremantle's luck was good and on May 11, 1863, he crossed safely.

So the perceptive English traveler was gone from the west into the heart of the Confederacy and the glamor area of the war. In the eastern theaters of conflict decisive things were happening; afar in the western sector raw ragamuffins played at soldiers and had no audience to care.

There were, however, vital things to be learned in the Trans-Mississippi, for in that sprawling vastness came the first hints of how the war would end.

Western troubles began with the first skirmishes of the war. They were far advanced by the late months of 1862 when Jefferson Davis agreed to a new western command structure. The stimulus came from many frightened citizens and politicians of the states apparently forgotten across the river. Steadily Yankee power had increased in the lower Mississippi area, naval units had proliferated, small raiding parties harassed the country along tributary streams in east and west Louisiana as far north as Natchez—by the beginning of 1863, the Mississippi was almost a Federal highway. All that was left to the Rebels was a hundred-mile stretch of the river between Vicksburg and Port Hudson, and even that segment suffered increasing incursions from gunboats.[31]

Left to itself, the Trans-Mississippi west would simply drift away. Some kind of remote control had to be exercised to keep this vast domain in the war. Western advocates in the Confederate Congress suggested different schemes, but most agreed on a basic requirement: a semiautonomous area under unified control.[32]

The President was receptive to the suggestions of Western Congressmen and spokesmen for the Indian nations. Already persuaded to surrender much military authority to General Johnston, he easily accepted the need to create another satrapy for another general. So urgent were problems in the area across the Mississippi, though, that Davis decided on a radical administrative rearrangement. As contact with the west was virtually impossible, Davis sent representatives of the War, Treasury, and Post Office Departments to erect a shadow government in the Trans-Mississippi region. He tried to assure unity of purpose among the Confederate and state civil officers and the myriad military leaders by assigning General Edmund Kirby Smith as supercommander of everything west of the river. With luck these special arrangements could weld the country together and prevent disaster.[33]

Luck was running poorly for the South. By the time Kirby Smith took charge of his domain in February 1863, long neglect had created chaos beyond one man's repair and patterns of disarray were entrenched. Evidence was on every hand: Sibley's fruitless expedition and Van Dorn's disaster at Elkhorn in early 1862 worked a pervasive demoralization in the troops of the new department; good order and discipline became quaint phrases and a mockery in practice; distance contributed to fragmented martial organization and raised a formidable barrier to any corrective measures; isolated posts, stations, divisions, and regiments boasted an aggresisve self-sufficiency.

This aggressive independence could not be blamed on anybody. It was a reaction to apparent indifference in Richmond. When repeated calls for help brought no response from the central government, Western states had been forced to fight their own war. Texas, for instance, sought to solve its military problems through a State Military Board and to protect its exposed Indian and Mexican frontiers with the Texas Frontier Regiment.[34] Arkansas, threatened with invasion on two sides, became increasingly chary with manpower and finally opposed removal of its troops.[35] Indian Territory lapsed into a vicious sort of intertribal civil war. In short, the strengths and resources of the section were siphoned away in a self-defeating cycle of local responses to local problems, and the Western Confederacy virtually stopped contributing to the South's war effort.[36]

Few things could have helped the Yankees more than this disarray in the west. Federal operations remained unified, and pressure on the Gulf coast, in northern Arkansas, and along the Mississippi increased as Southern cohesion declined. As enemy incursions multiplied, Western resentment of Richmond's inattention smoldered. Occasionally the President had sent a new commander across the Mississippi but never any reinforcements. And for each general bestowed on them, Westerners were expected to send regiments and more to help Virginia.

And now, at a crisis time along the Mississippi, when Grant and Sherman along the river and Rosecrans in Tennessee were threatening to cut the South in twain, Davis resorted to the traditional sop: one general came West. True, Kirby Smith rated several cuts above the mediocrities that had come before him—he was a hero of First Manassas and of the Battle of Richmond, Kentucky— but he came alone. More irritating still was the fact that he came with great pretensions and limitless paper power.

Like all his predecessors, those castaways from fame, Kirby Smith had no appreciation of his place and situation. His staff officers were mostly men from the east whose longings stayed behind them. General and entourage had no understanding of the people they were to save, no grasp of the way the war had gone with them, no feel for the ground. That things were vastly awry in this "other Confederacy" its protectors had to learn.[37]

There was, for instance, the question of law. Never the most law-abiding section of the old Union, the west was now torn by brigandage. In places where local authority still counted, laws were respected, but the respect faded with distance. Everywhere a kind of irreverence was paid to Confederate statutes, especially the conscription laws. Impressment and war taxes met resentment from people who felt forgotten. Some laws were simply ignored. War profits were legitimate where combat came rarely, hence certain criminal statutes were in abeyance. Since fortunes were involved in the Mexican cotton trade, regulation restricting cotton acreage did not apply. There was an obvious corollary: public cotton was private business.[38]

If General Kirby Smith was shocked by the condition of his command he concealed it well. Soon it became apparent that he was a perceptive man who would bend to reality, yet he was no weakling.

Reforms reflecting the General's concern for military efficiency went into effect all across the Trans-Mississippi. He consolidated the scattered western departments into one, then subdivided it into districts, each with a commander of his choice.

Texas, his strongest state, he put in charge of popular "Prince John" Magruder. Flamboyant, gregarious, theatrical Magruder might be, but he had certain compensations—loyalty and a willingness to fight. His earlier lapses in Virginia, which damned him to the fringes of fame, were erased at Galveston, where, recapturing the city and taking the *Harriet Lane,* he showed the dash and valor that won him his sobriquet.

Indian Territory was a mess. Stand Watie, the Cherokee brigadier, commanded a good brigade and had the confidence of his people. But the other nations distrusted him and would resist his control of the entire district. One man seemed able to hold Indian loyalty and instill order in the Territory: General Samuel Bell Maxey, a Texan with a sound service record. He took the job.[39]

Arkansas posed special problems. General Theophilus Holmes held doddering sway in the state. Resistance to change was his weakness, but it endeared him to many Arkansans who feared the future. Holmes, for the moment, stayed.[40]

No general in his senses would want command in western Louisiana. Federals raided along the Mississippi, up every tributary, every bayou; bands of blue pillagers roamed the plantation country and scourged it with fire. They met little organized opposition. Men were scarce here, most of them gone to the eastern Rebel armies. Old men, boys, a few stray state militia units made feeble resistance. Confederates were increasingly unpopular in the district; whoever got the command must be a kind of zealot, a man to snatch energy from weariness and loyalty from lethargy. Richard Taylor, Louisianian, hero of Stonewall Jackson's valley campaign, seemed to be the obvious choice. Familiar with the land and people, he had won new friends with harassing operations against the Federals near New Orleans. Kirby Smith hesitated, for Taylor's fame, family connections, and assertiveness might make him a rival. In the absence of any other likely candidate, Taylor received the assignment.[41]

His command structure reorganized, Kirby Smith set about building an army. First he had to discover exactly what manpower was available—and this proved impossible. Existing units kept casual records; formal returns were sporadic, unreliable, based largely on hopes instead of facts. At best guess there were possibly 50,000 Confederate soldiers in the Trans-Mississippi Department. Most of these were organized into cavalry units, since marching seemed peculiarly unsuited to Westerners.[42] A few infantry divisions could be found, some of them extremely good. Artillery units were scarce; some batteries were strong in men and cannon, some woefully weak, others figments of the imagination. Men, horses, and guns had been strewn around the west according to whims of various commanders.

Kirby Smith met the problem of army reorganization with energy. Conscription officers fanned into the whole department; camps of instruction sprang up near the larger cities; drilling and artillery practice began. And many sacrosanct cavalry companies, so long the preserve of caste and privilege, were dismounted; the men went into the infantry, the horses to artillery or supply service.[43] A growing army demanded increasing supplies. Old logistical arrangements were too small, and new channels of procurement and distribution had to be created. In any plan of logistics money was the first essential. But treasury agents in the Trans-Mississippi—civilians sent from the East, and others appointed by Kirby Smith—proved amazingly inept. Currency raced from the presses at a rate to shame Eastern printeries—and no one counted the total. Reams of notes wafted around the west, and for a time an area chronically short of money basked in affluence.[44] Soon prices rose to match inflation and the public's confidence waned. Some solid medium must be found to prop the economy. Kirby Smith and his financial advisers profited from Eastern errors: they recognized that cotton was the surest Rebel wealth. Private stocks were tapped to provide public bales for shipment to Mexico. Once there, the cotton was exchanged for commodities and army supplies, which filtered into Texas commercial channels and lent some confidence to consumers. It was a sound move and it might have pointed the way to salvation for the national economy. But in the end it failed, because of competition between multiple government agencies, profiteering, speculation, and thievery, and when it failed it ruined a last chance to win the people's faith. Sadly for the Trans-Mississippi Department, failure came before the full fruits of the cotton-purchasing system were realized.[45]

Confederate officials at Shreveport did not rely wholly on Mexico for money or supplies. Kirby Smith recognized early the advantage of sending agents to Cuba, the British West Indies, and to Europe, armed with cotton certificates and ready to compete with Yankee traders and other Rebel purchasers. Competition between Southern procurers would drive prices up, shorten tempers, and defeat any over-all logistical plan; but the Trans-Mississippi apparently had already been dropped from national plans and had to fend for itself. Precedents, too many of them, could be cited for direct action in Kirbysmithdom. Many states owned blockade runners that ran regular schedules to the Islands, took out state cotton, and brought in state supplies. This annoyed the Quartermaster General, the Chief of Ordnance, the Commissary General, even the Secretary of War, but the business flourished.[46]

While efforts at external supply continued, attention focused on domestic production in the larger towns of Texas and Arkansas. San Antonio boasted a long martial history; there a substantial arsenal had made guns for years; there, too, quartermaster and commissary officers had developed systems of purchase and transportation. This old Spanish city would be an adequate base depot for most of central, west, and south Texas. Little Rock, too, had an arsenal, not in such good repair or so well equipped, but important to the armament of Confederate Arkansans. Fort Smith traditionally supplied Old Army expeditions journeying into the Indian country, and its system of procurement continued. North Texas, southern Arkansas, and western Louisiana were supplied from Shreveport and Marshall, Texas. Much materiel went up to Jefferson, Texas, and filtered from there into north Texas and Indian Territory.[47]

As a general pattern of logistics evolved, questions of special supply multiplied. Where could guns, small arms, and ammunition be found? These were basic needs beyond the magic of makeshift; lead, powder, and metal could scarcely be conjured. For a time ordnance officers snatched lead from southern Missouri, some from Arkansas; army authorities encouraged powder mills of all sorts virtually anywhere; iron, copper, and much saltpeter came from Europe to Matamoros, Mexico, and on into Texas. Arsenals were enlarged and new shops established to convert raw materials into finished munitions. The Tyler, Texas, Armory, specializing in Rebel copies of the Enfield, ranked among the best in the Confederacy.[48]

Dry goods were provided by careful scavenging and by putting state prisoners to work as textile hands. Medicines remained a constant bane, but attempts at manufacturing were partly successful. Arkadelphia, Arkansas, developed a large Confederate Medical Laboratory, notable for a heroic blue mass, a strangely diluted castor oil, and resourceful, amorous pharmacists.[49]

Logistics in the Trans-Mississippi developed into nimble, hand-to-mouth efficiency. But Western supply officers were no more able than their eastern counterparts to build stockpiles; everything went to immediate consumption.[50] And in the end, of course, there was not enough of anything. Yet it is true that troops in Texas and Arkansas, even in ravaged West Louisiana, ate better, looked better, and fared better longer than their confreres in the east.

Better conditions should have ensured an effective war role for Kirby Smith's men, and there is no doubt that shortly after his arrival, Smith did achieve impressive improvements. Morale rose, recruiting increased, the flow of supplies to military and civilian markets quickened; military administration took on new smartness; even civil affairs assumed a kind of hopeful confusion. All of which pleased the general's people and inspired the government in Richmond to hope that as chaos faded the west might send troops and supplies to the eastern armies.[51]

Troops and supplies were not sent. The men enrolled by conscription, the munitions bought and fabricated, the sacrifices of all the westerners were not put to any constructive use. There were hints of this languorous trend as early as the summer of 1863. As Grant's threats to Vicksburg mounted, President Davis, Secretary Seddon, and General Johnston all called on Kirby Smith for help. Vicksburg's safety was as vital to Kirby Smith as to the President, but while the general acknowledged his duty, he argued his inability to help.

Later, when order and some discipline returned to Kirbysmithdom, greater assistance would surely come for the hard-pressed armies under Johnston and Lee. Assistance did not come later. A few peripheral operations along the river, one or two isolated and feeble attempts at harassing maurauding Yankee raiders, were the best the west could do in the way of grand war. Yet when it came to self-defense, Smith's forces gave a good account of themselves. When General Nathaniel Banks launched an invasion of Louisiana in April 1864, Confederate troops concentrated rapidly, met him at Mansfield, Louisiana, and in the major battle fought west of the river wrecked his expedition. Properly inspired, the Army of the Trans-Mississippi could match the best in the east.[52]

What was wrong in the land beyond the river? A good deal. Far removed from hard war, the Trans-Mississippi seemed likely to avoid the full reaches of ruin. In this favored circumstance fortunes might be made in trading cotton with Confederates and Yankees alike. All things balanced, the Trans-Mississippi could hardly afford to help the Confederacy.

Such cynical self-seeking characterized a minority of westerners, but they were vocal and blessed with Kirby Smith's tacit support. Struggle as he might, he yielded at last to western nationalism and became a sort of benevolent despot concerned more with the safety of his subjects than the welfare of his country. And why not? Close association made him a Trans-Mississippian, gave him the values and prejudices of his flock. In due course he was fully converted to a different patriotism in which victory was survival.

What happened to Kirby Smith and his department cast a shadow over the whole Confederacy. A social dry rot cut through the west, eroded will power, sloughed morals and values, brought confusion and a fading faith in the future. People and institutions were worn, tarnished, and strained.

If this slow decay worked eastward, how long before the end?

God's Consequences

She was a lovely, golden-haired pixie with shining eyes and a loving smile—and she had a special status at Headquarters, Second Corps, Army of Northern Virginia, because of her good friend, Stonewall Jackson. Their friendship amused the general's staff; he had obviously fallen for Jeanie Corbin. Almost every afternoon, when army work ended for a while, she would come from the Corbin plantation house to Jackson's little "office" in the yard and sit at his feet to listen or to watch him cut out long regiments of paper soldiers. No other six-year-old Southern girl had so talented a friend as General Stonewall. She loved him. Jackson loved her. Almost the age of his own beloved and lamented daughter, Jeanie brought light and life to winter camps. Little things fascinated her: small stories he remembered, a glittering bit of gilt on the cap J. E. B. Stuart had given him, the paper soldiers she called her "army." Sweet, trusting, and innocent Jeanie made war remote.

Winter added to the sense of peace. Jackson's men were in quarters near the old Fredericksburg battlefield; the rest of Lee's army camped farther up the Rappahannock. Food and fuel were chronically scarce, shoes and clothes and blankets worth fortunes, but spirits ran high. Snowball fights raged between different units, card games passed evening hours, and young men had no time to worry. Such tedium was left to the officers.[53]

Officers worried a good deal, especially generals. Hunger and cold and ennui were deadly enemies that weakened men and filled hospitals. Brigade, division, and corps commanders spent long hours seeking bare necessities of field life. Jackson paid special attention to supply details. Weak men were weak fighters; stamina came with physical strength. Sadly enough, his concern and that of Lee himself produced barely enough food for short rations. All of middle Virginia apparently had been drained of animals and grain; even grass for the cavalry was scant. Those hardy Rebels who survived the Fredericksburg winter learned the horrors of Valley Forge.[54]

Comforts aside, the army's general situation was good. After smashing Burnside's assaults at Fredericksburg in December 1862, Lee's army remained near the town to guard the routes to Richmond. Its presence guaranteed the capital's security, for the Army of Northern Virginia had become the world's most renowned fighting force. Proof could be glimpsed at Lee's modest headquarters. Itinerant officers from far corners of the globe descended on the newest genius of the art of war. Even the enemy conceded Lee's greatness, and that fact lent special impact to his army.

So did the fame of his immediate subordinates. James Longstreet, who led the First Corps, earned distinction for steadiness in action and for baffling stolidity. He had also earned the admiration of his men.[55]

Stonewall Jackson, Second Corps commander, ranked a world hero almost equal to Lee. Swift marches, smashing blows, stubborn defense, matchless sense of battle, these were Jackson's hallmarks. Scarcely anyone knew him save his wife, Mary Anna, and little Jeanie, but he commanded the worship of his men. Few soldiers have the magic of making men more than themselves; Jackson did.

Everyone now had a snatch of knowledge about the army led by this daring trinity. Lee's dauntless scarecrows were bravery's hope against fate.

When winter broke, fate began to close in on some of Lee's men. Spring came, signs of it, in March; rains soaked the roads, drenched the somber forests, and took away the last rimes of frost. Always in central Virginia spring is spectacular. Green comes swiftly to grass and shrubs, skies clear, expectation charges the air.

Spring of 1863 brought new expectations to the Rappahannock Valley. Across the cold river on the northern slopes above Fredericksburg, Federal camps began breaking. The great Army of the Potomac stirred from hibernation and made ready to try its new commander, Joseph Hooker. Rebels knew little of the cocky general called "Fighting Joe." Rumors had him a reckless boaster bloated with ambition but combative and courageous. All expected him to lead his fresh ranks to battle and to defeat.

With the first let-up of the cold, Stonewall Jackson broke up housekeeping in the Corbin yard and moved headquarters closer to his front. Command seemed easier from a tent in the field. He found the Second Corps spoiling for war. Ranks were nicely full, ammunition was plentiful, and clothing, shoes, and rations were almost adequate. All the omens looked good. And then, on a blustery March day, came heartbreak. A courier rode to the general's tent and told him Jeanie Corbin was dead—she had caught cold and went swiftly. Her death cut harshly through the preparations for slaughter; it turned General Stonewall's thoughts to a Christian's small mortality.

Early in the morning of April 29, Federal cannon boomed along the Rappahannock, hordes of bluecoats milled on the Falmouth heights. Hooker opened the spring campaign. Momentary puzzlement about his plans faded with news from cavalry scouts: heavy Yankee columns were snaking upriver, apparently bent on crossing somewhere beyond Lee's left flank. The best ford would take the bluecoats into an area known as the Virginia Wilderness. Part of the Army of Northern Virginia must march swiftly to check Hooker there, in woodland that would crowd his troops and turn numbers into losses. As expected, the assignment went to Jackson's Second Corps. Quickly Stonewall's veterans took the road. They had an easy, shambling gait born of hard experience, and they covered ground. Behind them a force stayed to hold the Fredericksburg lines should Hooker's river march be a ruse.

After quick marching, Jackson's vanguard took position at the edge of the Wilderness and watched the road leading from the forest to Fredericksburg and Richmond. But Hooker delayed, his men mired in the river crossing, then clustered in confusion as the brush and the trees closed around them. The chance was too good to miss; Jackson decided to probe into the Wilderness and fight Hooker while he was still caught in a maze. The move had prompt rewards.

Unnerved in strange terrain, Hooker dug in—and lost the initiative to Lee and Jackson. No sooner did Lee learn of Hooker's hesitation than he brought most of the rest of his army to the Wilderness and pinned the Yankees firmly in their hasty works.

Delay in the Yankee front would cost the Confederates their advantage, and Lee looked anxiously for a route to Hooker's rear. The plan working in his mind had little theory to sustain it. He intended to divide the smaller Confederate Army—60,000 against 130,000— hold the Federals pinned with part of it, and send the rest around behind them. If Hooker suddenly doffed his fears and struck at either segment of Lee's army, awesome defeat might befall the South. But Lee gauged his enemy with deadly insight. There were flaws in Hooker's character made worse by dense and sodden woods. He would cower rather than attack. Everything depended on finding a road behind the Federals; given such a road, the Army of the Potomac would be caught in a Rebel vise and squeezed into extinction or routed shamefully back across the Rappahannock.

There was such a road. A trace, not marked on most maps, was found by Jackson's wizardly Topographical Engineer, Jed Hotchkiss. Promptly Lee called Jackson to a fateful conference in the Wilderness. Could he take the Second Corps—more than two-thirds of the Rebels on the field—work around Hooker, and attack before the rest of the army was ruined? Yes. The order was given. On May 2, 1863, properly before dawn, as suited Stonewall Jackson, his corps began its greatest march, and his last.

All day the men toiled on a miry track, often they were certainly seen, but steadily onward they marched. No alarm or harassment hindered them, and at last, almost ten hours and fifteen miles later, they deployed to the right rear of Hooker's army. The Rebel line was long, stretching far on either side of the pike leading through the hamlet of Chancellorsville, and the ranks were double, treble in places. Afternoon weather that May was warm, the march made everyone weary. But when the bugle rang the charge late in the day all the fatigue was gone. Screeching their blood-chilling Rebel yell they began advancing through the underbrush. Slowly at first, as skirmishers ran ahead, then momentum built and they began to run, fire sporadically, race at the low log works in front of the Flying Dutchmen, the luckless Eleventh Federal Corps. Yankees saw them belatedly, hasty efforts to change front brought disorder, a scattering of shellbursts bloated over the onrushing Rebels. Nothing stopped them; they bunched, their banners clustering in a wave of red; they charged bayonets, screamed their way into the Union lines, carried them, and raced after the broken foe. Darkness and the confusion of success finally halted the drive. By then Hooker's army was pinched into a hairpin, the apex south, the open angle to the river. His hope lay in attacking, but he stood behind works and cannon. One final charge might cut him off from the river. Jackson decided to organize that charge.

To make sure of his ground, he rode with a small party through the moon-splotched night, on beyond his lines to a place where he could hear the enemy, their axes falling, their oaths and cries and orders. Turning his dumpy Little Sorrel he rode back toward his lines. It was pitch black on his stretch of road, men everywhere were nervous, jittery fire rattled in the night. A challenge was called and, before his answer, a volley came—and he was down, hit in a hand and an arm, victim of a Rebel picket.

Command passed hastily to A. P. Hill, who was promptly wounded, then to Robert Rodes, who had so gallantly led the first charge that afternoon. And later it went to the usually dashing trooper with flowing beard, plumed hat, and constant laughter, but Stuart now anguished with fears for his friend Stonewall.

Back to a house the general was taken, his right hand was dressed, his left arm was amputated. As word of his condition seeped across the dark woods a dread anguish oppressed the army. He was somehow more than mortal, he was a kind of greatness. God would not take him from a land so much in need. Lee put his feelings clearly: "He has lost his left arm, but I have lost my right."

Hooker was beaten, his weakened army hurled back beyond the Rappahannock. But the cost to the South was terrible. On Sunday, May 10, 1863, Stonewall Jackson roused briefly from the stupor of pneumonia, announced his happiness to die on Sunday, remembered that "Duty is Ours, Consequences are God's," called A. P. Hill to the front, ordered his quartermaster, Major Harman, to hurry up the wagons, and then saw the everlasting victory: "Let us cross over the river and rest in the shade of the trees."[56]

What he saw was joyful, but his death gave his country a look at God's consequences, and the vision was bleak and lonely.

CHAPTER SEVEN

"Oh! Wherefore Come Ye Forth, In Triumph from the North"
—MACAULAY

"Where's the Fun, the Frolicking . . . Gone! Gone!" [*Mike Fink*]

It chanced that the mythical Sut Lovingood, on one of his peregrinations, traveled with President-Elect Abraham Lincoln, and the trip made a vivid mark, if not on literature, at least on Sut. "Linkhorn" had the looks of a dodger: "His mouth, his paw, and his footses am the principal features, and his striking point is the way them-there legs of his'n gets into his body. They goes in at each edge sorta like the prongs goes into a pitch fork. Of all the durned, scary-lookin, ole cusses for a President ever I seed, he am decidedly the durndest. He looks like a yaller ladder with half the rungs knocked out." Association with so grotesque a figure bothered Sut not at all. He was fairly grotesque himself, a "nat'ral born durn'd fool," who lumbered into somber moments and reduced them to grisly comedy. Sut's crudity might offend fastidious gentry, but he was beyond insulting. A native cunning, a mountain-hewn roughness and racy style, these were his defenses against fashion. And they made him a hero to many wartime Southerners. People can identify with a confessed spoiler, a man warring against fortune and losing.[1]

George W. Harris's stories of Sut Lovingood spread across the South in the newspapers and in small books, but mostly in the telling. Much of the humor of Sut's outrages came in the telling, in the fearsome folk dialect that tied him to his mountain home. Dialects were common in the Confederacy. Soldiers from the high country showed it in a quaint, slurry language with traces of almost English measure. Those from the lowlands, from the plantation climes of the Deep South, spoke in soft, muffled words, lazy and cotton-blown. Outcountry men, the "po' whites" who raged at the world, these spoke in baffling "cracker" tongues—an exotic made-up speech of mixed words and slurs and dropped letters that barely escaped gibberish. People were products of place, and place showed in talk; so dialect was important—it fixed a man's firmament.

And because dialect had a utility of sorts, a humor built around it had compulsion. Later scholars who buried their lives in studying such matters as storytelling, those book folk would say that dialect humor was transitory, a crude stage in the making of American thought. That is as it may be to thinkers, but to the people hearing and reading the dialects, Sut's doings, the hilarious escapades of that great influencer Captain Simon Suggs, and the martial evasions of Billy Fishback were funny. All these Southern heroes were miserable, inflicted as much of the same on others as possible, and survived by luck, art, and disdain for manners. War makes cant of custom, and those who break custom may be a new breed of winners. And there is a naughty gaiety in shattering the old. Humor is like ready money; it serves its time.

Some of those later serious students of humor would say that war made Southerners happy with misery and made them see fun in agony. But students can misread things and be wrong in large ways. There are similar myths about the Old West. Remember the antics of the "alligators" and "hell roarers" of the rivers, the tremendous and undoubted deeds of Mike Fink and his friends, the particular hugeness of Davy Crockett's courage? And there were notable violences and cutting moments in the hunting and Indian-fighting escapades of such Eastern folk as Natty Bumppo and Daniel Boone.

Southerners were great on humor. They enjoyed jokes, and many were renowned yarn spinners. Most of the great taletellers—and the ranks would include that rising Westerner, Mark Twain—enlarged on absurdities, on right men in wrong places, on the good falling in with the evil, on bad fortune touching everybody else.

War affected fun. In the midst of death, humor was found in ways of escaping death, of deluding Satan's envoys, or simply in prolonging the misery of life. Many Confederate soldiers were great storytellers, some were surpassing jokers, a few ranked as humorists.

Most semipermanent camps spawned army newspapers, often handwritten, one-page sheets specializing in advertisements and jokes. Butts of these gibes were the great archetypes of armies: bad officers, mulcting quartermasters, sutlers in quest of astonishing profits. Egregious these jokes often were, the kind that rely on exaggeration for emphasis, but they reflected the mood of troops. Nothing brought a quicker laugh from a bivouac than the sarcastic cry, "Mister, here's your mule!" It was a taunt to all visiting contractors or commissaries, those desk troopers who journeyed rarely to the armies and then always well mounted. Oddly enough their sleek horses tended to wander around the camps, followed by a welter of hints as to their whereabouts. So helpful a motto deserved wide popularity, and "Mister, here's your mule" found its way to music and song.

Much camp humor was topical. One Southern satire on army life, though, transcended the Confederacy, the war, even the times, and rings fresh with every war. Charles H. Smith's *Bill Arp, So Called* has a droll irony to it that still pillories foppish officers and makes comics of regimental rascals. Arp is the protagonist, the sufferer, the "high private's" idol. He is a pawn of fate; things go directly awry whenever he arrives on the scene. Other times and other armies have had Arp's counterpart—the American GI's "Sad Sack" and "Willie and Joe," Czechoslovakia's "Good Soldier Schweik"—they are all fate's discards and they have that one essential of true comedy: a touch of pathos.

Pathos figured prominently in the stories about Sut and Johnson Jones Hooper's great Captain Suggs, as well as in the pages of the ubiquitous Arp. Sadness came to be much of Confederate life. With summer of 1863 drawing on, the casualty lists lengthened, the dirge drummed dully in town and countryside. And the long trains came with their refuse from the battlefields, with the broken humans who were useless now to Mars. Arms and legs were most commonly absent, but there were deeper wounds, unseen, that haunted eyes and hearts, wounds of the spirit, the evilest wounds, for they sloughed the good in men.

Behind the lines the South became a kind of hospital with maimed and crippled and blind everywhere. It seemed as though some terrible mutation had swept the country and changed the figure of humanity. For a brief time when the killing and wounding were new, there was repugnance at the sight of ruined friends, brothers, lovers—but there is a limitless awe in people when they meet the fruits of bravery, an awe that makes beauty out of ruin. This different vision at last affected most of the country. The rich and the well-born met reality the hardest. Gay blades who graced cotillions, rode to hounds, drank gentlemanly draughts in clubs, and paid chivalric court with verse and lyre and hand-holding, these dandies when they returned home were often scarred and partial men. Their plight had a poignance beyond suffering; gone was the shining image of the splendid young men. With the image went some measure of the South. The good and the beautiful were mortal, after all.

Sometimes suffering makes men—and women. As the maimed shambled back, ladies across Dixie shivered aside horror and learned a changing sort of love. A case to prove the point: Later in the war, after Chickamauga, General John B. Hood, "Sam" to his friends, recovered from the loss of a leg and began to circulate in Richmond society. He met and fell in love with Sally Buchanan Campbell Preston, "Buck" to her friends, and paid desperate court. He failed to win her hand, but the romance waxed hot for many gossipy months. Buck was one of the true beauties of the capital and the country, a haughty, well-connected girl who strewed swains as she went. She resisted Hood, shared her family's doubts of his lineage, shied at his disfigurement. But she was fascinated. Hood was an authentic hero, a general on the rise; his long, sad face, soulful eyes, his candor all appealed. Once, when some of her girl friends were comparing notes about their butchered lovers, Buck broke and cried a protest: "Don't waste your delicacy! Sally is going to marry a man who has lost an arm, so he is also a maimed soldier, you see; and she is proud of it. The cause glorifies such wounds. . . . Tudy has her eye on one who lost an eye!"[2]

Death and maiming and feminine sacrifice, these are heady ingredients for romance. Romance ran deep in Southern blood; this churning strain was nourished by Sir Walter Scott's glorification of chivalry in his Waverley novels, nourished, too, by the gentry's courtly manners, by strange devotion to the protocols of the *geste*. So much creatures of fancy, Southerners were incorrigible sentimentalists. They basked in sacrifice, in engulfing tragedy; they identified with martyrs and, prophetically perhaps, with lost causes. Stories of Bonnie Prince Charlie's defeat at Culloden dimmed many a Rebel eye; he rode against odds and was gallant. Gallant is an especially Southern word. It has meanings beyond definition; to the tuned ear it brings echoes of Bruce's pipes at Bannockburn, of bugle notes floating before the Light Brigade at Balaklava; it reaches brave hearts and leads them. There would be, in the end, a special poignance to this word.

While the war wracked on, gallantry counted in the Confederacy. It runs through most Southern music and lends bravado to bad meter; it shines out from countless old picture frames and sometimes makes bad paintings bearable; it is a running counterpoint in Southern verse, occasionally rising off key; but gallantry was the essence of Southern war and hence was frequently the core of Confederate art.

Before the war the South boasted some few accomplishments in artistic lines. Certain nonhumorous Southern writers were achieving national status. Charleston, South Carolina, always questing for culture, probably garnered the best literary coterie anywhere in the South. For years such hard-working writers as William Gilmore Simms, Paul Hamilton Hayne, and Henry Timrod struggled against isolation, apathy, and the amused toleration of the local sophisticates. Hayne and Timrod dabbled in versifying, a wastrel's craft, but their dabbling did produce the good though short-lived *Russell's Magazine,* a literary journal edited by Hayne. These three won increasing admiration beyond the confines of their city-state. Simms, a curious blend of artist and politician, wrote furiously in all reaches of prose. By nature a novelist, he also wrote essays, articles, and numerous reviews, and won space in the leading literary magazines of the nation. None of these Charlestonians qualified as a hack; none was yet to number with the great.[3]

War might change their status, not only personally but also artistically. War's touch on the Charleston trio worked variously. Hayne, desperately sensitive and never master of his hopes, rose slightly above himself and wrote some strong war verse.[4] Timrod, a strange, romantic, and shining mind, took anger at the North, and set the South's place in the world with two poems of lasting beauty— "The Cotton Boll" and "Ethnogenesis." Timrod found love in war, love for the Confederacy, and the melody ringing in his heart broke forth in pride. Simms, at a guess the most likely to flourish under harsh stimulation, strangled with his country's suffering; his talents quenched, he wrote little during the conflict.

Beyond Charleston were other Southern literary figures who worked throughout the war years. Among the noted novelists was John Esten Cooke of Virginia; a soldier with Lee, Cooke captured for generations of readers the joys and troubles of army life. *Surry of Eagle's Nest* (1866) and *The Wearing of the Gray* (1867) won him lasting American renown. Augusta Jane Evans Wilson, of Mobile, had earned fantastic popularity as an authoress. In 1855 she published her best-selling *Inez, A Tale of the Alamo,* and in 1859 offered a glorification of religious faith in *Beulah.* An ardent secessionist, Miss Evans became a fire-eating Confederate nationalist. Service in Southern hospitals gave her special knowledge of army horrors. She sought to give the brave graycoats some glimpse into the reasons for fighting, and in 1863, published *Macaria: or, Altars of Sacrifice.* Some felt this book a triumph of moralizing, the best sort of propaganda. Propaganda it surely was, a tome filled with boastful assertions of Southern rights, snide shafts at the abolitionist Union. *Macaria* enjoyed unique success because it was just the sort of cheerless tale to fascinate the morbid. But it was also a pillar of Confederate morale.[5]

Outlets for the Southern literary muse were few and hardly flourishing. Of these, Richmond's venerable *Southern Literary Messenger* had the best reputation. Once edited by Poe himself, the journal claimed readers—a corporal's guard—even in the North. War cut the *Messenger*'s tiny subscription list further, but did not extinguish its light until very near the end. George W. Bagby was the wartime editor; he supported President Davis and opened his columns to an important serial history of the war. The remaining space was occupied with stories, essays, and poems.[6]

Below Virginia, two journals were worthy of note: the *Southern Field and Fireside,* published in Augusta, and *De Bow's Review* of New Orleans, perhaps the most remarkable of all periodicals circulated in Dixie. *Southern Field and Fireside* catered to interest in agricultural matters and was read avidly by farmers and planters. It kept going through most of the war.[7] *De Bow's Review,* a handy statistical and general magazine of business and farming, "refugeed" to Richmond when New Orleans fell, appeared spasmodically until late 1863, and then vanished—a strange end for a project spawned by secession's greatest statistician, James Dunwoody Brownson De Bow.[8]

Heroic effort produced a few new magazines in the Confederacy, but only the popular *Southern Illustrated News* flourished to the point of expansion. Others like Joseph Addison Turner's *Countryman* struggled nobly during the war but barely eked out survival.[9]

Confederate newspapers varied in quality from excellent (Richmond's *Enquirer, Dispatch, Whig,* Charleston's *Courier,* and Augusta's *Constitutionalist*) to mediocre (Atlanta's *Southern Confederacy,* Charleston's *Mercury,* Mobile's *Register,* Houston's *Tri-Weekly Telegraph*) to treasonable propaganda sheets (Raleigh's *Standard*). Columns in the press continued the South's lively political tradition. Editors exercised their freedom of expression virtually without hindrance; some encouraged the war effort by supporting Davis's administration; others sniped at the President to the point of sedition.

Edward Pollard's *Daily Richmond Examiner* soon became a vitriolic antiadministration paper that offered comfort to Davis's enemies throughout the war. Pollard, journalist and historian, wrote bitterly about poor Southern leadership and set a lamentable precedent of disaffection. War news caught readers, and many Rebel papers provided competent battle accounts from field correspondents. The Confederate States Press Association linked the country in a telegraphic news service.

War forced many papers to "refugee" or to suspend. Those that persisted were plagued by chronic labor and material shortages. Gradually pages shrank in number and size until most dailies and weeklies sported a single folio. Advertisements proved the main source of money for the press, but as goods dwindled, so did the need to hawk wares. Subscriptions were uncertain guarantees of continuation. But Rebel newsmen matched the zeal of their Yankee brethren and kept many papers printing to the end.[10]

Like literary folk, artists suffered sharp survival pangs. Never a noted haven for painters, the South counted few and almost none of note. Those few in the Confederacy were engulfed by war and reacted as their writing brethren. Some were overwhelmed by the horrors they saw and shrank from recalling them. Others were seared by war and impelled to creation. Much of the finest work done by Confederate artists records army scenes. Adalbert Volck's political caricatures are vital historical documents. He had an easy grace of line that caught men's airs and slouches and gave them life. A few of his pencil portraits are unique—they freeze forever the face of crisis.[11] Volck pictured life behind the lines, while Louis Montgomery, a soldier in the Washington artillery, caught the angular beauty of cannon, the strange repose of gunners, the indolence of caisson teams with sure strength—and yet few knew him or his work, and he wanders on to history a fading anonym.[12]

Artists reflect their culture: Confederate artists were romantic sentimentalists, quick to catch pathos for posterity. Consider the fantastic popularity of one picture, a large, sprawling scene by Rebel artist William Washington, called "The Burial of Latane." Latane was an authentic hero, the one casualty suffered in J. E. B. Stuart's first "Ride Around McClellan"—that glorious tour of Rebel cavalry all around the Union Army on the Virginia Peninsula, June 12, 1861. The young lieutenant was, of course, gifted, well born, noble, and cut off in the fullness of promise. He was buried near Richmond in a lovely mansion yard surrounded by drooping shrubs and somber lady mourners. Even the little girl who gazed on the grave was sober and forlorn. What artist could miss the scene, tears and heartbreak, a hero's bier? This tragic moment Washington caught in classical strokes, and his painting traveled the Southland over. Copies can still be found in attics and other hiding places.

Unlike some Southern writers, Southern artists were uninspired, even by war, and their work was largely mediocre. Why? Possibly because art had no real admirers in the ante bellum South and there was no tradition to develop.

Reaction to art is a matter of taste. Southern taste setters were sparse and were usually classically trained in European mold. While most Rebel states boasted some attempt at public systems, education was fairly restricted. War broke up many colleges, even the South's famous military academies; students and faculties simply closed their doors and marched away. Secondary schools were hard hit by teacher and student ennui and by a sudden and peculiar shortage—suitable textbooks became almost unfindable. Most schoolbooks had been shipped from the North and often contained subtle abolitionist poison. Southern books by Southerners were needed, and some were written. Scattered titles illustrate the patriotism poured into little Rebels.

A *Dixie Speller* assessed war guilt simply: "If the rulers in the United States had been good Christian men, the present war would not have come upon us." A Confederate geography for primary grades talked of Yankees as "ingenious, and enterprising, and . . . noted for their tact in 'driving a bargain.' They are refined, and intelligent on all subjects but that of negro slavery, on this they are mad." Southerners, in contrast, were "High minded and courteous." The Confederacy, said the author, "is at present a sad country, but Preident [sic] Davis is a good and wise man, and many of the generals and other officcrs [sic] in the army, are pious. There are many good praying people in the land; so we may hope that our cause will prosper. 'When the righteous are in authority, the nation rejoiceth; but when the wicked bear rule the nation mourneth.' Then remember, little boys, when you are men, never to vote for a bad man to govern the country."[13] These diverting lessons left a scar on a whole generation.

Other types of Confederate amusement left scars, but hardly such lasting ones. The nature of the war and the increasing stranglement of the blockade forced a special kind of public amusement on Confederates—theatricals. Plays and musicals had always been well attended in the South; the larger towns all boasted theaters of some kind. Traveling troupes were welcomed and well patronized; visiting divas and noted artists were lionized. But taste was unpredictable. Shakespeare might draw crowds in Richmond but play to empty galleries in Raleigh, even Charleston. Audience vagaries aside, the South had a theatrical tradition and war increased demand. There is a comforting escape in mime and music, and when death stalked the land, escape became essential to life.

Many actors went North at the war's beginning, but the hardy few remaining made up in energy their lapses in craft. And they served a patriotic purpose. Along with the standard offerings of traveling and repertory companies (Greek drama and Shakespeare), timely plays by Southern authors filled most engagements. In time, Southern propaganda pieces were the featured attractions, a circumstance which should have extinguished the theater. Only the most self-sacrificing Southerner should have been able to stomach an evening of such chauvinistic offerings as John Hill Hewitt's *King Linkum the First,* Joseph Hodgson's *The Confederate Vivandiere,* J. J. Delchamps's *Great Expectations: or, Getting Promoted,* and yet audiences came and clapped and enjoyed.[14] In the late reaches of the war, when the cast of fate was clear, few questioned the quality of escape. A moment's laughter, a tear for the race, a mummer's recall of happiness, these mattered. And so Confederate players were great successes—their footlights caught at gladness and eased a country's woe. When it all was over, these nimble stage folk shifted character and adopted Uncle Tom.[15]

Perhaps the most constant diversion available to an embattled people was music. Southerners loved songs and good tunes. It was a trait accentuated in Protestant hymns and at revivals. Music meant much to the slaves of the South; chants, songs, shouts, and calls played large parts in their lives. Evenings in the "quarters" were lightened by dancing and singing. Soldiers found a kind of solace in song. Campfire groups lifted voices in remembrance of Mother, Sister, Home, in grief for lost friends, wives, and sweethearts.[16]

Music is sometimes the mirror of an era. It was for the Confederate era. The maudlin, the sentimental, the hopeful, the fearful, the for'orn, all the Southern moods were caught in Southern music. When the war was young and hopes were still high, Rebel tunes showed gaiety and certitude. Dixie's need for soldiers found first voice in song:

> Southrons, hear your country call you!
> Up! lest worse than death befall you!
>   To arms! to arms! to arms! in Dixie!
> Lo, all the beacon-fires are lighted,
> Let all hearts be now united!
>   To arms! to arms! to arms! in Dixie![17]

Dreariness and penury caught up with hope and youth. When the war was pretty much the whole of life, the people's music and verse changed:

> The homespun dress is plain, I know,
>   My hat's palmetto, too;
> But then it shows what Southern girls
>   For Southern rights will do.
> We send the bravest of our land
>   To battle with the foe,
> And we will lend a helping hand;
>   We love the South, you know![18]

As death scourged the country and casualty lists filled the newspapers, words and music rang a dirgelike mourning. In songs for the dying and the dead, Confederate music was touching. Lyrics of *The Southern Soldier Boy* caught the grief of a nation:

> Young as the youngest who donned the gray,
>   True as the truest who wore it,
> Brave as the bravest he marched away,
>   Hot tears on the cheeks of his mother lay.
> Triumphant waved our flag one day,
>   He fell in the front before it.
>
> CHORUS:
>
> A grave in the wood with grass o'ergrown,
> A grave in the heart of his mother,
> His clay in the one, lifeless and lone,
> But his memory lives in the other.[19]

Then at the final, beaten-down last, when the boys were soldiers and the veterans gone, then, when Lee gave up the war there was a last song:

> I can never forget the day Lee
>   And the soldiers had to part,
>   There was many a tear to wipe away,
>   And many a sad and weary heart.[20]

Old words and rhythms faded, drums stilled, bugles rang no more —all the music stopped. Other music came in time, and tunes were part of Southern life again. But sounds of the old world were lost, lost in a rummage of echoes.

"And I Will Bring Down Their Strength to the Earth . . ."
[Isaiah 63:6]

General John C. Pemberton had a quiet man's manners; he was dignified, cautious, a bit chilly. And he had a flaw to bother his men—he was a Pennsylvania Yankee. Not that there was disloyalty in him; his whole career attested Southern patriotism. President Davis had faith in Pemberton and sent him to the defense of Mississippi and especially of Vicksburg with confidence. By any test he justified the President's choice. He had deftly foiled Sherman's amphibious attempt to land at Chickasaw Bluffs and hence support Grant's land offensive against Vicksburg in late 1862. Grant's probe was halted at Holly Springs, Mississippi, December 20, 1862. Pemberton's great victory at Chickasaw Bluffs came on December 29.

Some Federal operations, however, had been beyond any Confederate's control. On March 8, 1863, Grant's engineers began digging a canal which, they hoped, would divert the Mississippi and leave the South's great bastion literally high and dry. Pemberton could do nothing to stop this project; the diggings were beyond the range of his formidable batteries sweeping the river.

Other things he might have done. He should have pushed cooperation with Kirbysmithdom across the river; he might have made a greater effort to work with an anguished Joe Johnston. Pemberton did neither. There was a nettle in him that chafed for glory and he had Johnston's own resentment of superiors. Sadly for the South he also had Davis's ear, and when the President made his Western tour late in 1862, a conference with Pemberton revealed that Johnston's fear of competition was justified. Read a querulous letter Pemberton sent to the President after Davis departed the army, a letter carefully calculated to fan discontent with Johnston:

> Since Genl. Johnston established his Head Qrs. in this city [Jackson, Mississippi] I have found myself virtually superseded in command of the Department, and can make no movement of troops unless with his sanction. It is true that up to this time Genl. Johnston has not prohibited any action I have proposed to take, yet in several instances our views have differed as to the propriety or necessity of such action. . . . In my recent interview with your Excellency I was impressed with the idea that it was not your intention to supersede me in the immediate command of this Dept., and I believe that I have already said enough to bring the subject to your consideration.[21]

Attitudes in war are often of final importance. Who could guess the possible tensions behind Pemberton's complaint? At some crucial moment, would resentment lead him to recklessness, even to insubordination? Probably not, but a crisis surely was building, and there would be testing of everyone's nerves.

Grant's canal proved useless, and after prodigious excavations, the whole dredging scheme was canceled.[22] Once convinced that engineers and great shovels could not supplant hard fighting, Grant took a different tack. Marching his men down the west bank of the river—the bank that Kirby Smith should have harassed constantly— he asked the navy to run Vicksburg's batteries with gunboats and troop transports. On the night of April 16 the sneaking began; ghostly black hulls slipped downriver in darkness, they were spotted, the big guns boomed, red rockets careered over the Mississippi, and the flotilla churned in a slice of hell. Damage was appallingly light; the fleet had made the trip! Grant wasted no time. Men were crossed to the eastern shore between Vicksburg and Port Hudson, and an expedition launched inland thrust its way northeastward in an attempt to cut Vicksburg off from behind.

Confederate reaction was slow; the whole scheme was fantastic and caught Pemberton off guard. He had sent some men to Port Hudson, had reduced his own strength to do it, and was painfully aware of his plight. If Grant's army of no less than 45,000 managed to straddle the railroad from Vicksburg to Jackson, Pemberton would have to make an agonizing decision—get out of the city and fight Grant inland, or hole up behind formidable entrenchments and stand siege.

Everything depended on Grant and on the speed of his campaign. He was no dawdler. Breaking his army in two, he sent one wing to hit the railroad at Edward's Depot while the other wing, under Sherman, marched on Jackson. Forced to action, Pemberton made the right move. Out of Vicksburg he came, determined to engage the enemy and thwart a siege by victory in the field. If things had worked out for him, if he could have risen above uncertainties— and, it must be said, above probable resentments—he might have been the hero of the war. But—and with good soldiers like Pemberton who elude greatness, there is always a "but"—Grant gave no time for pondering.

In a matter of weeks it became clear to Johnston that the only hope for Mississippi, for Vicksburg itself, lay in combining the tiny force he had scratched together near Jackson with Pemberton's army; with this joint force Grant's divided army might be beaten piecemeal. Johnston was right. He had the perspective of total western command and knew one chilling fact more clearly than anyone else: if Grant bottled Pemberton's men in the Vicksburg lines, chances of lifting the siege were poor. Bragg's army had already sent south all available men; cavalry was frighteningly scant in the Department of the West; most of the guns and ammunition currently on hand were stored in Vicksburg—everything dictated prevention rather than cure. Orders went from Old Joe to Pemberton, orders directing the vital junction of force. Pemberton found himself in a special torture. He knew Johnston was right, even began to ease eastward to carry out the plan, but he was hesitant and slow. Was his delay necessary or was it the result of warring with himself?

At last the President removed the agony. Vicksburg, said the Chief Executive, was indispensable, must be held at all costs, everything must be subordinated to its defense. Now Pemberton could either go back to the entrenchments or join Johnston. Either course could be construed as defending Vicksburg. But caution overrode reality, and the general stopped his eastward ooze and headed back for the city. It was a fateful decision, one that Johnston could scarcely believe. And yet it made a kind of sense. A tense and desperate President could not accept the abandonment of a last firm grasp on the river, not even for strategic reasons. Doubtless Old Joe was right in saying that Grant's army was the real objective of Confederate operations, but for this moment a symbol triumphed over sense.

Once Pemberton made his choice, the outcome could be read almost by the textbook. True, he almost ruined the symmetry of it all by losing the major battle of Champion's Hill on the return to Vicksburg. But he did get his army back, and on May 18, 1863, Grant's men snaked into positions ringing the town. The siege was on.

Sieges have a fascination for history. Troy, Acre, Carcassonne, Sevastopol, and countless others all have their page of glory. Reasons for glorification are obscure, for with rare exceptions sieges are tedious things of starvation, thirst, heroism, and defeat. Vauban, the great French engineer, devised virtually foolproof ways to break into strong points, and his lessons were certainly known to West Pointers in both North and South. Grant obviously knew the technique. He had no doubts about the task ahead of him. Vicksburg's defensive works ranked with the best ever constructed; they ringed the city from a point above it on the Mississippi, all around the land side to a point on the river below, and they were some nine miles long. Great care had been lavished in selecting the lines; they ran along ridges and high delta ground, were revetted and bastioned at turning points, had clear fields of fire improved by redans and lunettes, and were held by some 35,000 veterans with numerous heavy guns. If a quick assault failed, the siege would be long and wearing.

A quick assault on the 18th of May failed, another on the 22nd met equal slaughter, and Grant settled to business. Lines of contravallation, trenches facing Rebel works, were constructed; they were strong and well protected with bombproofs, communicating trenches, and embrasures for field guns. At the same time, Grant put some of his men to work digging lines of circumvallation, works facing behind the Federals, designed to foil efforts at siege lifting. This added precaution was rare, but Johnston lurked somewhere in Mississippi, and he was a dangerous man to have loose in the rear. Secure now front and back, Grant had no concern for the outcome—he knew.[23]

Concern lay heavy over Pemberton's headquarters, over Vicksburg's lines, over the citizens who huddled in caves along the bluffs overlooking the river. Daily bombardment ravaged the streets of the upper town, chipped away buildings, smashed homes and stores, wreaked ruin everywhere. Constant cannonading frayed nerves, banished sleep for some, eroded morale. Morale also eroded in direct ratio to the fading food supply. Vicksburg had been stocked for a two months' siege, Pemberton hoped, but consumption ran higher when nerves were torn and the siege was tight.[24] Almost nothing got into the town. This year there was no heroic little ironclad *Arkansas* to run the gantlet of the Yankee river flotilla as had happened a year before.[25]

Days became endless stretches of bleary wakefulness streaked with raids, tunneling, another assault try, and waiting—waiting for the food to go and for weakness to wilt resistance.

By the first of July Pemberton had lost hope. Johnston had been trying to gather enough men to attack Grant, distract part of his army, and let Pemberton slip out, but only 25,000 Rebels had gathered at Jackson.[26] Even with so few, Johnston was coming, told Pemberton his plans in a dispatch that never arrived, and when, at last, Johnston marched, he learned he was too late.[27] On July 4, 1863, Pemberton gave up the city. Terms were as usual with Grant, unconditional surrender. Johnston raced toward Jackson to escape the backwash.

Vicksburg cost 30,000 men, almost 45,000 stands of arms (many of them excellent, imported Enfield rifles),[28] stocks of powder, little food save the uneaten mules.[29] But figures are misleading. Much more went with the city: a last cling to the river, for alone Port Hudson was doomed; a dream of impregnability; and worst of all, a whole army. Months would pass before exchanges could bring the men back and many would never return.

Real costs were compounded of other statistics, too, statistics tabulated afar in Pennsylvania.

Stonewall Jackson's death had forced General Lee to a drastic shake-up in the command structure of his army. From the traditional two corps he created a third and put it under Jackson's old subordinate A. P. Hill. The hard-hitting Second Corps went to Stonewall's trusted lieutenant Dick Ewell. Old Pete Longstreet—that bluff, stubborn, reliable fighter with a smoldering thirst for fame—still led the tough First Corps. In the weeks after Chancellorsville the army mended from battle, refitted with the best a poor land could afford, and recruited. Manpower by now had become an acute problem. Thin ranks imposed caution on Lee's generals and on the commander himself. Casualties might not be replaceable.

These were weeks of careful thought for Lee. Well he knew the audacity demanded of the weaker side; he was determined not to waste the fruits of Chancellorsville. With the Army of the Potomac routed again and rebuilding, with Hooker's star eclipsed, the time for decisive blows had come. But how to deliver them and where? Longstreet suggested detaching some troops (perhaps his own?) to Bragg's aid in Tennessee for a thrust toward Cincinnati.[30] Rumor had it that Beauregard, the tarnished paladin, suggested reinforcing Pemberton to protect Vicksburg. Lee conceded the logic of both plans, but offered his own: Vicksburg could be aided as much by an invasion of Pennsylvania as by direct support. Up from Virginia, once more across the Potomac, the renewed and victorious Army of Northern Virginia might capture Harrisburg, Philadelphia, might put even Washington under tribute. No specter more dread could come to the North; great cities lost to the Rebels might take the heart from the Yankee war effort. Successful invasion might win European recognition. Even now a Southern friend in Parliament moved to acknowledge Confederate independence. There were so many possibilities to the plan that Lee urged it on the President.[31]

In late May all possible uses of Lee's army were discussed by the Confederate cabinet. The outcome was obvious: if Lee wanted to invade Pennsylvania, who would deny him? So it was that in June 50,000 toughened veterans crossed the Potomac at Williamsport. Lee had a gambler's streak, and he meant to stake everything on one venture. If he could maneuver the shattered foe into retreat, good; if he had to meet the foe, equally good. His gaunt gray men were winners; perhaps at their best they were invincible, for they had never failed him.

Of Lee the men had no doubts at all. Anything he asked they would do. Jackson's men had been reputed willing to charge hell itself for Stonewall; Lee's would storm the gates of heaven for Marse Robert! Pennsylvania might qualify as a kind of paradise. It was guarded by half-trained and skittish militia and seemed open to easy plucking. And if the Army of the Potomac came, the game would be more exciting. Lee's men knew they could win.

Yankees thought so, too, at least most of the men in the damned ranks of Hooker did. Their dapper general strutted still, but the stuffing had gone out of him. He lapsed to the role of organizer. Some of the men wanted McClellan back; he had stopped the Rebs before. Some wanted to go home, a few thought the war was "gone up," and a small clan thought they might stop Lee.

Lincoln faced again the dread of defeat. There was a dismal familiarity to the waiting. He tried to make his army ready by removing Hooker and putting George Gordon Meade in command. But it was altogether an uncertain move. Meade had a soldier's bearing, but was phlegmatic, had a relatively undistinguished military record in the Seminole and Mexican wars, and might not nerve up to battle. At least he was new, and the army needed something different. And he was careful, which was good. No rash moves seemed likely from him; he kept the status quo, wasted no time on shuffling subordinates. He had to learn the army, and until he did he would let it run along. While he was learning it, things caught up with him.

While Lincoln waited he received an interesting sign from the South. Alexander Stephens, an old acquaintance, wanted to come up to Washington for a talk. Word had it he carried a letter from Jeff Davis, who bridled his punctilio and signed it merely as the commander of forces opposed to the United States Army. There ought to be nothing lost in a chat, but the cabinet vetoed the meeting. It was just as well; Stephens could say nothing that the North could accept; Lincoln had no concessions for the Rebels. Talk could wait on the outcome of Lee's invasion. Lincoln might be asking a conference soon enough.[32]

A good deal of remembrance clouds the summer invasion of Pennsylvania. People later recalled omens and dreams and strange flights of birds that purported great events. Such memories are the clutter of history; they make things bigger than they were. At least it can be said that the men who marched northward with Lee had no more than usual foreboding, no more than usual hope. Discipline was rigid; Marse Robert wanted no chicken stealing or fence filching; things taken for rations would be paid for or certified. Southern troops were gentlemen.[33]

The weather cooperated and men enjoyed the march. In Yankee-land everybody had so much! Farms bulged with grain and animals and produce. Some few people were friendly, but most were angry and pouted at the invasion. Here and there children waved the Stars and Stripes, which always brought smiles and approving words from the strange skeletal men in tattered gray.

Although the army counted itself well spruced, it was a matter of definition. Some of the men marching northward needed shoes, others needed hats. Not many months before one brigade of Lee's army had 141 men unshod and 188 "nearly so."[34] It was rumored that the lack of shoes brought on the trouble. Some of A. P. Hill's men meandered toward the little hamlet of Gettysburg on July 1 in quest of footgear.[35] In Gettysburg the Rebel van ran into Federal cavalry, began skirmishing, and called for infantry, and before long a full-scale fight flared along the hills near the town. Troops pitched in on both sides; A. P. Hill's corps got into action, finally drove the Federals through Gettysburg up Cemetery Hill. By this time Ewell's corps was pretty much on hand and the moment looked good for one final assault to carry the hill and rout the Yankees.

According to many memories, a lot of men there that day thought Old Jack would have stormed the hill and won the war on the spot. Ewell was no Jackson and he took the blame for uncommon caution on July 1. A solid thrust at the high ground would have been sound tactics; there is just the chance, though, that it would have been a mistake. Fresh Federal troops are alleged to have been on top of the hill.[36]

There is a strange vagary to memories. Men in high places have greater imprecision in recall than lesser folk. Possibly the great have more to forget. At any rate generals of the South record Gettysburg so differently that it may have been a great number of battles jumbled together. Time played tricks on some of them. In places of hot fighting, time telescoped and things happened in blinding sequence. Where men waited with the ageless unrest of armies, time languished and the sun hung sullen in the sky. So time is a variable at Gettysburg.

Some things are certain. Among them the awful inconvenience of the battle to Lee and to Meade. Neither wanted the fight where it happened, again if recollection is right. Lee's reasons are clear. Jeb Stuart with most of the cavalry had galloped off on a lark toward Baltimore—Jeb had a passion for catching Federal wagons. But he was a master of reconnaissance and now he was urgently needed as the eyes of the army. Without accurate scouting information, Lee could scarcely guess Meade's concentrations. Beyond Stuart's absence was the inconvenience of the field selected by the battlers of July 1.

When Lee reached the field he found his men thronging along Seminary Ridge, a range somewhat less imposing than Cemetery Hill, but sufficient to beat back anyone foolish enough to attack. The line as it filled in was about three miles long and it curved sharply through the outskirts of Gettysburg around to the base of an eminence called Culp's Hill. The Confederate line of battle snaked south of the town and faced east. Some circumstances of deployment were difficult. Federals held the inner lines, which meant that Ewell's men on the left, in the town and on in front of Culp's Hill, could not see Longstreet's men on the extreme right. Hill's men in the center had a fine view of the field, but discovered that their part of Seminary Ridge cut back away from a direct front at the enemy. Lee's lines were imperfect and awkward.

Many in the higher echelons of the army shared Lee's irk at the position. Longstreet, who arrived later than he should have, showed no enthusiasm at all for the ground in front of his command. Great boulders were ahead, reaching up the approaches to a mound called Big Round Top that seemed to anchor the Federal left flank. To the left of that and certainly commanding the whole Yankee position was Little Round Top. Both these hills were scrubby and rough. Getting at them would be extremely difficult, especially if the boulders were staffed with sharpshooters. A survey of his front convinced Longstreet that some other spot should be found for fighting.

Later he remembered thinking seriously about other places, especially after his corps drove at Little Round Top on July 2, came close to the peak, ran into concentrated cannon fire (from hastily summoned batteries), and streamed back chastened.[37] A few remembered other fights on the second day; some had feelings of doom. Many things were out of joint. General Lee was nervous, somewhat brusque, and withdrawn.[38] The ubiquitous Colonel Fremantle, who had made it all the way to Pennsylvania, thought that Lee had done his job by getting the army to the field; the fighting was up to the generals.[39] A. P. Hill seemed in one of his funks, mad at someone, probably Lee. Hill had a running quarrel with superiors. Longstreet, usually firm and hearty, looked worried. In the ranks on the night of July 2 there was considerable disquiet. Off in the field in front of Hill nervous skirmish fire could be heard; Ewell pushed a desperate and forlorn assault on Culp's Hill that shattered the night for Gettysburg's citizens and ended in a wash of blood for his soldiers.

Sunshine. Many men noticed it on July 3, sunshine and the curious quiet of a field almost ready for battle. Lee had made up his mind. Brushing aside Longstreet's plan to flank the Federals around their left, he had fixed on smashing the Yankee center. It was a plan defying logic. Why hit the one surely untouched Union corps on the field? Why attack frontally against large numbers of guns? Confidence is part of the answer. Lee believed in his men. Necessity is another part of the answer. Stuart was around somewhere behind the enemy now, close but not yet up. It mattered where he was, for his columns would guard the army's wagon trains if the Confederates changed position.[40] And there was one overriding reason—the nature of Robert E. Lee. He had come this far; his army was at its finest pitch and gear; two indecisive days had earned nothing save casualties; no equal chance might come again; if the army went back, the North would take heart and the South quail. For the man who had said at Fredericksburg, "It is well that war is so terrible—or we should grow too fond of it,"[41] only one choice was open. Attack the Union center; force the issue now.

Men recalled their places that day—recalled, too, that Southern guns bristled everywhere in the lines (there were 142 of them[42]) and that the sun etched things sharply. It was a strange kind of day, one fragmented by small memories. Men noted again the flights of birds, some listened to a band playing in Pettigrew's brigade, many lay on the soft ground and waited as Federal shells probed the trees on Seminary Ridge, and many of them died. One, a sergeant of Company A, 14th Tennessee, could hear, years later, the things he said to himself. June Kimble was his name, his was the center regiment in Archer's brigade, and he was curious. In a lull after the bombardment that morning he walked to the fringe of the woods and looked at the place his men would go. Guns crowning the Federal hills, the little clump of trees that fixed so many an eye that day, the whole position lay shimmering far away across almost a mile of open, rolling land. There, up there, into that line of black guns behind the low stone wall, there his men would go. Kimble was scared, almost sick at the sight, and began mumbling to himself: "June Kimble, are you going to do your duty today?" And he answered, "I'll do it, so help me God."[43]

Porter Alexander of Longstreet's artillery remembered the thunderous, awesome Rebel bombardment that consumed ammunition in the early afternoon, remembered, too, being stunned when Old Pete later virtually fixed responsibility for the attack on him. Longstreet sulked in disapproval; Fremantle eagerly sought a vantage point to watch; Lee vanished from prominence; Sergeant D. B. Easley, Company H, 14th Virginia, closed files and watched for skulkers; George Pickett watched his division and some men from Hill's corps line up for a charge. Grandly mounted, Pickett talked with Longstreet during a momentary lull in noise, scratched a brief note to his fiancée, and rode to lead one of gallantry's last great gestures.[44]

The Rebels came out of the trees at about 3:15. Yankees could count the battle flags, and there were many; the formation was trim and the march began slowly to allow for distance and rising ground.

Some changes in direction were accomplished easily by the 15,000 of Pickett's charge, and the lines of battle bunched slightly. Silence. Federal gunners waited for closer range. Steadily now the Johnnies marched, lines dressed and closing. Off to the right of them some long-range cannon boomed; a few marchers fell. Across a small stream they went, through a fence, then straight up the hill toward the trees, the guns, the lurking infantry. Cadence was kept and the steady pace covered ground. Men remembered how it was on the way; to some the silence crowned the world, then it broke in a clap so awful it was more than sound, in a roar so angry it was tangible, in an endless crack of doom. Shells raked the Rebs now, cut gaps in their serried ranks; the gaps closed, the lines moved on, faster; men leaned forward against some great wind that beat at them; up the hill they went, bunching more as Yankee batteries took them in flank, ate away the outward fringes of Pickett's command, and chopped hungrily at lives. Without knowing it they were running, crouched, bayonets flashing, flags waving, and they began their Rebel yell. In musket range of the stone wall and the clump of trees they halted, some of them, to fire; took a withering volley right in the face, recoiled, went on, and carried the wall. Then the charge faded in carnage and countercharge. A handful, some thought as many as 300, rode the South's tide to its height; most of the handful died in an angle by the fated clump of trees.[45]

Back down that awful slope the rest of the grayclads fled, razed and raked and maimed again. And when at last the race was done, a scant 5,000 of Pickett's original 15,000 returned.

Memories are vivid about the aftermath. Many saw Lee at his best; he took the blame: "All this is my fault. Too bad! Too bad! Oh, too bad!" he said, as if a *mea culpa* would excuse such wholesale waste.[46] Meade wasted a chance for counterattack, and two days later Lee began the long journey back to Virginia.

Four days of July shattered the Confederacy. People read the dreary lists of dead and wounded, gasped at news of Lee's hospital train—a line of blood-spattered wagons seven miles long. Vicksburg, too, had its mourners. There were many in the country who glimpsed the impact of those four days and who tried to see a balance of profit and loss: 30,000 men lost at Vicksburg, 20,000 killed, wounded, captured at Gettysburg; 45,000 arms lost at Vicksburg, 25,000 at Gettysburg—along with the oddments that strew battlefields. Against such losses what balance could be struck? Vicksburg gone and with it all sure contact with Kirbysmithdom; Gettysburg lost and "Lee's Miserables" turned back to Virginia. The only balance was woe. Lee offered to resign; the President said he had no general he trusted more, and Marse Robert kept his army.[47]

People fond of rhetorical questions might ask if July's first days marked the beginning of the end. A dazed Confederate government had no time for such grim speculation. The only issue was survival and assessment. How had such disaster happened? Was something wrong with the army, the administration? Had human frailty brought the South so low? Frailty, of course, there was, human and materiel. Defeats were partly caused by pettiness in high places, personal quirks, but more by obvious deficiencies in manpower, supplies, and transportation. Could a ravaged land provide replacements?

"Firmness Does Better Than Concession with the Americans. . . ."
[Lord Lyons]

He looked like a great rascal, had a high forehead, flowing locks, and dark, snapping eyes that gazed sharply at the world above a rogue's mustache. For years he languished as a member of the United States Lighthouse Board, but he went South with the war and accepted a naval commission from Jefferson Davis. All some men need for greatness is a chance, and Raphael Semmes was such a man. Confederates all glowed with pride at his exploits in the little *Sumter,* and when he commanded a larger, swifter vessel, they expected miracles. They got them. In July 1862 he assumed command of a rakish, trim ship built in England and known cryptically by her ways number, *290.* Since Victoria's Foreign Enlistment Act forbade construction of warships for belligerents,[48] Southern agents in England contracted for "merchant vessels." It was a known fact that Captain James D. Bulloch, Confederate States Navy, was busy placing such orders in Britain and Scotland.[49] Yankee diplomats knew his ulterior designs but were pressed to prove their suspicions. They almost succeeded with the mysterious *290* taking shape in the huge

Laird yards near Liverpool. But before the facts were all gathered, *290* slipped from her ways, ostensibly on a shakedown cruise. She never came back.[50]

A modern vessel, *290* sported both steam and sail and made quickly for the Azores, where she received a naval crew, armament, a new name, and a new captain. Man and vessel were equal to each other.[51]

Deeds done by Semmes with the C.S.S. *Alabama* were world renowned. In two years of constant cruising, the *Alabama* captured sixty-five Yankee ships.[52] Plagued always by inability to send prizes to Confederate ports, Semmes burned many of his captures, but never did unnecessary violence to their crews. Violence he saved for the Yankee merchant fleet, and in time he virtually drove it from the seas.[53] Such scourging did he achieve that the United States fumed in anger at the English for letting his ship escape. After the war the issue of the *"Alabama* claims" clouded British-American relations for years. The *Alabama*'s operations certainly clouded British-Confederate relations. Aware of the kind of horror the daring Rebel commerce raiding policy could wreak, Yankee diplomats pushed desperately for seizure of all "merchants" building for the South. It was a delicate issue. Law officers of the Crown insisted on proof of perfidy, a nicety that enraged United States Ambassador Charles Francis Adams. Proof was a matter of conviction; he knew the purpose of all the vessels in ways along the Mersey and the Clyde. And there was more than bluster behind Federal ire. Secretary Seward breathed war freely in conversations with British Ambassador Lord Lyons. The United States would "defend itself if vessels for the Confederates should escape from British ports, either in the United Kingdom or the Colonies."[54]

British statesmen were piqued by Yankee bellicosity but understood the cause. Ambassador Lyons, under the eye of Seward and obviously impressed, suggested the ships be taken, but so deftly that the Federals would not "think that they had gained their point by threats."[55] Nothing Britain did should indicate any truckling. "All my experience," said Lyons, "goes to prove that firmness does better than concession with the Americans. It is well to build a golden bridge for the retreat of their National Vanity, but not to yield in essentials.''[56] It was a point to remember in dealing with Confederates, too, for they shared the American boorishness in international relations.

Obviously it was safer to be tough on the Confederates; threats to Mason about the ships sounded serious. He objected and sent his objections to Richmond, and President Davis took the only recourse open: in September 1863 he was ready to expel the British consuls still assigned to Southern ports. Relations with Britain were deteriorating rapidly, a circumstance that boded ill for recognition. And yet the South could hardly blink at overt insults abroad. At home, interference by British consuls in recruiting could not be tolerated. Without dignity there could be no claim to independence.[57] And the chances for recognition were not extinguished, not as long as Napoleon III remained loyal.

In point of fact, he acted like the loyalest of Southerners. It was one of his more irritating traits as far as Lords Palmerston and Russell were concerned. Several times through 1863 the Emperor suggested recognition or mediation.[58] In late summer, a spy reported to the British Foreign Office an alarming conference at Saint-Cloud:

> Yesterday another Meeting of Ministers was held in the morning, at which the Emperor presided. The two principal objects, which were discussed, related to *the Policy,* which the Cabinet of the Tuilleries [sic] should pursue, both with reference to the *American* Question, as well as to the *Polish Question.*
>
> With respect to the former . . . the Recognition of the Confederates as Bellingerents [sic] was a long time under discussion. It appears that the Emperor, in order to avoid the inconveniences which might arise through a *too direct* and *premature resolution,* has decided to adopt a provisionary course, which is to consist, in making the actual Government of Mexico to be the *first* to recognize the Southern States, that this Government should open diplomatic relations with them, and should invoke the assistance of the Emperor, in case the Cabinet of Washington should come forward with any obstacles, or should combat such an initiative.[59]

Mexican connivance at Southern independence sounded like a Bonapartist plan, and it might have worked. But Britain steered clear of assistance. One thing was sure about the Emperor of the

French; he dreaded isolation. If Britain acted, he would act, but his special commitment in Mexico depended too much on the acquiescence of the Lion to permit much adventure. And Britain was not going to act.

Napoleon hoped, however, that Britain might be maneuvered into aiding the South. With that hope in mind, he granted a surprising interview to two British subjects, members of Parliament, who also were friends of the Confederacy. On June 22, 1863, the three conferred at length on the matter of recognition. The Englishmen reported a widespread rumor that His Majesty was opposed to Southern independence and that "if the Emperor would declare that he proposed to recognize the South [a Parliamentary motion for recognition] by Her Majesty's Govt would be carried by a great majority."

Napoleon made no blunders, offered no proposals to the unofficial visitors; he did reiterate his Confederate sympathies, and he promised to join Britain in any move to end the American War and to inform Palmerston privately of his readiness to act.[60] The whole matter was complicated by the incredible bumbling of one of the English visitors, John A. Roebuck.

Roebuck was a strange and unpredictable man. As far as his Southern hopes went, he had done pretty well in Paris.[61] Obviously the Emperor could not open negotiations with him, but had gone almost that far. Careful presentation of the resolution suggesting cooperative recognition might succeed. James Mason had high hopes, as did Slidell; Henry Hotze waxed jubilant. Freedom had almost come! But everyone misjudged Roebuck. On June 30 he offered his resolution in Parliament (over the government's private objections) and debate began. It must be said of John Roebuck that he was eager in debate. Almost brimming with excitement he began to leak secret confidences from Napoleon: "He said to me," and "I told his Majesty." Soon everyone in Commons surely assumed him a flunky of the French. In his hands high diplomacy became low farce.[62]

On July 13 Roebuck withdrew his doomed motion, and the chance for recognition, like so much that summer, faded into the limbo of Confederate might-have-beens. In a way they were linked together, the might-have-beens of Gettysburg, of Vicksburg, of Roebuck's misguided motion. There is evidence that Gettysburg and Vicksburg directly affected the matter of recognition. Lyons spotted the importance of Lee's repulse and explained it to Lord Russell on July 6, 1863: Lee's men, he said, "must have lost the feeling of superiority to the enemy, which constituted a great part of their strength."[63] A few weeks later Palmerston put the importance of that awful first week of July clearly enough: "It would not be very logical to acknowledge . . . Independence [of the Confederate States] at the moment when they are less prosperous in their war than they have been for some time."[64]

There were a few diplomatic tricks left for the French and the Confederates, but they would fail. Britain was the key, and stayed aloof.

Judah Benjamin recognized by mid-August that the South had sustained a diplomatic defeat to rank almost with the Vicksburg-Gettysburg combination. Evidence came in the form of British refusal to permit delivery of the famed Laird rams, two powerful ironclads obviously built for war. Word was out that Her Majesty's government intended to detain them; there was precedent in the earlier seizure of the *Alexandra*. Although the *Alexandra* was finally released, the policy could not be missed. Secret orders to take the Laird ships were sent from Whitehall, and the Confederate Navy scored a near miss.[65]

Confederate authorities could see little point in continuing friendship with a Britain so eager to do Seward's bidding. Secretary of State Benjamin at last directed James Mason to abandon his London mission, a tacit rupture of relations with England. Later, in October 1863, the Confederate cabinet approved expulsion of the British consuls and so cut virtually all formal contact with Perfidious Albion.

Informal contacts increased. With the King Cotton myth now exploded, with much wishful thinking deflated, Benjamin guessed Southerners might be ready for secondary diplomacy on a grand scale. Commercial activities increased substantially. Officers of the newly created Bureau of Foreign Supplies purchased or impressed cotton for the government, sent it to such ports as Wilmington, North Carolina, Mobile, Alabama, Fernandina, Florida, and Charleston, where it was shipped aboard blockade runners to Confederate agents in the islands. Much of this system was not new, but the emphasis on it took new dimensions. Energy, money, and manpower were channeled at last to a systematic evasion of the blockade and to a skillful use of cotton as foreign exchange.[66]

President Davis had opposed open trading in cotton as long as it had any leverage as diplomatic blackmail. Now he relented and approved the purchases of government blockade runners, government cotton, and the management of foreign and domestic transportation to expand importations. The best evidence of his approval was permission to use naval officers as blockade-running captains![67]

Redoubled commercial efforts required more ships, more exports, more agents in the islands, a general overhaul of domestic transportation. These, in turn, required money. And for once in the history of the Confederacy, it looked as though money would be available. A good deal of planning had gone into finding money for 1863. Past experience forecast failure of the general tax bill that year, and despite initial successes the yield proved poor. But Congress had listened to a proposal for a foreign loan, even though Benjamin must have been behind the scheme and he was the most disliked man in Richmond. At any rate, the President wanted to try for foreign assistance, so did hard-pressed Secretary Memminger in the Treasury. Closeted in secret session, Congress considered proposals, fixed on the offer of Emile Erlanger & Co. of Paris, and on January 29, 1863, passed "An Act to authorize a foreign loan."[68]

Erlanger & Co. were willing to lend the South a good deal of money. Apparently this respected financial house felt sure of Confederate victory and hoped to be the European creditors of the new nation. Possibly—a few thought so—the growing affection of young Frederick Erlanger for John Slidell's lovely daughter opened family coffers. But the Confederate Congress simply could not nerve up to a long-standing national debt—think of posterity! Instead of borrowing enough to ensure winning, Congress asked only $15 million. Mystifying ramifications surrounded the loan; it would be backed by Confederate cotton bonds, which had much attraction in Europe; interest payments were guaranteed; and the Messrs. Erlanger were assured of a high commission. When the loan was offered in March, it attracted much attention, held around par for a time, and seemed a fine adjunct to the Southern quest for recognition.

News of Gettysburg and Vicksburg rocked the market and the loan plummeted—the baneful effects of that July week seemed endless. Desperate, Confederate agents abroad reinvested some proceeds to bull the value of Southern bonds, but the price fell with Southern fortunes. Estimates of receipts from the loan vary, but considering expenses incidental to sustaining the bonds, interest, and commissions, it is probable that the Confederacy received about $6 million in cash.[69]

Sudden money proved a sudden embarrassment to James M. Mason. For two years he had been banker to all Confederates abroad, a hectic role he filled adequately. During that time he procured most supplies for the South through S. Isaac, Campbell & Co. and Fraser, Trenholm & Co. of Liverpool. These firms sold cotton coming from the South, credited Mason with the receipts, and paid on his order. In simpler days of moderate poverty this system had succeeded. The two companies cooperated with Mason, even advanced funds against future cotton shipments, and provided almost everything ordered by government agencies. Now, though, rumors of money brought swarms of spenders. Apparently every agency of every state in the South sent agents to Europe with long lists of vital necessities—all to be bought with Erlanger proceeds. There were more agents than Mason could see, more claims than he could honor; he called for help.

In May, an agent to manage the Erlanger loan arrived in England. Colin J. McRae, Alabama businessman and industrialist, seemed an odd choice for the task. About his only qualifications were a capacity to profit from the war and membership in the Confederate Congress. But he proved tough and successful. From the outset he insisted on method; all accounts would clear through him; all receipts and disbursements were his responsibility. Tradition makes him a model administrator, a magician who snatched order from chaos. Possibly. But he was mettlesome and stubborn, often assertive of authority and sure of his judgment in matters far beyond his ken. A human weakness for flattery led him sometimes to poor judgment and wastefulness. But in the main, he deserves praise. Certainly after his arrival on the scene Confederate affairs in England and Europe achieved a kind of system.[70]

He was right about blockade running. From his early days in office he urged Richmond authorities to reorganize the whole business of importation. Good officers with the power to act must be stationed along the supply routes to the South. Additional ships must be purchased until at last a great fleet of them plied the lanes between the islands and Wilmington or Charleston; blockading squadrons must be outnumbered by blockade runners. More than that, space on each vessel must be reserved for government freight—it would be a kind of tax in kind for the privilege of trade.[71]

He failed to get all the improvements he wanted, but significant changes were made. A new blockade-evasion system evolved under McRae's careful eye. Early in 1864 a Bureau of Foreign Supplies, under Thomas L. Bayne, put order and discipline into cotton procurement east of the Mississippi, organized shipping details at various ports, and hence gave McRae a reasonably reliable basis of credit. He, in turn, reorganized relations with brokerage houses, kept close accounts, and infused a businesslike air into all foreign purchasing.[72]

Largely because of the 1863–64 reorganization, blockade running became one of the most successful operations of the Confederate government. Why? Probably because there were no precedents to ensnarl the agents, the financiers, the captains, and the crews. They did what they had to do and with ingenuity. Statistics prove the over-all efficiency of blockade running: 330,000 small arms imported from 1861 to 1865 for the government, perhaps another 270,000 for states and private firms; 624,000 pairs of boots; 378,000 blankets; and during the period of December 1863 to December 1864 alone, 1,933,000 pounds of saltpeter, 1,507,000 pounds of lead, 8,632,000 pounds of meat, 520,000 pounds of coffee. Myriad other items came into the South during the war in substantial quantities, enough to prove the vitality of a system that provided much but never enough.[73]

The task of sealing off the South with its vast coastline was superhuman; not even the Federal navy could meet the challenge. How many runners got through during the war? Estimates vary, but the late Frank L. Owsley, a leading authority on foreign purchasing, surmised that in 1861 Yankee blockaders caught one out of ten runners; in 1862, one out of eight; in 1863, one out of four; in 1864, one out of three; in 1865, after most Confederate Atlantic ports were gone, one out of two—for a wartime average of one out of six.[74]

These impressive figures argue that the South made the best possible use of blockade running, but this is debatable. There is evidence that some of the states, particularly North Carolina with its fabulously successful runner *Advance*, did better with less. Many captains and private entrepreneurs complained that Confederate authorities constricted the Yankee cordon tighter with endless red tape, with confusing regulations, even with unnecessary impressment of cargo space. Certainly bureaucratic snarls developed. And until the general reorganization of foreign purchasing and trade came in mid-1863, inequities and problems multiplied.

But could it have been otherwise? Blockade running grew apace with emergency; it was a spawn of war. A few Confederate leaders had historical knowledge of earlier blockades, but none of it helped —there had never before been a blockade of this scope. When, at last, the government would take an obvious step in February 1864 and nationalize foreign commerce by the famous "blockade statutes," the strongest advocates of order among shipowners became the loudest critics of "centralism."

Still, Benjamin's commercial diplomacy proved brilliant. If his reputation were measured by this alone, he would rank with the world's Richelieus. Reputations, though, are not seen piecemeal; they mark a whole career, and so Benjamin comes to history as a failure. A luminous failure, to be sure, for he was the subtlest Confederate—but a failure, nonetheless. Is the verdict just? Does casting him against the odds change the degree of his failure? Sadly enough, no. For Benjamin failed even before the odds went against him, failed in imagination. Guile, deviousness, and brilliant craft he had, but vision was denied him. A confidant of the President's, Benjamin had his chance to persuade a policy of cotton shipment early in the war, a policy of barter and trade and commercial amity when the South still could win friends in the world. Later, when it was too late, he doubted cotton's sway and suggested commercial ties with France. This was the way of expediency.[75]

And so diplomacy became incidental to the war. The outcome rested where it always had: on the Confederate infantrymen. They were fewer and weaker than before, but they were still the best hope.

CHAPTER EIGHT

"The Sun Can Never Dip So Low"

—LORENA

"Bread or Peace"

Mrs. Mary Jackson caused the trouble. She was big, with "strong features, and a vixenish eye," and she was hungry. Most of the women who heard her that morning of April 2, 1863, shared her hunger. They had gathered in Richmond for a peaceful church meeting, but Mrs. Jackson took the floor, brandished a bowie knife and a six-shooter, and told them all what they must do: demand food from Richmond's authorities. Food was in the city; the government had it, speculators and crooked commissaries had it, and must be made to sell it at fair prices or lose it to force. The crowd spilled from the church and moved toward Capitol Square, picked up on-lookers and thrill seekers, and at last marched to the Governor's Mansion. John Letcher listened to the ladies' complaints, offered sympathy but no food, and the crowd turned ugly. Boys and men joined the women. Mary Jackson, sporting a tall white feather in her hat, led a march down Ninth Street, past the War Department, and onto Main Street. There in the midst of the shops and stores and bakeries all order vanished and a wild, ravening mob sacked and pillaged everywhere. Screaming "bread," waving all kinds of weapons, swept along in the hysteria of hunger and violence, the women cleaned out food stores, broke into clothing, jewelry, and shoe shops, and took anything that struck their fancy. Nothing was spared; the City Hospital lost 310 pounds of beef! As the madness grew a spirit of vengeance seemed to grip the mob. Riot verged on revolution.

Hasty efforts were made to halt the rioters, to check wreckage. An official from the YMCA urged the mob to "come to the rooms of the Association," where food was available,[1] but few heard him. Mayor Joseph Mayo and the governor mixed with the mob and tried to restore order; their voices were lost in turmoil.

At last the City Battalion appeared; the governor threatened to have the troops open fire unless the rioters dispersed. Fear congealed action momentarily. Before Letcher was forced to prove his threat, President Davis arrived on the tense scene. He climbed on a dray between the soldiers and the people, held up his arms for silence. Hisses greeted his appeal, sullen voices threatened to roar again. The President told the mob to cease lawlessness, emptied his pockets of money for any takers, then took out his watch, looked at the ranks of the City Battalion, and called an ultimatum: the rioters had five minutes to disperse. No one moved. The commander of the troops ordered his men to load and to fire when the time was up—still no one moved. The mob bunched, the troops stood with muskets loaded, the President looked at his watch, and the minutes ticked away. There was no missing the impact of the moment: the government was staked on stopping the riot. If the people rushed the troops, the war was all but lost. At the last moment, the mob broke and the crisis ebbed.[2]

Richmond's rulers writhed in shame. It was monstrous that the Confederacy's capital should spawn such anarchy. Hasty word went to city papers in an attempt to keep news of the riot from the enemy. "The unfortunate disturbance which occurred to-day," explained an Assistant Adjutant General to the editors, "is so liable to misconstruction and misrepresentation abroad that I am desired by the Secretary of War to make a special appeal to the . . . press at Richmond, and earnestly request . . . [no] reference directly or indirectly to the affair."[3] Among the capital's citizens the incident served as proof that "aliens" and other outcasts were despoiling the country. And there were fears of other riots.

President Davis knew that the riot was not an isolated disturbance, that a general scarcity sparked similar outbreaks elsewhere. There was, for instance, the case of Mobile. Food shortages there had become so acute that placards with the ominous motto "Bread or Peace" had mysteriously appeared on street corners. Similar trouble erupted in several other cities. This kind of protest had grim overtones. Hunger was the deadliest foe of morale. And glib explanations to the contrary, hunger existed in the South. It affected not only the citizens but also the armies. Soldiers bore it better than civilians; discipline quieted complaints, discipline and the fortitude of Rebels. Somehow something must be done to increase the food supply.[4]

The necessity was obvious enough, but the methods were obscure. Constant efforts were made by the Commissary Department and by state and local agencies to provide food for the country, but scarcity increased. Why? Causes were almost too involved for understanding. Inflation, debilitated railroads, scant supplies of wagons and horses, dishonest supply officials, all these were obvious factors of famine. But there was an overriding cause. Lucius Northrop, the master curmudgeon presiding over the Commissary Department, explained it clearly as early as October 1862:

> The loss of crops in the districts north of Lat 32° of the cotton state[s] & those of So W Va & parts of Tennessee & the devastation of those yet in our hands will make meat scarce for want of grain to fatten the animals. . . . Every exertion it is believed will be inadequate to obtaining a sufficiency of salt meats to sustain armies of strength equal to keeping in check the . . . enemy.[5]

Loss of territory reduced food sources, which in turn weakened the armies, which in turn lost more territory—a vicious circle had begun in the Confederacy. If there was not enough food available within the contracting borders of the South, improvements in logistical system would achieve nothing; the outcome would obviously be starvation. Was the situation as desperate as the curious misanthrope guarding the larder indicated? It seemed incredible that a huge agricultural land pretty well converted from cotton to food production verged on hunger. Had the produce loan, the tax in kind, impressment, scavenged the country clean? Again this seemed incredible, considering the public skepticism heaped on all these measures. Had Northrop possibly misplaced the food of the South, lost it beyond his narrow vision? He had the kind of mind that reduced order to bureaucracy and made simplicity a vice, so he was capable of such a stupendous loss. From the beginning of the war he planned to draw supplies from Tennessee, Kentucky, and other border areas; when they were lost, his plans were lost. An overriding rigidity denied him alternatives; no other plan occurred to him. Variations on his original scheme taxed the limits of his mind. If such alternatives as enemy trade failed, the fault lay with retreating generals, not with Northrop. His attitude is understandable since he found rectitude in ruin.[6]

All of which tended to cast some doubt on Northrop's perception. Comparisons always went badly for the Commissary General, although he seemed deft enough to survive them, even when congressional committees pointed to success in other supply departments and questioned failure in his own. Still, in the long summer and fall of 1863, comparisons reflected heavily against the Subsistence Department, especially comparisons with the Ordnance Department.

Some people in the government found Chief of Ordnance Josiah Gorgas too cold for friendship. He seemed lost in a kind of grim aloofness and appeared perpetually irritated. Close scrutiny showed him almost Spanish-looking, despite his Dutch name, and Southerners all had suspicions about foreigners. Combine his looks with his Yankee origins and suspicions increased. Yet who could deny his ability? Behind that high forehead, those sober eyes, worked a mind of genius. Guns, cannon, powder, the myriad requirements of combat, had somehow been provided in a land lacking tools or shops or mechanical traditions. Gorgas was responsible. Since no domestic sources of munitions existed at the beginning of the war, Gorgas's task appeared to be a good deal tougher than Northrop's.

How was it the crisp Yankee administrator succeeded where the carper failed? A few might argue that Yankees were just better businessmen, had more devotion to organization than their lazing Rebel brethren. There was enough truth to this to be embarrassing, but energetic organization alone would not have made a genius of

Gorgas. His achievements were the fruits of high art and broad vision. Never shackled to a logistical plan, never a prisoner of prejudice, Gorgas cast always for new ideas, new systems—his eye scanned alternatives constantly. Aware at the outset that foreign purchases were the best initial source of munitions, he launched a comprehensive campaign of cotton exportation and blockade running. The first suggestions that the government own and operate ships as a means of broadening the supply base came from Gorgas. With the tacit approval of President Davis, Gorgas bought ships, found cotton, sent agents to Bermuda and Nassau, even urged Navy Secretary Mallory to put Naval officers in charge of blockade runners and persuaded his brother-in-law, a lieutenant in the Confederate Navy, to command the *Cornubia!*[7] All of this brought the Ordnance Department rich rewards.

Part of the rewards, though, came in wake of the thorough reorganization of foreign purchasing. For some time Caleb Huse, the able ordnance purchasing agent sent abroad in 1861, had needed help with shipping details. Now that Colin McRae had charge of financial matters in England and Europe, Huse could devote himself exclusively to finding potential sources of Rebel arms and supplies. Money would be provided by McRae, shipping details would be handled by such ordnance agents in Bermuda as Major Norman Walker, in Nassau and Cuba by Louis Heyliger. System was McRae's religion; it was Gorgas's life.[8]

System in finding and issuing ordnance spread far beyond matters of foreign supplies. External sources were only one facet of Gorgas's procurement pattern. No matter the glittering prospects of purchases abroad, the Chief of Ordnance understood that domestic production must be the mainstay of the department. While home factories and shops were developing and expanding, he would rely on Europe and on the enemy. Careful scavenging gleaned rich rewards after each battle; swarms of Rebels ransacked the fields in search of discarded Yankee arms, jettisoned caissons, and abandoned guns. Bluecoats were splendid providers, and for the first two years they were the South's best reliance for munitions—importations ran a lagging second.

Domestic production continued the main hope of Gorgas and the

War Department. Successive war secretaries supported the sober Chief of Ordnance in his constant quest for Confederate factories and shops. Armories, arsenals, depots were expanded and improved. A great powder works established by Colonel George W. Rains, at Augusta, Georgia, rivaled Britain's renowned Waltham Abbey powder plant. Colonel John W. Mallet's Central Laboratories, in Macon, produced spectacular innovations in artillery and achieved standardization of musket cartridges.[9] Colonel James Burton's armory in Macon employed hundreds and produced a variety of ordnance items.[10] Gorgas kept his service modern. Countless potential furnaces, forges, mines, and smelters were encouraged by the Ordnance Department; small rolling mills and private armories boasted expansionist dreams. There was no denying that the government's need for ordnance offered fabulous chances for speculation. Official contracts were obvious prizes—along with money, they brought large fringe benefits.

Gorgas welcomed the help of private contractors but learned quickly their unreliability, as many of them failed and begged to be annexed by the military. When the bureau obliged there were outraged cries of state socialism from state-rights politicos, but results overrode objections. And the Ordnance Department showed results. Gorgas, in a rare moment of self-satisfaction, once boasted the achievements of his bureau:

> I have succeeded beyond my utmost expectations. From being the worst supplied of the Bureaus of the War Department it is now the best. Large arsenals have been organized at Richmond, Fayetteville, Augusta, Charleston, Columbus, Macon, Atlanta and Selma, and smaller ones at Danville, Lynchburgh and Montgomery, besides other establishments. A superb powder mill has been built at Augusta, the credit of which is due to Col. G. W. Rains. Lead smelting works were established by me at Petersburgh, and turned over to the Nitre and Mining Bureau, when that Bureau was at my request separated from mine. A cannon foundry established at Macon, Columbus, Ga., and at Augusta; a foundry for shot and shell at Salisbury, N.C.; a large shop for leather work at Clarksville, Va.; besides the Armories here and at Fayetteville, a manufactory of carbines has been built up here; a rifle factory at Ashville (transferred to Columbia, S.C.); a new and very large armory at Macon, including a pistol factory, built up under con-

tract here and sent to Atlanta, and thence transferred under purchase to Macon; a second pistol factory at Columbus, Ga.;—All of these have required incessant toil and attention, but have borne such fruit as relieves the country from fear of want in these respects. Where three years ago we were not making a gun, a pistol nor a sabre, no shot nor shell (except at the Tredegar Works)—a pound of powder—we now make all these in quantities to meet the demands of our large armies.[11]

All supply departments shared the pattern of increasing nationalism. Quartermaster officers assumed control over much of North Carolina's large textile industry; meat-packing plants and food processors suffered direction by the Commissary General; private laboratories and chemical plants became part of the Medical Department.[12] Reasons for this trend were obvious, if dismal. Faced with rising costs, shortages of skilled and unskilled labor, of food, clothing, and transportation, contractors defaulted on deadlines, incurred penalties, and went under. In the wake of enlarged government control over manufacturing came some improvement in management of plants and resources and some differences in production. Coordination of production permitted rational logistics.

For the most part, government agents were subtle in management techniques. Outright assumption of private plants was usually avoided. Company officers and employees were encouraged to remain and supervision came in thin disguise: money went in swelling volume to efficient plants; owners who proved willing to work patriotically found raw materials and transportation mysteriously handy. Against those misguided companies reluctant to accept Confederate contracts, the government aimed an irresistible weapon —control over manpower.[13] Conscription and exemption laws gave the War Department power to channel men into the ranks of armies or of industry, and the power was deliberately used. Raw coercion had unpleasant overtones, but necessity makes its own virtues.

Some officials guessed that production was only one facet of the burgeoning supply emergency by late 1863. They were right. Inflation damaged government credit and hampered procurement of raw materials all across Dixie. Scarcity of money drove ordnance officers, quartermasters, commissaries, all supply folk, to the dubious use of "certificates of indebtedness." These government promissory notes were supposed to replace official currency, but people resisted them with considerable gusto. Any government forced to a system of public IOU's had a chancy future. The certificates were a kind of counterfeit, and they produced a Confederate variation on Gresham's law—they drove goods out of circulation. More than that, as the Treasury Department encouraged purchasers to offer bonds in lieu of either notes or certificates, trade diminished. Years later a careful student of Rebel economics would say that "the resort to irredeemable paper money and to excessive issues of such currency was fatal, for it weakened not only the purchasing power of the government but also destroyed economic security among the people. In fact, there seems to be nothing vital that escaped its baneful influence."[14]

Scant funds directly affected the most important element in logistics—transportation. Improvements in procurement and production methods, careful management of the skilled worker pool, adequate provisions for feeding and clothing laborers, all these things would be meaningless if transportation failed. By mid-1863, there was a good chance that the horse shortage would cripple wagon transport and that the railroads would collapse.

Diligent searching for horses and mules produced barely enough for military needs. After Gettysburg and Vicksburg most of the horses were gone; a minimum supply for the armies was found. Mules could replace them, but mules, too, were few. Natural livestock increase lagged far behind consumption. Remount depots scattered behind the armies worked wonders of resuscitation but could not provide surpluses adequate for both military and civilian needs. The result was obvious enough: fewer wagons reduced the mobility of men and supplies in the field and balked logistical efforts throughout the nation.[15]

Railroads were the essential of nationwide supply. Trainmen thought money the great panacea and demanded constantly increased funds for repairs of cars and track. Would money have worked the miracle of preservation necessary to an efficient rail system? Probably not. Railroad companies suffered all the troubles of the Confederate economy in microcosm. No matter the expedients—the short lines hastily rigged to bridge gaps, the patched, coddled, and cajoled engines, the different gauges, the borrowing and lending of cars and engineers and trainmen, the juggling of rates and special fees, the encouragement of the Railroad Bureau in the Quartermaster Department—there were not enough trained railroaders, trains, or shops in the South to survive a long war.

Railroad officials and quartermaster officers charged with managing rail transport knew the limitations from the beginning of hostilities. But hopes for quick success cloaked fears for the future. In the weeks after Vicksburg and Gettysburg, those weeks of hard assessment of potential, the limitations became frighteningly clear. Virginia's tracks were worn and battered by usage and destruction; the rails running south and west from Richmond were equally worn and badly overcrowded; deeper in the South, feeder lines to the coast were rusting or yielding iron to the trunks; rolling stock was rickety, wheels wobbled, engines wheezed and labored slower; and with each retreat tracks and cars were lost. Since replacements were virtually impossible and repairs doubtful, everything depended on skillful conservation of remaining equipment. A general plan of railroad management offered the best hope for military transportation, but the government shied from such massive nationalism. Half measures were adopted: the Railroad Bureau worked to win cooperation from the railroad companies, flattered, wheedled, pleaded with presidents and superintendents for trains and priority for official shipments. Higher rates for troops and freight, details of engineers and mechanics, appeals to duty, all were tried.

Owners and operators of railroads were not brigands; they had their share of patriotism. But they found themselves in a unique position. The armies, the country, all the commerce of the nation depended on them for survival. Private shippers offered incredible prices for freight space; cotton speculators promised virtually anything for delivery of bales at Wilmington, Charleston, Mobile, and other ports. Government agents simply could not match the private competition, and the war needs notwithstanding, private freight often rode ahead of munitions and medicines. This kind of thing had to stop, else it would be impossible to recoup the losses of July 1863.[16]

Constant badgering by the Quartermaster General and other bureau chiefs finally got results. By secret act in May 1863, Congress empowered the War Department to seize and manage railroads, regulate freight schedules, and interchange rolling stock. There was one sop to Georgia in the law: no road owned or operated wholly by a state could be touched, so Joe Brown's line was safe.[17]

At last there was a chance of logic in railroad management, but more should have been done. Instead of providing for seizure of railroads in emergencies, the government should simply have assimilated them into the war effort—later, when it scarcely mattered, the Confederate Congress would go that far.[18] For the moment, the law seemed adequate. The Railroad Bureau could threaten impressment and hence compel much cooperation. Under Major F. W. Sims, an able man who grasped the obvious—"our needs are beyond belief"[19] —the bureau achieved a semblance of order. Trains ran more promptly to army railheads, government shipments moved, trainmen did stupendous deeds with weary equipment. By the winter of 1863–64, though, a kind of subtle sloth settled over the lines; wear and fatigue eroded order and energy. Heavy traffic on trunk lines warped beds and ties, cut U rails, and bent T rails, and accidents increased. Working parties were few, overburdened, and careless. Speed limits declined until, at last, ten miles an hour courted destruction.

Still, through the hard days of late 1863, the winter, spring, and summer of 1864, Rebel trainmen proved the value of railroads in modern war. They brought Longstreet's corps from Virginia in time for the Battle of Chickamauga in September 1863; they hauled just enough men and guns and forage and medicine to keep Johnston's Army of Tennessee on the defensive during the summer campaign of 1864; they carried sufficient food to give Lee's starvelings a daily ration of one handful of parched corn and a spoonful of brown sugar in the last stages of the siege of Richmond.[20] Breakdowns and Sherman's "bummers" interfered, but Confederate railroadmen pulled some of Beauregard's men from Charleston and some of Hardee's from Savannah and concentrated these remnants ahead of Sherman in North Carolina; and at the absolute end they sent a munitions train to meet Lee's retreating army at Amelia Station and a ration train toward Appomattox. Rebel railroads almost beat the odds, almost supported the war. Spread too thin, run too far, they brought diminishing returns from dwindling resources and wrote a tantalizing chapter in the history of Confederate logistics. Just a few more engines, cars, and trainmen, just a few more might have . . .[21]

Rail lines were the arteries of the South; when they atrophied, decay set in, decay that became chronic, pervasive, strangled the efforts of all supply bureaus, stalled commerce, halted the mail, and sapped the nation's will. The conclusion seems obvious: railroad failure wrecked Confederate logistics. Unfortunately the conclusion is not sound. A large factor in failure was the absence of a comprehensive logistical system in the wartime South. Economic planning came piecemeal, almost spasmodically and in response to crises.

Partial planning came because a reluctant administration and a conservative Congress could not quite face the supply needs of modern war, could not fasten order on a reckless people. Individualism hung on as a fetish of that old-time democracy the Rebels fought to save. Another fetish of that democracy was the Minuteman tradition—each man takes up arms at country's call and each man is his own leader in an army of patriots. What need among these for discipline or cadence? Britain's rigid legions had quailed against such men of independence. Southerners were fighting for the cause of their fathers and so were armored in the right. These fancies were grand, the principles were perfect, the rhetoric was soothing, but the South was out of time.

New values brought new realities. History had passed the antique hero by and left him, an island, far behind. Wars now were systems of people and engines of force, and their essence was mass. This horrid proposition the South could scarcely accept; it conjured an alien world of bigness without regard for men. It happened that erosions of conflict pushed the South at last to one of history's poignant choices: fight on as men of principle, as defenders of liberty, and lose the war; fight the way of the enemy and lose the future. Southerners tried to slip the choice, to fight both ways, and lost both the war and the future. But they saved a legend.

"I Want Some Valiant Soldier to Help Me Bear the Cross. . . ."

Some of Nathan Bedford Forrest's men were dismounted, in a favorite way of the general, strung out in the woodland like skirmishers, and they groped toward Chickamauga Creek in northern Georgia. Somewhere in the dark country ahead lay elements of Rosy Rosecrans's victorious army, that stylish aggregation which had maneuvered Bragg and the Army of Tennessee out of Chattanooga and threatened a march straight on through Atlanta. It looked strikingly as if the winning time had run out for Rosecrans, though, on that morning of September 19, 1863. Forrest's tough dismounted troopers were the vanguard of an attacking Rebel army. After much marching, countermarching, and retreating, Bragg had set his mind forward. With typical precision he had begun plotting Rosecrans's ruin in mid-August, and if such subordinates as D. H. Hill, Simon Bolivar Buckner, and that tardy Arkansan T. C. Hindman had been quick, if Bishop General Polk had not relied on his own limited revelations, victory probably would have crowned at last the sufferings of the Army of Tennessee.

But there was too much talking in the army's high command. Mary Chesnut put the problem aptly: "Bragg always stops to quarrel with his generals."[22] True enough. Bragg fostered much of his own trouble. A stickler for discipline in the ranks, he asked advice too often from his generals. Nothing seems to have fascinated him more than the prospect of a council of war. Napoleon had contempt for military consensus, but some generals need the comfort of consultation. Bragg's worst error lay in taking a good deal of the advice he got. Which proved that he lacked understanding of his Southern confreres—once unburdened of caution in council, Bragg's generals followed their own prejudices. Unhappily for Bragg he seems to have had more than his share of competing brilliance. That brilliance blinded, finally, and led to considerable trouble.

In mid-September, an incredible chance had come to Bragg, a

chance to do something no other Rebel general had yet done: destroy a Federal army. If all went according to plan, the frustrations of 1863 might vanish in the smoke over Chickamauga. A wrecked Yankee army would change the pattern of the war.

Bragg aimed at cutting the road behind the Federals—their escape route to Chattanooga—and at locking them in a closed valley. Trapped by mountains and Confederate guns, Rosecrans's men would wither away. Rosy had done pretty well, though, once he caught the drift of Bragg's intent and had concentrated as best he could along Chickamauga Creek in an attempt to keep open the road behind him. The stage was almost arranged for battle.

Battles are not really subject to plans. They generate a will of their own and unravel without logic. Chickamauga proved no exception. All the plots and wishings of the commanders ceased to have meaning when Forrest's troopers stalked the woods near the small, meandering creek. Sunshine filtered slanting rays of motes and light through the trees around the Rebs; everywhere there was the cold stillness, the silence veterans hear, then the pop-popping of skirmish fire, the sudden volleys of massed infantry, the roar and clangor of iron and guns and yelling men. Troops from George Thomas's big corps were in the woods; they were in line and they were fighting. So the battle happened. Plans and hopes and art yielded to surprise and to the tough character of soldiers. About all the generals could do now was hurry their men forward, watch, listen, and perhaps assure defeat.

Bragg really had the best of the situation, though he could not guess it when the action began. Rebels almost outnumbered the Yankees on the field. Reinforcements from Knoxville and from Mississippi swelled the gray ranks to nearly 63,000, which would have matched Rosecrans's numbers, but the Confederates had a surprise for the enemy coming by rail. All the way from Virginia, down on a great circuit through the Deep South (a detour imposed by Burnside's recent cutting of the line from Richmond to Knoxville and Chattanooga) on that circuit came the 12,000 veterans of Longstreet's corps from Lee's army. It was a heroic trip, one fraught with delays, car changes, popular demonstrations at way stations, bountiful handouts, and bone-wearing fatigue.[23] It was also a railroad miracle, one that proved the uses of trains in troop movements. Late coming as they were, some of Longstreet's divisions arrived in Bragg's camps on the morning of September 18, and when they came, the odds were shifted. And so there was confidence among Forrest's men when they probed those fateful woods.

On their side, the Federals owned a miracle, too, a miracle of marching by Thomas's corps. Like all great marches it stretched back in the memories of men for years and grew longer, less tolerable with each telling, but it was worthy of its myths. All night Thomas's men toiled, four divisions of them, until hours blurred into a garish horror of roads, guide fires, and endless steps. Not a man among them fresh, they reached the crucial position east of the road to Chattanooga before dawn on the 19th, met Forrest's skirmishers, forgot numbing fatigue, and set about combat.

Some things run common to battles—among them a kind of bunching. Where there is pressure the troops collect in a mass, and pressure that day was on the Federal left. Rosecrans shifted men as fast as possible from his distant right, upstream, down to Thomas's hard-pressed line. Bragg sent increasing numbers in behind Forrest and built a considerable power on the field. All day the action for the road flared. Thomas's command huddled in a shallow kind of crescent and stood off the Rebs. Men knew little of the battle; their small slice of war was bounded by woods and clearings and an awful, crowning sound. Some recalled later that the air seemed filled with moaning lead, that metal scythes sawed trees and shrubs in strangely level patterns, that no space was free of bullets.[24] Up against the knolls held by Thomas went the Rebs, back again into the hissing foliage; up once more and back, in a macabre seesaw of charging death. Heat rose with the sun and the shooting, water was scarce, wounded streamed to the rear in milling confusion, until at last night spread mercy on the battlefield.

Battle nights have oddities of moon and smoke and fires and strange hushes midst the dead. Preying through the gloom are old fears and horrors, and even the bravest are haunted. Dawn is long in coming and it brings death once more. Some men brood on nights like that, some are numbed to sleep, a few keep sentry on the shadows, and some are apt to pray. Generals ponder in a battle's wake, and plot to change the odds. Rosecrans talked in weary council and sought men to send to Thomas. None doubted Bragg's intent—all day he tried to reach the road and he would try with morning.

Across the leveled trees, beyond the corpses in the bush, Bragg arranged his ranks anew and changed his general's tasks. Bishop Polk, a fighter when the decision had been cast, would strike at dawn where Thomas was and push on toward the road. When Polk's grayclads charged, Old Pete would hurl his men against the enemy right; no respite would permit a shifting of the Yankees from one flank to the other. If both attacks succeeded, the Federals might be surrounded.

Polk jumped off late, but when he went, he went hard, with all the terrible force of Murfreesboro. As that eerie Rebel yell rang through the woods and Thomas's men shrank in front of a withering charge, it looked for a time as though Rosy was ruined. Graycoats were out beyond his left, snaking in toward the road behind his lines. He had reacted quickly early in the morning and sent men to help Thomas in those crucial hours while Polk delayed the charge and the added strength prevented immediate disaster.[25] But strident calls from Thomas for help pushed the Union commander into further rash withdrawals. One of these withdrawals, an entire division, left a gap in the Federal line which offered Longstreet a supreme opportunity: squarely toward the gap stormed his five divisions.

The Army of Northern Virginia did things well; Longstreet's men acted quickly, as a unit, and they charged with the discipline of Gettysburg. Through the Federal lines they went, splintered Rosy's front, drove a third of his army in rout from the field, and turned to harass the hill held by Thomas.

Luck had it that Rosecrans was caught in the rout of his men, that he left the battle and went all the way to Chattanooga, and that he thought his army ruined. There was logic in the assumption, and he would have been right save for Thomas's stand on Snodgrass Hill. There that afternoon the wrecked flotsam of an army gathered; there Thomas's own unbroken men held on against the most searing assaults of the war. The afternoon dwindled down to darkness and the lines held. And yet the field was all but lost. Only the thinnest thread of ground was open to the rear; that thread parted often in the afternoon, tied, and parted again, until finally Thomas took his dazed men along it to safety in the darkness. History chooses heroes often by the way they meet disaster, and for his deeds that day Virginian George Thomas won his page as the "Rock of Chickamauga."

In the haphazard camps of victory that night of September 20–21, Bragg's men rested in uncertain glory.

Slowly in the days following the battle, Bragg pulled his divisions to the mountaintops surrounding Chattanooga. First hopes that a beaten Rosecrans would evacuate the city faded as the Federals lingered. Both armies were almost inert. Confederate casualties came close to 18,000, Federal casualties neared 17,000.[26] With Rebel cannon atop the lofty ridges that ran some four miles along the riverfront, Rosecrans found himself virtually trapped. One road remained open, but wagons traveled at the drivers' risk; Rebel interdiction fire threatened starvation. Nobody in his right mind was going to lead the beaten Federals up against Bragg's perched followers, so it seemed that Chattanooga would finally fall to siege.

Jefferson Davis rejoiced at the Chickamauga victory and sent an enthusiastic message of congratulation to the Army of Tennessee. Lincoln and the North writhed in anger over the disparity between Rosecrans's promises and his achievements. After brilliant maneuvers which had warped Bragg out of Tennessee, the Federal Army lay beaten and disheartened and the grayclads held a springboard to the North. There were no real reinforcements to send out to Chattanooga in time to prevent Bragg's invasion—if he moved with reasonable speed.

Still, as far as many Southerners could see, Bragg had too large a penchant for basking, and he lingered peacefully in his crow's-nest headquarters overlooking his prize. The view was captivating enough, and bemusing. Spread before the worn Rebels was the Tennessee River. It made a huge oxbow south of the city and cut sharply back north. Around the western fringes of Chattanooga itself, the river ran a slightly crescent course. Through a cut in Rebel-held Missionary Ridge two ribbons of iron ran southwestward to a Chattanooga depot and then onward by the river to the foot-hills of Lookout Mountain. Both rail approaches were covered by Confederate cannon. Chattanooga was handsome, a growing metropolis with some burgeoning industry. A few of the buildings showed signs of war, but for the most part, Bragg's veterans could look longingly at comforts down below them. Rosy's discomfort added to the beauty of the scenery. Locked in, he manned picket lines and redoubts but lay obviously at bay. A sudden thrust down the mountains and the prize would be Confederate.[27]

But Bragg made no moves, sudden or otherwise. Reasons for things Bragg failed to do are always clouded by excuses. Rarely mistaken, he was often mistreated—by his subordinates, by the government, surely by fate. In the post-Chickamauga assessment, he had good cause for relaxing in lofty isolation. Transportation was scarce, he had no pontoons for crossing the Tennessee, ammunition was low after heavy fighting, his cavalry was scattered and needed forage and mounts, his men were on short rations, and he felt compelled to replenish his army before taking the field. Which is to say that even if Rosecrans had abandoned Chattanooga, Bragg felt unready to invade Tennessee. He simply had too few supplies for a campaign. And there was also the question of men; no reinforcements made up battle losses. Almost all the spare troops at President Davis's command had come up before the battle, and what was done by the Army of Tennessee would have to be done with the men at hand.

All of this the President clearly understood when he reached Bragg's headquarters on October 9, 1863. He had praise for the deeds of the army[28] and a cold eye for the troubles surrounding his general. Troubles were hard to separate from Bragg; he attracted them with morbid gusto. His worst troubles always had to do with people, usually underlings. In this particular month, with one of the great chances of the war spread before him, his troubles focused on his generals. As he thought about it, almost every one of his corps and "wing" commanders did him wrong. Polk and D. H. Hill looked to be the worst offenders, but incipient mutiny flickered through all the high command.

Sensitive ever of tender honors, the President tried forthrightly to meet the personnel crisis of the army. With the tactlessness of the truly shy, Davis made a botch of his mission. At a meeting of all the high brass, Davis asked each in turn if the army should have another commander. It must have been a hideous moment for many of them, since Bragg sat there staring them squarely in the face, but they spoke honestly and all said "yes." A consensus of reasons developed, the chief one being that Bragg simply could not do the job. Neither Bragg nor the President could have been much surprised at this open vote of no confidence; most of these men had signed a round robin urging their leader's departure shortly after the battle of Chickamauga. Now the whole sordid mess was in the open, opinions were clear, and everything was up to the commander in chief.[29]

Davis knew his dilemma. If Bragg went, who would take his place?

There were two obvious candidates, officers of sufficient rank for army command: Johnston and Beauregard. Johnston's misanthropy and unhappy experience in Mississippi debarred him; besides, he had constantly supported Bragg, and now appeared involved in a sniping campaign to exonerate himself of Vicksburg's fall by fastening the disaster on Davis.[30] Beauregard looked even less attractive. He had commanded the Army of Tennessee much earlier and had apparently bequeathed its high command a legacy of raucous disorder. Within the army itself were competent men, notably Polk, but his appointment would destroy Bragg's reputation. In the end Davis did the only possible thing—he kept Bragg. Polk departed to another command, as did D. H. Hill, and with some sullen rumblings the remaining generals accepted the inevitable.

All of this vastly depressed the President. Constantly urging the need for cooperation and self-denial for the good of the cause,[31] the Chief Executive could scarcely believe the animosity riddling the Army of Tennessee. Sadly this chronic complaining had infected even the placid Longstreet.[32]

Still, there were patriots to be found. The people who came to the stations as the President's train journeyed back southeastward toward Charleston had the old zest of better times; crowds cheered the President, children lavished garlands on him, and that special feeling of being the nation's own returned. And there were the soldiers, those gallants of the Tennessee Army who endured and kept faith with the cause. When the commander in chief had visited their mountainous camps, they cheered him and he cherished mightily the welcome of heroes.

Strength came from touches with the people. In the labyrinths of Richmond's bureaucracy, trapped in daily crisis, Davis sometimes lost the feel of the country. Worried and vexed by the petty climbers of martial society, he relaxed amid civilians and gained hope. He glimpsed poverty's inroads everywhere and felt the general weariness, but the firm acceptance of privation as the cost of independence touched him deeply. Acceptance was a sentiment he shared. By the time his train reached Charleston on November 2, his spirits were up. To a large crowd, including Mayor Macbeth, Pierre Soulé, and General Beauregard, Davis offered remarks termed "brilliant" by a *Courier* reporter who recorded them sporadically.[33] The President waxed eloquent about history; he was, after all, in the South's most history-conscious city, a place filled with descendants, and he knew the value here of ancestral compliment. Every true Carolinian claimed at least spiritual kinship with John Calhoun, and the President artfully invoked the great man's shade: "If it be that the departed spirit can look down upon the events of life with what interest can we not believe he views our present struggle, and in our trial watches over us with all a guardian angels [sic] care." Here in this fighting city the "revolution" began, and no gallant son of the Palmetto would defame the honor of the place. Charleston, the President believed, would not be captured, despite all the Yankee venom loosed upon it. South Carolinians would never let it go. And they would do all their duty everywhere: they never quailed. "We will have more glorious names to record and proud incidents for our descendants. The new has overshadowed the old. Every man has now an opportunity to carve out his own name and fame, and to be the author of his own history. We all like to trace back to the fame of our fathers and to leave some glorious record for our descendants." There was an undertone to the speech of peculiar interest: history as prediction. Southerners believed in the past as the sure path of the future; as long as there was precedent, there was certainty. It was an important assumption.

Davis had made other important assumptions, assumptions about what should be done with Bragg's army. Inactivity saps energy and makes good men lazy. There was no doubt that the enemy would make great efforts to do something about Chattanooga; a direct assault on the city looked impossible and unnecessary. And so it occurred to the President that part of the army might be detached to harass that old bumbler Burnside out of Knoxville, an achievement which would not only hearten the South but reopen vital rail connections to the East. The plan struck Bragg favorably—most Presidential plans did—and he sent Longstreet off toward East Tennessee with an army of his own.

A curious jealousy ruffled relations between Bragg and Longstreet (probably Old Pete's disgust over recent operations was thinly disguised), and it led to a virtual collapse of communication. There may have been another factor in the problem: the structure of the Confederate high command. Longstreet, who had long coveted a chance at an independent role, may have assumed that as an army leader he now had no superiors save the President and the Secretary of War, and there was ample precedent to make him think so. Bragg, on the other hand, regarded Longstreet's force as a detachment from the Army of Tennessee and hence felt he still had control over its operations, for which, too, there was precedent enough. At any rate, Longstreet slogged off along the mountaintops to a rendezvous with inertia. A lingering siege of Knoxville proved fruitless, and Longstreet sulked in grim isolation. Bragg heard nothing specific from his lost lieutenant, and at last his temper broke. Complaints went to Davis, who tried some long-distance soothing. While this quixotic correspondence smoldered, General U. S. Grant retrieved the initiative.

Tarnished Rosecrans had been sacked, and in his place was Thomas. Sherman arrived with some western divisions, and things started humming in Chattanooga. The "cracker line"—the one open road—functioned and supplies arrived. There was a change in hope: Grant. He was now commander of a vast domain extending far beyond the Chattanooga camps, and he was a man for doing. Men knew it and knew, too, that Thomas was from the same mold. What could be done about Bragg would now be done.

On November 24, 1863, it became clear that very much could be done about those Rebels sitting in haughty splendor midst the clouds. That day men under Old Joe Hooker marched out on the road to Lookout Mountain, the extreme left of Bragg's line where he commanded the great oxbow in the Tennessee; then they swung around to a kind of frontal assault and carried the pinnacle. It was no real job—too few Confederates were there to make a fight of it— but the task was vastly heartening to the bluecoats. With morning of the 25th, a Federal banner could be glimpsed on Lookout, and both armies marveled at the stamina of the victors in the Battle Above the Clouds. The real battle was still to come. Grant had erred in reconnaissance, thought Bragg's right flank rested where, in fact, it did not, and on the 24th sent Sherman to carry it. The assignment was impossible. Pat Cleburne's immovable veterans easily held Tunnel Hill and stopped Sherman's attack. Next morning, while so many looked at the new flag over the field, Sherman was again repulsed.

While Sherman's men stumbled back from their bloody encounter, Grant made a second error, and won the battle. Thinking that Bragg was shifting men from the Rebel center to Cleburne's assistance on the right—which he was not—Grant directed Thomas's men to attack straight at the middle of the Confederate army. He wanted a diversion to pin Bragg's men in position, and ordered the trenches at the base of the ridge taken. Confederates evacuated the exposed trenches and fell back to the crest of Missionary Ridge. Rebel guns raked the attacking bluecoats, razed the ground behind them, and left them only one route of escape—forward. Up the slope they came, and as they came, something happened which had never happened before: an unreasoning, amorphous panic engulfed the Rebel ranks. When the Yankees neared the top of Missionary Ridge, Bragg's center cracked, his army broke in two and streamed southeastward. Not all of the army was wrecked, but enough to ruin any hope of stopping the retreat. All the way back to Dalton,

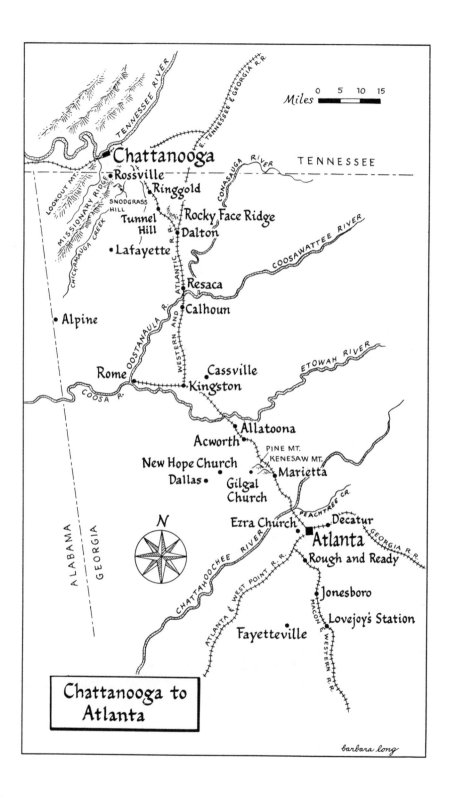

Miles 0 5 10 15

TENNESSEE RIVER

E. TENNESSEE & GEORGIA R.R.

TENNESSEE

Chattanooga

•Rossville

LOOKOUT MT.

SNODGRASS HILL

MISSIONARY RIDGE

•Ringgold

CONASAUGA RIVER

Rocky Face Ridge

Tunnel Hill

CHICKAMAUGA CREEK

•Dalton

•Lafayette

COOSAWATTEE RIVER

Resaca

OOSTANAULA R.

WESTERN AND ATLANTIC R.

•Calhoun

• Alpine

ETOWAH RIVER

Rome

•Cassville

COOSA R.

Kingston

•Allatoona

Acworth•

PINE MT.
KENESAW MT.

New Hope Church
•

Dallas•

•Gilgal
Church

Marietta

PEACHTREE CR.

Ezra Church

N

Decatur

Atlanta

GEORGIA R.R.

ALABAMA

GEORGIA

CHATTAHOOCHEE RIVER

Rough and Ready

Jonesboro

ATLANTA & WEST POINT R.R.

MACON & WESTERN R.R.

Lovejoy's Station

Fayetteville

Chattanooga to
Atlanta

barbara long

Georgia, the melee went, and only the intrepid rear-guard fight by Cleburne's division fended total ruin.

Grant should have pressed the advantage but lapsed for a moment into the sloth which so often mocks a victor. He rationalized: supplies were short, wagons scarce, and there was the problem of Burnside's Knoxville defense. Who would complain if the Yankees rested?[34]

Most of the complaining was done in the South. There, anyone with a grain of military grasp caught the awful import of Bragg's failure. And at last he lost his command to General William J. Hardee. A scant two months had passed, and in that time Dixie's hopes rose briefly like the phoenix and were ashes once again. The enemy would call the next rounds in the West.

When things had soured before in the Western theater, the country had looked to Virginia for a saving victory. It was natural because of Lee. More and more the people came to cherish him, to identify the cause with him, to make him a symbol of survival. Part of the burden, of course, his army shared; it grew in the hearts of Confederates to be the buckler of a nation. The man and his army were special. Gettysburg might be explained as one of those freaks of the gods, a caprice of fate to test the South. What was happening was simple enough—Lee and his men were becoming the whole of the cause.

Lee must have glimpsed the patterns of apotheosis, but there was no vanity in him and no sham. He accepted what he could not change and pursued his steadfast duty. More clearly than others he knew the ravages worked on him and on his men. Gettysburg was more than a defeat, it was a symptom of disease endemic in the South, a disease that weakened as it ravaged. It was hard to isolate, its duration uncertain; and if unchecked, its results were fatal—it was attrition. An army reflects national health fairly accurately, and Lee's army suffered after Gettysburg. Lee fought the suffering, did everything possible to bring more men to his ranks, find food sufficient to repress hunger, badger clothes and socks and shoes from quartermasters, medicines from the Surgeon General, worked to keep his men healthy and alert. Living conditions slowly improved late in the summer, though the daily army ration remained laughably small. Slowly ranks expanded, depots filled, and morale improved. The men were ready for almost anything.[35]

Were the officers ready? It was a real and unnerving question. Attrition had whittled grimly at the upper echelons of command through the fierce campaigns of 1862 and early 1863; Gettysburg took a toll of brigade and division commanders, and now there was a crisis of command. Where were new generals coming from? A system of natural selection had prevailed before; battle separated good and bad commanders, the good were promoted, and there was continuous improvement in leadership. But too many now were dead or maimed. Which meant that the new generals came up too quickly, without experience, and without skills. In the early months of fall Lee reorganized his army and found it almost strange. Old units still were present, familiar flags stood muster, and old veterans touched their forelocks as he passed—but the generals? War is youth's opportunity and Lee accepted that; still, with the shrewd teachings of the ranks, with the instant aging that comes in battle, the army might season its tyro generals and be much as it had been.[36]

Much depended on opportunity. Given the right kind of contact with the enemy, sufficient room for error, the new generation would learn. Summer and fall were happily easy for Lee's army. It lay in camps along the Rapidan and guarded the way to Richmond. Lee wanted to use the army, to harass George Meade's legions, but Longstreet's absence in Tennessee made him cautious. Meade might come to him.

Meade came late in the year, just about the moment Bragg's men were running from Missionary Ridge. The Army of the Potomac crossed the Rapidan on another thrust for Richmond. Suddenly Lee had a chance to help Longstreet and Bragg, perhaps to save the west. Through a series of circumstances Meade exposed his army badly and Lee made ready to smash it. He planned as usual—a flanking move to turn attention, attacks front and rear if possible. Behind Meade was a river, and his army might be trapped the way Hooker's should have been at Chancellorsville. Old plans went awry with the new command system. Orders were not executed as before, confusion spread, maneuvers failed, and Meade slipped the coils set for him at Mine Run. Lee read the lesson of Mine Run: some quality of skill was gone from the army, a deftness missing that no gallantry could balance. His men fought as always, with *élan* and courage, but their leaders used them poorly. Over the army that winter, especially over headquarters, there was gloom and weariness.[37]

All the problems of Lee's army, all the problems of the country, could be solved with more men. But manpower was at a critical ebb. The problem had become tangled with a matter of morale. In better times men maimed and wounded chafed to rejoin their units in the field; now a wound sufficient for hospitalization was a ticket out of the war. Increasing numbers of absentees without leave appeared on army rolls, and the word "deserter" lost much of its shame.[38] As attrition cut more deeply into the ranks, Confederate military authorities looked squarely into an almost empty country. Where were the replacements?

Patriots at home always had a ready answer to this embarrassing query: another draft law, another summons from President and governors, and the nation would rise up. After the rhetoric stilled, the ranks remained thin. A serious effort had been made to reorganize the conscription business at the top, and Bragg had been busy enrolling men on his own. But results indicated population bankruptcy.[39]

It was the kind of crisis to discourage men already in the ranks. Anyone could see that emergency measures were needed; what ought to be done provided a lively matter for talk. Talk in the camps of the ravaged Army of Tennessee grew fairly particular. With a new commander, Joe Johnston, a spirit of adventure excited the corps and division leadership. On the night of January 2, 1864, a week after Johnston had taken command of the army near Dalton, Georgia, he called a meeting of his generals. When they had all gathered, the nature of the council came clear and amazed many. That tough, fighting Irishman Pat Cleburne stood up and began reading a lengthy memorandum that advocated arming the slaves. General William Bate's reaction is worth recalling:

I confess I was not only surprised, but grieved as the "unrolling of the scroll" revealed its hideous and objectionable features. The proposition itself—the source whence it emanated—the place where, and the persons befor[e] whom it was presented—the infamous avowal of its author and advocates, and the apparent foothold it had gained among men in whose judgment and patriotism I reposed confidence, alarmed me.

I thought I knew the temper of the troops, and felt it was an entering wedge which if driven, in these disjointed times, would rift and scatter our Army, defeating the very object it proposed to secure. I regarded, at the time, and do now, the seductive argument with which it is interwoven, as the rose, beneath which, the serpent of Abolitionism coiled. Pluck it, and you lay bare a political hydra, the deformity of which is shocking to contemplate. Its propositions contravene the principles upon which I have . . . acted—asks to discard our received theory of government—destroy our legal institutions and social relations, which . . . would result in breaking down all barriers between the black and white races.[40]

Others reacted with equal horror to this radical proposal. General W. H. T. Walker, able division commander, took personal offense at the suggestion, and two days after the night conference at Johnston's headquarters circulated a letter to officers of like antipathy. He compiled an impressive bundle of negative reactions, presented them to Old Joe, was told that official channels were not open to an unofficial communication, and sent his brief of disgust privately to President Davis. Here was the touchiest of issues, one that searched the soul of the country. The President greeted Walker's communication with careful respect, but his reaction lacked the fiery outrage which might have been expected. Thanking Walker for the information, the Chief Executive said that such an issue could hardly be discussed openly without injury "to the public service," and he added that "I have concluded that the best policy under the circumstances will be to avoid all publicity, and the Secretary of War has therefore written to General Johnston requesting him to convey to those concerned my desire that it should be kept private."[41] If such mildness seemed surprising, Davis's reasoning was sound. Never one to deny the South any workable advantage, he had some knowledge of the fighting qualities of slaves—he had led some of his own against a group of saboteurs on his and his brother's plantations in Mississippi[42]—and he had healthy respect for Cleburne and others who sponsored the suggestion. Probably he also knew of Johnston's growing conviction that slaves must be used more effectively in supporting the Confederate armies. Then, too, there was another consideration: arming the slaves might have to be advocated sometime in the future, and if private discussion smoothed the way, the future would be easier.[43]

Those who considered the manpower problem with seriousness knew the sanity of the proposal to arm the slaves. There were legitimate fears working against the use of blacks as soldiers, fears reflected in the worrisome comments permeating Mary Chesnut's diary and in the increasing strictures put on free Negroes and slaves on plantations. Fears were natural—the specter of the Haitian uprising against the French still haunted Southerners. But the fears had little genuine basis. Where Federal armies came, slaves deserted their masters; where Confederate control was secure, so was slavery.

Many whites found this surprising—a fact which perhaps tells volumes about the Southern guilt complex. But example after example showed the general loyalty of slaves. Mary Chesnut's Lawrence remained faithful throughout the war, kept money safe for his absent master, and looked out for his mistress when necessary. Some slaves served almost as auxiliary soldiers, assisted their masters in battle, and showed a steadfastness under fire that once even brought the admiration of Stonewall Jackson. Not a few blacks protected their masters from capture by the enemy, showed special concern for family property, and did much of the behind-the-lines work that helped continue the war.

This is not to say that all slaves were docile or unswervingly loyal to the Confederacy. Often docility cloaked eagerness to escape to the Yankees, and often vengefulness replaced servility. Booker T. Washington recorded that "in one way or another, many of the slaves of the plantations managed to keep pretty good track of the movements of different armies, and after a while it began to be whispered that soon all slaves were going to be free." Elaborate grapevine systems evolved, which kept slaves aware of the progress of Union armies and of the prospects of freedom. As news of Union progress traveled along the grapevine, Washington observed, "there was more singing than usual. It was bolder, had more ring, and lasted later into the night." A new word was coined to describe a slave who had important news of the war, news received from whites or read somewhere, hard, reliable news—such a messenger was called "greasy," and was welcomed warmly. Most of the slaves were aware of the war, of its trends, and were intensely interested—but they remained largely loyal.

Why? What sort of urge kept the Negro population orderly and useful to the South? Many suggested answers have been advanced by later students of the war. Among these is the interesting suggestion that blacks simply did not think of revolting—patterns of Negro-white etiquette were so ingrained that disloyalty rarely occurred to black men. "Slavery was an institution established in the tradition and habits of both races," said one student, "and institutions withstand for a long time the winds of doctrine and the gusts of opinion—even the shock of war."[44]

Fear of possible trouble, though, inhibited Confederate use of Negroes in critical jobs—or seemed to inhibit their use. Popular rumor had it that Negroes remained on the plantations or did the usual city work; some worked on fortifications when called out by Confederate authorities or rented by their masters. A few were used in hospital service, and at last in special army functions. But beyond carefully screened activities, Negroes were considered the great mismanaged resource.[45]

In reality far more direct use was made of Negroes than scholars report. In Virginia alone, Negroes were employed in virtually every government plant, depot, or agency—enough to constitute a healthy adjunct to the Confederate payroll in the state. Elsewhere skilled Negro workers were sought avidly, their masters compensated for their time, and their skills applied in ordnance and machine shops run by the army and navy. Service by Negroes as laborers, teamsters, trainmen, and animal handlers was expected and almost universal across the South.

In retrospect it seems clear that without the active aid of countless Negroes, the Confederate war effort could not have persisted beyond 1863. Black cooperation may not have always been voluntary, may have been sometimes reluctantly rendered, but it was essential to the Confederacy. Where cooperation was a willing offering to the South, it lent a special and peculiar grace to the cause of Confederate independence.

Using Negroes as soldiers posed unusual problems in philosophy, in economics, and in social control. When General Johnston discussed black troops with his generals in early 1864 the time was too early, hope too high, for serious acceptance of a scheme to reconstruct Southern society.

But at any rate, it seems clear that Joe Johnston achieved his purpose. He had opened the subject and tacitly accepted the most extreme view of slave use in the war, and so felt justified in a restricted application of the scheme. To friend Louis Wigfall of the Senate, he wrote two days after the fated conference with his generals: "I propose to substitute slaves for all soldiers employed out of the ranks on detached service, extra duty, as cooks, engineer laborers, pioneers, or on any kind of work. Such details for this little army amount to more than 10,000 men. Negroes would serve for such purposes better than soldiers."[46] It was a sound plan and one that grew in the minds of the President and others as the year wore on.

Yankee perfidy had already made slaves into soldiers; the Confederacy could do no less. Those who wailed that the suggestion struck at the heart of the South's society must consider a fundamental question: were they fighting for slavery or independence? New divisions of valiant soldiers might guarantee victory.

"Davis, Our Loved President"

Winter seemed a poor time for a meeting of Congress. Now, in the dead of 1863's harsh cold, Richmond offered less hospitality than usual. Congressmen drifting into town in late November and early December could reflect on the price of living, and if they were of a penitential cast, they might feel the sting of works undone. Prices rose in ratio to the printing rate, goods and food grew scarcer, services too dear for purchase, and lodgings cost a sizable fortune. Worst of all, fuel could hardly be had for any sum, and the cold lingered as an enervating chill that lurked always in the marrow. It was a cold beyond normal, a tangible gnawing that seemed almost something of the spirit.

At any rate, Congressmen competed for everything in town. Many gravitated to the bigger hotels, the Ballard House, the Exchange, the Spotswood; more clustered in rooming houses, where living presumably was cheaper. But nothing was cheap. Coffee now ran to $8 a pound in Richmond, beef to $1.25; butter $4, eggs $3 a dozen, and, as a government official complained, "clothing is unobtainable."[47]

Facts of livelihood impressed on Congressmen the dire emergency engulfing the Confederacy. They soon grew touchy, eager to rearrange things and to get right with the voters. Much good could come from the proper sort of enthusiasm, but there were certain currents of legislator opinion running dark and bothersome. Rumblings of unrest across the nation focused on elected representatives, and these rumblings had alarming overtones. People across Dixie, those same people Davis had seen and heard during his swing out to the west, people everywhere were scared, scared by the way the war was going, scared by penury, starvation, a growing regimentation of life, by incesssant conscription, impressment, taxation, and the long trend of losing. In a few places, notably North Carolina, whispers of peace were spreading.

All the fears and frustrations of the electorate had affected the congressional elections of 1863. These elections sputtered across the South from June until November—there was no specific date set for them—and revealed clearly the anguish of the country. They had the usual flair and bombast of Southern politics, but there were differences from the past. The whole political process had altered. For two years a façade of unity muffled unrest and opposition to the national administration. Sporadic complaints were voiced in Congress against various war measures urged by the Executive, but no cohesive bloc formed to thwart Jefferson Davis.

In the wake of that first July week of 1863 had come a shift of balances. Now the President was a magnet of attack because survival was the issue. Those who hesitated to berate Davis personally had no qualms about quibbling with policies. The reason is obvious: policies were failing, hence were easy targets for abuse. No candidate worth his salt could miss the chance. Patriots rallied to the moment and dozens of antiadministration politicians took the stump. These men pretty well reflected the confused aims of the people: some wanted a hard war to the finish; some, a hard war with light burdens; others, almost any path to peace.[48]

In a way the 1863 elections were unique in American experience—the candidates fixed on issues and argued them furiously. Suspension of the writ of habeas corpus irked many campaigners. Conscription and exemption laws were grist for everyone; complaints of unfair enforcement, of diminishing personal liberties, of class favoritism, rang loudly from the Atlantic seaboard to Texas. Even former advocates of conscription scurried to cover and avowed disbelief.[49] Much political capital was made from the South's whirling inflation. Speakers scolded the Treasury Department, Congress, and the President for weak tax laws, for haphazard monetary planning, and for almost criminal maladministration of what plans were enacted, and scored solid points. Some candidates in the Deep South talked of using cotton as the basis of currency and called for the government's purchase of the national crop, at suitably compensating prices.[50]

All of these issues showed critics how far the government had strayed from the design of the Fathers at Montgomery, how tragically the South had followed Lincoln's example of centralism. One, especially, proved how cynically the administration had flouted state rights. The writ of habeas corpus ranked as the Anglo-Saxons' greatest victory over tyranny; it was considered the surest protection of the common man. In the North, as every Southerner knew, Lincoln had suspended the writ at dictatorial will. While Jefferson Davis had not yet gone so far, he had several times asked congressional permission to deny the writ and had imposed martial law in various parts of the country where courts were at least partially functioning. The trend rather than the fact boded the future. Unchecked, Davis and his henchmen might wreck liberty's last bastion.

Events more than issues wrote the outcome of the elections. The voters engaged in the politics of protest. Most Confederates had no will to destroy the government, most supported the war but they did want relief. And a change of leaders seemed the best way to get it. So new leaders were elected. The Second Congress, when it assembled in May 1864, would be vastly different. Critics would be heard.[51]

The election had an immediate effect on the members of the First Congress gathering for their last session. Many members were strong proponents of a Davis war, had supported all the nationalistic measures offered by his Administration, and believed still that a strong federal government was the only hope for independence. But even the staunchest pro-Davis men could not ignore the voter's vacillation. Time for change was at hand.

Even before Congress met it was clear how the political winds were running. War Clerk Jones wrote with righteous gloom in early December that "to-morrow Congress assembles. It is to be apprehended that a conflict with the Executive will ensue—instead of unanimity against the common enemy—and no one living can foretell the issue, because no one knows the extent of capacity and courage on either side."[52]

Courage the President had in uncommon quantity; capacity he had developed considerably in the war. There was no doubt that he would resist a runaway Congress. The question was how? Did Davis have the finesse for the moment? Could he unbend and cajole? Most Congressmen would answer no. Some of them already branded him a bayonet ruler, a burgeoning dictator, "King Jeff the First"; a few disliked him personally and hence saw no virtues at all; others recalled slights or slurs that rankled. One, Thomas Withers of South Carolina, carried a long grudge against Davis from the 1850's and it warped his judgment.[53] Henry Foote's enmity dated from a first fight with the President when both men were in the United States Congress.[54] Louis Wigfall, progressively irritated as the President ignored his advice, had turned from fan to foe and declared at last that Davis was crazy.[55] A general feeling of alienation spread and damaged congressional relations. Davis brought much of this on himself by secrecy and superiority. He had a zealot's intolerance and a patriot's haste, and worst of all, he knew he was right. The conviction gave him irritating insolence and drove one Congressman to say "it will do my very soul good to *rebuke* him. . . ."[56] Late in

December 1863, during a heroic recital of Davis's inadequacies, Foote announced that if the South must have a dictator, he much preferred General Lee![57]

A scattered few in congressional circles respected Davis's dedication. There were even members who glimpsed a greatness in him born of trouble. Where lesser men quailed at the long roll of attrition, wavered as the nation withered, the President met every crisis calmly and with grace. This fortitude, this courage, impressed Navy Secretary Mallory, who remembered it always:

> He could listen to the announcement of defeat, while expecting victory, or to a foreign dispatch destructive to hopes widely cherished, or to whispers that old friends were becoming cold or hostile, without exhibiting the slightest evidence of feeling beyond a change of color. . . . Under such circumstances, his language temperate & bland, his voice calm & gentle, & his whole person at rest, he presented rather the appearance of a man, wearied & worn by care & labor, listening to something that he knew all about, than of one receiving ruinous disclosures.[58]

Now, in the last days of 1863, Jefferson Davis was tired, his unfailing courtesy tinged with exhaustion. In his lofty and remote office comfort was denied him; so much needed doing and so few were left who helped. Congressmen were problems. They each had small desires and narrow views and together they offered more woe than wisdom. They wanted courting and entertaining, they talked of patronage and local bills while disaster surrounded them.

On December 7, 1863, President Davis laid before the balky legislators his plan to prolong the war. The message was a careful document that faced reality. Defeats, failures, and weaknesses were confessed in a message that called for a hard dose of discipline. Aware of all the complaints from the people, the President did not yield to panic. More conscription, stricter exemptions, more taxation, more belt-tightening, more sacrifice was the program. Foreign relations had deteriorated, and increased self-reliance was the result. Hopes for peace were wasted in so cruel a war; the enemy gave no hint of listening to propositions involving Confederate independence, and no other terms were acceptable to the South. So the war must go on until God blessed the efforts of "men who have given all they possessed to the righteous defense of their inalienable rights, their homes, and their altars."[59]

Congress understood the message clearly enough. The President expected a working session, and he wanted quick action. Action came quickly, but not constructively. The unyielding program asked by Davis gave Congress little room to maneuver. Administration advocates, and there were some, felt vulnerable to constituent attack, and opponents were uncomfortable in the role of slackers. Debates were angry and personal.[60] Reluctant at first to strike directly at the President, Senators and Congressmen aimed at his cabinet and soon fixed on Secretary Memminger as a likely villain. Up from the Treasury Department came an elaborate funding proposal; it was involved, technical, and designed to reduce the paper currency stifling commerce. It happened that luckless Memminger was right this time—his grasp of finances had improved with inflation—and he urged a plan which might have worked. But Congress could not yet believe the scope of the war. Accusations of incompetence were hurled in both houses, past failures were resurrected, and Memminger thought of resigning.[61]

Not content with harassing one member, Congress made a direct assault on the whole cabinet. On December 10, Senator Waldo Johnson of Arkansas introduced a bill to fix the tenure of cabinet officers at two years. Here was an open thrust at the President, but the Judiciary Committee approved. The right of removal was preserved to the Chief Executive, while Congress merely sought to exercise its privilege to regulate government departments. Pro-administration men rallied to the cause, and Johnson's bill was not brought to a vote.[62]

This kind of sniping showed Congress in an aggressive mood. Members were willing for the first time to insinuate congressional control over Executive matters, perhaps even to take a hand in running the war. There were ways in which such control might be managed. Confederate Senators and Congressmen were fascinated with investigating things; committees surveyed Mallory's Navy Department and Benjamin's alleged malpractice in the State Department, and while generally careful with conclusions, these committees interfered with government business. Special investigations of the Commissary and the Quartermaster Departments showed just how much damage Congress could work. Both departments were splendid targets for legislative snoopers, and they were studies in paradox. Colonel Northrop's grossly incompetent handling of the problem of starvation earned legions of dedicated enemies, while Colonel Myers was a good administrator resented by the President. Northrop survived the investigation long enough to achieve infamy by failure. Myers, whose real crime seems to have been a reference to Mrs. Davis's "squawlike qualities," became an unwilling sacrifice to congressional ambition. Efforts by congressional friends to get him promoted over presidential inertia failed and finally cost Myers his job.[63] The whole trend was dismal. Internal squabbling only comforted the enemy. Dual command of the war effort would bring chaos beyond even Southern dimensions.

At last the wayward legislators began legislating, and by the time the session closed on February 18, 1864, they had written an impressive number of laws. Conscription and exemption exhausted hours of debate. In the end the conscript age was changed to include all white men between seventeen and fifty, substitutes were no longer permitted, and those who had employed them became eligible for enrollment.[64] Congress would not yield total manpower management to the Executive, and so the practice of class exemptions continued, although the Secretary of War was given power to detail skilled workers from the army. Attempting to use every available man, Congress created an invalid corps in which partially disabled officers and men were accepted for limited service and often did heroic duty.[65]

In the monetary realm Congress did poorly. Intricacies of public finance eluded most of the lawyers and merchants, and they trimmed their views to soothe people at home. Still, some important additions to revenue could be expected from a direct 5 percent tax on all kinds of personal property—presumably including slaves—and from an excess-profits tax on joint stock companies.[66] The most important piece of financial legislation was "An Act to reduce the currency and to authorize a new issue of notes and bonds," enacted on

February 17, 1864.[67] This law, in effect, removed one-third of the currency from circulation. New notes were ordered printed and exchanged for old, at various places and times; attractive inducements were dangled for those willing to accept bonds instead. In theory, the law would reduce the outstanding $973 million in notes by $300 million, but the theory was never fully tested, since no one knew how much money actually was exchanged. And there was a catch to the prospective benefits, one which remained hidden to the public—reduction amounted to partial repudiation.

Some Congressmen of foresight argued that the South should change the base of its economy from gold to cotton or tobacco, or both. These were the real securities of the nation. But Southerners instinctively valued everything in gold, it was a tradition difficult to change.

Once they plunged into economics, lawmakers were diligent. Monetary value depended on much besides the amount of negotiable currency in circulation. Trade and commerce served as partial props to credit. Commerce had been getting out of hand as private blockade runners took increasingly less interest in public cargoes. Government freight piled up along the Wilmington and Charleston and Mobile docks, while private cotton shipments cleared readily. Agitation from Ordnance, Commissary, and Quartermaster officials finally produced two important laws that all but nationalized foreign trade. Blockade runners were required to give space to government freight on outbound and inbound voyages. Strict limitation was placed on luxury importations so that food, munitions, and medicines could take precedence on all ships.[68]

At long last, after bitter wrangling, Congress gave President Davis the power to suspend the hallowed writ of habeas corpus until the next session.[69] It marked a victory for the administration, but the price may have been too high.

By any standard the session was an administration success. Carping, complaints, opposition, delay, all had been overcome, and most of Davis's legislation became law. But now the problem of survival was inexorably his. Congress had given him what he asked, or most of it, and if his program failed, the reckoning would be grim.

And the program failed. It failed because casualties and desertion outran conscription; because money rests on confidence, and hope was fading; because private greed negated public trust; and because the Southern sun was setting.

CHAPTER NINE

"Unconquered and Unconquerable Hearts"

—JEFFERSON DAVIS

The Iron Grip of Numbers

Braxton Bragg was in Richmond. Rumor had it that the President summoned him to a high position suited to his peculiar talents. Which led to considerable speculation. The country already boasted its surfeit of croakers and even a coward or two; and numerous generals were natural losers. What was Bragg to do? The answer, when it came, defied logic, defied even the bounds of nonsense. Jefferson Davis made him Chief of Staff to the President. Adjutant General Cooper issued a brief order announcing that Bragg was "charged with the conduct of military operations in the armies of the Confederacy."[1] In light of those words the assignment had a bizarre lucidity, because Bragg's growing talent was for mischief and now he could lavish it on all Rebel armies.

Fortunately Bragg's arrival in the councils of power coincided with so much good news that he was almost lost in a spreading euphoria.

Early in 1864, the Federals flexed their armies on all fronts and ran squarely into trouble. Sherman and William Sooy Smith planned a joint thrust at Meridian and on toward the great cannon foundry at Selma, but Smith met Forrest's men at Okolona, Mississippi, and retired, and the whole expedition fizzled.[2] At the same time a forlorn column under General Truman Seymour trudged into the sandy interior of upper Florida in an attempt to encourage Unionists; the "invasion" engaged flies, snakes, endless boredom, and at last a ragtag force, mostly Georgians, under General Joseph Finegan. In a pitched battle at Ocean Pond near Lake City on February 20, Seymour lost a third of his force and fled with the rest toward Jacksonville.

In March, a major invasion of Kirbysmithdom began under General Nathaniel Banks. His army was big, well organized, and burdened with equipment, and his plan exceeded his capacity. Had he done all he hoped, Banks would have joined with another Union force coming down from Arkansas and sliced the Trans-Mississippi to pieces. All this ambition came to grief in the battle of Mansfield, Louisiana, in April when Kirby Smith smashed Banks back toward New Orleans.[3]

A Federal probe through the Shenandoah Valley was blunted at New Market on May 15 in one of the most stirring battles of the year. A small force under General John C. Breckinridge attacked a larger army commanded by General Franz Sigel, and at a critical moment four companies of VMI cadets smashed the Yankee front in a gallant charge.[4]

Enemy activity spread beyond the armies. Admiral David Farragut's fleet dared both sea mines ("torpedoes") and Admiral Franklin Buchanan's ironclad *Tennessee* to carry Mobile's outer harbor on August 5, 1864. The city was saved (was held by General Dabney Maury's little army until April 12, 1865), but the port closed and the loss proved critical.

On the high seas the *Alabama* prowled, frightened shipping far beyond her range, and at last challenged the U.S.S. *Kearsarge* to a quixotic duel off Cherbourg on June 19, 1864. The *Kearsarge* was protected by a kind of chain mail, and she finally battered Semmes's gallant vessel to the bottom. Other Rebel cruisers followed the *Alabama*'s sparkling wake—the C.S.S. *Stonewall,* a giant ironclad, escaped England in January 1865 and sailed to Cuba in time to surrender with the South in May 1865. The last Confederate banner flew on the cruiser *Shenandoah*'s mast. She ranged the Atlantic and Pacific in late 1864 and early 1865, and struck colors in Liverpool, November 6, 1865.[5]

Several attempts at amphibious warfare were made, including some frustrating fights around Albemarle Sound in North Carolina.

But there, at any rate, the Confederates seized the initiative, used a little jerrybuilt ironclad called the *Albemarle* as an adjunct to a land force, and recaptured Plymouth.[6] Bolder strikes for New Bern failed. But successes so far indicated 1864 might be a Rebel year. Southern successes might influence the Northern elections scheduled for the winter.

Still, all this Federal activity bothered the new director of Confederate military operations. So much energy expended in so many theaters indicated that the Federals must have a plan for the spring and summer. Bragg had shrewd strategic sense—it was his best talent—and he worried about possibilities. Better, he thought, for the South to strike, to follow up these early successes and to dislocate Federal plans, far better than to wait. President Davis agreed —the offensive-defense remained his constant hope—but there simply was no chance present for a sustained Confederate offensive. Bragg, after surveying the Rebel armies, reluctantly agreed. Lee's men rested along the Rapidan in fine spirits but wretched condition. Food in scourged Virginia had vanished, rail lines were overtaxed, and the army's daily ration diminished until scurvy plagued the ranks.[7] Although A. P. Hill's and Ewell's corps were recruiting, the rolls showed more troops absent than present. With Longstreet's corps still truant in Tennessee, the Army of Northern Virginia could scarcely muster 40,000 men.[8] Things were worse in Georgia. The Army of Tennessee counted 36,111 present, and 69,514 present and absent.[9] Scattered cavalry troops added another 5,000 to the effective total. Some reinforcements had been sent to the main field armies; others would go when found. A critical horse shortage reduced the mobility of the armies and restricted use of artillery. Severe logistical snarls sapped the strength of men and animals and forced the South to the defensive. This dismal fact both Davis and Bragg accepted for the moment, but hoped for some miraculous change.

"Sherman's Darling Yankee Boys Will Never Reach the Coast. . . ."
["Marching Through Georgia"]

Dalton, Georgia, sprawled in unkempt squalor. Mud, red and oozy, marked its streets, mud that slithered into shoes and boots and colored floors and walls, a heroic kind of mud. The Western and Atlantic railroad ran along the eastern edge of town, and the depot sat dank and lonesome. Out east from the tracks the Georgia countryside sulked in wintry grayness. Hills rocky and reddish rolled down toward the Conasauga River. Rising grandly west of town was Rocky Face Ridge, a mountain that ran along a north-south line as far as a man could see.[10] Between the ridge and the town, tents were scattered haphazardly in a virtual ocean of muddy water. Rain fell in sheets, gusts whipped it at anyone unfortunate enough to be out. Joseph E. Johnston was one of the unfortunates. His train rolled into Dalton Depot on December 27, 1863, and squeaked to a halt, and he stepped into the mud and the awful dreariness. For Johnston, though, the scene was shining—he had come to take command of the Army of Tennessee, and he was alive again.

This job suited his training, his temperament, and his ambition, and he was happy. Quickly he learned the low morale, the heavy gloom, of the men and changed it all with discipline. Parades were ordered, men encouraged to care for themselves, their guns, and their quarters and to think like soldiers. Veterans responded to that kind of sense and soon gave their hearts to the little general.

While he rebuilt the spirit of the army, Johnston learned a good deal about its heart. General William J. Hardee, a caretaker commander who shirked responsibility but coveted glory, greeted his successor gleefully and told him the tragic story of Missionary Ridge and its aftermath. No other Confederate army had come so low. Richmond authorities seemed convinced that the army was sound, that it had recruited above its pre-Chickamauga strength and could take on all comers at any time. Hardee knew better, as did Generals Cleburne and Walker, Bate, C. L. Stevenson, all those who joined the retreat to winter quarters. One thing told it all: the men welcomed winter and relief from war. That was disturbing. Poor living conditions magnified depression. If the Georgia state railroad could increase its trains, or could bring more food, clothing, and equipment from Atlanta, spirits would improve. But the heart of an army was revealed in its readiness to fight. Would the Army of Tennessee fight? That could only be answered in battle. Johnston thought fight was in his men. They were ashamed of Missionary Ridge and wanted a chance at redemption. Time would soothe anguish and restore courage.

Winter passed slowly. Supplies were always the problem, supplies and the missives from Richmond. The President and Secretary Seddon inundated Army Headquarters with letters filled with wild expectations, detailed lessons in tactics, querulous disagreements with Johnston's assessments of his situation, and endless promises— promises of men, horses, munitions. Precious little aid of any kind ever came; instead Johnston had to send some of his small army off to help Polk against Sherman's Meridian raid and some of his cavalry into the country in quest of forage. Morale did improve, despite chronic penury.

Out beyond Rocky Face the enemy gave signs of action. Johnston kept a wary scout on the Federals, knew when Sherman took charge, and warned the President that the spring offensive would be fearsome because of enemy strength. Could more men be sent to Georgia? Some few came; Polk returned Hardee's corps, and small brigades were shipped from Charleston, but these additions barely kept pace with disease and detachment. They were reinforcements, however, and they brought grandiose plans from Richmond. Why not take the offensive, Johnston was asked by Davis and Seddon, beat Sherman to the attack, join with Longstreet's 14,000 in east Tennessee, and cut a swath through Kentucky to the Ohio? A kind of Beauregardian whimsey tinged this question, and it must have given Old Joe some wry amusement. What would he use for transport, he asked in rebuttal, where were those promised men and horses and guns, where were the rations for the march? Ammunition was barely adequate now for defense, food at a danger level, wagons used in shifts, ambulances virtually immobile. Far more immediate was another question: could the army retreat intact when Sherman came?[11]

Johnston's questions always irked the President—they were never the optimistic kind that looked forward. A seed of distrust sown long ago sprouted during that long winter and flourished with Johnston's hesitancy in the spring. Would nothing move the man? Appeals, virtual orders, suggestions ran against Joe Johnston's will. He would move when the odds were his, a sentiment above reproach in normal circumstances. But would the odds ever be right again for the South?

Sherman ended all the criminating. Fixing on the Army of Tennessee and its Atlanta base as his objectives, he struck at Rebel positions atop Rocky Face on May 5, followed with probing attacks along the mountain, and at last moved to flank the Dalton line. Johnston beat off the first attacks but started his trains south along the W&A tracks—he could do nothing else in face of almost 100,000 bluecoats.[12] And on May 12, he began one of history's great retreats. Slowly, grudgingly, back he went toward Atlanta, halting where the ground was good, standing when the odds were for him, slipping back ahead of flankers, keeping always between the Yankees and Atlanta. With a sure grip on his men and with a marvelous sense of timing Johnston made his retreat a deadly process, turned it to a type of offense. He taught valuable lessons in tactics and maneuver as he stung Sherman at Resaca, stalled him near Cassville, made the Etowah River almost an impossible barrier, and at last seized dominating ground on Kenesaw Moutain. By the end of June Sherman was closer to Atlanta but not to victory—both of his objectives lay beyond his grasp. Wary now of Old Joe's mettle, Sherman used superior numbers to flank the Kenesaw lines, the positions near Pine Mountain, where General Polk was killed, and the lines at Gilgal Church, and finally crossed the Chattahoochee in July. Still victory was denied him. Johnston's intact army manned powerful entrenchments ringing Atlanta and waited eagerly for battle. A mistake was all the Rebels needed to make Sherman's summer a colossal ruin.

A mistake they got, but the wrong kind. On July 18, at a moment when Johnston was preparing a sharp counterattack and when Sherman's fate alarmed all the North, at that crucial moment, President Davis gave General Hood command of the Army of Tennessee.[13]

Some of Davis's reasons were sound, some complicated. Johnston kept too much to himself, refused to tell his plans, would not pledge to hold Atlanta even to General Bragg, who journeyed down to see him. There was prudence in such reticence, for Johnston had no devotion to ground and doubtless would have maneuvered anywhere to strike Sherman fatally—if he had to give up Atlanta, he would give it up. Once Sherman's army disappeared, the city would be again Confederate.

The decision had come hard to the President. True, he disliked and distrusted Johnston, but these were not sufficient reasons for the most dangerous action a president can take—changing generals in mid-campaign. Later it would become clear that Davis suffered evil advice. Bragg, who advocated the dismissal, probably did so partly from jealousy of his old friend, partly from covetousness. General John B. Hood, one of Johnston's most trusted corps commanders, veteran of Lee's army, famous leader of the Texas Brigade, man of thwarted talent, wanted the command himself and secretly derided his superior. Only the fact mattered. Johnston was out, Hood was in, and a vast fear seeped through veterans so often the victims of ambition.

There are sometimes sequels to injustice, and those who cherished hatred for Hood might have taken heart at the fullness of his fate. He took the army into hard fighting, attacked Sherman from the lines twice, was repulsed both times, abandoned Atlanta on September 2, and pulled the remnants of the army south to refit for another tilt with destiny. He was not wholly mad; his plan to attack Sherman's communications, to get on the road back to Chattanooga, and to strike up toward the great Union base at Nashville had the merit of daring. Jefferson Davis let him try it, and in November he crossed into Tennessee, wasted the best of his army in a useless attack on Franklin, and at last clamped a partial siege on Nashville. George Thomas broke the siege in December and broke Hood's army in the battle; bits and pieces of it streamed back toward the Gulf, and the bedraggled survivors sang a wry ditty of despair:

> And now I'm going southward
> My heart is full of woe
> I'm going back to Georgia
> To see my Uncle Joe[14]

Those men would see their Uncle Joe again and would know a fuller woe. While they were up in Tennessee, Sherman reached the coast.

"A smoky . . . Indian summer" [J. B. Jones]

One thing could be said for the war—it was distressingly demo-cratic. Inconvenience fell on rich and poor. The rich complained the loudest; after all, accustomed comfort is sternly missed. But wealth still had its compensations, and the fact rankled with the poorer folk. One wealthy man of Georgia confessed the situation to the Secretary of War in July 1864; he complained that although his own nine sons were in the army, he could have bought their exemption. Around him many wealthy fathers and rich slackers were buy-ing freedom from service. Sales of indulgences had been organized so well that an informal price schedule was common knowledge.[15] Which implied a sad decay in the morals of certain government offi-cials, but also implied the continuance of some "amenities" in the country.

Amenities were fewer, though, than ever. As Sherman's big army came slowly down toward Atlanta, a queasy shifting began. Many families in north Georgia, even in the upper reaches of Alabama, packed up valuables and began moving. Interior places that looked safe bulged with these new refugees. Numbers of the dispossessed boasted impeccable lineage and venerable homesteads, and there were attempts for class to keep to class. Still, a welcome went to all the war's castaways, and character came to count a good deal more than pedigree.[16]

Shock waves of invasion ran far ahead of Sherman's men. Disloca-tion of everything could be glimpsed not only throughout Georgia but also in South Carolina and northward toward Raleigh. Con-federate and state authorities would have to find alternatives for the postal service, telegraphic communications, express deliveries, train connections. Considerable desperation confused supply officers in the Deep South. Should Sherman push through Atlanta into the heart of Georgia, he might raze the great ordnance plants in Macon, Augusta, and Columbus, might cut all connection between the Army of Northern Virginia and the Confederacy's heartland. If he came irresistibly toward the Atlantic, supplies must somehow con-tinue to reach the South's main field armies. Systems of procure-ment, manufacture, and distribution must flex to the emergency.

All of which made sound rhetoric but avoided the hard truth that supply systems were already stretched beyond capacity and no flexibility was left in them. An emergency of Sherman's magnitude simply defied imagination—any attempt to cope with it was like scheming against the Great Flood.

Still, in that tremulous late spring, Sherman's meaning was obscure and the South's chances remained hopeful. Good Southern soldiers could be trusted to fend off the Yankees.

Other enemies were less easily handled. Behind the Confederate armies, citizens must rise to the challenge of peace talk, disloyalty, and treason. The trouble was that challenge remained vague, clouded in logical doubts and partial truths, and too often wore the face of friendship. With the opening of the Yankee summer offensives came a respite in peace sentiments in Georgia and North Carolina, where the boldest "reconstructionists" lurked. But it would smolder and break out hotter than before when the fighting turned against the Rebels. Sadly enough, much comfort came to the croakers from state executives. Zeb Vance of North Carolina and Joe Brown of Georgia kept up a running peace correspondence with the President through the spring and summer. Late the previous year Vance told Davis that the only way to remove North Carolina's discontent with the Confederacy would be to make "some effort at negotiation with the enemy."[17] Because Vance's comment reflected a growing sentiment, Davis answered him carefully. Obstacles to peace talks, said the President, were larger than Vance could guess.

> I cannot recall at this time one instance in which I have failed to announce that our only desire was peace, and the only terms which found a *sine qua non* were . . . "a demand only to be let alone." . . . Peace on other terms is now impossible. To obtain the sole terms to which you or I could listen, this struggle must continue until the enemy is beaten out of his vain confidence in our subjugation. . . . Till then all tender of terms to the enemy will be received as proof that we are ready for submission, and will encourage him in the atrocious warfare he is waging.[18]

Persuasive as Davis's answer might be, it irked Vance and others, seemed to show a dangerous rigidity in presidential thinking, and fed rising antiadministration sentiment.

In Georgia that sentiment received constant nourishment from a distinguished duo of disaffected politicians, Robert Toombs and Alec Stephens. Toombs's hopes dwindled as his military career withered, and he cast around for other causes. The Vice-President brooded in his remote lair and conjured visions of creeping dictatorship from Richmond. Occasionally darting forth to address the state legislature or other groups, Stephens preached loftily the doctrine of honor in adversity. What would it profit the South to win the war and lose its purpose? To which sterile logic there was an obvious rebuttal: what would it profit the dead to save purpose and lose the cause? But lawyers sometimes live in wondrous distortion and confuse abstraction with reality. Stephens was one of these. His preachings were not traitorous in purpose, only in result; his excuse was utterly legal—the important thing is intent! His high voice raised in criticism lent virtue to Joe Brown's totalitarian resistance to anything un-Georgian.[19]

As unhappiness increased with the plight of the war, men of good will lost faith in the cause and joined the carping. Resistance to Confederate laws flared in certain hill-country parts of Georgia and North Carolina.[20] When ordnance officers trekked into the mountains in search of copper coils from moonshine stills, they met the usual fate of "revenooers." When Medical Department men took the full production of legal distilleries, a natural resentment built to a small rebellion. Taxes were high, and were increasingly unpaid; tax-in-kind collectors met hostility, some of them violence; enrolling officers finally took military escorts with them on their press-gang rounds. Sometimes the courts joined the troublemakers. Usually the state judiciary supported the Confederate government, but in the wearing summer of 1864 notable lapses occurred. Most of these lapses centered on the use of habeas corpus as a way to avoid conscription.[21]

Davis reacted to all dissension in cold anger. Utterly devoted himself, he expected the same in every Confederate. Lesser mortals eluded his comprehension, and his venomous distaste for them spilled across page after page of correspondence. Especially in exchanges with Governor Brown did Davis vent his stilted patriotism, but he was up against a tough correspondent. Brown met Davis pen to

pen and their letters deserve recognition as primers of opposed constitutional philosophies—they were, in a way, "Con-Federalist
Papers."[22]

Something had to be done about low morale. Davis met the problem squarely. His letters across the Confederacy increased; influential men everywhere read the President's views on the war. Governors of all persuasions received courteous, sometimes pathetic
appeals for help; loyal ones who had sustained the government received Davis's warm praise. The President turned at last to public-
relations techniques. The columns of friendly newspapers were filled
with exhortations to rekindle the fires of resistance; teams of patriotic Congressmen went back to their constituencies having pledged
to speak widely on the need for renewed effort. But the wilderness
grew and the voices faded. Angry sounds of protest rang louder
everywhere.[23]

Nothing much could be done about the protests without attacking
the things that caused them, and the causes were beyond reach.
Poverty, the terrible grinding away of things and people and spirit,
the endless drab of life, the fear, the death: these were the causes.
Tragically, they were also effects, for the South by now had been
caught in a swirling cycle of wastage. About all the government
could hope for was a slackening of the downward trend. Brakes must
be applied somehow until the summer campaigns gave a chance for
political settlement.

Just how badly brakes were needed came clearly to Georgian
Warren Akin as he made his way to the first session of the Second
Congress. All the way from Oxford, Georgia, to Richmond he
glimpsed the wearing of the country. Trains were slow and rickety,
in places the old-style U rails were faced with sheet iron that rolled
under the trucks and speared through car floors, connections were
whimsical, schedules a joke, movement itself a miracle. Prices for
food and goods were high in the Georgia back country, prohibitive
in Atlanta, and fantastic closer to Richmond. Living conditions concerned Akin; he had a large family of his own, was a decent, conscientious Christian who took his election seriously. He had been a
Whig before the war, opposed secession, but followed Georgia to
whatever fate would come. In the 1863 elections his district sent him

to the Confederate House in the Second Congress, and his trip to the capital gave him more knowledge of the task facing the national legislators than he might have wanted. Everywhere were signs of exhaustion.

Once in those deliberative halls, Akin encountered a different exhaustion—the long, droning, picky debates over small importances. Oddly truncated, the summer session of 1864 lasted six weeks and produced little legislation. Laws passed were curiously short, missing those intricate paragraphs that earlier marked congressional style. Congress tinkered with taxes and currency manipulation. Perhaps Senators and Congressmen had run out of things to enact, but there were other possible reasons for such commendable brevity. Much verbiage was expended that summer in secret debate on two great issues: arming the slaves and peace.

Free Negroes and slaves were already serving in various menial capacities with the armies and on fortifications.[24] They had done fairly well and had convinced a good many doubters of their valor and competence. So the ancient objection to making them into soldiers faded a bit. President Davis, when he squelched the scheme of Johnston and some of his generals late in 1863, had purposely not ended discussion of Negro troops; argument had flared across the country for months. Editors, local politicians, and citizens had aired their prejudices, and contention continued in the halls of Congress. Behind the talk now was an aura of necessity. But Congressmen could not yet bring themselves to act forcefully on an issue that cut to the core of the nation, and they did nothing that summer.[25]

Peace was a different matter. In the hectic climes of Richmond everyone could see too starkly the urgent need for an end to war. Congressmen, who might cherish some claims to privilege, were cramped. They were badgered by constituents who wanted exemptions, details, or pardons for sons in the ranks. They suffered the squeeze of prices (Akin noted that he paid $2 for laundered socks, $1 for a washed and pressed handkerchief; a colleague noted that he paid $600 a month for a room and two meals),[26] and they looked on while the young recruits who mustered for the armies (the bright, fuzzy-faced boys, the South's "seed corn") marched off with fresh belief in glory. All these visions pointed to a hard truth: the South had mobilized just about everything, had committed all the blood and treasure in the country, and now lingered a hollow shell. Peace would lose its purpose if no one was left to share its joy.

What could Congress do for peace? Congress could talk much about it, could rant in endless secret conclave about motives and patriotism, could damn a stubborn President who refused negotiation, could wait. In June 1864 good news from Lee's front at Cold Harbor seemed to give a chance for honorable action. A resolution sponsored by Senator John W. C. Watson of Mississippi and a group of his friends was offered on June 2, a resolution suggesting that the government send peace commissioners to treat with Lincoln. Although many members shared the sentiments of this small minority, they could not support a document so clearly infringing the President's control over foreign affairs. The resolution, and another offered by Foote, the petrel of them all, failed.[27]

But the import was impossible to miss. Congressmen in growing numbers wanted a way out, and if the President did not find one, Congress might take the initiative. Little that happened in the halls of Congress missed the Chief Executive. He caught the drift of things and set about showing the legislators and the country the futility of peace talk. He got some help from certain editors who knew the absurdity of negotiating the extinction of the Confederacy.[28] And later in the year, when the Second Congress gathered for its last meeting, Davis would lay out grimly the requirements of peace.

In that summer there could be hope in Richmond, in Georgia, hope everywhere that old Confederate bravery would shift the paths of fate. There was really no other reliance. All the wisdom and the spirit, all the virtues had been spent. Everything had been done for independence that history told was needed, and now the South had careered on past history, past experience. What was happening in Dixie by summer of 1864 had never happened before to Americans. No traditions, no customs, no manners or methods were known for losing.

Sherman came down the tracks to Atlanta, and out from his army went bands of brigands called "bummers" who robbed and degraded the widows and orphans and aged, who burned houses and toppled monuments, and who killed far more than people. Gone with the ruins smoking in Georgia's summer air was much of America's innocence. No sorrow marred the spirit of Yankees on the march. They carried "freedom's flag" they thought, in that year of Jubilo.

Geometry of a Closing Circle

Something stirred the camps of the Army of the Potomac. Meade held his lines near the old Mine Run positions, but reinforcements poured into his camps, and much marching and countermarching could be glimpsed by Rebel vedettes at vantage points along the Rapidan. Rumors persisted that Grant himself was with Meade, that some form of condominium existed in the command structure of the army. The stumpy little general who chewed cigars, drank apocryphal gallons of whiskey, and looked perpetually like a disheveled circuit rider apparently attached himself to the Army of the Potomac as a participating observer. Meade kept direct command of the army, but the general in chief of the Armies of the United States peered closely over his shoulder. There may have been some friction in the arrangement, but for the moment none showed. What did show was energy, and by early May Meade counted 120,000 men in his ranks.[29]

Lee never wasted time. Throughout the spring he had worked to improve the condition of his men and to recruit his ranks. There were now clear limits to affluence among Confederate armies, but the Army of Northern Virginia looked and felt far better than it had in the cold reaches of winter. Men were filtering in, rations expanded with seasonal vegetables, and the horse supply improved. With Longstreet's corps back, Lee mustered slightly over 60,000 men—two to one, then, good Confederate odds.[30]

Early on the 4th of May Meade followed Hooker's old path into the Wilderness, and another phase of Grant's crusher offensive in east and west had begun. Serious fighting erupted on the 5th, confused, bitter woodland combat that shattered the Wilderness with shellfire and hissing lead. Night stalled the indecisive action, but morning of the 6th produced a full-blown crisis on the Rebel right. Into weak Confederate units still weary from the day before, a reinforced Union attack smashed smartly, broke the Rebel front, and almost cleared the way to surrounding Lee's army. At that touchy minute one of those incidents occurred that so often charmed the war: Longstreet's corps came trotting to the field, deployed with professional skill, and made ready to drive back the bluecoats. Some veterans of the Texas brigade spotted Lee as he watched anxiously, and they cheered him mightily. Caught up in the emotion of battle, Lee spurred Traveller forward to join in the Rebel charge. Go back! Go back! his soldiers cried, "Lee to the Rear!"[31] Their general safely away, grayclads stormed on to success. Part of Longstreet's command took a path around to the Union left, found Meade's exposed flank, and hit it with four brigades. Back in milling chaos the Federals ran, rolling up the line in mounting terror as they went; an incredible disaster was building for the Army of the Potomac. At that moment General Longstreet went down, accidentally wounded by one of his own, and momentum went out of the attack. Woods and the fear of shooting other comrades closing on the enemy from the other flank paralyzed further advance. What black omen could be seen in Longstreet's fall? He was wounded by his own men scarcely a mile from the spot where other Rebels had brought down Stonewall Jackson. As in that year before, there was another Rebel victory.[32]

The victory was not to be enjoyed as it had been before; Grant was of different stuff than Hooker and the others. To the surprise of everyone but Lee, the Union Army licked its wounds briefly and began moving southeastward toward Lee's right and rear. So began a deadly game of fight, flank, and fight again; a game not to end until the woods of Spotsylvania were flecked with the blood of thousands, until the North Anna and the Totopotomoy ran red, until the two armies faced each other across Lee's formidable works at Cold Harbor, near the old Seven Days' battlefields. Each battle raged fiercer than the last. Grant spent men like greenbacks, and "the butcher's bill" mounted in grisly casualty lists that shattered families all across the North.

On June 3, Grant ran the bill up another 6,000 or 7,000—he threw his whole army, the part of it that got going, into a frontal attack against some of the most sophisticated earthworks known to modern war. Lee's engineers had carefully laid out the Cold Harbor trenches, spotted fields of fire, revetted battery positions, and so arranged things that there were no real approaches. Bravery made one or two tiny dents in that honeycomb of death, but after no more than thirty terrible minutes, the attack had failed, failed midst such staccato, cadenced volleys that Lee remarked the sound was like sheets ripping in the wind.[33]

Again Grant refused to retreat. Writing Union Chief of Staff· Henry Halleck that "I purpose to fight it out on this line if it takes all summer," he planned another slipping move to Lee's right.[34] Lee this time was fooled. For three June days he lost the Union army. He suspected a flank movement, but Grant fuddled the situation with diversions. The plan was to threaten northern Virginia, bring a combination of expeditions together at the vital Rebel depot town of Lynchburg, and disrupt Lee's logistical network. This might compel a detachment of the Army of Northern Virginia and open the gates to Richmond. All of which might have worked, save for the splendid incapacity of the Union general David Hunter; Hunter bungled his approach to Lynchburg so completely, despite early successes, that valuable time elapsed and the initiative passed briefly to the gray army.

Before he snatched the initiative, Lee almost lost Richmond. Grant's scheme to fasten the Rebel capital in a circle of various Union forces produced a crisis of numbers. Hunter's army could not go unopposed, and Lee detached a small command under John Breckinridge to meet it; then came word that Sheridan's cavalry was galloping away from Cold Harbor toward Lynchburg and a junction with the wayward Hunter. Off in pursuit went Lee's troopers, under their new commander Wade Hampton, and on June 11, the Rebels turned the Yankees back at Trevilian Station.[35] Grant's continuing digging of trenches in front of the Army of Northern Virginia looked comforting; he apparently was going to sit awhile. In that respite, Lee acted to save Lynchburg. Breckinridge's efforts had been weak, and more men were needed to preserve central Virginia. Jubal Early, a veteran who rolled cigars in his mouth, cussed mightily, and fought like a demon when he served under Stonewall, took part of Jackson's old Second Corps, smashed Hunter in front of Lynchburg, and then took perhaps the biggest gamble of the war. Lee had given Old Jube wide discretion—if a chance for it opened, he could launch himself down the Shenandoah, cross the Potomac, and strike for Washington. That he did, with verve almost worthy of Stonewall; by mid-July his guns thundered at Washington's defenses and some of his sharpshooters leveled on a tall figure in a high hat standing on the parapets of Fort Stevens, but they missed Lincoln. Jubal's raid was diversion in the best tradition of the offensive-defense.[36] It drew a corps from Grant, another from the Gulf coast, but failed to relieve Richmond. And Richmond needed relief; it was under siege.

While Early still plodded northward, Grant began moving part of his army south of the James, filtered it past some Union positions between the James and the Appomattox, and suddenly appeared in great strength at Petersburg. Boldness almost won the war for him right there. Lee remained confused about the doings of the army in his front. Most of it seemed still in the lines, and no reliable intelligence could be gleaned from cavalry patrols or prisoners. The only Confederate who knew exactly the proportions of danger was Pierre Gustave Toutant Beauregard.

Fresh from a hilarious "bottling up" of a large Union force commanded by "Beast" Butler (infamous because of his New Orleans "Woman Order") at Bermuda Hundred, Beauregard was at Petersburg. Called from his splendid defense of Charleston, Beauregard had command of 2,000 men. With these he held four miles of light fieldworks around Petersburg. Against that tiny army on the morning of June 15, two Union corps advanced. Which would have been bad enough, had not the nature of Beauregard's force made the odds worse. A large segment of the Petersburg defenses was held by reserves, young and old men with little training and outmoded arms, and these nondescripts were led by one of the South's most lackluster generals, Governor Henry Wise. All in all, it was a strange and varying day. More than 40,000 Yankees were on hand, but mismanagement kept many of them useless. Attack after attack stormed the Rebel lines; the reserves hung on somehow until dusk. Then, with Southern ammunition almost gone, with casualties thinning the skeleton ranks to nothing, the Yankees broke into the trenches. Hot fighting raged in the ditches, but Petersburg was virtually "gone up." If it went, Richmond, too, was gone, for Petersburg anchored the southern defenses of the capital. But it did not go. At another of those moments when the fates have almost made their choice, a division came from Lee. Not because he knew yet that Grant was slipping from him, but just to humor Beauregard, Lee sent back a division he had previously borrowed from Petersburg. It came in time to seal the breach. For three more searing days Petersburg held out without reinforcements. Beauregard put no more than 15,000 up against 40,000, 50,000, finally 65,000 Federals. Lee remained unsure of the situation and Beauregard improvised desperately. New lines were spotted, staked out; during the night of the 17th–18th Rebels gave up their threatened positions and pulled into shortened trenches. Messengers went to Lee several times that night, all with the same message: Grant's whole army would storm Petersburg in the morning, and Beauregard could not save the city. Help must come.

By early morning of the 18th Lee had made up his mind and gone south. Troops from the Army of Northern Virginia poured into the Petersburg lines all during the 18th, took up positions assigned by Old Borey, and beat off a general attack by 90,000 men. By day's end the lines were solid and would hold. They would hold against thousands more, would be extended south of Petersburg, then sharply westward along the Southside Railroad until they became a ten-mile labyrinth of ditches, bombproofs, communicating gullies, lunettes, and redans, and they would sustain a nation for nine heroic months. Much of the credit was Beauregard's; during one of the war's worst crises he proved greater than he guessed. Some credit went to that unsung band of irregulars, those civilians in reserve who gave special burnish to the Minuteman tradition.[37]

Now, though, the crisis had passed and there was breathing time, a time to cast a balance on the summer. Richmond was besieged, but Lee's army lay intact. Grant's circle was not yet perfect. With men enough to fill the losses, the South might yet survive.[38]

A Last Charade in Richmond

At least the weather mellowed. When Congressmen clotted again in Richmond for the second session of the Second Congress an unseasonal warmth livened the city. But livening was now a matter of semantics; shabbiness was everywhere. Things were a good deal less coherent than when Congress had last met in May 1864. Prices were climbing steadily as inflation ran unchecked. Patches and mends were seen in everyone's clothes. And by the time Congress convened on November 7, 1864, most of the country was gone.

Nine days after the Southern legislators met, Sherman began his march from Atlanta to the sea, and he wrought ruin where he went. A sixty-mile swath of desolation trailed behind him: houses, factories, barns, livestock, contrabands, all the means of living were forfeit to his men. "War," he said, "is Hell," and no man proved it more conclusively. As for war, his was sound, the exact kind to win against a weaker foe. If his tactics lacked some quixotic fairness, lay it to the age. Old things were passing. When he reached the coast near Savannah and occupied that proud Georgia city on December 21, he presented it to Lincoln as a Christmas present.

Nothing could be done to stop him; Congress noted his progress in agony. Sherman's old nemesis, the Army of Tennessee, by now was ruined at Nashville and streaming back in frazzled remnants; only small Rebel units attempted to harass the Union flanks. These tatterdemalions were brushed aside. General William Hardee, who had struggled to hold Savannah, evacuated his 10,000 men to South Carolina. Once to the sea, where would Sherman turn? It was a question that terrified the Deep South. " 'Ware, Sherman, 'Ware, Sherman," was a frightening cry to thousands of civilians fleeing before that moving blue stain.[39] Sherman knew his task was easy because the opposition never mattered; he also knew that he was doing his job, that he was gutting the Confederacy.

With the western army gone and with Sherman searing the vitals of the nation, Congress sat in Richmond determined to legislate. Laws would somehow charm men from homes, guns from ships, and food from some imagined granaries. It was mad, of course, the hopeless dream of desperation. By the end of December Richmond was really all there was, Richmond and that little iron band with Lee. Laws could be passed and postures taken and many bitter words hurled in blame, but Richmond stood alone.

Intruding on the dream of resurgence was the news. Slowly the great circle closed in. In those dim times of truth, Congressmen sought ways to change the trends. Sadly for their history they fixed on the President as the cause of all the ruin and spent great venom on that anguished man. His war plan had miscarried; it must have been wrong. Critics in the country had been right: Davis was a despot, more power-mad than patriotic. Perhaps even now something might be saved from the debris of the South. Peace must be tried in earnest, while the Rebels still had an army. So strident were the calls in Congress for negotiations that Davis's calm reminders of reality were lost.

Still, he might have prevailed had not that noisome Missourian Frank Blair come through the lines to talk about peace. Blair claimed he wanted to look for papers lost in Early's raid to Washington, but he met with Davis and asked for peace conditions. Would Davis consent to talk with Yankee leaders? He would, either in Washington or Richmond, or some neutral ground. Blair's mission mystified most Richmonders, but rumors charmed facts and hope soared. Davis remained skeptical. It would all depend on one thing: would the North concede Confederate independence? The hard-worn President doubted it.

Blair went back to Washington, then returned to Richmond with a message from Lincoln: he would talk. Still doubtful, Davis appointed three commissioners to discuss peace, and he picked them with some care. Since the Vice-President was unexpectedly in Richmond and was a loud advocate of talk, he could go; along with him the distinguished Virginian R. M. T. Hunter to watch the honor of the Old Dominion; and the third man would be that old negotiator John A. Campbell, whose past experiences in Washington intrigue might be valuable.

Out of it all came a strange meeting in Hampton Roads on the morning of February 3, 1865. The three Rebel commissioners arrived (after some *opéra bouffe* formalities) aboard a steamer. There they found William H. Seward and Abraham Lincoln. Wasting little time on preliminaries, all got down to business. The discussion lasted "several hours" and, according to the Rebel delegates, "was both full and explicit." Lincoln would not yield recognition, insisted on the disbanding of forces in arms against the Union, and declined to consider individual state overtures. If peace came to a reunited country, he would, said the Northern leader, use the power of pardon liberally. While the conversation progressed, the Southerners were shown a copy of a proposed Constitutional amendment ending slavery, or "involuntary servitude," in the United States.[40]

So there was no door open. Davis might be pardoned a slight satisfaction. Holding out against the Federal armies was the only way to peace. Redoubled efforts were essential. And the sentiment spread. For a tiny moment the old fire of war flickered brightly once again. Southerners were not yet beaten, certainly not in spirit. To a huge crowd gathered in Richmond's African Church on February 6, Davis made a fiery, moving speech that impressed even his bitterest critic, Edward Pollard of the *Examiner*. Turn out half the men absent from Lee's army, and Grant would reel back to Yankeeland.[41] On the 9th another African Church meeting lasted the day and people heard Benjamin, Hunter, and others preach a new dedication to victory. The strength was in the country, according to the rhetoricians; let the people bring it out. There were other gatherings in the days after Hampton Roads. Speakers were sent back to the country with a call for renewal. Even morose Robert Toombs bestirred himself to eloquence in announcing the South could, if it would, whip "forty Yankee nations."[42] Governors rallied to the cause with patriotic proclamations,[43] and then came the pledges from the soldiers, from those ragged few who held the lines while all the talk meandered. Regiments and brigades passed resolutions of loyalty and promised their devotion to the death. Some of the fieriest sentiments came from Pickett's Division, from men in his charge that day at Gettysburg. Veterans would do their duty; the country could do no less.[44]

Resolutions were encouraging, but facts demoralizing. Bits and pieces of the country fell away in a strange kind of breaking; the

Confederacy seemed to be sloughing apart. Oddly enough in this extremity even old heroes lost their touch. John Morgan (whose escape from the Ohio penitentiary in November 1863 thrilled the South) had galloped once more to Kentucky with hopes for good recruiting. Some quality had gone from his veterans, through carelessness many were surprised and captured, and back home came Morgan much bedraggled. Even prisoners were an unexpected problem. Tucked remotely away in the backwoods fastness of southwestern Georgia lay Andersonville Prison, presided over by Major Henry Wirz. Large segments of Northern opinion condemned all Rebel prisons and guards, but the storied atrocities of Wirz and his "plug-uglies" made Andersonville a special inferno. Open, a swampy plot cut by a sluggish stream that turned putrid with human refuse long before it cleared the yard, the prison was bordered by a gruesome "deadline" beyond which no prisoner might go and remain alive. Rations and medicines were appallingly scant, and in the summer of 1864 the place became crowded with bluecoats shipped from Richmond's packed dungeons and with men from Sherman's fringes. Sanitation vanished, men contracted all kinds of epidemic diseases and suffered the ills that hunger spawns, and more than 12,000 died.[45] Wirz got the blame, not all of it deserved.

Confederate prisons fell largely under the harsh hand of General John Winder, the hated policeman of Richmond. Despite his unattractive firmness, Winder did his best to obey Confederate law and to give every Yankee prisoner the same rations as Rebel soldiers, but the regular ration was so small that it seemed like starvation fare to the bluecoats. Conditions were improved as much as possible at Andersonville, but before any real improvements in housing and medical care came, Sherman's vanguard threatened the prison and the inmates were distributed across the Deep South—some of them wandered much like Southern refugees. They had to be guarded, fed, and attended, and they were a large bother. If the Union authorities had not peremptorily stopped exchanges, the bother would have been easier, but Grant's policy was to deny the South the aid of its men in Union prisons, even if faithful Yankees suffered for it in the South. Then, too, Southern reluctance to exchange Union black troops and insistence on forcing repatriation of Rebels who had "turncoated" helped break down the exchange system.

The Confederate Congress did all it could to liberalize treatment of prisoners and in March 1865 even appropriated money to buy United States postage stamps to improve prisoner mail service.[46] This might have looked a small bit of flummery to casual observers, but the implications of that act are worth considering—it showed that Congress could swallow sovereignty for the sake of human beings.

Panic filtered into the late stages of the congressional session. Somehow confidence must be restored to the country. How? Two obvious moves by Congress might help: make General Lee commander in chief of the Confederate armies, and arm the slaves.

From the earliest days of the session—earlier, for that matter— certain members had pointed with disgust at Davis's military blunders: lost land, affection for Bragg and Northrop, the failure of the 1863 offensive, the daily glimpse of defeat. Take away some of his authority, these critics said, give it to a trusted soldier, and things had a chance to come right. Lee was the man in everyone's mind. But an attempt to create a military czar would attack directly the President's constitutional prerogative. A bill to create the office of general in chief appeared in the Senate, was debated, and was tabled —respect still protected Davis. But opponents refused to quit. A Senate resolution "advising" the Chief Executive to appoint Lee a supercommander, Joseph E. Johnston again to lead the fragments of the Army of Tennessee, and Beauregard over South Carolina passed by a 14–2 vote. Here was a serious show of congressional power—members were about ready to run the war. Davis worked quickly to avoid a clash over principle and in one of his finer moments accepted a law creating the office of general in chief.[47] He had no doubts of Lee and recognized him as his best ally. The Senate's belief that the country might rejoice in the reassignment of Johnston was officially ignored by the President.

Lee accepted the new post with accustomed modesty and pledged himself to do the President's bidding, as Davis knew he would.[48] Not long after assuming the office of supreme commander, Lee assigned Joe Johnston to his old army and told him to "drive back Sherman."[49] Too late, said Johnston "to expect me to concentrate troops capable of driving back Sherman,"[50] but he would try. For Old Joe there would be one final brush with glory.

Satisfied with command decisions, Southern lawmakers set about the difficult business of arming the slaves. Through the long months of 1864 the issue had burned across the country; all the arguments about constitutional obstacles, moral questions, and military needs were heard. Necessity slowly ended hesitation, and at last even the stalwart men with Lee raised their voices in approval; they would fight alongside slaves, but Negroes must join quickly or the cause was lost. For once Congress and the Executive were in tune on something. Davis had been in favor of putting slaves in the ranks for months. The main impediment he saw was the matter of freedom. Was it sensible to enroll slaves without a promise for the future? In his opening message to the session November 7, 1864, the President explained his views: "A broad moral distinction exists between the use of slaves as soldiers in defense of their homes and the incitement of the same persons to insurrection against their masters. The one is justifiable, if necessary, the other is iniquitous and unworthy of a civilized people."[51] Privately, the Chief Executive explained his faith in Negro soldiers.[52]

There were some touchy constitutional problems to consider. Could the Confederate Congress draft slaves? That right seemed inviolably reserved to the states. If so, then the Confederacy could levy a quota on the states. But all of this awaited firm decision by the Congress, and firm decision had gone with certainty of the future. What would the people say? Was there agreement enough on this fundamental change in the social order? Davis secretly believed the country would agree to anything save subjugation and had sent Duncan Kenner in February to Britain with a question: would Britain grant recognition in exchange for abolition? If so, the South would free the slaves! Although the President had no constitutional authority to make such a pledge, he thought he would be exonerated in wake of independence.[53] But this was incidental to the main question of Negro soldiers.

Congress sidled from the issue and talked endlessly. Finally the

state of Virginia acted. After passage of a law making slaves liable
to state military service, Governor "Extra Billy" Smith offered to
supply Virginia's quota.[54] Davis was pleased, suggested that volunteers would be better, and hoped Congress would do its duty. Congress did, after it learned the opinion of the greatest remaining
Confederate, Robert Lee. Lee, in a letter to Virginia legislators,
declared himself eager to have Negro troops. When he heard that
Negro soldier bills had actually come up for congressional debate,
he added his voice in support:

> I should . . . prefer to rely upon our white population to preserve
> the ratio between our forces and those of the enemy. . . . But in view
> of the preparations of our enemies, it is our duty to provide for con-
> tinued war and . . . I fear that we cannot accomplish this without
> overtaxing the capacity of our white population. . . . If it end in sub-
> verting slavery, it will be accomplished by ourselves, and we can devise
> the means of alleviating the evil consequences to both races. I think . . .
> we must decide, whether Slavery shall be extinguished by our enemies
> and the slaves be used against us, or use them ourselves at the risk of
> the effects which may be produced upon our social institutions. My
> own opinion is that we should employ them without delay.

Any humane view of the matter, it seemed to Lee, dictated freedom
as reward for enlistment.[55]

So it was done. On March 13, 1865, Congress passed and the
President approved "An Act to increase the military force of the
Confederate States." A compromise of various bills, the law authorized the Chief Executive to ask slaveowners for as many
Negroes between eighteen and forty-five as were needed to save the
armies. Freedom for service was not promised, but generally assumed. A few companies of colored infantry were raised and drilled
in Richmond, to the surprise of gawking citizens, but the whole
expedient was tried too late.[56]

Wrangling over major issues left just enough time for congressional harassment of the President. A major target for abuse was the
cabinet, and so offensive did the criticism grow that Secretary Seddon resigned the War Portfolio. He quit, he said, because the Virginia delegation criticized the ministers, and that seemed to him an

expression of no confidence. Seddon was the wrong man. Congress really was after Benjamin. He had survived the furor of a year before, which brought the downfall of Memminger and the appointment of George Trenholm to the Treasury Department. His relentless affability frayed taut congressional nerves increasingly, and at last he became the symbol of evil. Privately Benjamin offered his resignation to relieve pressure on Davis, and was refused.[57]

Stung by winging the wrong bird, Congressmen shifted attack to bureau heads and found the hunting bountiful. Colonel Northrop's fatuous achievements by now were legendary; starvation stalked Lee's trenches in testimony to Northrop's reign. He had to go. This time Davis could not save him, and in February his place was taken by Colonel I. M. St. John, late of the Nitre and Mining Bureau. There was, in all this pettiness, some finical satisfaction, and Congress licked its chops.

Concern about supplies was justified. They were simply running out. When Fort Fisher, guarding the harbor of Wilmington, North Carolina, fell to a fierce attack on January 15, 1865, the Confederacy's last port was closed. Self-reliance had come with a vengeance. Critical shortages accelerated to outright dearth. Such commonplaces as nails became objects of jealous contention; acid for telegraph batteries was lent from office to office;[58] paper was used more thoroughly than before. Sherman had complicated the entire logistical snarl. He kept moving northward from Savannah, to Charleston, and into North Carolina. Ordnance installations in Georgia were either cut off from Lee's army or forced to tortuous lines of communication. Columbia, with valuable munitions and medicines, was in Sherman's way, and went to the torch.[59] Other threatened depots were deliberately abandoned or destroyed in the path of invasion.

All of which revealed a terrible truth: the South was beginning to consume itself.

Surrounded by the spreading shambles Congress remained true to the mirage that buoyed Richmond. On March 14, 1865, a Joint Resolution was adopted which put the fading Southern dream in curiously poignant words:

> *Resolved by the Congress of the Confederate States of America,* That while Congress regrets that no alternative is left to the people of the Confederate States, but a continuance of the war or submission to terms of peace alike ruinous and dishonorable, it accepts in their behalf the issue tendered them by the authorities of the United States Government, and solemnly declares that it is their unalterable determination to prosecute the war with the United States until that power shall desist from its efforts to subjugate them, and the independence of the Confederate States shall have been established.[60]

So saying, Congress adjourned on March 18, 1865. It never met again. When the members left, Richmond was much as it had been before they came. All the talk and lawmaking consumed time and newsprint but made no changes in reality. Reality lay out from Richmond and along the ditches that stretched to Petersburg. The future rested with the thin gray men who trusted Robert Lee.

"Duty Faithfully Performed" [*General Order No. 9, ANV*]

A good many remembered the kind of day it was that Sunday. "Bright and beautiful," noted War Clerk Jones. As on other pretty Sundays, Richmonders bedecked in their worn finery journeyed to church. An alarm just at dawn scarcely raised an eyebrow in the battle-wise capital; it signaled another local emergency in the lines that would be dealt with as all others. The President, alone these days since his family had gone south, went to St. Paul's where he had been confirmed thirty-four months before and listened to the good Dr. Charles Minnegerode's elevating drone.[61] Almost in mid-sentence the sermon stopped as a messenger bent over the President and escorted him from the church. Other men left other churches. Soon all of Richmond knew the worst: Lee had telegraphed that his lines were broken, he could no longer cover the capital and it must be evacuated by nightfall! Confusion began slowly, eddied along main avenues, and brought dazed people out. Panic simply did not come. Everyone seemed to know that they were not going to get out, that such limited transport as could be gathered would take important people and papers away. In government offices the situation did get sticky; clerks and officers raced about to little purpose;

papers were shuffled, spilled, and crammed into boxes. Orders concerning evacuation procedure were given: The tobacco, some of which was claimed by France, would be burned—no, it would be soaked with turpentine.[62] Arsenals and ordnance works would not be blown up—no, they would be. Trains would or would not run; civil employees of the government with families in town were urged to stay.

All the anguish of every lost hope gathered over the White House that Sunday. Rushing, confusion, rumors, expectations, dread, all plagued the President. Faithful friends suddenly feared to know him, and that brought the old stiff smile—people scarcely changed. Time trembled and little things took on great import; it was important to pack the things Varina wanted, but suddenly everyone was interested in his own problems and help melted. The President had too many public duties, he left what he could not carry. Surprised and muddled he was, but less so than most. He knew how closely ruin clutched the city, had known for weeks. The cold reports of supply chiefs, which he had asked for in February, told him the future. The South had gone beyond resources, and the end could be measured in the storehouses.[63] And yet he was not ready for it now; no man is ready for the real finish. He knew that still in the hearts of the Confederate people there was the stuff of winning, that in the fullness of crisis all the croakers and the carpers, the gossipmongers and the profiteers would see the doom they were ringing down and would repent. If that repentance came quickly and completely, the Confederacy might live. As he gathered the Executive papers he would need, the people who must go with him, something very human happened to Jefferson Davis. He stopped seeing the inevitable and began to believe in another future. In this other future the Confederacy would win and be free. It was a deep and moving conviction and it lent him a certain grandeur as he walked through the ruin of his life.

The government, such parts of it as made the train, went that night to Danville.[64] Friendly, sympathetic folk made the President's party welcome, and for a moment the flight stopped. Davis wanted desperately to stay in Virginia, he thought it vital to keep a corner of the Old Dominion lest a peace party take it from the Confederacy.

To show his purpose he set up a temporary capital in Danville and got the bureau chiefs who were with him to do business as usual. Now, though, the tokens of civil government seemed empty gesturing. Everything hinged on the armies.

Hours and then anxious days passed while the President waited for word from Lee. Johnston's troubles were too well known; Sherman was pushing the tiny little Army of Tennessee backward toward Virginia, and in time it might camp in the President's front yard. Not much had been done to stop Sherman, and this time Davis could hardly blame Old Joe. Confederate forces in the Carolinas could not have counted more than 25,000 men. With that small force, though, Johnston had tried desperately. At Bentonville, North Carolina, in mid-March, he struck at Sherman's divided columns. Once again the tattered battle flags went forward, the tiny brigades fixed bayonets, the Rebel yell echoed, and Johnston's army charged. The Army of Tennessee swept the field that day in one last round of glory. But there was no strength for the victory needed and the only way was back. Now those tired legions who had marched so long, so far, were back near Durham Station, North Carolina. Old Joe talked of a convention or armistice with Sherman, and it might be that now all those bloody miles and roads had reached an end.

Davis hoped not. He waited for word from the country's greatest army and from General Lee. While he waited he wrote his last state paper and his best. In the eloquence of anguish he called his people to redeem their dead with dedication. There was ardor in his heart that the haughty often know and he put it now in words:

Danville, Va., April 4, 1865

To the People of the Confederate States of America

The General-in-Chief of our Army has found it necessary to make such movements of the troops as to uncover the Capital, and thus involve the withdrawal of the Government from the city of Richmond.

It would be unwise, even if it were possible, to conceal the great moral, as well as material injury to our cause that must result from the occupation of Richmond by the enemy. It is equally unwise and unworthy of us, as patriots engaged in a most sacred cause, to allow our energies to falter, our spirits to grow faint, or our efforts to become relaxed, under reverses however calamitous. . . . It is for us, my countrymen, to show by our bearing under reverses, how wretched has been the self-deception of those who have believed us less able to endure misfortune with fortitude, than to encounter danger with courage. . . . If by stress of numbers, we should ever be compelled to a temporary withdrawal from her [Virginia's] limits, or those of any other border State, again and again will we return, until the baffled and exhausted enemy shall abandon in despair his endless and impossible task of making slaves of a people resolved to be free.

Let us not then respond [sic], my countrymen, but, relying on the never failing mercies and protecting care of our God, let us meet the foe with fresh defiance, with unconquered and unconquerable hearts.[65]

Six days after he wrote this message he heard from Lee. The night that Richmond was evacuated, the Army of Northern Virginia had moved southwest along the railroad toward Burkeville. Lee hoped somehow to escape Grant's hordes and link with Johnston. Perhaps the combined armies could beat Sherman and change the balance of the war. All kinds of small impediments plagued the retreat. Word was that a train of rations waited at Amelia Court House, and rations were vital. The men were trench-weary and unused to long marching and had eaten little for months. Food would restore morale and then the army would be hard to stop. There was a train at Amelia, but it carried ammunition. Not far south, and barring the way into Danville, was a heavy curtain of Grant's cavalry. West, then, Lee turned his army, and sent for a commissary train to meet him at Farmville. After four days' trudging the ranks were numb and dazed; men kept marching because they were with Lee. Sights along the columns saddened the commanding general. Those veteran corps shrunken now to brigades, those special men—many of them with him on the fields of the Seven Days, into Maryland, with Stonewall in the Wilderness—were tired and gaunt and drawn out beyond mortality. Some uncommon lapse occurred, and Ewell's men were trapped in a big fight near Saylor's Creek; most were captured. Onward still the others went, found the train at Farmville; Longstreet's frenzied scarecrows milled around it, broke into cars, threw out rations, and then heard the sharp popping skirmish fire of Yankee cavalry. A hasty rear-guard fight raged, the train and the rations were lost, and the army marched on toward Appomattox

Court House. Hunger became tangible. Hope now centered on food, on reaching Lynchburg's stores and then perhaps turning South or going on to the mountains of southwest Virginia. Off on the left flank Hampton reported great clouds of blue horsemen, stalking, blocking the way to Johnston. Hunger and now fatigue riddled the ranks. Steadily the effective strength melted away.

On the night of April 7, General Billy Mahone, a Virginian with battle distinctions beyond counting, asked the Union general in his front for an hour's truce to care for his wounded. During the lull, a courier rode in from the Federals with a letter for General Lee. It was from Grant, and it proposed that the time had come for the Confederates to give up. Lee considered his reply. No, he said, the Army of Northern Virginia was not yet brought so low. But perhaps talk about a general settlement might be fruitful. Grant had no authority to talk of anything beyond Lee's army. Lee was careful to keep contacts open, watched his language. Grant did the same. Both men were realists, both without a sense of glory, both in favor of saving lives.[66]

The march went on, resolved now in a strange, unequal race for Appomattox Station. By morning of Sunday, April 9, the race went to General Phil Sheridan's blue cavalry. His men captured a ration train, the one hope that had kept Lee's thin troops going.[67] Before the news reached the Rebels, Lee had learned something about the cause. One of his generals told him bluntly the nature of things: "There is no country . . . for a year or more. You are the country to these men. They have fought for you. They have shivered through a long winter for you. Without pay or clothes, or care of any sort, their devotion to you and faith in you have been the only things which have held this army together. If you demand the sacrifice, there are still left thousands of us who will die for you."[68] Sobered and quiet, Lee pondered this truth. Another of his officers offered a suggestion. The army should break up, scatter into the hills, try to reassemble under Johnston or just fight on as guerrillas—that kind of smoldering war would finally sap the Northern will. Lee thought this over, too, and then put his philosophy of life into the answer: "We must consider . . . the country as a whole. Already it is demoralized by the four years of war. If I took your advice, the men would be without rations and under no control of officers. They would become mere bands of maurauders. . . . We would bring on a state of affairs it would take the country years to recover from." Younger men, the General said, might enjoy bushwhacking, all he could do would be to "go to General Grant and surrender myself and take the consequences of my acts."[69] The man who offered the plan remembered Lee's words always: "He had answered my suggestion from a plane so far above it, that I was ashamed of having made it."[70]

There was going to be one last fight. Only 9,000 effective infantry answered roll now, but a conference of generals on Saturday night concluded that the army must do everything to escape. John Brown Gordon, he of the hitched shirtsleeves and fiery eye, would lead his corps against the enemy's Appomattox positions in the morning. If a way through could be found, there still could be another ending. With their usual verve, Gordon's corps attacked at Sunday's dawn on April 9, 1865. That hunched scurry once again, those starry rags flapping, the familiar yell, that splendid courage that never quailed, that old touch of victory—all of it was there that morning, and the Union front broke, two guns were captured. For one tantalizing moment the escape road was open, and then it closed as heavy blue columns arrived. So there was nothing left but a talk with General Grant.

Small details often etch great moments. Again the weather was remembered; it was a sparkling spring day, clear and bright. Then there was the house where Lee and Grant met around noon; it belonged to Wilbur McLean, and surely he was the most war-bedeviled man North or South. Beauregard had used his other house as headquarters at First Manassas. And of Lee and Grant themselves, that day, a good deal is recollected. Lee had Grant on looks; his headquarters wagon had burned on the retreat, and all he had was his best gray uniform and in the sunlight it showed to good advantage. Grant appeared informal as ever, but there was a quiet dignity to him. Several generals stood in the room where the two commanders talked, and these witnesses recalled things variously, but they all noted an atmosphere of restrained courtesy. Grant did no boasting, Lee no asking. A bit of reminiscing started the meeting. Both chieftains talked of old wars and of the United States Army. Grant had some terms; Lee thought them generous, and suggested that his men owned their horses. Grant understood, agreed they should keep the animals, and Lee said the terms would be helpful "and will do much toward the reconciliation of our people." And it was over.[71]

Lee walked out, mounted Traveller, and rode alone to his lines. Veterans saw him, the lowered shoulders, the tragic face, and they knew; they clustered around his horse, they touched him, they mumbled things. And he rode on to his wagon. By arrangement, the Army of Northern Virginia would march out with colors to stack arms the next day. During the afternoon Grant sent rations to Lee's men and stopped incipient cheering in the Union camps, and both armies mingled.

To any who read the terms Lee signed that day, one paragraph might have brought interest: "Each officer and man will be allowed to return to their homes, not to be disturbed by the United States authority so long as they observe their paroles and the laws in force where they may reside." General Grant pledged himself to prevent reprisals—it was the most important fact of reconciliation.[72]

Monday was the day, and those few men left on the Southern side knew it would be hard; they had lost, the gall tasted, and they wept, many of them. By some terrible cast of fate General Lee had surrendered and the war for them was over. With elegant simplicity General Lee bade farewell to those good soldiers, spoke his affection for them, and saved a shred of honor. Those men of Lee's were the winnowed ones who stayed on for the end. They were proud, and they showed it as they fell in for that last parade. They would have liked to look better, but the tatters, rag-soled shoes, and riddled flags would do. Men of Gordon's Corps went first; their tall general led them. At the head of the corps marched the proudest unit of the army, a tiny fragment of the Stonewall Brigade. Out from the Rebel lines, along the serried ranks of the enemy they went, shifting to carry arms, the marching salute; the enemy shifted, too, and the gray men stacked arms. Others came, the line moved steadily, and then there were no more.[73] Over the field for a moment there was a strange silence—an age had stood review and gone on to memory.

* * *

Davis would not believe it for a while; would try to work south to Johnston. And when at last Old Joe gave up, too, and surrendered his incredible 14,000 to Sherman on April 26, a shattered President still journeyed on toward something. A vision it was, a vision of renewing the war in the Trans-Mississippi. The vision blurred, though, in the wilds of North Carolina and in Georgia as Davis saw the dissolution all around. Bitter vision it became when he glimpsed, too, some joy in peace. The South was finished with fighting.

In those last days Davis gained another dignity. He planned secretly how to end the war according to the constitution. Perhaps if he resigned the states might each conclude a treaty. It was legal and proper that he should think this way, for he was the President and could not yield.

On May 10 at Irwinsville, Georgia, he was captured with his wife and a small staff. In that last moment there was irony; he wore a shawl and some sort of coat, and it led to a persistent story that he was dressed as a woman and tried to flee.[74]

So the dream was lost for Davis, his country, and his people. Davis would suffer two prison years, win a mite of martyrdom, and last out his life as the symbol of the defeated South. The South would suffer a dozen years of Reconstruction, generations of poverty, and the humility of being beaten. Confederates would suffer the wound of losing, and would nurse the wound in anger until anger became pride.

At last a legend would arise, a legend of honor and duty, of sacrifice against great odds, a legend that would pit gallantry against impersonal force.

Acknowledgments

This book has been so long in the making that I offer thanks to legions of people. There are, of course, special folk who have aided, cajoled, persuaded, listened, encouraged through many years, and these I thank especially. Among them is the coterie of friends clustered in the Jefferson Davis Association offices at Rice University—Gene Riddle (without whom not), James McIntosh, Mary Castaneda, Kathleen Davis—whose assistance transcends mere gratitude.

My colleagues in the history department of Rice University, especially Dr. Floyd Lear (who read the manuscript and whose aid through the years has been constant), Dr. Harold M. Hyman (who also read the manuscript), Dr. Ira Gruber, Dr. Hardin Craig, Jr., Dr. Charles Garside, have been patient and understanding. I am deeply indebted to them all.

Professor T. Harry Williams of Louisiana State University read the manuscript and listened to various theories and ideas at various pre-football parties. I am constantly in his debt.

Lynda Lasswell of the Jefferson Davis Association, my research assistant, worked on the notes and on difficult problems of research. I can never repay her kindness and her diligence.

Other research assistants were especially helpful: Lyn Dumenil and Larry Turner of Rice University both worked on various problems, and Miss Dumenil prepared most of the notes. Steve Shannon, a graduate student in history at Rice, performed special research tasks without adequate notice, and always performed them well.

Jackie Miller Church did yeoman service in typing, checking, and editing. Lucille Echohawk also assisted with typing.

Friends in the historical guild offered their usual willing aid—among them: Allan Nevins (who has helped always and generously), Ray Billington, John Pomfret, Jay Luvaas, Bell I. Wiley, Richard Harwell, Thomas

L. Connelly, Haskell M. Monroe, Jr., Emory M. Thomas, Will Holmes, Michael Davis, James Chumney, Sharon Hannum, Archie McDonald, James L. Nichols, Barnes F. Lathrop.

Special thanks are due to the grants-selection committee of the Henry E. Huntington Library for a summer research grant, which made possible vital work in the library's impressive Civil War collections. I am equally indebted to the American Philosophical Society for a summer grant which made possible work in British sources.

This book could hardly have been finished without the generosity of the Board of Governors of Rice University, who made research funds available on a long-term basis.

Historians are always in the debt of archivists and librarians. My sincere thanks go to Sarah Jackson and Karl Trever of the National Archives, who gave of their vast knowledge and their time; to Richard O'Keeffe, Librarian of Fondren Library, Rice University; to Gilberta Zingler, chief of acquistions in the Fondren Library; to the entire staff of Fondren Library; to the staff of the Huntington Library; the staffs of the following university libraries: Duke, Emory, Georgia, North Carolina (especially the Southern Historical Collection), Southern Methodist, Texas, Tulane, Virginia, William and Mary.

As usual, the staffs of the Library of Congress and the National Archives were very helpful.

My family has been unfailingly polite about this book. Daughters Nita and Nancy and son Frank have suffered the outrage of a "writing" parent with understanding; mother and father have encouraged as ever; mother-in-law and father-in-law have aided and abetted; my wife, Susie, has lent her special "listening ear" to years of the Confederacy.

And I want to express apprecation to my editor, Herman Gollob, and his assistant, Linda Taylor, who not only kept the faith but converted others.

What good there may be in this book is the result of the aid of all these who have helped—the bad is my sole doing.

Notes

Chapter One: "The South, the Poor South . . ."

1. For general coverage of party history through the prewar years, see Allan Nevins, *Ordeal of the Union*, 2:452–86; and Roy F. Nichols, *The Stakes of Power*, pp. 54–62, 73–84.
2. For general discussions of slavery and the plantation system, see Eugene D. Genovese, *The Political Economy of Slavery*, pp. 243–87; Clement Eaton, *A History of the Old South*, pp. 380–96; Stanley M. Elkins, *Slavery: A Problem in American Institutional and Intellectual Life*, *pp.* 37–80, 206–22; Ulrich B. Phillips, *American Negro Slavery* pp. 261–90, 359–401.
3. W. J. Cash, *The Mind of the South*, p. 63.
4. Clement Eaton, *A History of the Old South*, pp. 267–72; Clifford Dowdey, *The Land They Fought For*, pp. 14–22. For a recent evocation of the spirit of Nat Turner's insurrection, see William Styron, "This Quiet Dust," pp. 135–46.
5. For a careful analysis of this nationalistic sentiment, see Avery O. Craven, *The Growth of Southern Nationalism*.
6. Wendell H. Stephenson, *A Basic History of the Old South*, p. 64.
7. For the impact of the *Liberator*, see John L. Thomas, *The Liberator*. For Garrison's role in the reform movement, see Russell B. Nye, *William Lloyd Garrison and the Humanitarian Reformers*. A competent recent biography of Garrison is Walter M. Merrill's *Against Wind and Tide*.
8. For the story of the abolitionists told from their point of view, see Dwight L. Dumond, *Antislavery*.
9. See Frank E. Vandiver (ed.), *The Idea of the South*, pp. 43–55; Jesse T. Carpenter, *The South as a Conscious Minority, 1789–1861: A Study in Political Thought*. See also Clement Eaton, *The Freedom of Thought Struggle in the Old South*, pp. 148–58.
10. See for example E. M. Coulter, *John Jacobus Flournoy*, pp. 11–31; Russell B. Nye, *Fettered Freedom*, pp. 57–69, 140–43.
11. The confusing details of church separation in the antebellum years are given in William Warren Sweet, *The Story of Religion in America*, pp. 412–99. Specific problems plaguing one denomination are analyzed in

Haskell M. Monroe, Jr., "The Presbyterian Church in the Confederate States of America."

12. For the closing of the Southern mind, see Clement Eaton, *Freedom of Thought in the Old South*, pp. 36–47.

13. Sarel H. Eimerl, "The Political Thought of the Ante-Bellum Fire-Eaters."

14. For details of Calhoun's life and thought, see Gerald M. Capers, *John C. Calhoun, Opportunist;* Margaret Coit, *John C. Calhoun, American Portrait;* Richard N. Current, *John C. Calhoun;* Charles M. Wiltse, *John C. Calhoun.*

15. See Dwight L. Dumond (ed.), *Southern Editorials on Secession*, pp. 151–59.

16. William W. Freehling, *Prelude to Civil War.*

17. For details of the conventions, see Allan Nevins, *The Emergence of Lincoln*, 1:203–28, 261–86; William B. Hesseltine (ed.), *Three Against Lincoln*, pp. 3–140; Roy F. Nichols, *The Disruption of American Democracy;* Ollinger Crenshaw, *The Slave States in the Presidential Election of 1860*, pp. 11–16.

18. Dumond (ed.), *Southern Editorials on Secession*, pp. 159–62.

19. For a discussion of secession and some of its causes, see Chauncey S. Boucher, *The Nullification Controversy in South Carolina;* Avery O. Craven, *Civil War in the Making* and "Background Forces and the Civil War," pp. 5–18; Ulrich B. Phillips, *The Course of the South to Secession;* Kenneth M. Stampp, *And the War Came;* Alexander H. Stephens, *A Constitutional View of the Late War Between the States*, 1.

20. For a careful study of the Montgomery debates, see Albert N. Fitts, "The Confederate Convention," pp. 83–101, 189–210.

21. Lynda J. Lasswell, "Jefferson Davis and the Mississippi Rifles in the Mexican War."

22. For Davis's speech, see [E. A. Pollard], *Echoes from the South*, pp. 72–76.

23. Jefferson Davis, *The Rise and Fall of the Confederate Government*, 1:231; Varina Howell Davis, *Jefferson Davis, Ex-President of the Confederate States of America*, 1:13–33; William E. Dodd, *Jefferson Davis*, pp. 222–25; E. M. Coulter, *The Confederate States of America, 1861–1865*, p. 26; Hudson Strode, *Jefferson Davis, American Patriot*, pp. 401–407.

24. Coulter, *The Confederate States of America*, p. 26.

25. Mary Boykin Chesnut, *A Diary from Dixie*, pp. 5–22.

26. Charles R. Lee, Jr., *The Confederate Constitutions*, pp. 60–81, 82–122; *Journal of the Congress of the Confederate States of America, 1861–1865*, 1:41, 45, 72; James M. Matthews (ed.), *Statutes at Large of the Provisional Government of the Confederate States of America*, stat. 1, chap. 1 ("An Act to Continue in force certain laws of the United States," approved February 8, 1861).

27. Frank Moore (ed.), *The Rebellion Record*, 1:44–45 (pages not consecutively numbered).

28. For the controversy surrounding the question of Memminger's nomination, see Mary Chesnut, *A Diary from Dixie*, p. 385.

29. Joseph T. Durkin, *Stephen R. Mallory*, pp. 130–35.

30. Ben Procter, *Not Without Honor*, pp. 129–31; Jefferson Davis, *Rise and Fall*, 1:242.

31. Mary Chesnut, *A Diary from Dixie*, p. 77; Edward Younger (ed.), *Inside the Confederate Government*, pp. xxiv, 100.

32. Mary Chesnut, *A Diary from Dixie*, p. 6.

33. Jefferson Davis, *Rise and Fall*, 1:232–36.

34. Hugo Schlatter and Arthur P. Van Gelder, *History of the Explosives Industry in America*, p. 107; *Eighth Census of the United States, 1860: Manufactures*, pp. 715–18; Clifford and Elizabeth Lord, *Historical Atlas of the United States*, pp. 70, 73; Frank E. Vandiver, *Ploughshares into Swords*, pp. 55–65.

35. Jefferson Davis, *Rise and Fall*, 1:311–13; W. Adolphe Roberts, *Semmes of the Alabama*, pp. 37–38; Vandiver, *Ploughshares*, p. 58.

36. Caleb Huse, *The Supplies for the Confederate Army, How They Were Obtained in Europe and How Paid For*.

37. Lord Lyons to Russell, 9 April 1861, Russell Papers, Public Record Office, London, PRO 30/22/35.

38. Matthews (ed.), *Statutes, Provisional Government*, p. 92.

39. Jefferson Davis, *Rise and Fall*, 1:244–46. Free navigation and elimination of trade barriers were ensured by early acts of the Provisional Congress. See specifically "An Act to declare and establish the Free Navigation of the Mississippi River," approved 25 February 1861, in *Statutes, Provisional Government*, stat. 1, chap. 14, and "An Act to Modify the Navigation Laws and Repeal All Discriminating Duties on Ships or Vessels," approved 26 February 1861, in *ibid.*, chap. 15.

40. Jefferson Davis, *Rise and Fall*, 1:246.

41. See L. E. Chittenden (ed.), *A Report of the Debates and Proceedings in the Secret Session of the Conference Convention, for Proposing Amendments to the Constitution of the United States, held at Washington, D.C., in February, A.D. 1861*.

42. See W. A. Swanberg, *First Blood*, pp. 229–31; Jay Monaghan, *Diplomat in Carpet Slippers*, pp. 54–55; A. K. McClure, *Lincoln and the Men of War Times*, p. 71. See also John G. Nicolay and John Hay, "Abraham Lincoln: A History," pp. 429–36.

43. Lord Lyons to Russell, 7 January 1861, in Russell Papers, PRO 30/22/35.

44. *Id.* to *id.*, 26 March 1861, in *ibid.*

45. Stampp, *And the War Came*, pp. 156–58, 205, 223, 226, 241–51.

46. For the address, see Roy P. Basler (ed.), *The Collected Works of Abraham Lincoln*, 4:249–71, especially p. 266.

47. *Ibid.*, 4:323.

48. William Y. Thompson, *Robert Toombs of Georgia*, p. 168. The Sumter crisis and especially the historiography of war guilt is covered in Richard N. Current, *Lincoln and the First Shot*. The Confederate dilemma is best presented in Ludwell H. Johnson, "Fort Sumter and Confederate Diplomacy," pp. 441–77. Perhaps the best general account of the Sumter episode is Swanberg's *First Blood*. See also Allan Nevins, *The War for the Union*, 1:39–70.

49. R. U. Johnson and C. C. Buel (eds.), *Battles and Leaders of the Civil War*, 1:75–82.

50. Ruffin to "Dear Sir," 30 January 1863, in Extra Illustrated Edition of *Battles and Leaders*, 2: facing p. 79, Henry E. Huntington Library, San Marino, California. This special edition, containing many original documents, is identified by the number 298000.

Notes

Chapter Two: "Cast upon the Winds and Waves"

1. Roy P. Basler (ed.), *The Collected Works of Abraham Lincoln*, 4:331–33.
2. Howard K. Beale (ed.), "The Diary of Edward Bates, 1859–1866," pp. 173–75, 198–99, 201; Allan Nevins, *The War for the Union*, 1:119–36; Jay Monaghan, *Civil War on the Western Border, 1854–1865*, p. 158.
3. E. M. Coulter, *The Civil War and Readjustment in Kentucky*, chaps. 2–6; *Journal of the Congress of the Confederate States of America, 1861–1865*, 1:536–43; Nevins, *The War for the Union*, 1:129–36; *War of the Rebellion*, ser. 1, vol. 2, pp. 179–88.
4. *Journal of the Congress*, 1:479–83; Wilfred Buck Yearns, *The Confederate Congress*, pp. 39–41.
5. For treaties between the Confederate States and the Indian nations, see James M. Matthews (ed.), *Statutes at Large of the Provisional Government of the Confederate States of America*, pp. 289–411.
6. Joseph E. Brown to Davis, 28 February 1861, in Keith Read Collection, University of Georgia; Dunbar Rowland (ed.), *Jefferson Davis, Constitutionalist*, 5:67, 78; *Statutes, Provisional Government*, stat. 1, chap. 22.
7. Rowland (ed.), *Jefferson Davis, Constitutionalist*, 5:78.
8. "An Act recognizing the existence of war between the United States and the Confederate States; and concerning letters of marque, prizes and prize goods," in Matthews (ed.), *Statutes, Provisional Government*, stat. 2, chap. 3; "An Act to make further provision for the public defence," in *ibid.*, chap. 8.
9. E. M. Coulter, *The Confederate States of America, 1861–1865*, pp. 328–32; Frank E. Vandiver, *Ploughshares into Swords*, pp. 60, 63, 81–82; A. B. Moore, *Conscription and Conflict in the Confederacy*, pp. 357–58; statistical table of Confederate manpower, compiled by T. L. Connelly, in writer's possession.
10. Edward Younger (ed.), *Inside the Confederate Government*, p. 100; J. B. Jones, *A Rebel War Clerk's Diary*, 1:37–38.
11. Charles B. Dew, *Ironmaker to the Confederacy*, p. 86.
12. Alfred Hoyt Bill, *The Beleaguered City*, pp. 45–61; Emory M. Thomas, "The Confederate State of Richmond," pp. 14–27.
13. Mary Boykin Chesnut, *A Diary from Dixie*, p. 51.
14. Matthews (ed.), *Statutes, Provisional Government*, p. 165.
15. Hudson Strode, *Jefferson Davis, Confederate President*, pp. 77–89; Jefferson Davis, *The Rise and Fall of the Confederate Government*, 1:339–40.
16. [Henry Timrod], *Poems of Henry Timrod, With Memoir and Portrait*, pp. 8–9.
17. Ulrich B. Phillips, *Life and Labor in the Old South*, pp. 301–302.
18. Clement Eaton, *Freedom of Thought in the Old South*, pp. 144–61. For an interesting view of Calhoun and the South, see Gerald M. Capers, *John C. Calhoun, Opportunist*.
19. Rowland (ed.), *Jefferson Davis, Constitutionalist*, 5:102–104; *Richmond Enquirer*, 30 May 1861. See also Matthew P. Andrews, *The Women of the South in Wartime*, and Katherine M. Jones, *Heroines of Dixie*.
20. *Richmond Dispatch*, 30 May 1861; Thomas, "Confederate State of Richmond," pp. 37–38.
21. Stanley Kimmel, *Mr. Davis's Richmond*, pp. 13–14.
22. Thomas, "Confederate State of Richmond," pp. 16, 21–26.

23. Atlanta *Southern Confederacy,* 26 April 1861.
24. Douglas Southall Freeman, *R. E. Lee: A Biography,* 1:chaps. 28–30.
25. Vandiver, *Ploughshares into Swords,* pp. 67–73.
26. Frank E. Vandiver, *Mighty Stonewall,* p. 138; Gilbert Govan and James Livingood, *A Different Valor,* p. 35.
27. Vandiver, *Mighty Stonewall,* pp. 144–47.
28. Joseph E. Johnston, *Narrative of Military Operations Directed During the Late War Between the States,* pp. 15–20; Clifford Dowdey, *The Land They Fought For,* pp. 111–112.
29. Govan and Livingood, *A Different Valor,* pp. 14–15.
30. See "An Act to raise Provisional Forces for the Confederate States of America, and for other purposes," Matthews (ed.), *Statutes, Provisional Government,* stat. 1, chap. 22; "An Act to provide for the Public Defence," *ibid.,* chap. 26; "An Act for the establishment and organization of the Army of the Confederate States of America," *ibid.,* chap. 29.
31. The tradition of Southern superiority in general officers is hardly supported by a look at Eliot Ellsworth, Jr., *West Point in the Confederacy,* and Ezra Warner, *Generals in Blue.*
32. John Hope Franklin, *The Militant South,* pp. 63–79.
33. T. Harry Williams, *P. G. T. Beauregard, Napoleon in Gray,* p. 66.
34. Williams, *Beauregard,* p. 75.
35. *Ibid.,* pp. 66–68.
36. A. B. Roman, *The Military Operations of General Beauregard,* 1:70.
37. For a survey of Beauregard's activities in the period before First Manassas, see Williams, *Beauregard,* pp. 66–80.
38. *Ibid.,* p. 75.
39. R. U. Johnson and C. C. Buel (eds.), *Battles and Leaders of the Civil War,* 1:179n; Coulter, *Confederate States,* pp. 72, 424.
40. Johnson and Buel (eds.), *Battles and Leaders,* 1:124–25; Vandiver, *Mighty Stonewall,* p. 147.
41. Matthews (ed.), *Statutes, Provisional Government,* stat. 2, chap. 3.
42. *Ibid.,* stat. 3, chap. 23; Richard Todd, *Confederate Finance,* pp. 25–36, 82–84, 130–36; John C. Schwab, *The Confederate States of America, 1861–1865,* pp. 1–18.
43. *Regulations of the Confederate States Army for the Quarter Master's Department,* pp. 10–12, 94–95; Dowdey, *Land They Fought For,* p. 103; Bell I. Wiley, *The Life of Johnny Reb,* pp. 24–25.
44. Coulter, *Confederate States,* map between pp. 354 and 355; Angus J. Johnston, II, *Virginia Railroads in the Civil War,* map, p. 3; Robert C. Black, III, *The Railroads of the Confederacy,* map, p. 61.
45. Roman, *Military Operations of Beauregard,* 1:71–75; Johnston, *Narrative,* pp. 23–24, 36–40; Williams, *Beauregard,* pp. 66–80.
46. Freeman, *Lee,* 1:529–30.
47. Jefferson Davis, *Rise and Fall,* 1:347–348; *War of the Rebellion,* ser. 1, vol. 2, pp. 934, 937; Williams, *Beauregard,* pp. 72, 79.
48. Johnson and Buel (eds.), *Battles and Leaders,* 1:175–77; Bruce Catton, *Mr. Lincoln's Army,* pp. 198–99.
49. *War of the Rebellion,* ser. 1, vol. 2, p. 478.
50. The main sources used in constructing the account of the Battle of First Manassas were Douglas Southall Freeman, *Lee's Lieutenants,* 1:chap. 5; Williams, *Beauregard,* chap. 5; Johnston, *Narrative,* chap. 2; Joseph M.

Hanson, *Bull Run Remembers;* Robert M. Johnston, *Bull Run, Its Strategy and Tactics,* chaps. 6–10.
51. Vandiver, *Mighty Stonewall,* p. 161.

Chapter Three: "A Knack of Hoping"

1. Mary Boykin Chesnut, *A Diary from Dixie,* p. 86. See also Richmond *Enquirer,* 23 July, 1861.
2. Mary Chesnut, *A Diary from Dixie,* p. 96.
3. A Richmond Lady [Sally Brock], *Richmond During the War,* p. 65; Mary Chesnut, *A Diary from Dixie,* pp. 104, 116, 119, 124, 125; Alfred Hoyt Bill, *The Beleaguered City,* pp. 68, 78, 116, 126, 129, 137; Emory M. Thomas, "The Confederate State of Richmond," pp. 62–72.
4. Mary Chesnut, *A Diary from Dixie,* p. 70.
5. T. Harry Williams, *P. G. T. Beauregard, Napoleon in Gray,* pp. 90–91; Frank E. Vandiver, *Mighty Stonewall,* pp. 167–68; Jefferson Davis, *The Rise and Fall of the Confederate Government,* 1:352–53; Joseph E. Johnston, *Narrative of Military Operations Directed During the Late War Between the States,* pp. 57–65; A. B. Roman, *The Military Operations of General Beauregard,* 1:114–19.
6. Jefferson Davis, *Rise and Fall,* 1:355.
7. See Charleston *Mercury,* 10 August 1861.
8. David Donald, *Lincoln Reconsidered,* pp. 90–95; T. Harry Williams, *Americans at War,* pp. 68–71; J. F. C. Fuller, "The Place of the American Civil War in the Evolution of War," pp. 316–25.
9. T. Harry Williams, *Lincoln and His Generals,* pp. 3–14, 291–314; Frank E. Vandiver, *Rebel Brass,* pp. 3–22.
10. Davis to Dabney H. Maury, 2 August 1875, doc. NI 725, Henry E. Huntington Library, San Marino, Calif.
11. Lincoln's proclamation of blockade is in Roy P. Basler (ed.) *The Collected Works of Abraham Lincoln,* 4:338–39. See also Davis's message to the Confederate Congress, 29 April 1861, in Dunbar Rowland (ed.), *Jefferson Davis, Constitutionalist,* 5:79; Gov. F. W. Pickens to Davis, 16 April 1861, *ibid.,* pp. 62–63; Frank L. Owsley, *King Cotton Diplomacy,* pp. 19–20.
12. The Yancey-Rost-Mann mission is admirably covered in Owsley, *King Cotton,* 52–84.
13. See Vandiver, *Rebel Brass,* pp. 79–126.
14. Slidell to S. L. M. Barlow, 20 July 1861, in Barlow Papers, Huntington Library.
15. Diary of Thomas Bragg, 5 December 1861, 14 January 1862, Southern Historical Collection, University of North Carolina.
16. See Charles W. Ramsdell, "The Confederate Government and the Railroads," pp. 794–810; Robert C. Black, III, *The Railroads of the Confederacy,* pp. 1–11; E. M. Coulter, *The Confederate States of America, 1861–1865,* map between pp. 354 and 355.
17. Charles W. Ramsdell, "General Robert E. Lee's Horse Supply, 1862–1865," pp. 758–77; *Eighth Census of the United States, 1860: Agriculture,* p. cviii.
18. Ramsdell, "Lee's Horse Supply," pp. 763–64; Frank E. Vandiver, *Ploughshares into Swords,* pp. 125–26.

19. Frank E. Vandiver, "Jefferson Davis and Confederate Strategy," pp. 19–32.
20. See Davis to the Confederate Congress, 18 November 1861, in Rowland (ed.), *Jefferson Davis, Constitutionalist,* 5:170.
21. James M. Matthews (ed.), *Statutes at Large of the Provisional Government of the Confederate States of America,* stat. 1, chap. 21; stat. 2, chap. 11; stat. 3, chap. 23; John C. Schwab, *The Confederate States of America, 1861–1865,* pp. 6–8; Richard Todd, *Confederate Finance,* pp. 25–36.
22. Todd, *Confederate Finance,* pp. 31–42; Diary of Thomas Bragg, 5, 7, December, 1861; Ralph Andreano, "A Theory of Confederate Finance," pp. 21–28; Matthews (ed.), *Statutes, Provisional Government,* stat. 2, chap. 24, act approved 16 May 1861.
23. J. S. Calver and J. M. Bennett to President and Directors of the Bank of Pittsylvania, Treasury Office of Virginia, 17 May 1861, Brock Collection, Box 205, Huntington Library.
24. Schwab, *Confederate States,* pp. 106–10.
25. Matthews (ed.), *Statutes, Provisional Government,* stat. 3, chap. 23.
26. Diary of Thomas Bragg, 5, 7 December 1861. See also Thomas L. Connelly, *Army of the Heartland,* pp. 200–201.
27. John S. Ford, *Rip Ford's Texas,* pp. 338–40; Walter Prescott Webb, *The Texas Rangers,* pp. 205–20; Ray C. Colton, *The Civil War in the Western Territories,* pp. 121–24.
28. Mary E. Massey, *Refugee Life in the Confederacy,* pp. 1–10.
29. J. B. Jones, *A Rebel War Clerk's Diary,* 1:75.
30. R. U. Johnson and C. C. Buel (eds.), *Battles and Leaders of the Civil War,* 2:135–42.
31. *New York Times,* 17, 18 November 1861; New York *Tribune,* 18 November 1861; *Zeitung* (Vienna), 28, 30 November and 1, 8 December 1861; Evan John, *Atlantic Impact,* pp. 6–10; Thomas L. Harris, *The Trent Affair,* pp. 98–101; Philip Van Doren Stern, *When the Guns Roared,* pp. 89–90; Jay H. Schmidt, "The Trent Affair," pp. 10–17; U.S. State Department, *Correspondence Relative to the Case of Messrs. Mason and Slidell;* "Prolege," *A Legal View of the Seizure of Messrs. Mason and Slidell;* Lynn Case, "La France et l'affaire du 'Trent,'" pp. 57–86; Charles F. Adams, "The Trent Affair," pp. 540–62; Sir John Wheeler-Bennett, *A Wreath to Clio,* pp. 110–27.
32. Jones, *War Clerk's Diary,* 1:93.
33. Lord Lyons to Russell, 23 December 1861, Russell Papers, Public Records Office, London, 30/22/14. For further details on British attitudes during the *Trent* crisis, see Lord Bloomfield to Russell, 28 November 1861, 9 January 1862, *ibid.,* 30/22/40; Lord Cowley to Russell, 29 November 1861, *ibid.,* 30/22/56; Palmerston to Russell, 9, 10, 13 January 1862, *ibid.,* 30/22/22; Russell to Palmerston, 20 December 1861, Palmerston Papers, Broadlands Archives (used by permission of Earl Mountbatten of Burma). See also Owsley, *King Cotton,* pp. 77–84, and E. D. Adams, *Great Britain and the American Civil War,* pp. 205–43.
34. See J. B. Jones's succinct summary: "Now we must depend upon our own strong arms and stout hearts for defense," 1 January 1862, *War Clerk's Diary,* 1:103.
35. Quoted in Sir James Fergusson's account of his visit to the Union and Confederate Armies, Edinburgh, 11 November 1861, attached to a letter from Lord Derby to Palmerston 13 November 1861, Palmerston Papers.

36. Palmerston to Russell, 10, 13 January 1862, Russell Papers, 30/22/22.
37. Owsley, *King Cotton*, pp. 146–47.
38. *Ibid.*, p .67.
39. *War of the Rebellion*, ser. 4, vol. 2, p. 227; Vandiver, *Ploughshares into Swords*, pp. 88–90.
40. Owsley, *King Cotton*, pp. 79–81, 240–42.
41. This idea certainly occurred to some English lawmakers. See *ibid.*, p. 245.
42. Coulter, *Confederate States*, p. 289. See also Owsley, *King Cotton*, chap. 8; Hamilton Cochran, *Blockade Runners of the Confederacy*, pp. 63–65; Francis B. C. Bradlee, *Blockade Running During the Civil War, and the Effect of Land and Water Transportation on the Confederacy*.
43. Admiral Hobart Pasha [Augustus Charles Hobart-Hampden], *Sketches from My Life*, pp. 87–158.
44. Thomas E. Taylor, *Running the Blockade*, pp. 48–54.
45. *Ibid.*, p. 85.
46. Frank E. Vandiver (ed.), *Confederate Blockade Running Through Bermuda, 1861–1865*, pp. xvii, xxi–xxii; Duke of Newcastle to Lieutenant Governor of the Bahamas, 15 October 1861, in Governor of Bahamas Letters Received from the Colonial Office File, 1823–1863, Government House, Nassau; Robert Carse, *Blockade*, pp. 9–10, 59, 142; Don Higginbotham, "A Raider Refuels: Diplomatic Repercussions," pp. 129–41.
47. Vandiver (ed.), *Blockade Running*, p. xvii; Taylor, *Running the Blockade*, p. 64.
48. Vandiver (ed.), *Blockade Running*, p. xxii.
49. *Ibid.*, pp. xxii–xxiii.
50. See Mary Elizabeth Mitchell Book, p. 25 (typescript in Southern Historical Collection, University of North Carolina Library).
51. For a description of Davis in August, see *ibid.*, p. 31; for a description of the dinner, see Diary of Thomas Bragg, 30 November 1861; for a description of the effects of neuralgia in one of Davis's eyes, see W. H. Russell, *My Diary North and South*, p. 173.
52. Douglas Southall Freeman, *R. E. Lee: A Biography*, 1:554–604.
53. Clement Eaton, *A History of the Southern Confederacy*, p. 51; Robert S. Henry, *The Story of the Confederacy*, pp. 74–79; Virgil C. Jones, *The Civil War at Sea*, 1:26–86.
54. Rowland (ed.), *Jefferson Davis, Constitutionalist*, 5:175.
55. Johnston, *Narrative of Military Operations*, p. 98.
56. Bell I. Wiley, *The Life of Johnny Reb*, pp. 327–28.
57. *Ibid.*, pp. 132–33; Coulter, *Confederate States*, pp. 328–30.
58. Matthews (ed.), *Statutes, Provisional Government*, stat. 1, chap. 29; *Regulations of the Confederate States Army for the Quarter Master's Department*, p. 81.
59. Wiley, *Johnny Reb*, pp. 134–35; Douglas Southall Freeman, *R. E. Lee*, 2:493–94.
60. L. B. Northrop, "A Comparative View of Commissary Supplies and Resources . . ." [November 1862], Brock Collection, Box 284, Huntington Library.
61. Johnston, *Narrative*, pp. 98–99 and n.
62. Davis to Johnston, Aug. 20, 1861, in Rowland, *Jefferson Davis, Constitutionalist*, 5:123.
63. H. H. Cunningham, *Doctors in Gray: The Confederate Medical Service*,

chaps. 9, 10; Wiley, *Johnny Reb*, pp. 254–67; D. E. Huger Smith, Alice R. Huger Smith, A. R. Childs (eds.), *Mason Smith Family Letters, 1860–1868*, pp. 103–38.

64. Cunningham, *Doctors in Gray*, pp. 151–53; Charles W. Ramsdell, *Behind the Lines in the Southern Confederacy*, pp. 36–39; Bell I. Wiley, *The Plain People of the Confederacy*, pp. 26–27. See also *The Medical and Surgical History of the War of the Rebellion*.

65. W. R. Brandriff to Messrs. Brock White & Co., 7 May 1863, Brock Collection, Box 285, Huntington Library; Cunningham, *Doctors in Gray*, pp. 146–50; *War of the Rebellion*, ser. 4, vol. 1, pp. 59–61, 1041; *ibid.*, vol. 2, pp. 79, 442, 467, 569, 1024.

66. Cunningham, *Doctors in Gray*, pp. 50–52.

67. Mary Chesnut, *A Diary from Dixie*, p. 116.

68. Rowland (ed.), *Jefferson Davis, Constitutionalist*, 5:148.

69. Frank E. Vandiver (ed.), "A Collection of Louisiana Confederate Letters," pp. 952–53, 966–68.

70. See, for example, Joseph E. Brown to Davis, 28 February 1861, and H. V. Johnson to Davis, 11 November 1861, Keith Read Collection, University of Georgia Libraries; Resolution, Georgia House of Representatives, 11 November 1861, Telamon Cuyler Collection, University of Georgia Libraries; Davis to John Letcher, 13, 14 September 1861, Rowland (ed.), *Jefferson Davis, Constitutionalist*, 5:131, 132; Davis to Gov. Thomas O. Moore, 26 September 1861, *ibid.*, p. 136; Davis to Gov. Claiborne Jackson, 21 December 1861, 8 January 1862, *ibid.*, pp. 183, 184; Davis to Weldon N. Edwards, President, N.C. Convention, 15 February 1862, *ibid.*, p. 193; Davis to W. W. Avery, 18 February 1862, *ibid.*, pp. 195–96. See also Diary of Thomas Bragg, 17 January 1862.

71. Diary of Thomas Bragg, 17 January 1862.

72. Virgil C. Jones, *The Civil War at Sea*, 1:198–207; Jones, *War Clerk's Diary*, 1:103; Diary of Thomas Bragg, 7 February 1862.

73. Jones, *War Clerk's Diary*, 1:105.

74. Diary of Thomas Bragg, 7 February 1862.

Chapter Four: God and the Weakest Battalions

1. Diary of Thomas Bragg, 31 January 1862, Southern Historical Collection, University of North Carolina.

2. Frank E. Vandiver, *Mighty Stonewall*, pp. 192–95.

3. Thomas L. Connelly, *Army of the Heartland*, pp. 96–99; R. U. Johnson and C. C. Buel (eds.), *Battles and Leaders of the Civil War*, 1:545–46.

4. Connelly, *Army of the Heartland*, pp. 106–7, 116–25; Stanley F. Horn, *The Army of Tennessee*, pp. 80–100; Johnson and Buel (eds.), *Battles and Leaders*, 1:362–72, 398–429; Diary of Thomas Bragg, 10, 16 February 1862; J. B. Jones, *A Rebel War Clerk's Diary*, 1:110–11.

5. Diary of Thomas Bragg, 7, 10 February 1862; Richmond *Whig*, 10, 11, 12, 13 February 1862; Richmond *Enquirer*, 11, 14 February 1862; Jones, *War Clerk's Diary*, 1:104, 109; Virgil C. Jones, *The Civil War at Sea*, 1:385; Wilfred Buck Yearns, *The Confederate Congress*, pp. 141–42; *Journal of the Congress of the Confederate States of America, 1861–1865*, 5:25, 28, 238–43.

6. Dunbar Rowland (ed.), *Jefferson Davis, Constitutionalist,* 5:216–17.
7. Martin H. Hall, *Sibley's New Mexico Campaign,* pp. 83–103, 141–60, 202–26; Ray C. Colton, *The Civil War in the Western Territories,* pp. 13–99; Johnson and Buel (eds.), *Battles and Leaders,* 2:103–11.
8. Gov. F. R. Lubbock and others to Davis [28 July, 1862], in Rowland (ed.), *Jefferson Davis, Constitutionalist,* 5:301–3.
9. Johnson and Buel (eds.), *Battles and Leaders,* 1:314–37; Jay Monaghan, *Civil War on the Western Border, 1854–1865,* pp. 236–41; Robert G. Hartje, *Van Dorn,* pp. 137–61.
10. Johnson and Buel (eds.), *Battles and Leaders,* 1:465–610; Connelly, *Army of the Heartland,* pp. 151–75; Horn, *The Army of Tennessee,* pp. 122–43; A. B. Roman, *The Military Operations of General Beauregard,* 1:283–325; T. Harry Williams, *P. G. T. Beauregard, Napoleon in Gray,* pp. 133–40; Charles P. Roland, *Albert Sidney Johnston, Soldier of Three Republics,* pp. 326–46.
11. Charles L. Dufour, *The Night the War Was Lost,* pp. 64, 337, discusses the importance of the Leeds Foundry.
12. *Ibid.,* pp. 344–54; Jones, *War Clerk's Diary,* 1:108–9, 135–36. For Lovell's Court of Inquiry, see *War of the Rebellion,* ser. 1, vol. 6, pp. 555–643, 646, 647, 650.
13. Richmond *Whig,* 26, 28, 29, 30 April 1862; Richmond *Enquirer,* 25, 29 April 1862; *War of the Rebellion,* ser. 1, vol. 6, pp. 555–643.
14. *Official Records of the Union and Confederate Navies in the War of the Rebellion,* ser. 1, vol. 7, pp. 32–44; Johnson and Buel (eds.), *Battles and Leaders,* 1:692–711; J. Thomas Scharf, *History of the Confederate States Navy from Its Organization to the Surrender of Its Last Vessel,* pp. 167–238; Harrison A. Trexler, *The Confederate Ironclad "Virginia" ("Merrimac"),* pp. 32–45.
15. Jones, *War Clerk's Diary,* 1:116; Robert D. Meade, *Judah P. Benjamin,* pp. 208–32.
16. *Ibid.,* pp. 207–29, 233–43; Edward A. Pollard, *The Lost Cause,* pp. 210–13; Frank E. Vandiver, *Rebel Brass,* pp. 45–48; *War of the Rebellion,* ser. 1, vol. 9, pp. 183–91; Jones, *War Clerk's Diary,* 1:119; Diary of Thomas Bragg, 21 February and 18 March 1862; John S. Wise, *The End of an Era,* pp. 176–78.
17. Rowland (ed.), *Jefferson Davis, Constitutionalist,* 5:205; *War of the Rebellion,* ser. 4, vol. 1, p. 963.
18. Freeman, *Lee,* 2:25–27.
19. *Ibid.,* pp. 28–29.
20. *Journal of the Congress,* 2:106.
21. Richmond *Whig,* 31 March 1862; Harrison A. Trexler, "The Davis Administration and the Richmond Press, 1861–1865," p. 183; Charleston *Courier,* 18 April 1862.
22. "Proceedings of the Confederate Congress," 45:26–27.
23. James M. Matthews (ed.), *Statutes at Large of the Confederate States of America,* I Cong., stat. 1, chap. 31.
24. *Ibid.,* chap. 74, "An Act to exempt certain persons from enrollment for service in the Armies of the Confederate States." This act exempted from service the physically unfit; employees of the Confederate Government; the judicial and executive officers of state governments; members of the federal and state legislature; all Confederate and state official clerks; all mail

carriers, ferrymen on post routes; all pilots and those engaged in marine service on river and railroad routes: all telegraph operators; all clergymen; all iron miners and furnace and foundry operators; all journeymen printers engaged in printing newspapers; all presidents and professors of colleges and academies; all teachers of more than twenty students; superintendents, nurses and attendants in public hospitals and lunatic asylums; teachers in institutions for the deaf, dumb, and blind; one pharmacist in each apothecary; superintendents and operators in wool and cotton factories.

25. Rembert W. Patrick (ed.), *The Opinions of the Confederate Attorneys General, 1861–1865*, pp. 94–99.

26. *Jeffers v. Fair*, 33 Ga. 347 (1862); *Ex Parte Coupland*, 26 Tex. 387 (1862); *Ex Parte Hill*, 38 Ala. 429 (1863); *In Re Bryan*, 60 N. C. 1 (1863); *Simmons v. Miller*, 40 Miss. 19 (1864); *Ex Parte Bolling in re Watts*, 39 Ala. 609 (1865); J. B. Robbins, "Confederate Nationalism," chap. 4. See also A. B. Moore, *Conscription and Conflict in the Confederacy*. See also William M. Robinson, Jr., *Justice in Grey*, pp. 209–436; and J. G. deRoulhac Hamilton, "The State Courts and the Confederate Constitution," pp. 433–42.

27. *War of the Rebellion*, ser. I, vol. 12, pt. 1, p. 385.

28. Freeman, *Lee*, 2:1–7.

29. For general discussion of the Valley campaign, see G. F. R. Henderson, *Stonewall Jackson and the American Civil War*, pp. 165–370; Douglas Southall Freeman, *Lee's Lieutenants*, 1:312–488; Lenoir Chambers, *Stonewall Jackson*, 1:463–597; Frank E. Vandiver, *Mighty Stonewall*, pp. 221–83; Henry Kyd Douglas, *I Rode With Stonewall*, pp. 35–94; John H. Worsham, *One of Jackson's Foot Cavalry*, pp. 66–107; Archie P. McDonald (ed.), "The Journal of Jedediah Hotchkiss, June, 1861–August, 1862"; Johnson and Buel (eds.), *Battles and Leaders*, 2:282–313.

30. Jefferson Davis, *The Rise and Fall of the Confederate Government*, 2:123; Gilbert Govan and James Livingood, *A Different Valor*, p. 156.

31. Johnston's Fabian tactics have caused much biographical controversy. See, for example, Clifford Dowdey, *The Land They Fought For*, pp. 131–32; Joseph E. Johnston, *Narrative of Military Operations Directed During the Late War Between the States*, pp. vii–xxxi.

32. Freeman, *Lee's Lieutenants*, 1:154–55.

33. Jefferson Davis, *Rise and Fall*, 2:129.

34. Mary Boykin Chesnut, *A Diary from Dixie*, pp. 94–95.

35. *Ibid.*, p. 95.

36. *War of the Rebellion*, ser. 1, vol. 11, pp. 39–71; Freeman, *Lee*, 2:122–219; Johnson and Buel (eds.), *Battles and Leaders*, 2:347–62; Clifford Dowdey, *The Seven Days*.

37. Richmond *Whig*, 1–4 July, 1862; Richmond *Enquirer*, 1, 4, 8 July 1862.

38. For general accounts of the Cedar Mountain and Second Manassas campaigns, see Freeman, *Lee's Lieutenants*, 2:16–51, 120–52; Henderson, *Stonewall Jackson*, 2:89–177; Vandiver, *Mighty Stonewall*, pp. 337–74; Freeman, *Lee*, 2:256–349; Johnson and Buel (eds.), *Battles and Leaders*, 2:449–538; Douglas, *I Rode With Stonewall*, pp. 120–45; Worsham, *Foot Cavalry*, pp. 108–35; Edward J. Stackpole, *From Cedar Mountain to Antietam*, pp. 1–287. See also *War of the Rebellion*, ser. 1, vol. 12, pt. 2, pp. 132–239.

Chapter Five: "They Have Made a Nation"

1. Mountague Bernard, *A Historical Account of the Neutrality of Great Britain During the American Civil War,* pp. 135–36; Lord Palmerston to Lord John Russell, 16 April 1861, Russell Papers, Public Record Office, London, PRO 30/22/14; Palmerston to Russell, 9 July 1861, *ibid.,* PRO 32/22/21; Lord Lyons to Russell, 16 May 1861, *ibid.,* PRO 30/22/36; Lyons to Russell, 29 October 1861, *ibid.,* PRO 30/22/28; Palmerston to the Duke of Newcastle, 1 September 1861, Palmerston Papers, Broadlands Archives (used by permission of Earl Mountbatten of Burma); Duke of Argyll to Palmerston, 2 September 1862, *ibid.;* Russell to Palmerston, 17 September 1862, *ibid.;* William Gladstone to Palmerston, 25 September 1862, *ibid.;* Lord Clarendon to Palmerston, 16 October 1862, *ibid.;* Russell to Palmerston, 25 May 1865, *ibid.;* Gladstone, "Memorandum on the War in America," printed for cabinet use ("Secret"), 25 October 1862, in *ibid.*
2. Frank L. Owsley, *King Cotton Diplomacy,* pp. 250–91, 332, 337.
3. Russell to Palmerston, 17 September 1862, Palmerston Papers.
4. C. F. Adams, *Charles Francis Adams,* p. 280; John Mosley, *The Life of William Ewart Gladstone,* 2:70; Gladstone to Palmerston, 25 September 1862, Palmerston Papers; Gladstone to Russell, 17, 21 October 1862, Russell Papers, PRO 30/22/19; *The Times* (London), 8 October 1862.
5. See Gladstone to Russell, 17, 21 October 1862, Russell Papers, PRO 30/22/19; Palmerston to Russell, 12 October 1862, in *ibid.,* 30/22/22, in which the Prime Minister says: "It is clear that Gladstone was not far wrong in pronouncing by anticipation the National Independence of the South." See also Argyll to Russell, 11 October 1862, *ibid.,* PRO 30/22/25, in which the Duke says: "I have been reading Gladstone. I am afraid that one phrase in his speech ('made a nation') will be an embarrassment."
6. Joseph M. Hernon, Jr., "British Sympathies in the American Civil War: A Reconsideration," pp. 356–67; Royden Harrison, "British Labour and the Confederacy," pp. 78–105.
7. See *The Index* (London), 1862–1865. See also Stephen B. Oates, "Henry Hotze: Confederate Agent Abroad," pp. 131–54. See also Henry Hotze, *Three Months in the Confederate Army,* Introduction and notes by Richard B. Harwell (University, Ala., 1952), introduction; and Owsley, *King Cotton Diplomacy,* pp. 170–71.
8. Owsley, *King Cotton Diplomacy,* pp. 377–79.
9. Lord Granville to Lord John Russell, 29 September 1862, Palmerston Papers.
10. Argyll to Russell, 15 October 1862, Russell Papers, PRO 30/22/25.
11. Palmerston to Russell, 21 October 1862, *ibid.,* PRO 30/22/14.
12. See Julian Fane to Russell, 18 September 1862, *ibid.,* PRO 30/22/41.
13. Argyll to Russell, 11 October 1862, *ibid.,* PRO 30/22/25. Argyll cites Richard Cobden's concern with the corn supply. See also Paul W. Gates, *Agriculture and the Civil War,* pp. 226–28.
14. For detailed accounts of the Battle of Sharpsburg (Antietam), see Frank E. Vandiver, *Mighty Stonewall,* pp. 390–400; Shelby Foote, *The Civil War, a Narrative: Fort Sumter to Perryville,* pp. 681–702; Douglas Southall Freeman, *R. E. Lee,* 2:367–414; Freeman, *Lee's Lieutenants,* 2:203–25; Hal Bridges, *Lee's Maverick General: Daniel Harvey Hill,* chap. 7.
15. Wood Gray, *The Hidden Civil War,* pp. 124–30, 166–69, 179–84; E. M.

Coulter, *The Confederate States of America, 1861–1865,* pp. 536–37; Robin Winks, *Canada and the United States: The Civil War Years.*

16. Dunbar Rowland (ed.), *Jefferson Davis, Constitutionalist,* 5:338–39.
17. Stanley F. Horn, *The Army of Tennessee,* p. 172.
18. For some indications of Bragg's character, see Don Seitz, *Braxton Bragg;* Horn, *The Army of Tennessee,* pp. 110–14; Grady McWhiney, "Controversy in Kentucky," pp. 5–6; Jefferson Davis, *Rise and Fall of the Confederate Government,* 2:383–84; T. R. Hay, "Braxton Bragg and the Southern Confederacy," pp. 294–95; Thomas L. Connelly, *Army of the Heartland,* pp. 205–6.
19. Jefferson Davis, *Rise and Fall,* 2:75.
20. For summaries of Bragg's Kentucky venture, see Seitz, *Bragg,* pp. 168–201; Connelly, *Army of the Heartland,* pp. 221–67. Connelly's account is a skillful blend of many sources and clear narrative, and it provides fresh insights into lingering historiographical problems.
21. George B. McClellan to William H. Aspinwall, 26 September 1862, in R. U. Johnson and C. C. Buel (eds.), *Battles and Leaders of the Civil War* (Extra Illustrated Edition, New York, 1887–1888), VIII, document facing p. 546. This special edition, containing many original documents, is in the Henry E. Huntington Library, San Marino, Cal., and is identified by the number 298000.
22. See James G. Randall, *Constitutional Problems Under Lincoln,* pp. 371–90; Randall, *Lincoln, The President,* 2:151–72, 3:225; *New York Times,* 23, 24 September 1862; Youngstown *Mahoning Sentinel,* 24 September 1862; Washington, D.C., *Daily National Intelligencer,* 23, 24 September 1862; Davenport (Ia.) *Daily Democratic News,* 24 September 1862.
23. Bell I. Wiley, *Southern Negroes, 1861–1865,* pp. 38–40; Charleston *Courier,* 24 September 1862.
24. George P. Sanger and others (eds.), *The Statutes at Large, Treaties, and Proclamations of the United States of America, 1789–1873,* 12:319, 589–92.
25. Clement Eaton, *A History of the Old South,* 2d ed., pp. 252–55, 344–45, 359, 505; W. J. Cash, *The Mind of the South,* pp. 124–27.
26. Miles Mark Fisher, *Negro Slave Songs in the United States,* p. 119.
27. Mary Boykin Chesnut, *A Diary from Dixie,* pp. 281–82.
28. Richmond *Dispatch,* 29 January 1863.
29. Virginia Clay-Clopton (Mrs. Clement Clay), *A Belle of the Fifties,* p. 179; Clifford Dowdey, *The Land They Fought For,* pp. 238–39; John C. Schwab, *The Confederate States of America, 1861–1865,* pp. 165–85; Charles W. Ramsdell, *Behind the Lines in the Southern Confederacy,* pp. 19–35; J. B. Jones, *A Rebel War Clerk's Diary,* 1:257.
30. H. H. Cunningham, *Doctors in Gray,* pp. 151–53. See also Gov. Joseph E. Brown's message to the Georgia Assembly, 25 March 1863, in which he urges revision of the laws against distilling because "I am satisfied that a large portion of the potatoe [sic] crop, most of the dried fruit, and a considerable quantity of the molasses in the State, have been, and are being distilled. Under pretence of distilling these articles, it is also said, that quantities of corn are being used by distillers, who keep their doors closed, and refuse to admit visitors who might testify against them." *Journal of the Senate at an Extra Session of the General Assembly of the State of Georgia,* p. 7.
31. D. E. Huger Smith, Alice R. Huger Smith, and A. R. Childs (eds.), *Mason Smith Family Letters, 1860–1868,* p. 28.

32. Dee A. Brown, *The Bold Cavaliers,* pp. 141–43.
33. *Ibid.,* p. 204.
34. For Morgan's Indiana-Ohio raid in June and July, 1863, see *ibid.,* pp. 177–229; Cecil F. Holland, *Morgan and His Raiders,* pp. 223–49; George D. Mosgrove, "Following Morgan's Plume Through Indiana and Ohio," pp. 110–20; A. C. Quisenberry, "Morgan's Men in Ohio," pp. 91–99; Allan Keller, *Morgan's Raid.*
35. Horn, *The Army of Tennessee,* pp. 194–95; Robert S. Henry, *"First With the Most" Forrest,* pp. 115–21.
36. See R. U. Johnson and C. C. Buel (eds.), *Battles and Leaders of the Civil War,* 3:600–34; Horn, *The Army of Tennessee,* pp. 190–210. Bragg's report of the Battle of Murfreesboro is printed in *War of the Rebellion,* ser. 1 vol. 20, pt. 1, pp. 663–75.

Chapter Six: A Look over Jordan

1. See Gov. Joseph E. Brown's Annual Message to the Georgia Assembly, 5 November 1863, in *Journal of the House of Representatives of the State of Georgia, at the Annual Session of the General Assembly, 1863,* p. 10.
2. See Ella Lonn, *Salt as a Factor in the Confederacy,* pp. 19–53; Charles W. Ramsdell, *Behind the Lines in the Southern Confederacy,* pp. 19–20; John C. Schwab, *The Confederate State of America, 1861–1865,* pp. 267–68.
3. Charles W. Ramsdell, "The Control of Manufacturing by the Confederate Government," pp. 231–49.
4. Ramsdell, "General Robert E. Lee's Horse Supply, 1862–1865," pp. 763–64; Frank E. Vandiver, *Ploughshares into Swords,* pp. 200, 223, 232–33; Ramsdell, *Behind the Lines,* pp. 16, 18.
5. Pp. 636, 678–79, 471–73; H. H. Cunningham, *Doctors in Gray,* pp. 146–50; Ramsdell, *Behind the Lines,* p. 15; W. R. Brandriff to Messrs. Brock White & Co., 7 May 1863, Brock Collection, Box 285, Henry E. Huntington Library, San Marino, Calif.
6. Josiah Gorgas Circular, 29 December 1863, Letters Rec'd by Confederate Sec. of War (1861–1865), doc. GWD 71, Confederate Records, National Archives; Frank E. Vandiver, "Makeshifts of Confederate Ordnance"; Mary E. Massey, *Ersatz in the Confederacy,* pp. 79–98.
7. E. M. Coulter, *The Confederate States of America, 1861–1865,* p. 137.
8. Dunbar Rowland (ed.), *Jefferson Davis, Constitutionalist,* 5:396–415.
9. *Southern Historical Society Papers* 47 (1930), 114–16.
10. The tax in kind met considerable approval in the South. See Alexander H. Stephens to Davis, 20 June 1863, Keith Read Collection, University of Georgia Libraries.
11. James M. Matthews (ed.), *Statutes at Large of the Confederate States of America,* I Cong., stat. 3, chap. 38.
12. *Ibid.,* chap. 10.
13. See A. B. Moore, *Conscription and Conflict in the Confederacy,* pp. 131–47; Statistical table of Confederate manpower, compiled by T. L. Connelly, in writer's possession.
14. *War of the Rebellion,* ser. 4, vol. 1, p. 1081; Moore, *Conscription,* pp. 45–46.

15. *Confederate Statutes,* I Cong., stat. 3, chap. 80; *Southern Historical Society Papers* 48 (1941), 20–25, 33–36, 88–89, 95–96, 104–7, 129–32, 136, 155–61, 166–68, 195–200; Wilfred Buck Yearns, *The Confederate Congress,* pp. 79–81.
16. T. L. Connelly, *Army of the Heartland,* pp. 187–280, describes the condition of the army and its commanders with admirable depth and clarity. See also Leonidas Polk to Davis, 27 September 1863, Autograph File, Dearborn Collection, Harvard University Library; William M. Polk, *Leonidas Polk,* 2:209–11.
17. See Gov. F. R. Lubbock to Jefferson Davis, 28 July 1862, 27 March and 13 July 1863, in Rowland (ed.), *Jefferson Davis, Constitutionalist,* 5:300, 454–57, 544–45; Lubbock and others to Davis [28 July 1862], *ibid.,* pp. 301–3.
18. Clifford Dowdey, *The Land They Fought For,* pp. 231–32; Rembert W. Patrick, *Jefferson Davis and His Cabinet,* pp. 127–31; Archer Jones, *Confederate Strategy from Shiloh to Vicksburg,* pp. 51–88; Frank E. Vandiver, *Rebel Brass,* pp. 30–31, 51–53; Edward Younger (ed.), *Inside the Confederate Government,* pp. 28–29.
19. Jones, *Confederate Strategy,* pp. vi, 96; Frank E. Vandiver, "Jefferson Davis and Unified Army Command," pp. 30–34; Vandiver, *Rebel Brass,* pp. 51–57; Vandiver, "Jefferson Davis and Confederate Strategy," pp. 30–31.
20. Vandiver, "Davis and Unified Command," pp. 29–31; Vandiver, *Rebel Brass,* pp. 34, 51–59; Jones, *Confederate Strategy,* pp. 94–98; Joseph E. Johnston to Louis T. Wigfall, 8 March 1863, Wigfall Family Papers, typescripts, Archives Collection, University of Texas; Joseph E. Johnston, *Narrative of Military Operations Directed During the Late War Between the States,* pp. 149–50.
21. Johnston, *Narrative,* pp. 163–64; Johnston to Wigfall, 14 February, 4, 8 March, 27 December 1863, Wigfall Family Papers.
22. Johnston to Wigfall, 8 March 1863, *ibid.*
23. Johnston to Wigfall, 4, 8 March and 12 August 1863, *ibid.*
24. Johnston to Wigfall, 14 February 1863, *ibid.*
25. Walter Lord (ed.), *The Fremantle Diary,* pp. 7–8.
26. *Ibid.,* pp. 41–42. See also San Antonio *Weekly News,* 9, 16 April 1863.
27. Lord (ed.), *Fremantle Diary,* p. 55.
28. *Ibid.*
29. *Confederate Statutes,* I Cong., sess. 3, Joint Resolution no. 8, 1 May 1863; Lord (ed.) *Fremantle Diary,* p. 52. See also A. F. Muir, "Dick Dowling and the Battle of Sabine Pass," pp. 399–428.
30. John Q. Anderson (ed.), *Brokenburn,* pp. 172–270.
31. See Richard Taylor, *Destruction and Reconstruction,* p. 137; William T. Windham, "The Problem of Supply in the Trans-Mississippi Confederacy," p. 154; Edward Cunningham, *The Port Hudson Campaign, 1862–1863.*
32. Gov. F. R. Lubbock and others to Davis [28 July 1862], Rowland (ed.), *Jefferson Davis, Constitutionalist,* 5:301–3.
33. Florence E. Holladay, "The Powers of the Commander of the Confederate Trans-Mississippi Department, 1863–1865," pp. 282, 288–98; John N. Cravens, *James Harper Starr,* pp. 138–42.
34. Charles W. Ramsdell, "The Texas State Military Board, 1862–1865," pp. 253–61.
35. H. Flanagin to Jefferson Davis, 5 January and 26 June 1863, Autograph File, Dearborn Collection, Harvard University; Davis to Flanagin, 15 July 1863, in A. W. Bishop Papers, Buffalo and Erie County Historical Society,

Buffalo, N.Y.; Joseph H. Parks, *General Edmund Kirby Smith, C.S.A.*, pp. 307–11; Davis Y. Thomas, *Arkansas in War and Reconstruction, 1861–1874*, pp. 253–54.

36. Holladay, "Powers of Commander of Trans-Mississippi," p. 282; Parks, *Kirby Smith*, pp. 280–82; Jay Monaghan, *Civil War on the Western Border, 1854–1865*, pp. 278–79.

37. Parks, *Kirby Smith*, pp. 306–44.

38. Frank L. Owsley, *King Cotton Diplomacy*, pp. 127–45; Samuel B. Thompson, *Confederate Purchasing Operations Abroad*, pp. 111–27; Windham, "Problem of Supply," p. 153.

39. Annie H. Abel, *The American Indian as Participant in the Civil War*, pp. 313–20; Abel, *The American Indian Under Reconstruction*, pp. 40–47.

40. Gen. William R. Boggs, *Military Reminiscences of Gen. Wm. R. Boggs, C.S.A.*, pp. 55–56, 296.

41. Boggs, *Reminiscences*, pp. 55, 57–58; John D. Winters, *The Civil War in Louisiana*, p. 320; Richard Taylor, *Destruction and Reconstruction*, pp. 116–30; *Official Records, Armies*, ser. 1, vol. 22, pt. 2, pp. 1128–42.

42. Stephen B. Oates, *Confederate Cavalry West of the River*, p. 121. See also X. B. Debray, *A Sketch of the History of Debray's (26th) Regiment of Texas Cavalry;* [J. P. Blessington], *The Campaigns of Walker's Texas Division;* Lester N. Fitzhugh, *Texas Batteries, Battalions, Regiments, Commanders, and Field Officers, Confederate States Army, 1861–1865.*

43. Oates, *Confederate Cavalry*, p. 155.

44. *The Confederate Almanac for 1865*, pp. 38–39; John C. Schwab, *Confederate States*, pp. 165–67; Charles W. Ramsdell, "Texas from the Fall of the Confederacy to the Beginning of Reconstruction," p. 200.

45. Parks, *Kirby Smith*, pp. 283–305; Thompson, *Confederate Purchasing*, p. 126; James L. Nichols, *The Confederate Quartermaster in the Trans-Mississippi*, pp. 53–82; Robert W. Delaney, "Matamoros, Port for Texas During the Civil War," pp. 473–87; William Diamond, "Imports of the Confederate Government from Europe and Mexico," pp. 497–503. See also, *Journal of the Congress of the Confederate States of America, 1861–1865*, 6:58, 116, 154, 485, 493, 7:669, 682.

46. Thompson, *Confederate Purchasing*, pp. 7, 22, 114–27; Nichols, *Trans-Mississippi Quartermaster*, pp. 65–68; Frank E. Vandiver (ed.), *Confederate Blockade Running Through Bermuda, 1861–1865*, pp. 43, 47–49, 82–83; T. Conn Bryan, *Confederate Georgia*, p. 148.

47. Nichols, *Trans-Mississippi Quartermaster*, pp. 9, 19–22, 41; Windham, "Problem of Supply," pp. 149–68.

48. See Letter Book of Col. G. H. Hill, in Confederate Records, National Archives (Records of the Ordnance Bureau, chap. 4, vol. 147).

49. W. R. Brandriff to Messrs. Brock White & Co., 7 May 1863, Brock Collection, Box 285, Huntington Library. Brandriff, a pharmacist himself, confessed special interest in the young ladies of Arkadelphia.

50. Windham, "Problem of Supply," pp. 165–68; Nichols, *Trans-Mississippi Quartermaster*, pp. 103–6.

51. Oates, *Confederate Cavalry*, p. 156.

52. Ludwell H. Johnson, *Red River Campaign*, pp. 128–45; [Blessington], *Campaigns Walker's Division*, pp. 182–92; Winters, *Civil War in Louisiana*, pp. 340–47.

53. Bell I. Wiley, *The Life of Johnny Reb,* pp. 37, 63; Frank E. Vandiver, *Mighty Stonewall,* pp. 449–51.
54. D. S. Freeman, *R. E. Lee,* 2:493–95.
55. H. J. Eckenrode and Bryan Conrad, *James Longstreet,* pp. 136–50; James Longstreet, *From Manassas to Appomattox,* pp. 297–321.
56. Vandiver, *Mighty Stonewall,* pp. 455–94; R. U. Johnson and C. C. Buel (eds.), *Battles and Leaders of the Civil War,* 3:172–223.

Chapter Seven: "Oh! Wherefore Come Ye Forth, In Triumph from the North"

1. George W. Harris, *Sut Lovingood,* pp. 221–22; Hennig Cohen and William B. Dillingham (eds.), *Humor of the Old Southwest,* pp. 156–249; Charles H. Smith, *Bill Arp, So Called;* Edmund Wilson, *Patriotic Gore.*
2. Mary Boykin Chesnut, *A Diary from Dixie,* p. 395.
3. See Daniel M. McKeithan (ed.), *A Collection of Hayne Letters,* pp. xv–xviii; Jon Louis Wakelyn, "William Gilmore Simms," pp. 1–6.
4. Clement Eaton, *A History of the Old South,* pp. 447–49; Henry Timrod, *The Collected Poems of Henry Timrod.*
5. E. M. Coulter, *The Confederate States of America, 1861–1865,* p. 513; Clement Eaton, *A History of the Southern Confederacy,* pp. 223–24.
6. Eaton, *Southern Confederacy,* p. 226; Wilson, *Patriotic Gore,* p. 498.
7. Eaton, *Southern Confederacy,* p. 226.
8. *Ibid.*
9. *Ibid.,* pp. 226–27.
10. London *Index,* 27 November 1862; Coulter, *Confederate States,* pp. 493–506; H. A. Trexler, "The Davis Administration and the Richmond Press, 1861–1865," pp. 177–95; J. Cutler Andrews, "The Confederate Press and Public Morale," pp. 445–65; Thomas H. Baker, "Refugee Newspaper: The Memphis *Daily Appeal,* 1862–1865," pp. 326–44; Frank L. Mott, *American Journalism,* pp. 365–68.
11. Coulter, *Confederate States,* p. 491; Editors of American Heritage, *The American Heritage Picture History of the Civil War,* pp. 55, 84, 259, 408–9, 482, 499, 504, 510.
12. Coulter, *Confederate States,* pp. 490–91.
13. Marinda B. Moore, *The Dixie Speller, to Follow the First Dixie Reader,* p. 33, and Moore, *The Geographical Reader for the Dixie Children,* pp. 14–15.
14. See John Hill Hewitt, *King Linkum the First,* pp. 7–11.
15. Richard B. Harwell, "The Richmond Stage," pp. 295–96, 298.
16. Bell I. Wiley, *The Life of Johnny Reb,* pp. 151–58; H. M. Wharton, *War Songs and Poems of the Southern Confederacy, 1861–1865,* pp. 52–53, 59–61, 132–33, 192–94, 329–30.
17. Willard A. and Porter W. Heaps, *The Singing Sixties,* p. 48.
18. *Ibid.,* p. 349.
19. *Ibid.,* p. 256.
20. *Ibid.,* pp. 354–55.
21. Pemberton to Davis, 5 January 1862[3], in R. U. Johnson and C. C. Buel (eds.), *Battles and Leaders of the Civil War,* 2: document facing p. 474.

This special edition, containing many original documents, is in the Henry E. Huntington Library, San Marino, Cal., and is identified by the number 298000.

22. See *War of the Rebellion,* ser. 1, vol. 24, pp. 23–24, for Grant's admission that the canal scheme was a failure.

23. U. S. Grant, *Personal Memoirs,* 1:532–70; John C. Pemberton, *Pemberton, Defender of Vicksburg,* gives a partisan account of the entire Vicksburg campaign. The best recent treatment is Earl S. Meirs, *The Web of Victory.* On the campaign see also Bruce Catton, *Grant Moves South,* pp. 250–483; John D. Milligan, *Gunboats Down the Mississippi,* pp. 121–76; Sam R. Reed, *The Vicksburg Campaign, and the Battles about Chattanooga Under the Command of General U. S. Grant, in 1862–63,* pp. 3–164; Joseph E. Johnston, *Narrative of Military Operations Directed During the Late War Between the States,* pp. 174–204; Correspondence between Gen. Pemberton and Confederate War Department, 28 October 1862–10 May 1863, Brock Collection, Box 590, Huntington Library.

24. Mary E. Massey, *Ersatz in the Confederacy,* p. 57.

25. V. C. Jones, *The Civil War at Sea,* 2:189–202; *Official Records of the Union and Confederate Navies in the War of the Rebellion,* ser. 1, vol. 19, pp. 60–62.

26. Johnston, *Narrative,* p. 199.

27. *Ibid.,* pp. 203–4.

28. Josiah Gorgas, *The Civil War Diary of General Josiah Gorgas,* p. 55; Grant, *Memoirs,* 1:672.

29. Massey, *Ersatz,* p. 63.

30. James Longstreet, *From Manassas to Appomattox,* p. 327.

31. Douglas Southall Freeman, *R. E. Lee,* 3: chap. 3, in which Freeman carefully analyzes the reasons for the Pennsylvania Campaign.

32. Bruce Catton, *Never Call Retreat,* pp. 176–77.

33. Freeman, *Lee,* 3:53–54, 57.

34. Capt. J. H. Boughton to Maj. G[?]. Hale, 27 January 1863, Eldridge Collection, Box 151, Huntington Library.

35. Clifford Dowdey, *Death of a Nation,* pp. 48, 78, 91. Some Rebel troops were eager to find hats as well as shoes. See Freeman, *Lee,* 3:57.

36. See Kenneth P. Williams, *Lincoln Finds a General,* 2:689–90.

37. Longstreet, *Manassas to Appomattox,* pp. 352–53; J. B. Hood, *Advance and Retreat,* pp. 57–59.

38. See Walter Lord (ed.), *The Fremantle Diary,* p. 208; George R. Stewart, *Pickett's Charge,* pp. 93, 230; Dowdey, *Death of a Nation,* p. 257.

39. Stewart, *Pickett's Charge,* p. 230.

40. G. Moxley Sorrel, *Recollections of a Confederate Staff Officer,* p. 162.

41. John Esten Cooke, *A Life of General Robert E. Lee,* p. 184; also Freeman, *Lee,* 2:462.

42. Stewart, *Pickett's Charge,* p. 114.

43. *Ibid.,* p. 96.

44. *Ibid.,* p. 150; Dowdey, *Death of a Nation,* p. 267.

45. Frank A. Haskell, *The Battle of Gettysburg,* pp. 48–67. This is one of the most graphic of all battle accounts to come out of the Civil War.

46. Lord (ed.), *Fremantle Diary,* p. 215; Freeman, *Lee,* 3:134; Stewart, *Pickett's Charge,* p. 272.

47. Gorgas, *Diary,* p. 55; Lee to Davis, 8 August 1863, *War of the Rebellion,*

ser. 1, vol. 51, pt. 2, pp. 752–53; Davis to Lee, 11 August 1863, *ibid.*, ser. 1, vol. 29, pt. 2, pp. 639–40.

48. "Vigilans" (pseud.), *The Foreign Enlistment Acts of England and America,* pp. 21–22; Frank L. Owsley, *King Cotton Diplomacy,* pp. 418–22; Raphael Semmes, *Memoirs of Service Afloat During the War Between the States,* pp. 400–3.

49. *Official Records, Navies,* ser. 2, vol. 2, pp. 64–65, 66. For details of Confederate naval purchasing operations abroad, see James D. Bulloch, *The Secret Service of the Confederate States in Europe,* 1: Introduction, pp. 46–48, and *passim.*

50. Semmes, *Service Afloat,* pp. 402–3; Bulloch, *Secret Service,* 1:238–42.

51. Semmes, *Service Afloat,* pp. 402–3; Bulloch, *Secret Service,* 1:224–33, 238–39; J. Thomas Scharf, *History of the Confederate States Navy from Its Organization to the Surrender of Its Last Vessel,* pp. 796–97.

52. The number of captures is difficult to establish. Semmes, in his memoirs, is silent on statistics. Scharf offers a chart in *Confederate Navy,* p. 815, which lists 67 captures and two other ships "released." V. C. Jones, *Civil War at Sea,* 3:228, lumps the captures of the C.S.S. *Sumter,* and C.S.S. *Alabama* together for a total of 305 ships overhauled. Jefferson Davis, *Rise and Fall of the Confederate Government,* 2:254, puts the number of *Alabama* captures at 63. W. Adolphe Roberts, *Semmes of the Alabama,* pp. 282–83, gives a list of 68. E. M. Coulter, *Confederate States,* p. 305, claims 58 ships destroyed by Semmes. Eaton, *Southern Confederacy,* pp. 187–88, puts the number at 62. A seemingly official list in *Official Records, Navies,* ser. 1, vol. 3, pp. 677–81, puts the number of ships destroyed and ransomed at 65. The text follows this list.

53. See George W. Dalzell, *The Flight from the Flag,* pp. 128–35 for Anglo-U.S. relations. The book discusses effects of Confederate raiders generally.

54. Lord Lyons to Lord John Russell, 17 April 1863, Russell Papers, Public Record Office, London, PRO 30/22/37.

55. Lyons to Russell, 13 April 1863, *ibid.*

56. Lyons to Russell, 5 May 1863, *ibid.*

57. Hudson Strode, *Jefferson Davis,* p. 471.

58. Owsley, *King Cotton,* pp. 352–57, 376–83, 462–72, 484, and chap. 15.

59. Unsigned Dispatch, No. 6, 1/3 September 1863, Russell Papers, PRO 30/22/14.

60. Lord Cowley to Russell, 14 July 1863, *ibid.*, PRO 30/22/59.

61. Owsley, *King Cotton,* pp. 468–72.

62. *Ibid.*, pp. 474–76; Ephraim D. Adams, *Great Britain and the American Civil War,* 1:169–72.

63. Lyons to Russell, 6 July 1863, in Russell Papers, PRO 30/22/37.

64. Palmerston to Russell, 14 September 1863, *ibid.*, PRO 30/22/14.

65. "Vigilans," *Foreign Enlistment Acts,* pp. 30–78; Owsley, *King Cotton,* pp. 422–26 and chap. 13 *passim;* Bulloch, *Secret Service,* 1:376–460; Palmerston to Russell, 4 September 1863, Russell Papers, PRO 30/22/22.

66. See Frank E. Vandiver (ed.), *Confederate Blockade Running Through Bermuda, 1861–1865,* pp. xxvii–xxix, xxxv–xxxix.

67. Vandiver (ed.), "The Capture of a Confederate Blockade Runner," pp. 136–38.

68. Charles W. Ramsdell (ed.), *Laws and Joint Resolutions of the Last Session of the Confederate Congress, Together with the Secret Acts of Previous*

Congresses, pp. 164–65; Emile Erlanger to Davis, 31 March 1863, in Autograph File, Dearborn Collection, Harvard University Library.

69. Owsley, *King Cotton,* p. 404; Richard C. Todd, *Confederate Finance,* pp. 48–51; John Bigelow, *France and the Confederate Navy, 1862–1868,* p. 118; John C. Schwab, *The Confederate States of America, 1861–1865,* p. 42; Judith Anne Fenner, "Confederate Finances Abroad."
70. See Charles S. Davis, *Colin J. McRae,* pp. 21–23, 26–33, 36–48.
71. *Ibid.,* 51–54, 56; Vandiver (ed.), *Blockade Running,* pp. xxxv–xxxvii; Vandiver, *Ploughshares into Swords,* pp. 98–104; James M. Matthews (ed.), *Statutes at Large of the Confederate States of America,* I Cong., stat. 4, chaps. 23 and 24.
72. Vandiver, *Ploughshares into Swords,* pp. 102–3.
73. Vandiver, *Blockade Running,* pp. xxxi–xxxii, xxxvii–xl; Owsley, *King Cotton,* pp. 286–91; William Diamond, "Imports of the Confederate Government from Europe and Mexico," pp. 476–77, 495–96.
74. Owsley, *King Cotton,* p. 285.
75. Robert D. Meade, *Judah P. Benjamin,* p. 253.

Chapter Eight: "The Sun Can Never Dip So Low"

1. Judith W. McGuire, *Diary of a Southern Refugee During the War,* p. 203.
2. Accounts of the Richmond "bread riot" are remarkable for dissimilarity. The narrative in the text is an attempt to reconcile several sources: J. B. Jones, *A Rebel War Clerk's Diary,* 1:284–86; A Richmond Lady [Sally Brock], *Richmond During the War,* pp. 208–10; Josiah Gorgas, *The Civil War Diary of General Josiah Gorgas,* pp. 28–29; E. M. Coulter, *The Confederate States of America, 1861–1865,* pp. 422–23; Bruce Catton, *Never Call Retreat,* pp. 100–1; Emory M. Thomas, "The Confederate State of Richmond," pp. 151–55; William J. Kimball, "The Bread Riot in Richmond, 1863," pp. 149–54. See also Richmond *Examiner,* 6 April 1863.
3. John Withers to the Richmond Press, 2 April 1863, in *War of the Rebellion,* ser. 1, vol. 18, p. 958.
4. See Coulter, *Confederate States,* pp. 423–24; Edward Younger (ed.), *Inside the Confederate Government,* p. 47.
5. Endorsement by L. B. Northrop [3 November 1862] on G. W. Randolph to Jefferson Davis, 30 October 1862, in Brock Collection, Box 284, Henry E. Huntington Library, San Marino, Calif.
6. Douglas Southall Freeman, *R. E. Lee,* 2:494–95, 3:246, 332, 535–36.
7. Frank E. Vandiver (ed.), "The Capture of a Confederate Blockade Runner," pp. 136–38.
8. Frank E. Vandiver, *Ploughshares into Swords,* pp. 99–104.
9. J. W. Mallet, "Work of the Ordnance Bureau of the War Department of the Confederate States, 1861–5," pp. 1–20; *General Orders from the Confederate Adjutant and Inspector-General's Office, Series of 1863,* p. 234; Gorgas to Gov. John Milton (Florida), 5 July 1863, John Milton Letter Book (1861–1863), Florida Historical Society, St. Augustine, Fla., p. 394.
10. Vandiver, "A Sketch of Efforts Abroad to Equip the Confederate Armory at Macon," pp. 34–40.
11. Gorgas, *Diary,* pp. 90–91.

12. Charles W. Ramsdell, "The Control of Manufacturing by the Confederate Government," pp. 231–49; Vandiver, "Confederate Plans for Procuring Subsistence Stores," pp. 273–77; Josiah Gorgas, "Ordnance of the Confederacy, I, II," pp. 212–16, 283–88; Socrates Maupin to M. S. Valentine, Jr., 14 September 1863, Brock Collection, Box 286, Huntington Library.
13. See Ramsdell, "Control of Manufacturing," pp. 231–49, and Vandiver, "The Shelby Iron Company in the Civil War," pp. 71–72.
14. Charles W. Ramsdell, *Behind the Lines in the Southern Confederacy*, p. 85.
15. Ramsdell, "General Robert E. Lee's Horse Supply, 1862–1865," pp. 764–69.
16. Robert C. Black, III, *The Railroads of the Confederacy*, pp. 82–83; Angus J. Johnston, II, *Virginia Railroads in the Civil War*, pp. 174–95; *War of the Rebellion*, ser. 1, vol. 33, pp. 1276–77, 1279–80.
17. Black, *Railroads*, p. 164. The secret act was entitled "An Act to facilitate transportation for the Government," approved 1 May 1863. See C. W. Ramsdell (ed.), *Laws and Joint Resolutions of the Last Session of the Confederate Congress, Together with the Secret Acts of Previous Congresses*, pp. 167–69.
18. Ramsdell, "The Confederate Government and the Railroads," pp. 805–10.
19. F. W. Sims to G. Jordan, Jr., 18 June 1863, F. W. Sims Letterbook, Huntington Library.
20. Black, *Railroads*, pp. 215–24.
21. *Ibid.*, pp. 225ff; Ramsdell, "Confederate Government and Railroads," pp. 794–810; Sims Letterbook.
22. Mary Boykin Chesnut, *A Diary from Dixie*, p. 307.
23. James Longstreet, *Manassas to Appomattox*, pp. 436–39; Clifford Dowdey, *The Land They Fought For*, pp. 295–96; Shelby Foote, *The Civil War, A Narrative*, pp. 709–11.
24. See William M. Lamers, *The Edge of Glory*, p. 351.
25. Joseph H. Parks, *General Leonidas Polk, C.S.A.*, pp. 327–40.
26. For the Battle of Chickamauga, see R. U. Johnson and C. C. Buel (eds.), *Battles and Leaders of the Civil War*, 3:638–75; Longstreet, *Manassas to Appomattox*, pp. 445–60; Parks, *Leonidas Polk*, pp. 327–40; Lamers, *Edge of Glory*, pp. 325–61; Don C. Seitz, *Braxton Bragg*, pp. 338–76; Glenn Tucker, *Chickamauga*; Stanley F. Horn, *The Army of Tennessee*, pp. 239–74; Andrew Lytle, *Bedford Forrest and his Critter Company*, pp. 206–39; G. Moxley Sorrell, *Recollections of a Confederate Staff Officer*, pp. 179–89; *Official Records, Armies*, ser. 1, vol. 30, pt. 2, pp. 287–91, 523–26.
27. Horn, *Army of Tennessee*, pp. 276–82; Seitz, *Bragg*, pp. 377–82.
28. Dunbar Rowland (ed.), *Jefferson Davis, Constitutionalist*, 6:57ff.
29. Parks, *Leonidas Polk*, pp. 343–47, 349–50; *War of the Rebellion*, ser. 1, vol. 30, pt. 2, pp. 65–68; *ibid.*, pt. 4, pp. 742–43; Horn, *Army of Tennessee*, pp. 285–92; Longstreet, *Manassas to Appomattox*, pp. 465–66; Bruce Catton, *Never Call Retreat*, pp. 50–54, 253–54.
30. See Joseph E. Johnston, *Narrative of Military Operations Directed During the Late War Between the States*, pp. 205–61; Johnston to Wigfall, 3, 14, 27 December 1863, Wigfall Family Papers, typescripts, Archives Collection, University of Texas.
31. Rowland (ed.), *Jefferson Davis, Constitutionalist*, 6:54–56, 68–72.
32. Longstreet, *Manassas to Appomattox*, pp. 480–85; Catton, *Never Call Retreat*, pp. 251–52.
33. Charleston *Courier*, 3 November 1863.

34. Catton, *Never Call Retreat*, pp. 264–65; Seitz, *Bragg*, pp. 396–400; Horn, *Army of Tennessee*, pp. 298–304; U. S. Grant, *Personal Memoirs*, 2:75–84; Fairfax Downey, *Storming of the Gateway*, pp. 3–198; *War of the Rebellion*, ser. 1, vol. 31, pt. 2, pp. 598–609, 613–17, 631–32.
35. Freeman, *Lee*, 3:246–53.
36. Freeman, *Lee's Lieutenants*, 3: Introduction.
37. *Ibid.*, pp. 269–79; Freeman, *Lee*, 3:190–93; J. A. Early, *War Memoirs*, pp. 319–25.
38. For an offer of Executive amnesty to deserters, see Richmond *Enquirer*, 7 August 1863. See also Rowland (ed.), *Jefferson Davis, Constitutionalist*, 6:164–69; *Journal of the Congress of the Confederate States of America, 1861–1865*, 3:708–12; Wilfred Buck Yearns, *The Confederate Congress*, pp. 156–57; Albert B. Moore, *Conscription and Conflict in the Confederacy*, pp. 218–22.
39. Younger (ed.), *Inside the Confederate Government*, pp. 84–85; Statistical table of Confederate manpower, compiled by T. L. Connelly, in writer's possession.
40. Bate to General W. H. T. Walker, 9 January 1864, Johnson and Buel (eds.), *Battles and Leaders*, 16: document facing p. 428. This special edition, containing many original documents, is in the Huntington Library, and is identified by the number 298000.
41. Davis to Walker, 23 January 1864, in Rowland (ed.), *Jefferson Davis, Constitutionalist*, 6:159–60. For the fears of a Southern governor concerning this issue, see Isham G. Harris (Tennessee) to Davis, 16 January 1864, Autograph File, Dearborn Collection, Harvard University Library.
42. Davis to Campbell Brown, 14 June 1886, in Johnson and Buel (eds.), *Battles and Leaders*, 2: document facing p. 99, Huntington Library.
43. On the use of slaves in the army, see Rowland (ed.), *Jefferson Davis, Constitutionalist*, 6:394–97; *War of the Rebellion*, ser. 1, vol. 52, pp. 586–92; N. W. Stephenson, "The Question of Arming the Slaves," pp. 295–308; T. R. Hay, "The Question of Arming the Slaves," pp. 34–73; Bell I. Wiley, *Southern Negroes, 1861–1865*, pp. 111, 121, 149–58; Benjamin Quarles, *The Negro in the Civil War*, pp. 273–75; Charles H. Wesley, *The Collapse of the Confederacy*, pp. 144–66.
44. For the quotations from Booker T. Washington, see his *Story of the Negro*, 2:4–5, and his *Up From Slavery*, pp. 7, 19–20. For the quotation on slavery as a lasting institution, see Bertram W. Doyle, *The Etiquette of Race Relations in the South*, p. 107.
45. Charles H. Wesley, *The Collapse of the Confederacy*, *passim* and especially chap. 5.
46. Johnston to Wigfall, 4, 9 January 1864, Wigfall Family Papers.
47. Gorgas, *Diary*, p. 68, for prices. For details of congressional lodgings see Bell I. Wiley (ed.), *Letters of Warren Aiken, Confederate Congressman*, p. 5.
48. Yearns, *Confederate Congress*, pp. 49–50.
49. *Ibid.*, pp. 50–51.
50. *Ibid.*, p. 189; Coulter, *Confederate States*, p. 159.
51. Yearns, *Confederate Congress*, pp. 58–59, 225–27.
52. Jones, *War Clerk's Diary*, 2:112.
53. Mary Chesnut, *A Diary from Dixie*, p. 9.
54. Yearns, *Confederate Congress*, p. 220.

55. *Ibid.*, p. 221. See also Mary Chesnut, *A Diary from Dixie*, pp. 107, 233–34, 329.
56. Quoted in *ibid.*, p. 220. See also R. B. Rhett to L. T. Wigfall, 15 April 1864, Wigfall Family Papers.
57. Richmond *Enquirer*, 30 December 1863.
58. Diary of Stephen R. Mallory, 27 September 1865, typescript, Southern Historical Collection, University of North Carolina.
59. Davis to Congress, 7 December 1863, in Rowland (ed.), *Jefferson Davis, Constitutionalist*, 6:93–128. The quotation is on p. 128.
60. See, for example, *Southern Historical Society Papers* 50 (1953): 10–13, 18–24.
61. Rembert W. Patrick, *Jefferson Davis and His Cabinet*, pp. 226–31; Davis to Memminger, 21 June 1864, in Rowland (ed.), *Jefferson Davis, Constitutionalist*, 6:275–76.
62. *Journal, Confederate Congress*, 4:533; Patrick, *Davis Cabinet*, p. 47; Yearns, *Confederate Congress*, pp. 230–32; *Southern Historical Society Papers* 50 (1953): 24.
63. Yearns, *Confederate Congress*, pp. 232–34; Younger (ed.), *Inside the Confederate Government*, pp. xxiii, xxix; Jones, *War Clerk's Diary*, 2:131–32; Northrop to Davis, 6 August 1864, Autograph File, Dearborn Collection, Harvard Library.
64. James M. Matthews (ed.), *Statutes at Large of the Confederate States of America*, I Cong., stat. 4, chaps. 3, 4, 55.
65. *Ibid.*, chap. 56.
66. *Ibid.*, chap. 64.
67. *Ibid.*, chap. 63. See also Richard C. Todd, *Confederate Finance*, pp. 75–76.
68. James M. Matthews (ed.), *Statutes, Confederate Congress*, I Cong., stat. 4, chaps. 23, 24; Vandiver, *Ploughshares into Swords*, pp. 102–3.
69. James M. Matthews (ed.), *Statutes, Confederate Congress*, I Cong., stat. 4, chap. 37.

Chapter Nine: "Unconquered and Unconquerable Hearts"

1. J. B. Jones, *A Rebel War Clerk's Diary*, 2:157.
2. Robert S. Henry, *"First With the Most" Forrest*, pp. 228–33.
3. Joseph H. Parks, *General Edmund Kirby Smith, C.S.A.*, pp. 385–89; John D. Winters, *The Civil War in Louisiana*, pp. 340–47.
4. William Couper, *One Hundred Years at V.M.I.*, 2:266–312.
5. James D. Bulloch, *The Secret Service of the Confederate States in Europe*, 1:277–89; 2:68–105, 125–70; V. C. Jones, *The Civil War at Sea*, 3:215–28, 379–86; Cornelius E. Hunt, *The Shenandoah;* Stanley F. Horn, *Gallant Rebel*.
6. Jones, *Civil War at Sea*, 3:144–64.
7. *War of the Rebellion*, ser. 4, vol. 2, pp. 960, 970–71; Douglas Southall Freeman, *R. E. Lee*, 3:240–41, 246–51.
8. Freeman, *Lee*, 3:253.
9. Joseph E. Johnston, *Narrative of Military Operations Directed During the Late War Between the States*, p. 570.
10. See George W. Pepper, *Personal Recollections of Sherman's Campaigns in Georgia and the Carolinas*, pp. 56–57.

11. Johnston, *Narrative*, pp. 287–300; Johnston to Wigfall, 27 December 1863; 4, 9 January, 14 February, 6 March, 5, 23, 30 April 1864, Wigfall Family Papers, typescripts, Archives Collection, University of Texas.
12. William T. Sherman, *Memoirs of General William T. Sherman*, 2:24.
13. John B. Hood, *Advance and Retreat*, pp. 126–27.
14. Stanley F. Horn, *The Army of Tennessee*, pp. 394–404, 405, 406–18. The song is printed on p. 418.
15. Jones, *War Clerk's Diary*, 2:257.
16. See Mary E. Massey, *Refugee Life in the Confederacy*, pp. 124–25, 179–80.
17. Dunbar Rowland (ed.), *Jefferson Davis, Constitutionalist*, 6:141.
18. Davis to Vance, 8 January 1864, *ibid.*, pp. 143–46.
19. U. B. Phillips (ed.), *The Correspondence of Robert Toombs, Alexander H. Stephens, and Howell Cobb*, pp. 580–81, 586, 595, 608, 614, 628, 630, 639.
20. See, for example, Georgia Lee Tatum, *Disloyalty in the Confederacy*, p. 77 and *passim;* Frank L. Owsley, *State Rights in the Confederacy*, pp. 162–71, 208–18, 272–81.
21. Owsley, *State Rights*, pp. 203–18; E. M. Coulter, *The Confederate States of America, 1861–1865*, pp. 374–404.
22. See, for example, Rowland (ed.), *Jefferson Davis, Constitutionalist*, 5:254–62, 292–93, 490, 510, 6:141–42, 143–46, 158–59, 178–81; Phillips (ed.), *Correspondence of Toombs, Stephens, Cobb*, pp. 653–54, 660; Brown to Davis (telegrams), 28 June and 4 July 1864, Joseph E. Johnston Papers, Library of the College of William and Mary, Williamsburg, Va.
23. Rowland (ed.), *Jefferson Davis, Constitutionalist*, 6:220–23, 224–25, 235–36, 260–61, 268–69, 271–72, 272–73, 280–81, 306, 308–9, 400–1, 439–45.
24. James M. Matthews (ed.), *Statutes at Large of the Confederate States of America*, I Cong., stat. 4, chap. 74.
25. *Journal of the Congress of the Confederate States of America, 1861–1865*, 4:258, 7:247, 261–62, 526–28; N. W. Stephenson, "The Question of Arming the Slaves," pp. 293–304; T. R. Hay, "The Question of Arming the Slaves," pp. 50–62.
26. Bell I. Wiley (ed.), *Letters of Warren Akin, Confederate Congressman*, pp. 4–5, 13.
27. Wilfred Buck Yearns, *The Confederate Congress*, p. 176; E. C. Kirkland, *The Peacemakers of 1864*, pp. 218–20.
28. See, for example, Charleston *Courier*, 14 January 1864.
29. Bruce Catton, *Never Call Retreat*, p. 355.
30. Freeman, *Lee*, 3:263–68, 270n.
31. Douglas Southall Freeman, *Lee's Lieutenants*, 3:357.
32. James Longstreet, *From Manassas to Appomattox*, pp. 564–65; Freeman, *Lee's Lieutenants*, 3:342–72; Clifford Dowdey, *Lee's Last Campaign*, pp. 61–82.
33. Freeman, *Lee*, 3:386–91.
34. See Catton, *Never Call Retreat*, p. 361.
35. Frank E. Vandiver, *Jubal's Raid*, pp. 10–11.
36. *Ibid.*, pp. 173–74.
37. See T. Harry Williams, *P. G. T. Beauregard, Napoleon in Gray*, pp. 212–35; R. U. Johnson and C. C. Buel (eds.), *Battles and Leaders of the Civil War*, 4:540–44.
38. For effects of attrition, see Lee to Davis, 2 September 1864, Rowland (ed.), *Jefferson Davis, Constitutionalist*, 6:327–29.

39. See, for example, Joseph LeConte, *'Ware Sherman;* Mary Sharpe Jones and Mary Jones Mallard, *Yankees A'Coming;* Dolly Sumner Lunt, *A Woman's Wartime Journal.*

40. Kirkland, *Peacemakers,* pp. 222–58; Catton, *Never Call Retreat,* pp. 419–23; Rowland (ed.), *Jefferson Davis, Constitutionalist,* 6:465–78.

41. See the account of this address in Coulter, *Confederate States,* p. 553; Edward A. Pollard, *The Lost Cause,* pp. 684–85; Jones, *War Clerk's Diary,* 2:411, 415; Richmond *Examiner,* 7, 10 February 1865.

42. Coulter, *Confederate States,* p. 554, citing Athens *Southern Watchman,* 22 February 1865.

43. See Davis to Vance and John Milton, 21 February 1865, Rowland (ed.), *Jefferson Davis, Constitutionalist,* 6:483.

44. See patriotic resolutions from various units in Richmond *Examiner,* 8, 10, 11 February and later dates, 1865. For resolutions from Pickett's men, see *ibid.,* 14 February 1865. See also Resolutions passed by 2nd Va. Cavalry, Fitzhugh Lee's Division, 28 February 1865, in Brock Collection, Henry E. Huntington Library, San Marino, Calif.

45. Sources dealing with Andersonville and prisons in general are legion. Among the most helpful are Coulter, *Confederate States,* pp. 471–81; A. Cooper, *In and Out of Rebel Prisons,* pp. 41–104 (on Andersonville); H. M. Davidson, *Fourteen Months in Southern Prisons,* pp. 109–239 (on Andersonville); Morgan E. Dowling, *Southern Prisons, or Josie, the Heroine of Florence;* John McElroy, *Andersonville;* John L. Ransom, *John Ransom's Diary,* pp. 32–87; Ambrose Spencer, *A Narrative of Andersonville, Drawn from the Evidence Elicited on the Trial of Henry Wirz, the Jailer;* William B. Hesseltine, *Civil War Prisons,* pp. 133–58.

46. Charles W. Ramsdell (ed.), *Laws and Joint Resolutions of the Last Session of the Confederate Congress, Together with the Secret Acts of Previous Congresses,* pp. 139–40.

47. *Ibid.,* pp. 22–23.

48. *War of the Rebellion,* ser. 1, vol. 46, pt. 2, 1205; Freeman, *Lee,* 3:533–34; Rowland (ed.), *Jefferson Davis, Constitutionalist,* 6:479.

49. Johnston, *Narrative,* p. 587.

50. *Ibid.*

51. Rowland (ed.), *Jefferson Davis, Constitutionalist,* 6:396.

52. Davis to Campbell Brown, 14 June 1886, in Johnson and Buel (eds.), *Battles and Leaders,* 2: document facing p. 99, Huntington Library.

53. Frank L. Owsley, *King Cotton Diplomacy,* pp. 550–61; N. W. Stephenson, "Question of Arming Slaves," pp. 303–8; R. D. Meade, *Judah P. Benjamin,* pp. 306–8.

54. *War of the Rebellion,* ser. 1, vol. 46, pt. 3, p. 1315; Rowland (ed.), *Jefferson Davis, Constitutionalist,* 6:522, 523.

55. Lee to Andrew Hunter, 11 January 1865, *War of the Rebellion,* ser. 4, vol. 3, pp. 1012–13 (original in Eldridge Collection, Box 43, Huntington Library).

56. Coulter, *Confederate States,* pp. 266–68; Stephenson, "Question of Arming Slaves," pp. 307–8; Bell I. Wiley, *Southern Negroes, 1861–1865,* chap. 9. For the act, see Ramsdell (ed.), *Last Laws,* pp. 118–19.

57. Meade, *Judah P. Benjamin,* pp. 308–9.

58. Frank E. Vandiver, "Makeshifts of Confederate Ordnance," pp. 190–92.

59. Vandiver, *Ploughshares into Swords,* p. 261.

60. Ramsdell (ed.), *Last Laws*, pp. 134–35.
61. Jones, *War Clerk's Diary*, 2:465; Vandiver, *Ploughshares into Swords*, p. 266; Rembert W. Patrick, *The Fall of Richmond*, pp. 17–18.
62. Josiah Gorgas, *The Civil War Diary of General Josiah Gorgas*, p. 171.
63. *War of the Rebellion*, ser. 1, vol. 51, pt. 2, pp. 1064–68.
64. Patrick, *Fall of Richmond*, pp. 20–22; Gorgas, *Diary*, p. 179; Varina Davis, *Jefferson Davis, Ex-President of the Confederate States of America*, 2:583–86.
65. Rowland (ed.), *Jefferson Davis, Constitutionalist*, 6:529–31.
66. *War of the Rebellion*, ser. 1, vol. 46, pt. 3, p. 619; Freeman, *Lee*, 4:109.
67. Freeman, *Lee*, 4:140–41; P. H. Sheridan, *Personal Memoirs of P. H. Sheridan, General, United States Army*, 2:188–90; Bruce Catton, *A Stillness at Appomattox*, p. 374.
68. John S. Wise, *The End of an Era*, pp. 434–35.
69. E. P. Alexander, *Military Memoirs of a Confederate*, pp. 604–5.
70. *Ibid.*, p. 605. The events and comments in the text are an attempt to reconcile several sources. See variations in R. S. Henry, *The Story of the Confederacy*, pp. 463–64; Catton, *Never Call Retreat*, pp. 452–53.
71. See Freeman, *Lee*, 4:138–39; Catton, *U. S. Grant and the American Military Tradition*, pp. 128–29. There is a formidable literature dealing with Appomattox. For example, consult: John B. Gordon, *Reminiscences of the Civil War*, pp. 429–42; Alexander, *Memoirs*, pp. 598–614; Freeman, *Lee*, 4:117–48; Catton, *Stillness*, pp. 368–80; and Joshua L. Chamberlain, *The Passing of the Armies*; Johnson and Buel (eds.), *Battles and Leaders*, 4:729–53; U. S. Grant, *Personal Memoirs*, 2:483–98.
72. Freeman, *Lee*, 4:138.
73. See Davis to Varina Davis, 23 April 1865, Rowland (ed.), *Jefferson Davis, Constitutionalist*, 6:559–62.
74. *Ibid.*, pp. 568–85. There is much confusion surrounding the question of Davis's capture. Stories vary with eyewitnesses and inflate in recollection. Standard sources all cover the episode, but see in particular: Howard T. Dimick, "The Capture of Jefferson Davis," pp. 238–54; "Capture of Jefferson Davis, told by himself," typescript account in possession of Mr. Jefferson Hayes-Davis, Colorado Springs, Colo.; Julian G. Dickinson to Gen. J. H. Wilson, 5 July 1879, and Robert Burns to Gen. J. H. Wilson, 1 September 1879, both in the files of the Jefferson Davis Association, Rice University, Houston, Tex.

General Richard Taylor surrendered some 42,293 Confederate troops in East Louisiana and the Gulf Coast areas to Federal General E. R. S. Canby at Citronelle, Ala., May 4, 1865. General E. K. Smith surrendered some 17,686 men and the Trans-Mississippi Department to Canby at New Orleans, May 26, 1865.

Bibliography

Manuscript Collections

Bahamas, Nassau. Governor of the Bahamas Letters Received from the Colonial Office. Government House.

Broadlands Archives (England). Papers of Lord Palmerston. (Used by permission of Earl Mountbatten of Burma).

Buffalo, New York. Buffalo and Erie County Historical Society. A. W. Bishop Papers.

Florida Historical Society, St. Augustine. Governor John Milton's Letter Book, 1861–1863.

Georgia, University of, Libraries, Athens. Telamon Cuyler Collection. Keith Read Collection.

Harvard University Library, Cambridge, Massachusetts. Dearborn Collection.

Huntington, Henry E., Library, San Marino, California. Barlow Papers. Brock Collection. Eldridge Collection. Maury (D. H.) Papers. Sims (F. W.) Papers.

Jefferson Davis Association, Rice University, Houston, Texas. Papers of Jefferson Davis.

National Archives, Washington, D.C. Confederate Records, War Department.

North Carolina, University of, Chapel Hill, Southern Historical Collection. Diary of Thomas Bragg. Diary of Stephen R. Mallory. Mary Elizabeth Mitchell Book.

Public Record Office, London, England. Foreign Office Records (Lord John Russell).

Texas, University of, Archives, Austin, Texas. L. T. Wigfall Family Papers.

William and Mary, College of, Library, Williamsburg, Virginia. Joseph E. Johnston Papers.

Newspapers

Atlanta (Ga.) *Southern Confederacy.*
Charleston (S.C.) *Courier.*
Charleston (S.C.) *Mercury.*

Davenport (Ia.) *Daily Democratic News,* September 1862.
London (England) *Index.*
London (England) *Times.*
New York Times.
Richmond (Va.) *Dispatch.*
Richmond (Va.) *Enquirer.*
Richmond (Va.) *Examiner.*
Richmond (Va.) *Whig.*
Vienna (Austria) *Zeitung,* November and December 1861.
Washington (D.C.) *Daily National Intelligencer.*
Youngstown (Ohio) *Mahoning Sentinel,* September 1862.

Primary Sources: Books

Alexander, E. P. *Military Memoirs of a Confederate.* New York, 1910.
Anderson, John Q. (ed.). *Brokenburn: The Journal of Kate Stone, 1861–1865.* Baton Rouge, 1955.
Basler, Roy P. (ed.). *The Collected Works of Abraham Lincoln,* 8 vols. New Brunswick, N.J., 1953.
Beale, Howard K. (ed.), "The Diary of Edward Bates, 1859–1866," in *Annual Report of the American Historical Association* for 1930. Washington, D.C., 1933.
[Blessington, J. P.] *The Campaigns of Walker's Texas Division.* New York, 1875.
Boggs, Gen. William R., *Military Reminiscences of Gen. Wm. R. Boggs, C.S.A.* Durham, N.C., 1913.
[Brock, Sally]. *Richmond During the War: Four Years of Personal Observation.* New York, 1867.
Bulloch, James D. *The Secret Service of the Confederate States in Europe: or, How the Confederate Cruisers Were Equipped,* ed. Philip Van Doren Stern, 2 vols. New York, 1959.
Chamberlain, Joshua L. *The Passing of the Armies.* New York, 1915.
Chesnut, Mary Boykin. *A Diary from Dixie,* ed. Ben Ames Williams. Boston, 1950.
Chittenden, L. E. (ed.). *A Report of the Debates and Proceedings in the Secret Session of the Conference Convention, for Proposing Amendments to the Constitution of the United States, Held at Washington, D.C., in February, A.D., 1861.* New York, 1864.
Confederate Almanac for 1865. Houston, Texas, 1865.
Cooke, John Esten. *A Life of General Robert E. Lee.* New York, 1875.
Cooper, A. *In and Out of Rebel Prisons.* Oswego, N.Y., 1888.
Davidson, H. M. *Fourteen Months in Southern Prisons.* Milwaukee, 1865.
Davis, Jefferson. *The Rise and Fall of the Confederate Government,* 2 vols. New York, 1881.
Davis, Varina Howell. *Jefferson Davis, Ex-President of the Confederate States of America.* 2 vols. New York, 1890.
Debray, X. B. *A Sketch of the History of Debray's (26th) Regiment of Texas Cavalry.* Austin, 1884.
Douglas, Henry Kyd. *I Rode With Stonewall.* Chapel Hill, 1940.

Dowling, Morgan E. *Southern Prisons, or Josie, the Heroine of Florence: Four Years of Battle and Imprisonment.* Detroit, 1870.
Dumond, Dwight L. (ed.). *Southern Editorials on Secession.* New York, 1931.
Early, Jubal A. *War Memoirs: Autobiographical Sketch and Narrative of the War Between the States.* Edited by Frank E. Vandiver. Bloomington, Ind., 1960.
Eighth Census of the United States, 1860: Agriculture. Washington, D.C., 1864.
Eighth Census of the United States, 1860: Manufactures. Washington, D.C., 1865.
Fisher, Miles Mark. *Negro Slave Songs in the United States.* New York, 1963.
Ford, John S. *Rip Ford's Texas.* Edited by Stephen B. Oates. Austin, 1963.
General Orders from the Confederate Adjutant and Inspector-General's Office, Series of 1863. Columbia, S.C., 1864.
Gordon, John B. *Reminiscences of the Civil War.* New York, 1903.
Grant, U. S. *Personal Memoirs.* 2 vols. New York, 1885.
Harris, George W. *Sut Lovingood.* Edited by Brown Weber. New York, 1954.
Haskell, Frank A. *The Battle of Gettysburg.* Boston, 1908.
Helper, Hinton R. *The Impending Crisis of the South: How to Meet It.* New York, 1860.
Hewitt, John Hill. *King Linkum the First.* Edited by Richard B. Harwell. Emory University Publications, Sources and Reprints, Series IV. Atlanta, 1947.
Hobart Pasha, Admiral [Augustus Charles Hobart-Hampden]. *Sketches from My Life.* London, 1887.
Hood, John B. *Advance and Retreat: Personal Experiences in the United States & Confederate States Armies.* Edited by Richard N. Current. Bloomington, Ind., 1959.
Hotze, Henry. *Three Months in the Confederate Army.* University, Ala., 1952.
Huse, Caleb. *The Supplies for the Confederate Army, How They Were Obtained in Europe and How Paid For: Personal Reminiscences and Unpublished History.* Boston, 1904.
Johnson, R. U., and C. C. Buel (eds.). *Battles and Leaders of the Civil War.* 4 vols. New York, 1887–1888.
Johnston, Joseph E. *Narrative of Military Operations Directed During the Late War Between the States.* Edited by Frank E. Vandiver. Bloomington, Ind., 1959.
Jones, J. B. *A Rebel War Clerk's Diary.* Edited by Howard Swiggett, 2 vols. New York, 1935.
Jones, Mary Sharpe, and Mary Jones Mallard. *Yankees A'Coming: One Month's Experience During the Invasion of Liberty County, Georgia, 1864–1865.* Edited by H. M. Monroe, Jr. Tuscaloosa, Ala., 1959.
Journal of the Congress of the Confederate States of America, 1861–1865. 7 vols. Washington, D.C., 1904–1905.
Journal of the House of Representatives of the State of Georgia, at Annual Session of the General Assembly, 1863. Milledgeville, Ga., 1863.
Journal of the Senate at an Extra Session of the General Assembly of the State of Georgia. Milledgeville, Ga., 1863.
Lasswell, Lynda J. (ed.). "Jefferson Davis and the Mississippi Rifles in the Mexican War." Master's thesis, Rice University, 1969.
LeConte, Joseph. *'Ware Sherman: A Journal of Three Months' Personal Experience in the Last Days of the Confederacy.* Berkeley, Calif., 1938.

Longstreet, James. *From Manassas to Appomattox*. Edited by James I. Robertson. Bloomington, Ind., 1960.

Lord, Clifford, and Elizabeth Lord. *Historical Atlas of the United States*. New York, 1944.

Lord, Walter (ed.). *The Fremantle Diary: Being the Journal of Lieutenant Colonel James Arthur Lyon [sic] Fremantle, Coldstream Guards, on His Three Months in the Southern States*. Boston, 1954.

Lunt, Dolly S. *A Woman's Wartime Journal: An Account of the Passage over a Georgia Plantation of Sherman's Army on the March to the Sea, as Recorded in the Diary of Dolly Sumner Lunt*. Macon, 1927.

McDonald, Archie P. (ed.). "The Journal of Jedediah Hotchkiss, June, 1861–August, 1862." Master's thesis, Rice University, 1960.

McElroy, John. *Andersonville: A Story of Rebel Military Prisons*. Toledo, Ohio, 1879.

McGuire, Judith W. *Diary of a Southern Refugee During the War*. New York, 1868.

McKeithan, Daniel M. (ed.). *A Collection of Hayne Letters*. Austin, 1944.

Matthews, James M. (ed.). *Statutes at Large of the Confederate States of America*. Richmond, 1862–1864.

——. (ed.). *Statutes at Large of the Provisional Government of the Confederate States of America*. Richmond, 1864.

Medical and Surgical History of the War of the Rebellion. 3 vols. in 6. Washington, D.C., 1870.

Moore, Frank (ed.). *The Rebellion Record*. 11 vols. and supplement. New York, 1861–1871.

Moore, Marinda B. *The Dixie Speller, to Follow the First Dixie Reader*. Raleigh, 1863.

——. *The Geographical Reader for the Dixie Children*. 2d ed. Raleigh, 1864.

Official Records of the Union and Confederate Navies in the War of the Rebellion. 30 vols. and index. Washington, D.C., 1894–1927.

Patrick, Rembert W. (ed.). *The Opinions of the Confederate Attorneys General, 1861–1865*. Buffalo, N.Y., 1950.

Pepper, George W. *Personal Recollections of Sherman's Campaigns in Georgia and the Carolinas*. Zanesville, Ohio, 1866.

Phillips, Ulrich B. (ed.). "The Correspondence of Robert Toombs, Alexander H. Stephens, and Howell Cobb." In *Annual Report of the American Historical Association* for 1911. Washington, 1913.

[Pollard, E. A.] *Echoes from the South*. New York, 1866.

Porcher, Francis P. *Resources of the Southern Fields and Forests*. Charleston, 1869.

"Pro-lege." *A Legal View of the Seizure of Messrs. Mason and Slidell*. New York, 1861.

Ramsdell, Charles W. (ed.). *Laws and Joint Resolutions of the Last Session of the Confederate Congress, Together with the Secret Acts of Previous Congresses*. Durham, 1941.

Ransom, John L. *John Ransom's Diary*. New York, 1863.

Regulations of the Confederate States Army for the Quarter Master's Department. Richmond, 1864.

Roman, A. B. *The Military Operations of General Beauregard*. 2 vols. New York, 1883.

Rowland, Dunbar (ed.). *Jefferson Davis, Constitutionalist: His Letters, Papers and Speeches.* 10 vols. Jackson, Miss., 1923.

Russell, William H. *My Diary North and South.* Boston, 1863.

Sanger, George P., and others (eds.). *The Statutes at Large, Treaties, and Proclamations of the United States of America, 1789–1873.* Little, Brown Edition. 17 vols. Boston, 1850–1873.

Semmes, Raphael. *Memoirs of Service Afloat During the War Between the States.* Baltimore, 1869.

Sheridan, P. H. *Personal Memoirs of P. H. Sheridan, General, United States Army.* 2 vols. New York, 1888.

Sherman, William T. *Memoirs of General William T. Sherman.* 2d ed. 2 vols. New York, 1904.

Smith, Charles. *Bill Arp, So Called.* Atlanta, 1866.

Smith, D. E. Huger, Alice R. Huger Smith, and A. R. Childs (eds.). *Mason Smith Family Letters, 1860–1868.* Columbia, S.C., 1950.

Sorrel, G. Moxley. *Recollections of a Confederate Staff Officer.* Edited by Bell I. Wiley. Jackson, Tenn., 1958.

Spenser, Ambrose. *A Narrative of Andersonville, Drawn from the Evidence Elicited on the Trial of Henry Wirz, the Jailer.* New York, 1866.

Stephens, Alexander H. *A Constitutional View of the Late War Between the States.* 2 vols. Philadelphia, 1868–1870.

Taylor, Richard. *Destruction and Reconstruction.* Edited by Richard Harwell. New York, 1955.

Taylor, Thomas E. *Running the Blockade.* London, 1897.

[Timrod, Henry]. *Poems of Henry Timrod, With Memoir and Portrait.* Memorial Edition. Boston, 1899.

U.S. State Department. *Correspondence Relative to the Case of Messrs. Mason and Slidell.* n.p., n.d.

Vandiver, Frank E. (ed.). *The Civil War Diary of General Josiah Gorgas.* University, Ala., 1947.

———. (ed.). *Confederate Blockade Running Through Bermuda, 1861–1865: Letters and Cargo Manifests.* Austin, 1947.

"Vigilans" (pseud.). *The Foreign Enlistment Acts of England and America.* London, 1864.

War of the Rebellion: A Compilation of the Official Records of the Union and Confederate Armies. 70 vols. in 127 and index. Washington, D.C., 1880–1901.

Wharton, H. M. *War Songs and Poems of the Southern Confederacy, 1861–1865.* n.p., 1904.

Wiley, Bell I. (ed.). *Letters of Warren Akin, Confederate Congressman.* Athens, Ga., 1959.

Worsham, John H. *One of Jackson's Foot Cavalry.* New York, 1912.

Younger, Edward (ed.). *Inside the Confederate Government: The Diary of Robert Garlick Hill Kean.* New York, 1957.

Primary Sources: Periodicals

Gorgas, Josiah. "Ordnance of the Confederacy, I, II." *Army Ordnance* 16 (1936).

Mallet, John William. "Work of the Ordnance Bureau of the War Department

of the Confederate States, 1861–5." *Southern Historical Society Papers* 38 (1909).
"Proceedings of the Confederate Congress." *Southern Historical Society Papers* 45 [n.s. 7] (1925).
Vandiver, Frank E. (ed.). "The Capture of a Confederate Blockade Runner: Extracts from the Journal of a Confederate Naval Officer." *North Carolina Historical Review* 21 (1944).
————. (ed.). "A Collection of Louisiana Confederate Letters," *Louisiana Historical Quarterly* 26 (1943).

Secondary Sources: Books

Abel, Annie H. *The American Indian as Participant in the Civil War.* Cleveland, 1919.
————. *The American Indian Under Reconstruction.* Cleveland, 1925.
Adams, C. F. *Charles Francis Adams.* Boston, 1900.
Adams, E. D. *Great Britain and the American Civil War.* New York, 1958.
Andrews, Matthew P. *The Women of the South in Wartime.* Baltimore, 1927.
Bernard, Mountague. *A Historical Account of the Neutrality of Great Britain During the American Civil War.* London, 1870.
Bigelow, John. *France and the Confederate Navy, 1862–1868.* New York, 1888.
Bill, Alfred Hoyt. *The Beleaguered City, Richmond, 1861–1865.* New York, 1946.
Black, Robert C., III. *The Railroads of the Confederacy.* Chapel Hill, N.C., 1952.
Boucher, Chauncey S. *The Nullification Controversy in South Carolina.* Chicago, 1916.
Bradlee, Francis B. C. *Blockade During the Civil War, and the Effect of Land and Water Transportation on the Confederacy.* Salem, Mass., 1925.
Bridges, Hal. *Lee's Maverick General: Daniel Harvey Hill.* New York, 1961.
Brown, Dee A. *The Bold Cavaliers: Morgan's 2nd Kentucky Cavalry Raiders.* Philadelphia, 1959.
Bryan, T. Conn. *Confederate Georgia.* Athens, Ga., 1953.
Capers, Gerald M. *John C. Calhoun, Opportunist: A Reappraisal.* Gainesville, Fla., 1960.
Carpenter, Jesse T. *The South as a Conscious Minority, 1789–1861: A Study in Political Thought.* New York, 1930.
Carse, Robert. *Blockade.* New York, 1958.
Cash, W. J. *The Mind of the South.* Garden City, 1941.
Catton, Bruce. *A Stillness at Appomattox.* Garden City, 1952.
————. *Grant Moves South.* Boston, 1960.
————. *Mr. Lincoln's Army.* Garden City, 1954.
————. *Never Call Retreat.* New York, 1965.
————. *U. S. Grant and the American Military Tradition.* Boston, 1954.
Chambers, Lenoir. *Stonewall Jackson.* 2 vols. New York, 1959.
Clay-Clopton, Virginia (Mrs. Clement Clay). *A Belle of the Fifties.* New York, 1905.
Cochran, Hamilton. *Blockade Runners of the Confederacy.* Indianapolis, 1958.

Cohen, Hennig, and W. B. Willingham (eds.). *Humor of the Old Southwest.* Boston, 1964.

Coit, Margaret. *John C. Calhoun, American Portrait.* Boston, 1950.

Colton, Ray C. *The Civil War in the Western Terrorities: Arizona, Colorado, New Mexico, and Utah.* Norman, Okla., 1959.

Connelly, Thomas L. *Army of the Heartland: The Army of Tennessee, 1861–1862.* Baton Rouge, 1967.

Coulter, E. M. *John Jacobus Flournoy.* Savannah, Ga., 1942.

———. *The Civil War and Readjustment in Kentucky.* Chapel Hill, N.C., 1926.

———. *The Confederate States of America, 1861–1865.* Baton Rouge, 1950.

Couper, William. *One Hundred Years at V.M.I.* 4 vols. Richmond, 1939.

Craven, Avery O. "Background Forces and the Civil War." In *The American Tragedy,* edited by Bernard Mayo. Hampden Sydney, Va., 1959.

———. *Civil War in the Making.* Baton Rouge, 1950.

———. *The Growth of Southern Nationalism.* Baton Rouge, 1953.

Cravens, John N. *James Harper Starr.* Austin, 1950.

Crenshaw, Ollinger. *The Slave States in the Presidential Election of 1860.* Baltimore, 1945.

Cunningham, Edward. *The Port Hudson Campaign, 1862–1863.* Baton Rouge, 1963.

Cunningham, H. H. *Doctors in Gray: The Confederate Medical Service.* Baton Rouge, 1958.

Current, Richard N. *John C. Calhoun.* New York, 1963.

———. *Lincoln and the First Shot.* Philadelphia, 1963.

Dalzell, George W. *The Flight from the Flag: The Continuing Effect of the Civil War upon the American Carrying Trade.* Chapel Hill, N.C., 1940.

Dew, Charles B. *Ironmaker to the Confederacy: Joseph R. Anderson and the Tredegar Iron Works.* New Haven, 1966.

Dodd, William E. *Jefferson Davis.* Philadelphia, 1907.

Donald, David. *Lincoln Reconsidered.* New York, 1956.

Dowdey, Clifford. *Death of a Nation: The Story of Lee and His Men at Gettysburg.* New York, 1958.

———. *The Land They Fought For: The Story of the South as the Confederacy, 1832–1865.* Garden City, 1955.

———. *Lee's Last Campaign: The Story of Lee and His Men Against Grant, 1864.* Boston, 1960.

———. *The Seven Days.* Boston, 1964.

Downey, Fairfax. *Storming of the Gateway: Chattanooga, 1863.* New York, 1960.

Doyle, Bertram W. *The Etiquette of Race Relations in the South: A Study in Social Control.* Chicago, 1937.

Dufour, Charles L. *The Night the War Was Lost.* Garden City, 1960.

Dumond, Dwight L. *Antislavery.* New York, 1961.

Durkin, Joseph T. *Stephen R. Mallory: Confederate Navy Chief.* Chapel Hill, N.C., 1954.

Eaton, Clement. *Freedom of Thought in the Old South.* Durham, 1940.

———. *The Freedom of Thought Struggle in the Old South.* New York, 1964.

———. *A History of the Old South.* New York, 1954.

———. *A History of the Old South.* 2d ed. New York, 1966.

———. *A History of the Southern Confederacy.* New York, 1954.

Eckenrode, H. J., and Bryan Conrad. *James Longstreet: Lee's War Horse.* Chapel Hill, N.C., 1936.

Editors of American Heritage. *The American Heritage Picture History of the Civil War.* New York, 1960.

Eimerl, Sarel H. "The Political Thought of the Ante-Bellum Fire-Eaters." Master's thesis, Rice Institute, 1950.

Elkins, Stanley M. *Slavery: A Problem in American Institutional Intellectual Life.* New York, 1963.

Ellsworth, Eliot, Jr. *West Point in the Confederacy.* New York, 1941.

Fenner, Judith Anne. "Confederate Finances Abroad." Ph.D. dissertation, Rice University, 1969.

Fitzhugh, Lester N. *Texas Batteries, Battalions, Regiments, Commanders, and Field Officers, Confederate States Army, 1861–1865.* Midlothian, Texas, 1959.

Foote, Shelby. *The Civil War, a Narrative: Fort Sumter to Perryville.* New York, 1958.

———. *The Civil War, a Narrative: Fredericksburg to Meridian.* New York, 1963.

Franklin, John Hope. *The Militant South.* Cambridge, Mass., 1956.

Freehling, William W. *Prelude to Civil War: The Nullification Controversy in South Carolina, 1816–1836.* New York, 1966.

Freeman, Douglas Southall. *Lee's Lieutenants: A Study in Command.* 3 vols. New York, 1942–1944.

———. *R. E. Lee: A Biography.* 4 vols. New York, 1934–1935.

Gates, Paul W. *Agriculture and the Civil War.* New York, 1965.

Genovese, Eugene D. *The Political Economy of Slavery.* New York, 1965.

Govan, Gilbert, and James Livingood. *A Different Valor: The Story of General Joseph E. Johnston, C.S.A.* Indianapolis, 1956.

Gray, Wood. *The Hidden Civil War.* New York, 1942.

Hall, Martin H. *Sibley's New Mexico Campaign.* Austin, 1960.

Hanson, Joseph M. *Bull Run Remembers: The History, Traditions and Landmarks of the Manassas (Bull Run) Campaigns before Washington, 1861–1862.* Manassas, Va., 1953.

Harris, Thomas L. *The Trent Affair.* Indianapolis, 1896.

Hartje, Robert G. *Van Dorn: The Life and Times of a Confederate General.* Nashville, 1967.

Heaps, W. A., and P. W. Heaps. *The Singing Sixties: The Spirit of Civil War Days Drawn from the Music of the Times.* Norman, Okla., 1960.

Henderson, G. F. R. *Stonewall Jackson and the American Civil War.* American edition. New York, 1949.

Henry, Robert S. *"First With the Most" Forrest.* Indianapolis, 1944.

———. *The Story of the Confederacy.* Indianapolis, 1931.

Hesseltine, William B. *Civil War Prisons: A Study in War Psychology.* Columbus, Ohio, 1930.

——— (ed.). *Three Against Lincoln.* Baton Rouge, La., 1960.

Holland, Cecil F. *Morgan and His Raiders: A Biography of the Confederate General.* New York, 1942.

Horn, Stanley F. *Gallant Rebel: The Fabulous Cruise of the C.S.S. Shenandoah.* New Brunswick, N.J., 1947.

———. *The Army of Tennessee.* Indianapolis, 1941.

Hunt, Cornelius E. *The Shenandoah: Or the Last Confederate Cruiser.* New York, 1867.

John, Evan. *Atlantic Impact.* London, 1952.

Johnson, Ludwell H. *Red River Campaign: Politics and Cotton in the Civil War.* Baltimore, 1958.

Johnston, Angus J., II. *Virginia Railroads in the Civil War.* Chapel Hill, N. C., 1961.

Johnston, Robert M. *Bull Run, Its Strategy and Tactics.* Boston, 1913.

Jones, Archer. *Confederate Strategy from Shiloh to Vicksburg.* Baton Rouge, La., 1961.

Jones, Katherine M. *Heroines of Dixie: Confederate Women Tell Their Story of the War.* Indianapolis, 1955.

Jones, Virgil C. *The Civil War at Sea.* 3 vols. New York, 1960–1962.

Keller, Allan, *Morgan's Raid.* New York, 1961.

Kimmel, Stanley. *Mr. Davis's Richmond.* New York, 1958.

Kirkland, E. C. *The Peacemakers of 1864.* New York, 1927.

Lamers, William M. *The Edge of Glory: A Biography of William S. Rosecrans, U.S.A.* New York, 1961.

Lee, Charles R., Jr. *The Confederate Constitutions.* Chapel Hill, N.C., 1963.

Lonn, Ella. *Salt as a Factor in the Confederacy.* New York, 1933.

Lytle, Andrew. *Bedford Forrest and his Critter Company.* New York, 1931.

McClure, A. K. *Lincoln and the Men of War Times.* Edited by J. S. Torrey. Philadelphia, 1961.

Massey, Mary E. *Ersatz in the Confederacy.* Columbia, S.C., 1952.

———. *Refugee Life in the Confederacy.* Baton Rouge, La., 1964.

Meade, Robert D. *Judah P. Benjamin: Confederate Statesman.* New York, 1943.

Miers, Earl S. *The Web of Victory: Grant at Vicksburg.* New York, 1955.

Merrill, Walter M. *Against Wind and Tide.* Cambridge, 1963.

Milligan, John D. *Gunboats Down the Mississippi.* Annapolis, 1965.

Monaghan, Jay. *Civil War on the Western Border, 1854–1865.* Boston, 1955.

———. *Diplomat in Carpet Slippers: Abraham Lincoln Deals with Foreign Affairs.* Indianapolis, 1945.

Monroe, Haskell, Jr. "The Presbyterian Church in the Confederate States of America." Ph.D. dissertation, Rice University, 1961.

Moore, A. B. *Conscription and Conflict in the Confederacy.* New York, 1924.

Mosley, John. *The Life of William Ewart Gladstone.* 3 vols. London, 1903.

Mott, Frank L. *American Journalism: A History of Newspapers in the United States Through 250 Years, 1690 to 1940.* New York, 1941.

Nevins, Allan. *The Emergence of Lincoln.* 2 vols. New York, 1950.

———. *Ordeal of the Union.* 2 vols. New York, 1947.

———. *The War for the Union.* 2 vols. New York, 1959.

Nichols, James L. *The Confederate Quartermaster in the Trans-Mississippi.* Austin, 1964.

Nichols, Roy F. *The Disruption of American Democracy.* New York, 1948.

———. *The Stakes of Power.* New York, 1961.

Nye, Russell B. *Fettered Freedom: Civil Liberties and the Slavery Controversy, 1830–1860.* East Lansing, Mich., 1949.

———. *William Lloyd Garrison and the Humanitarian Reformers.* Boston, 1955.

Oates, Stephen. *Confederate Cavalry West of the River.* Austin, 1961.

Owsley, Frank L. *King Cotton Diplomacy: Foreign Relations of the Confederate States of America.* 2d ed. Chicago, 1931.

———. *State Rights in the Confederacy*. Chicago, 1925.

Parks, Joseph H. *General Edmund Kirby Smith, C.S.A.* Baton Rouge, La., 1954.

Patrick, Rembert W. *The Fall of Richmond*. Baton Rouge, La., 1960.

———. *Jefferson Davis and His Cabinet*. Baton Rouge, 1944.

Pemberton, John C. *Pemberton, Defender of Vicksburg*. Chapel Hill, N.C., 1942.

Phillips, Ulrich B. *American Negro Slavery*. Baton Rouge, La., 1966.

———. *The Course of the South to Secession*. Edited by E. M. Coulter. New York, 1930.

———. *Life and Labor in the Old South*. Boston, 1929.

Polk, William M. *Leonidas Polk: Bishop and General*. 2 vols. New York, 1915.

Pollard, Edward A. *The Lost Cause: A New Southern History of the War of the Confederates*. New York, 1867.

Procter, Ben. *Not Without Honor: The Life of John H. Reagan*. Austin, 1962.

Quarles, Benjamin. *The Negro in the Civil War*. Boston, 1953.

Ramsdell, Charles W. *Behind the Lines in the Southern Confederacy*. Baton Rouge, 1944.

Randall, James G. *Constitutional Problems Under Lincoln*. New York, 1926.

———. *Lincoln, The President*. Last volume with Richard Current. 4 vols. New York, 1946–1955.

Reed, Sam R. *The Vicksburg Campaign, and the Battles about Chattanooga under the Command of General U. S. Grant, in 1862–63: An Historical Review*. Cincinnati, 1882.

Robbins, John B. "Confederate Nationalism: Politics and Government in the Confederate South, 1861–1865." Ph.D. dissertation, Rice University, 1964.

Roberts, W. Adolphe. *Semmes of the Alabama*. Indianapolis, 1938.

Robinson, William M., Jr. *Justice in Grey: A History of the Judicial System of the Confederate States of America*. Cambridge, Mass., 1941.

Roland, Charles P. *Albert Sidney Johnston, Soldier of Three Republics*. Austin, 1964.

Scharf, J. Thomas. *History of the Confederate States Navy from Its Organization to the Surrender of Its Last Vessel*. Albany, N.Y. 1894.

Schlatter, Hugo, and Arthur P. Van Gelder. *History of the Explosives Industry in America*. New York, 1927.

Schwab, John C. *The Confederate States of America, 1861–1865: A Financial and Industrial History of the South During the Civil War*. New York, 1901.

Seitz, Don. *Braxton Bragg: General of the Confederacy*. Columbia, S.C., 1924.

Stackpole, Edward J. *From Cedar Mountain to Antietam*. Harrisburg, Pa., 1959.

Stampp, Kenneth M. *And the War Came*. Baton Rouge, La., 1950.

Stephenson, Wendell H. *A Basic History of the Old South*. Princeton, 1959.

Stern, Philip Van Doren. *When the Guns Roared*. Garden City, 1965.

Stewart, George R. *Pickett's Charge: A Microhistory of the Final Attack at Gettysburg, July 3, 1863*. Boston, 1959.

Strode, Hudson. *Jefferson Davis, American Patriot*. New York, 1955.

———. *Jefferson Davis, Confederate President*. New York, 1959.

Swanberg, W. A. *First Blood: The Story of Fort Sumter*. New York, 1957.

Sweet, William Warren. *The Story of Religion in America*. New York, 1930.

Tatum, Georgia Lee. *Disloyalty in the Confederacy*. Chapel Hill, N.C., 1934.

Thomas, D. Y. *Arkansas in War and Reconstruction, 1861–1874*. Little Rock, Ark., 1926.

Thomas, Emory M. "The Confederate State of Richmond: A Biography of the Capital." Ph.D. dissertation, Rice University, 1966.

Thomas, John L. *The Liberator*. Boston, 1963.

Thompson, Samuel B. *Confederate Purchasing Operations Abroad*. Chapel Hill, N.C., 1935.

Thompson, William Y. *Robert Toombs of Georgia*. Baton Rouge, La., 1966.

Todd, Richard. *Confederate Finance*. Athens, Ga., 1954.

Trexler, Harrison A. *The Confederate Ironclad "Virginia" ("Merrimac")*. Chicago, 1938.

Tucker, Glenn. *Chickamauga: Bloody Battle in the West*. Indianapolis, 1961.

Vandiver, Frank E. "Jefferson Davis and Confederate Strategy." In *The American Tragedy*, edited by Bernard Mayo. Hampden-Sydney, Va., 1959.

——. *Jubal's Raid: General Early's Famous Attack on Washington in 1864*. New York, 1960.

——. *Mighty Stonewall*. New York, 1957.

——. *Ploughshares into Swords: Josiah Gorgas and Confederate Ordnance*. Austin, 1952.

——. *Rebel Brass: The Confederate Command System*. Baton Rouge, La., 1956.

——. (ed.), *The Idea of the South*. Chicago, 1964.

Wakelyn, Jon. "William Gilmore Simms: The Artist as Public Man, a Political Odyssey, 1830–1860." Ph.D. dissertation, Rice University, 1966.

Warner, Ezra. *Generals in Blue*. Baton Rouge, La., 1964.

Washington, Booker T. *Story of the Negro*. 2 vols. New York, 1909.

——. *Up From Slavery*. New York, 1901.

Webb, Walter Prescott. *The Texas Rangers: A Century of Frontier Defense*. Austin, 1965.

Wesley, Charles H. *The Collapse of the Confederacy*. Washington, D.C., 1937.

Wharton, H. M. *War Songs and Poems of the Southern Confederacy, 1861–1865*. n.p. 1904.

Wheeler-Bennett, Sir John. *A Wreath to Clio: Studies in British, American and German Affairs*. New York, 1967.

Wiley, Bell I. *The Life of Johnny Reb: The Common Soldier of the Confederacy*. Indianapolis, 1943.

——. *The Plain People of the Confederacy*. Baton Rouge, La., 1944.

——. *Southern Negroes, 1861–1865*. New Haven, 1938.

Williams, Kenneth P. *Lincoln Finds a General: A Military Study of the Civil War*. 5 vols. New York, 1949–1959.

Williams, T. Harry. *Lincoln and His Generals*. New York, 1952.

——. *P. G. T. Beauregard, Napoleon in Gray*. Baton Rouge, La., 1954.

——. *Americans at War*. Baton Rouge, 1960.

Wilson, Edmund. *Patriotic Gore: Studies in the Literature of the American Civil War*. New York, 1962.

Wiltse, Charles M. *John C. Calhoun*. 3 vols. Indianapolis, 1944–1951.

Winks, Robin, *Canada and the United States: The Civil War Years*. Baltimore, 1960.

Winters, John D. *The Civil War in Louisiana*. Baton Rouge, La., 1963.

Wise, John S. *The End of an Era*. Reprint edition. New York, 1965.

Yearns, Wilfred Buck. *The Confederate Congress*. Athens, Ga., 1960.

Secondary Sources: Periodicals

Adams, Charles F. "The Trent Affair." *American Historical Review* 17 (1911–1912).

Andreano, Ralph. "A Theory of Confederate Finance." *Civil War History* 2 (1956).

Andrews, J. Cutler. "The Confederate Press and Public Morale." *Journal of Southern History* 32 (1966).

Baker, Thomas H. "Refugee Newspaper: The Memphis *Daily Appeal*, 1862–1865." *Journal of Southern History* 29 (1963).

Case, Lynn. "La France et l'affaire du 'Trent.'" *Revue Historique* 226 (1961).

Delaney, Robert W. "Matamoros, Port for Texas During the Civil War." *Southwestern Historical Quarterly* 58 (1954–1955).

Diamond, William. "Imports of the Confederate Government from Europe and Mexico." *Journal of Southern History* 6 (1940).

Dimick, Howard T. "The Capture of Jefferson Davis. *Journal of Mississippi History* 9 (1947).

Fitts, Albert N. "The Confederate Convention." *Alabama Review* 2 (1949).

Fuller, J. F. C. "The Place of the American Civil War in the Evolution of War." [British] *Army Quarterly* 26 (1933).

Hamilton, J. G. deRoulhac. "The State Courts and the Confederate Constitution." *Journal of Southern History* 4 (1938).

Harrison, Royden. "British Labour and the Confederacy." *International Review of Social History* 2 (1957).

Harwell, Richard B. "The Richmond Stage." *Civil War History* 1 (1955).

Hay, T. R. "Braxton Bragg and the Southern Confederacy." *Georgia Historical Quarterly* 9 (1925).

———. "The Question of Arming the Slaves." *Mississippi Valley Historical Review* 6 (1919–1920).

Hernon, Joseph M., Jr. "British Sympathies in the American Civil War: A Reconsideration." *Journal of Southern History* 33 (1967).

Higginbotham, Don. "A Raider Refuels: Diplomatic Repercussions." *Civil War History* 4 (1958).

Holladay, Florence E. "The Powers of the Commander of the Confederate Trans-Mississippi Department, 1863–1865." *Southwestern Historical Quarterly* 21 (1917–1918).

Johnson, Ludwell H. "Fort Sumter and Confederate Diplomacy." *Journal of Southern History* 26 (1960).

Kimball, William J. "The Bread Riot in Richmond, 1863." *Civil War History* 7 (1961).

McWhiney, Grady. "Controversy in Kentucky: Braxton Bragg's Campaign of 1862." *Civil War History* 6 (1960).

Mosgrove, George D. "Following Morgan's Plume Through Indiana and Ohio." *Southern Historical Society Papers* 35 (1907).

Muir, Andrew F. "Dick Dowling and the Battle of Sabine Pass." *Civil War History* 4 (1958).

Nicolay, John G., and John Hay. "Abraham Lincoln: A History." *Century Illustrated Monthly* 35 [n.s. 13] (1888).

Oates, Stephen. "Henry Hotze: Confederate Agent Abroad." *The Historian* 27 (1964).

Quisenberry, A. C. "Morgan's Men in Ohio." *Southern Historical Society Papers* 39 [n.s. 1] (1914).

Ramsdell, Charles W. "The Confederate Government and the Railroads." *American Historical Review* 22 (1917).

———. "The Control of Manufacturing by the Confederate Government." *Mississippi Valley Historical Review* 8 (1921).

———. "General Robert E. Lee's Horse Supply, 1862–1865." *American Historical Review* 35 (1930).

———. "Texas from the Fall of the Confederacy to the Beginning of Reconstruction." *Quarterly of the Texas State Historical Association* 11 (1907–1908).

———. "The Texas State Military Board, 1862–1865." *Southwestern Historical Quarterly* 27 (1923–1924).

Schmidt, Jay H. "The Trent Affair." *Civil War Times Illustrated* 1 (January 1963).

Stephenson, N. W. "The Question of Arming the Slaves," *American Historical Review* 18 (1913).

Styron, William. "This Quiet Dust." *Harper's Magazine*, 130 (1965).

Trexler, Harrison A. "The Davis Administration and the Richmond Press, 1861–1865." *Journal of Southern History* 16 (1950).

Vandiver, Frank E. "Confederate Plans for Procuring Subsistence Stores." *Tyler's Quarterly Historical and Genealogical Magazine* 27 (1946).

———. "Jefferson Davis and Unified Army Command." *Louisiana Historical Quarterly* 38 (1955).

———. "Makeshifts of Confederate Ordnance." *Journal of Southern History* 17 (1951).

———. "The Shelby Iron Company in the Civil War." *Army Ordnance* 31 (1946).

———. "A Sketch of Efforts Abroad to Equip the Confederate Armory at Macon." *Georgia Historical Quarterly* 28 (1944).

Windham, William T. "The Problem of Supply in the Trans-Mississippi Confederacy." *Journal of Southern History* 27 (1961).

Index